The Gospel of Family Planning

∴

The Gospel of Family Planning

∵

AN INTIMATE GLOBAL HISTORY

Nicole C. Bourbonnais

THE UNIVERSITY OF CHICAGO PRESS
CHICAGO AND LONDON

The University of Chicago Press, Chicago 60637
The University of Chicago Press, Ltd., London
© 2025 by The University of Chicago
All rights reserved. No part of this book may be used or reproduced in any
manner whatsoever without written permission, except in the case of brief
quotations in critical articles and reviews. For more information, contact the
University of Chicago Press, 1427 E. 60th St., Chicago, IL 60637.
Published 2025
Printed in the United States of America

34 33 32 31 30 29 28 27 26 25   1 2 3 4 5

ISBN-13: 978-0-226-84078-9 (cloth)
ISBN-13: 978-0-226-84080-2 (paper)
ISBN-13: 978-0-226-84079-6 (e-book)
DOI: https://doi.org/10.7208/chicago/9780226840796.001.0001

Library of Congress Cataloging-in-Publication Data

Names: Bourbonnais, Nicole C., author.
Title: The gospel of family planning : an intimate global history / Nicole C.
  Bourbonnais.
Description: Chicago ; London : The University of Chicago Press, 2025. |
  Includes bibliographical references and index.
Identifiers: LCCN 2024039135 | ISBN 9780226840789 (cloth) | ISBN
  9780226840802 (paperback) | ISBN 9780226840796 (ebook)
Subjects: LCSH: Family planning—History—20th century. | Birth control—
  History—20th century.
Classification: LCC HQ766 .B67 2025 | DDC 363.9/60904—dc23/eng/20240911
LC record available at https://lccn.loc.gov/2024039135

♾ This paper meets the requirements of ANSI/NISO Z39.48-1992
(Permanence of Paper).

Contents

Introduction · 1

CHAPTER ONE
Prophets · 25

CHAPTER TWO
Practice · 63

CHAPTER THREE
Crisis of Faith · 103

CHAPTER FOUR
Redemption? · 141

Epilogue · 183

Acknowledgments 187
Notes 191
Bibliography 241
Index 253

Introduction

Where do I start? I could tell you stories of contraband condoms hidden in a Jesuit priest's suitcase, of busloads of women arriving at a clinic to participate in a contraceptive research trial, of a man walking through the night, flashlight in hand, to attend a talk on family planning the next morning. I could tell you stories of women removing intra-uterine devices with their bare hands, of poor men undergoing vasectomies in return for cash payments. I could start with one woman, sterilized in the midst of a complicated labor. Maybe she signed off on the procedure willingly, happy to be rid of the constant threat of unwanted pregnancies, or desperately, in a moment of overwhelming pain and fear. Maybe it was done without her knowledge or consent, a tragic surprise to be discovered the next morning, or many years later, when her attempts to conceive failed over and over.

Each of these stories captures a different element of the twentieth-century family planning movement, a movement that brought liberation, devastation, and everything in between. This is an absurd history: of Disney films projecting the benefits of small families, of mobile clinics distributing contraceptives in village squares, of birds flying away with diaphragms hung out to dry. It is a messy history: of spermicidal foams bursting out of tubes, of washable condoms deteriorating in the heat, of expelled intra-uterine devices, of cramping, bleeding, and pain. It is an emotional history: of hope and disappointment, of compassion and suspicion, of personal bonds made and broken. It is a history both intimate and global, unfolding in the smallest of spaces—clinics, bedrooms, doorsteps—across the world, intentionally linked together by advocates who saw the need for family planning everywhere, for everyone, by any means necessary.

To understand this history, we could start with the leaders of the movement, the people who wrote essays extolling the value of small families, who published pamphlets outlining "modern" methods, who gave speeches at international conferences promoting the cause. Or we could start with the policymakers and experts, the people who headed the government programs and foreign aid agencies that funded the movement, developed new contraceptives, and designed model family planning clinics and communication strategies. As recent histories have shown, these actors were driven by a range of ideologies and political agendas: sexual liberation, women's rights, environmentalism, eugenics, population control. The lines between these ideologies could be thin: many prominent family planning activists drew on multiple arguments at once, linking the cause to everything from individual liberty to national economic growth to planetary survival. As a result, family planning became entangled in nearly every major geopolitical struggle of the twentieth century: colonialism, decolonization, the Cold War, globalization, calls for a fundamental reorganization of the global economy, the rise of transnational social activism.[1]

The leaders of this movement undoubtedly played a key role in transforming family planning from a fringe cause to a site of widescale state and international intervention over the course of the twentieth century. But family planning was never just an ideological debate or political agenda, never just the terrain of prominent activists or policymakers. It was also a daily *practice*, constantly made and remade through interactions between a host of intermediate actors—doctors, social workers, fieldworkers, consultants, nurses, and volunteers—and the women and men who variously sought out, engaged with, or resisted their efforts to preach contraception at home and abroad. *The Gospel of Family Planning* argues that the global family planning movement was shaped as much—if not more—by these intermediate actors and daily interactions. It is in the absurd, messy, emotional world of family planning practice—where global ideals met intimate lives—that this movement ultimately found its meaning.

Starting with the intermediate and the intimate allows us to see the much broader landscape of activism that propelled the movement forward in the twentieth century, the much more diverse personal, experiential, and spiritual concerns that drove an eclectic group of actors to see "the gospel of family planning" as not only a political agenda, but a matter of life and death. We can see the many layers of gendered labor that went into promoting the cause, and the frictions that arose when this simple prophecy confronted the much more complex material and social realities of people's reproductive lives. We can understand the critical role played by intermediate actors as both gatekeepers and allies to communities targeted by increasingly aggressive state population control programs over the course of the twentieth century. Finally, we can see how experiences on the front lines led some to abandon the cause of "family planning" altogether, joining movements for reproductive rights and reproductive justice that put forward much broader visions of reproductive freedom. Retelling this history

FIGURE I.1. "Interview on the front porch of a patient." Puerto Rico, c. 1960–1965. Source: Adaline Pendleton Satterthwaite Papers, Smith College Special Collections.

here, starting with the intermediate and the intimate sphere, thus allows us to understand more deeply where this movement came from, what it did, and where we go from here.

The Personal, the Political, and the Global

At first glance, family planning seems like an inherently personal subject: a set of decisions made by sexually active individuals to control whether, when, and how many children they have. These individual decisions, however, are shaped by forces that extend well beyond the bedroom. Technological and pharmaceutical markets shape what contraceptive methods are available. Community, cultural, and religious values shape what methods are acceptable. Gendered power dynamics in relationships influence who has a voice in the intimate sphere, who is able to assert their reproductive desires and in what ways. Larger social norms influence the meaning of family planning: whether it makes one a sinner, a responsible parent, a modern woman, or something else entirely. The choices we make in the bedroom can also be profoundly shaped by governments: by the public policies, health infrastructure, and educational systems that determine what

FIGURE I.2. Contraceptive methods, 1900–1950. Source: Dittrick Medical History Center, Case Western Reserve University.

contraceptive methods and family sizes are actually accessible/viable, for whom, and under what circumstances.

The relative impact of these different forces on our individual decisions differs across time and space. Throughout most of history, people around the world turned primarily to friends, families, and community members for advice on how to prevent pregnancy. They might have been told about periodic abstinence, withdrawal, or prolonged breastfeeding as ways to delay another child. They might have tried rudimentary condoms made of animal skin or pessaries to block the cervix, made of everything from honey to wax to lemon peels. They might have experimented with a range of herbs and concoctions rumored to have anti-fertility properties or used sticks or other objects to induce abortions. In the mid-nineteenth century, the vulcanization of rubber led to new preventative methods, including more effective condoms, the female diaphragm, and the cervical cap. Companies also marketed different "chemical" methods: spermicidal foams, powders, tablets, and sponges inserted into the vagina before sex. By the early twentieth century, several countries had active contraceptive markets; even the Sears catalogue sold "ladies' cup-shaped silk sponges" under the euphemism of "feminine hygiene."[2] Contraception had become commercialized.

It also became increasingly medicalized. Diaphragms and cervical caps were estimated at around 90 percent efficacy, but required a visit to a doctor's office or health clinic to be fitted to a woman's cervix, an uncommon experience for most people around the world in the early twentieth century.

The development of new methods for abortion, vasectomy, and tubal ligation in the mid- to late nineteenth century made these procedures increasingly safe, but only if done in a hygienic clinic by a skilled practitioner. These procedures were enhanced further in the mid-1940s with the introduction of penicillin and other drugs to control the risk of infection. Doctors in a number of countries also began to experiment with intra-uterine devices (IUDs) in the early twentieth century. They observed that inserting an object into the uterus—a metal or silver ring, for example—seemed to prevent conception, although the exact mechanism through which this process worked was unclear. IUDs were unique in separating birth control from the act of sex itself and offering long-term yet reversible protection, but they also came with a risk of infection and range of potential side effects.[3]

In any case, in most countries in the early twentieth century, illiteracy, a lack of public health infrastructure, and taboos around open discussions of sexuality meant that many people did not know about these methods or could not afford to access them even if they did. The idea of deliberately limiting reproduction also ran counter to many religious and cultural norms that viewed conception as a sacred act or a question of fate, and valued children as critical members of the family labor force, social support system, and/or networks of lineage. Certain methods, like the condom, were associated with the protection of venereal disease and prostitution, antithetical to respectable family life. Birth control advocates in the early twentieth century thus sought to both increase access to different methods and change ideas about family planning. They began to open small-scale clinics to insert diaphragms and provide other "modern" methods; by 1939, such services were being offered in at least twenty-five countries around the world.[4] They distributed pamphlets touting the economic, social, and health benefits of child spacing and outlining different methods available to those who could not reach clinics. They gave talks in public halls and village squares and visited women in their homes to extol the value of small families. They reached out to contraceptive manufacturers and conducted research trials of new methods. They conducted studies that showed the broader appeal of family planning in their countries, wrote letters to newspapers demanding support, and lobbied government leaders to endorse the cause. Along the way, they tried to normalize contraception, arguing that "family planning" or "planned parenthood" was modern, responsible, and in line with fundamental religious and moral principles.[5]

Activists also reached across borders from early on to connect with like-minded actors in other countries and spread their cause more broadly. Indeed, over the course of the last century, family planning became a particularly dense site of international activism. "Family planning missionaries" (as some called themselves) first began to fan out across the globe in the 1920s and '30s, connecting with local advocates and trying to spark discussion, attract publicity to the cause, and standardize contraceptive research and clinic practice. The creation of the International Planned Parenthood Federation (IPPF) in 1952 helped consolidate these informal networks from its headquarters in London and regional branches across the globe. American-based foundations like the Population Council (founded in 1952) and Pathfinder Fund (1957) also began to invest more heavily in family planning promotion and contraceptive research abroad. New methods like the birth control pill, a variety of plastic IUDs, the Depo-Provera shot, and the Norplant implant were developed with funding from these foundations and tested internationally from the mid-1950s onward. Large international aid agencies like the United Nations Fund for Population Activities (UNFPA), Swedish International Development Agency (SIDA), and US Agency for International Development (USAID) also became major donors to family planning programs, dramatically increasing the size and scale of the cause. By the mid-1960s, population had become a multimillion-dollar international aid industry.[6]

This rapid expansion of international aid corresponded with—and helped fuel—the rise of government population programs across the globe from the mid-twentieth century onward, starting with India in 1952. These programs dedicated resources to the study of population dynamics, the dissemination of family planning methods, and the promotion of small families. They

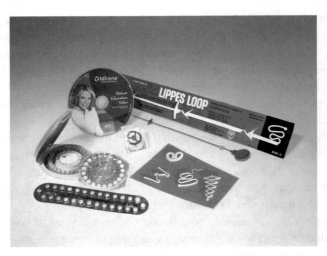

FIGURE I.3. Contraceptive methods, 1950 to present day. Source: Dittrick Medical History Center, Case Western Reserve University.

varied in size and scale. Some included the creation of thousands of state family planning clinics, billboards plastered across public spaces, mass sterilization and IUD camps, and aggressive campaigns to bring family planning into every home. Others were much more limited, consisting of a handful of clinical trials or demographic research studies done by a small cohort of interested actors. Either way, these programs operated on the assumption that the size of families was of interest to the state, and a sphere in which the government could and should intervene. In doing so, they mobilized "family planning"—the effort to limit/space children at the level of the family— toward "population control"—attempts to affect rates of reproduction and population growth on a national level.[7]

Why did people become so concerned with the size of other people's families, both within their own countries and on the other side of the world? As noted above, historians have identified a variety of ideological imperatives that shaped the work of some of the most prominent activists in the early twentieth century. Sex reformers like British advocate Marie Stopes argued that access to contraception was key to a satisfying sexual life and happy marital relations. Feminists like American nurse Margaret Sanger argued that it was essential to women's emancipation: no woman could be free unless she could control her reproductive body. But Sanger and Stopes also engaged actively with the eugenics movement, which reached its zenith in the interwar years just as the birth control movement was taking off. Drawing on theories of social Darwinism, eugenicists argued that a variety of traits—from intelligence to mental health to vague conceptions of "criminality" and "fitness"—were passed down from parents, and that societies should actively intervene to promote good "breeding" and prevent the reproduction of those deemed "unfit." For Sanger, Stopes, and other prominent advocates, spreading access to birth control provided a critical means to promote both a feminist and a "eugenic" future.[8]

The expansion of state interest and international aid for family planning was also profoundly influenced by concern over population growth and size. As scholars have illustrated, in the seventeenth and eighteenth centuries states began to see their populations less as a group of individuals and more as "a set of processes to be managed."[9] A number of European governments began to collect statistics on births, deaths, and population size more proactively to facilitate this management, both at home and in their expanding colonial empires in Africa, Asia, the Caribbean, and South America. Throughout much of this period, states were primarily concerned with increasing population size, deemed crucial to national/colonial power. But some commentators began to warn that too-rapid population growth could have dramatic consequences. In 1798, for example, English cleric

Thomas Malthus's *An Essay on the Principle of Population* argued that resources grew linearly while populations grew exponentially, leading to poverty, war, and misery. While Malthus himself promoted late marriage and abstinence, a transnational network of "neo-Malthusians" revived his core thesis in the late nineteenth/early twentieth century and called for more active interventions, including the mass distribution of contraceptives. Neo-Malthusian and eugenic arguments were often tightly linked, as commentators blamed everything from urban poverty in Europe to famine and political instability in the colonies on the "excessive" fertility of *certain* populations, defined by their race, class, ethnicity, and/or ability.[10]

The end of World War II only enhanced these fears. A wave of decolonization movements led to the unraveling of European colonial rule in Africa, Asia, and the Caribbean, disrupting the global political order. A very real rise in global population growth rates after the war provided fuel for neo-Malthusian arguments, despite the fact that this growth was due in most places to declining mortality rates, rather than birth rates per se. These concerns also intersected with an emerging environmentalist movement concerned with the impact of population expansion on natural resources and habitats. Warnings from prominent commentators like Fairfield Osborn and Hugh Moore helped fuel panic over an impending "population bomb" that would lead to the destruction of the environment, instability in the decolonizing world, and—in the context of the Cold War—a turn to communism. Many nationalist leaders within newly independent states also saw unrestricted population growth as a threat to their plans for postcolonial economic development, calling on citizens to limit their families in the name of national growth and "modernity." In this context, family planning became a presumably simple solution to the complex problems facing poor communities at home and abroad.[11]

This mix of ideologies and political imperatives has left a complicated historical legacy. In popular imagination, the history of family planning is often still portrayed as a story of liberation, of brave activists and technological advances that progressively freed sex from reproduction and women from the burden of uncontrolled childbearing. But several decades of historical scholarship have shown how these movements could just as easily become part of "an elitist agenda that actually restrained women from exercising control over their own reproductive capacities."[12] Indeed, eugenic and neo-Malthusian ideologies helped justify some of the most extreme forms of state intervention in modern history. Most infamously, they contributed to a wave of compulsory eugenic sterilization laws in the 1920s–1940s targeting disabled, institutionalized, racialized, and other vulnerable populations in a number of countries: Norway, Sweden, Japan, the United

States, Canada, Switzerland, Czechoslovakia, Yugoslavia, Hungary, Turkey, Latvia, and Cuba, among others. The dramatic ends taken by the Nazi regime in Germany (including forced sterilization and euthanasia) led to a backlash against eugenics in the 1940s, but targeted sterilization policies under different names continued in several countries well into the 1970s. Even after explicit policies were phased out, reports of coercive sterilizations in prisons, detention centers, and marginalized communities around the world continue to surface periodically, attesting to the enduring pull of eugenic ideologies.[13]

A number of state population programs that arose in the 1960s–1980s have also been charged with a range of ethical and human rights violations. The most visible examples include the mass sterilizations undertaken during the "Emergency Period" in India in 1976 (some eight million people in one year), reports of forced sterilizations and abortions in China under the One Child Policy, and the enforcement of the Indonesian family planning program by military personnel. Critics also cite a range of less dramatic but still highly unethical methods: distributing contraceptive methods en masse with little oversight, involving patients in research trials without their full awareness/consent, withholding state benefits from those with large families, setting targets to encourage nurses and doctors to insert IUDs more rapidly, and/or providing incentives to patients to use a particular method or undergo a sterilization. Like eugenic policies, these activities have largely targeted marginalized people, particularly women of color in both the Global North and Global South.[14] Far from a story of liberation, Matthew Connelly has thus described the history of population control as a story of "how some people have tried to control others without having to answer to anyone."[15]

As scholars have argued, these practices in many ways reflected the logical outcome of the dehumanizing language of eugenics and population control. Eugenics had "an evaluative logic at its core. Some human life was of more value—to the state, the nation, the race, future generations—than other human life."[16] Anthropologists describe this as "stratified reproduction": the process by which some categories of people are empowered to nurture and reproduce, while others are disempowered.[17] As Sanjam Ahluwalia argues, portraying poor and marginalized populations as "hypersexual and hyperfecund" demonizes them as drains on national resources and development, paving the way for aggressive interventions that privilege state interests over individual rights.[18] It also radically oversimplifies the causes of poverty and conflict. Betsy Hartmann notes that the neo-Malthusian equation is "compelling because of its simplicity. More people equal fewer resources and more hunger, poverty, environmental degradation, and political instability. This equation helps explain away the troubling human suffering in that 'other' world beyond the neat borders of affluence. By procreating, the poor create their own poverty. We are absolved of responsibility and freed from complexity."[19] This narrative diverts attention away from larger measures of social and environmental justice: land distribution, limits on consumption, employment creation, mass education, and health care.[20] The supposedly neutral language of population statistics and descriptions of family planning patients as contraceptive "users" also strips the women most targeted by these interventions of their humanity and complexity. Women's bodies are portrayed primarily as "a key political resource: available, malleable, and potent material to deploy in the biopolitical project of shaping the state's size, character, and place in the world."[21]

Scholars have further highlighted the colonial mentalities and structures underlying family planning and population movements, both before and after formal political decolonization. Colonial population programs were often cast in the language of a "civilizing mission," promoting the small, Western nuclear family as the norm and portraying all other family forms as "disordered,"[22] thus both drawing on and reinforcing colonial racial hierarchies. Many post-WWII international humanitarian and development organizations remained dominated by actors from North America and Europe, and promoted similarly universalizing models of "progress."[23] As Connelly illustrates, the post-WWII "population establishment"—the matrix of foreign aid agencies and elite foundations funding contraceptive research and population programs—was headed by a small group of "jet set" male elites from the Global North who saw themselves as entitled to dictate policies for the rest of the world. The dominance of American foreign aid, philanthropists, and experts in the field, in particular, tied the cause intimately to American neo-imperial domination in the Cold War period and beyond.[24]

Critiques of these programs were, of course, raised at the time. Indeed, family planning, population, and reproduction were sites of immense struggle throughout the twentieth century. Marxists, anti-colonial leaders, and anti-racist advocates across the globe challenged eugenic and neo-Malthusian theories from the outset, arguing that poverty and disorder had more to do with the combined forces of imperialism, capitalism, and racism than family size or population growth rates.[25] "Control de la natalidad" (birth control) became synonymous with American imperialism in parts of Latin America in the 1960s and 1970s, with advocates referred to disparagingly as "controlistas."[26] At the United Nations International Conference on Population and Development (ICPD) in Bucharest in 1974, a variety of leaders criticized the international population movement as a racist and imperialist project, popularizing the mantra that "development is the best contraceptive": in other words, economic advance would bring small families, rather than vice versa.[27] But critiques of population programs in the twentieth century also came from more conservative groups concerned with the threat posed by family planning to religious visions of sexuality and the family. While several Christian denominations had approved the use of contraceptives by married couples by the 1950s, the Catholic Church maintained a strict position against all artificial methods throughout the twentieth century. The Vatican's representation at the UN and connections to member-states with Catholic majorities allowed them to push back against conversations on family planning in international spaces. Indeed, opposition from Catholic member-states kept the World Health Organization (WHO) from intervening in the field of family planning until the late 1960s. Religious groups have also used the history of eugenics and coercive practices in population programs to push for policies that restrict access to family planning altogether or promote a pro-natalist agenda, viewing women as primarily—or compulsory—reproducers.[28]

The family planning movement thus has the unique position of having been consistently critiqued from both the left *and* the right. This created a particularly difficult political landscape for those actors in the twentieth century who were against coercive practices but still felt that family planning methods—under certain conditions—could provide valuable resources for women and families struggling to control their own reproduction. Socialist, anti-racist, and anti-imperialist feminists who supported access to contraceptive methods often found themselves attacked both by conservative actors for promoting the destruction of family values and by their "comrades" for selling out the class, race, or national struggle.[29] Feminists have also conflicted with one another over whether family planning programs run by the state and headed by male elites could ever offer liberation for women. Indeed, women's health movements emerging around the world in the 1970s and 1980s critiqued the patriarchal nature of the medical profession and the instrumentalization of their bodies toward state goals, creating their own networks to spread access to health information and support reproduction on women's terms instead. Others, however, argued that full detachment from the state would only leave these patriarchal structures intact, with particular consequences for those who depend on public services and whose interests could not be met by a small network of feminist clinics.[30]

In the 1980s and 1990s, networks of women from across five continents joined together across borders to try to reconcile these debates, challenge the international population establishment, and bring feminist principles into state and international programs. In the buildup to the next ICPD in

Cairo in 1994, they demanded an end to population control policies and the implementation of a "reproductive rights" approach, including the right to access safe, reliable contraceptive methods but also a much broader range of reproductive health services: prenatal, childbirth, and postpartum care; safe abortion; and treatment of sexually transmitted diseases, women's cancers, and infertility. They stressed that these services need to be women-centered and women-controlled, free from coercion and discrimination, and undergirded by a larger reorganization of the global economic and political order. They challenged the claim that overpopulation was the main cause of poverty, conflict, or environmental destruction, pointing instead to the role played by neoliberalism, destructive economic policies, military competition, and overconsumption.[31] In doing so, these activists both drew on and fed into the emerging "reproductive justice" movement led by women of color in the United States. Reproductive justice advocates explicitly merged the framework of reproductive rights with principles of social justice, calling for: (1) the right to have a child, (2) the right to not have a child, and (3) the right to parent a child in a safe and healthy environment, with access to the political and economic resources required to make these rights achievable.[32]

These movements made a number of visible gains in the late twentieth/early twenty-first centuries. The language of "reproductive rights" was adopted by the ICPD's Cairo Program of Action, signed by 179 member-states, and considered one of the most significant paradigm shifts in the international sphere in the twentieth century; some have described it as the moment in which the population movement was finally "redeemed."[33] Indeed, in the early twenty-first century most state and international aid programs adopted—at least officially—the language and approach of "reproductive rights" or "reproductive health" rather than "family planning" or "population control." The language of "reproductive justice" has also become increasingly prominent both within the United States and abroad. Still, reproductive politics remain fraught. On the one hand, feminists have questioned whether the incorporation of the language of reproductive rights and/or justice on the national and international level reflects a genuine commitment to the principles of these movements, or merely a discursive mask for the continuation of population control mentalities and projects. On the other hand, Cairo led to a widespread backlash among conservative groups locally and internationally, which are more coordinated and well funded than ever before. Indeed, recent backsliding on reproductive rights from Poland to the United States reminds us that people's ability to make decisions about their reproductive lives remains tenuous at best.[34]

In the past few decades, academic and popular studies have provided an increasingly rich understanding of the ways that something seemingly so simple—the control of conception—could become entangled in so many battles: over decolonization, communism, racism, patriarchy, religion, faith, development, and global security. They have done so through a variety of approaches: by tracing the international travels of prominent personalities like Margaret Sanger;[35] by following the spread of population thinking through international conferences and organizations;[36] by documenting how research organizations like the Population Council created and marketed new contraceptives like the IUD as a "method for the global masses";[37] and by mining the minutes, correspondence, and public writings of key American foundations and foreign aid agencies that funded population control internationally.[38] These studies provide us with a deep understanding of the ideological and political motivations that shaped the advocacy of those in positions of power around the world. But I wanted to know something a bit different: What did all of this look like in practice? Who did the daily labor of promoting family planning on doorsteps, in village squares, at community halls? What happened when these advocates, sometimes from distant parts of a country, sometimes from the other side of the world, showed up and started preaching the gospel of family planning? How did early advocates relate to one another across countries so deeply divided along so many lines? What was it like to try to use a spermicidal foam or a rubber cervical cap created in one part of the world in an entirely different context? How did the ideologies held by those at the helm of international aid agencies and population programs filter down—or not—into encounters between doctors and patients behind the closed doors of a clinic? And what compelled and enabled women to take their complaints not only to their individual doctors or clinics, but to the highest echelons of global power? In other words, how did the personal become political, then personal, and then political once more?

Intimate Global History

The kind of questions I'm interested in are usually best answered through local-level studies: of one country, one region, one program, even one clinic. Zooming in on this level allows us to look more comprehensively at the multiplicity of economic, social, cultural, political, and personal contexts that shape, as Carole Joffe puts it, "what family planning 'is' at any given moment."[39] Recent studies of Puerto Rico, Egypt, Mexico, South Korea, and Ghana, among others, have illustrated the diverse range of ideologies and actors that shaped how activism and state programs played out in any one country.[40] As Raúl Necochea López argues in his study of family planning in Peru, international organizations had to negotiate their interests with those of pre-existing local advocates, which included a diverse mix of physicians, eugenicists, feminists, pharmaceutical companies, military leaders, religious institutions, Catholic social reformers, and individual men and women who sought contraceptives.[41] These studies also show how the ideologies of those at the head of programs and clinics did not always filter down directly into practice. Despite the eugenic narrative of Marie Stopes in the public sphere, for example, her early clinics were rooted more firmly in women's needs and quality of care, regularly violating eugenic principles by providing working-class women with both birth control and infertility advice.[42] In black communities in the United States, birth control programs were likewise shaped not only by the eugenic and neo-Malthusian discourses of those who funded them, but also by the ideas of the black health professionals who implemented them and had their own motivations often rooted in maternal health and community uplift.[43]

These studies have also challenged the portrayal of women targeted by these programs as *either* liberated subjects *or* coerced hapless victims, as *either* acquiescing *or* resisting birth control.[44] In her careful examination of state eugenics in North Carolina in the twentieth century, for example, Johanna Schoen argues that medical technology "did not hold one meaning for all women," and invites us to look closer at "the ways in which women exerted control over their health and reproductive care, pointing to both the extent and the limits of women's agency."[45] As she points out, the very class, racial, and international inequalities that made marginalized women targets of family planning projects also often made them underserved by social and medical services, thus making them sometimes eager to seize on opportunities for free reproductive care.[46] Family planning programs—and even sterilization programs—could provide them with "a measure of reproductive control," though "not on their own terms."[47] Interviewing Puerto Rican women about their sterilization experiences, Iris Lopez likewise found that few saw themselves as having experienced either direct coercion or complete volition. Rather, their experiences existed on a continuum: they exercised *degrees* of constraint and freedom.[48] These studies allow us to consider in more depth under what circumstances, how, and in what ways programs could be liberating, coercive, or something in between.

These studies were immensely helpful to me in conducting my own first research project, on reproductive politics and practices in the Anglophone Caribbean. Here, too, birth control movements were promoted by colonial officials, white elites, eugenicists, and neo-Malthusians, but also by liberal nationalist leaders, socialist doctors, public health nurses, and black nationalist feminist organizers. Clinic records and letters from working-class women also illustrated the wide diversity of reproductive demands and experiences in the region.[49] Of course, to a great extent these experiences were shaped by the particular dynamics of this time and place. Still, I could not help but think of not only the commonalities between what I was reading about in other places, but also the connections between these different countries. Family planning activists from other countries would regularly crop up in my sources in the Caribbean; international contraceptive markets profoundly shaped what methods were available locally; international population consultants visited the islands and tried to promote models seen as universally applicable; Caribbean advocates in turn developed materials that were adapted and used in other contexts; and Caribbean women participated actively in early transnational reproductive rights networks. These realities seemed to beg for an analysis that went beyond the particular to look globally and transnationally, without losing sight of those actors and experiences that lay at the core of this story.

In other words, could one write a social history of this global movement, one which takes a broad international frame of analysis but focuses in on the everyday, with ordinary people and close encounters still front and center? Peter Stearns notes that international history and social history have not generally "mixed well," since the former has a tradition of focusing on state elites, diplomatic decision-making, global conferences, and "high politics": the seeming antithesis to social history.[50] But the dense connections between societies and the transmission of ideas that we see as "global history" occur not only in the high-level political sphere: they also happen through daily encounters between international aid workers and local communities, between advocates who exchange letters and gifts across borders, and among people who remain geographically locked in place but whose experiences are shaped by—and in turn shape—technologies and policies developed thousands of miles away. As Tehila Sasson argues, the global "could be produced in the most local and intimate spheres of everyday life, as much as it could take place in national and international spaces."[51] Capturing these more intimate elements of global phenomena requires us to look at "specific, traceable networks of connection and exchange that allow us to see effects on people caught up in them."[52]

This book takes up this call by focusing on two main networks of connection and exchange: first, among the cohort of nurses, doctors, social workers, volunteers, and fieldworkers who worked on the front lines of family planning and population control programs in the 1930s–1960s, and second, among the women's health, reproductive rights, and reproductive justice activists who emerged in the 1970s–1990s to challenge these paradigms. Many of these actors occupied an intermediate location, moving between small-scale clinics and international conferences while maintaining personal relationships that stretched across borders. As a result, their experiences allow us to hold global and local spaces—and the connections between them—within a single frame. I also use micro-history to dive deeper into these spaces. Micro-history starts with the examination of a small object—a single event, a person, a source—and extrapolates outward.[53] As Julia Laite argues, focusing in on this micro level can allow us to see "things that would be imperceptible in a different register: the subtle love between friends, brief flashes of agency and choice in a life constrained by poverty and gender inequality, the surprising connections between the global and the personal."[54] It allows us to produce historical analysis that is intimate not only in subject matter (in this case, family planning) but also in its attention to individuals, personal relationships, emotions, and close encounters.[55]

To find and trace these actors and stories, I have focused particularly on the materials of fieldworkers and consultants for organizations like the IPPF, Pathfinder Fund, and Population Council, contained in both organizational archives and personal collections. Their diaries and internal reports provide insight into both the mentalities and day-to-day work of those sent out to preach contraception abroad in the twentieth century. But their personal collections also contain newsletters tracking the development of family planning groups worldwide, correspondence with a much broader network of activists from different countries, and materials collected from local family planning associations, including pamphlets, promotional materials, and reports. These sources thus allow us to get both a bird's-eye view of the movement and a glimpse into the approaches and tensions shaping transnational relationships and family planning in practice. My understanding of the latter has also been greatly enhanced by the wealth of new research on local and national-level family planning programs produced in the past two decades, evident in the bibliography. These studies, written by scholars deeply immersed in local archives, allow us to both contextualize and sometimes counter the accounts contained in fieldworkers' archives. Finally, I have relied on oral histories, collected by other scholars and by myself, to explore the personal trajectories and subjective experiences of both family planning and reproductive rights activists.

Doing so has revealed a much broader landscape of activism surrounding family planning in the twentieth century. The following pages draw attention to the work of an extremely diverse cast of characters: doctors, nurses, social workers, midwives, charity ladies, local personalities, priests, nuns, registry clerks, teachers, and volunteers. These actors came to the movement for their own equally diverse set of reasons, including but not limited to the ideological imperatives of feminism, sex reform, neo-Malthusianism, and eugenics. I thus argue that family planning gained ground globally during this period not only because of the strength/spread of these ideologies but also because it tapped into a range of different local experiences, concerns, and agendas, not all of which can be reduced to "a prehistory of population control."[56] Family planning advocacy also took place in a variety of informal and everyday spaces. As Trent MacNamara has argued in the context of the United States, the spread of family planning was a "sprawling mass movement," produced through discussions in "kitchens, foundries, bars, churches, and picnic grounds."[57] In this book, I posit that this was also true on a global scale. For every prominent international personality who made controversial statements in the press during an international lecture tour, there were hundreds of other local enthusiasts offering family planning "quietly on the side"[58] as part of their medical or social work, handing out pamphlets to their friends and family, or raising the subject in their local church group or mothers' circle.

Another broad characteristic of this movement is a fairly clear gendered division of labor. If men dominated at the higher echelons (as heads of organizations, foundation board directors, ministers of population programs, official presidents of family planning associations) in most places, women dominated on the ground, disproportionately represented as doctors, fieldworkers, nurses, and volunteers conducting the often underpaid—frequently unpaid—practical work for the cause. While less visible when we look at legislative debates, minutes of board meetings, or international conferences, these women laid the foundation of most clinics/programs. They also formed their own transnational networks, maintained by correspondence, newsletters, gift-giving, personal favors, and gatherings in homes. They performed not only the physical labor of the movement (hanging posters, organizing village meetings, traveling long distances on bikes and motorcycles to meet mothers in their homes), but also the emotional labor, building the personal relationships that solidified ties across borders. This book thus further supports Aiko Takeuchi-Demirci's call to pay attention to the role of women as "key agents and facilitators of transnationalism."[59]

When these actors connected across borders, they appealed to affective bonds as much as—or even more than—a sense of ideological unity. In particular, at the level of the local advocate and the international fieldworker, there is a predominance of individuals who portrayed themselves as humanitarians, and particularly as maternalist humanitarians: acting out of concern for mothers, based on repeated and sometimes traumatic experiences witnessing maternal morbidity and mortality. In testimonials and oral histories, they portrayed their work as apolitical and grounded in experience, compassion, and basic ethical principles rather than a particular political agenda. Many saw it even as metaphysical, spiritual work: hence, the "gospel" of family planning, the language of "missionary" work and of "conversion" that prevailed in many family planning narratives. This orientation reflects in part the very real involvement of religious individuals in this movement. Indeed, if religious groups often appeared as the antithesis of family planning in the spaces of international politics, in practice the family planning movement drew in a range of Anglicans, Christian Scientists, Catholics, Buddhists, and Muslims alike who saw the work of family planning as compatible with their larger social and spiritual missions. For other advocates, the "gospel of family planning" was a metaphor, capturing the evangelical spirit of an otherwise secular message of modernity, development, and global humanity. Either way, the language of gospels and missions illustrates the deeply emotional nature of this work which, for many of those in the field, was seen not as a question of population statistics or nation-building, but as a matter of life and death.

To recognize the involvement of women and humanitarians— particularly in the early years of the family planning movement—is not, however, to downplay the reality of race, class, gender, and national inequality that fundamentally shaped this movement. Rather, the sources explored here allow us to see how these inequalities were present not only in the discourse of political leaders and ideologues, but also in the interactions between intermediary actors. If the sources are suffused with moments of empathy, compassion, and trust, they also bear witness to the frustration, aggression, and conflict that could erupt when utopian ideals of cross-class, cross-race, transnational cooperation confronted the reality of difference, inequality, engrained prejudice, and social distance. Advocates from different countries clashed at times over the goals and fundamental principles of the movement and the relationship between different levels of the movement hierarchy, leading to both political and personal conflicts. Many family planning advocates also found that their assumptions about what targeted communities wanted or needed, or how they should behave as recipients of aid, did not hold. Sometimes advocates were able to recognize and adapt to differing social needs or wants; at other times, they were so convinced of the strength of their prophecy that anything less than total acquiescence was read as ignorance or superstition. The sources illustrate that one need not be a fully committed eugenicist or neo-Malthusian to feel superior or impose paternalistic approaches. As Avishai Margalit points out: "Caring may easily play out at the expense of respect for the other person's autonomy."[60]

The sources explored here also allow us to see a broad range of experiences among those targeted by family planning programs. There is ample evidence here to show that in most places, there was some interest in family planning: the high rates of abortion in most countries suggest a desire for reproductive control, and many people actively sought out clinics and programs through their own initiative. Still, the sources show a wide variety of reactions. Some people walked miles to obtain methods; others hid when family planning prophets came knocking at their doors. Some tried diaphragms, foaming tablets, IUDs, and other methods until they found the one that worked; others took pills quietly from nurses and then fed them to the chickens. Some clearly found liberation through birth control; others were clearly coerced, tricked, or exploited in their encounters with these programs. Many had a deeply ambiguous experience: they were interested in the idea of family planning, but found the methods too difficult or ill suited for their lives; they came to clinics willingly but struggled to assert their needs and went away feeling disempowered; they had a good experience at the clinic but then faced resistance from their sexual partners back home. Sometimes, their needs and desires simply changed over time in ways that defied the linear predictions of family planning advocates. Again, at a most basic level, I hope the pages that follow illustrate the complexity of people's reproductive lives so often ignored in ideological tracts or political debates of the time that reduced women to "acceptors" or "resisters."

The sources explored here also provide convincing evidence of the fundamental inadequacy of universalist approaches to family planning promotion. Intermediary family planning advocates found it legitimately helpful to share information, materials, and strategies across borders, but frequently found that what worked in one place—small clinics, home visits, meetings in village squares, and so on—failed in another. Moreover, despite repeated claims to have found *the* method—the diaphragm in the 1920s–1930s, spermicidal foams and powders in the 1950s, the pill and the IUD in the 1960s–1970s, the shot or implant in the 1980s—the technological quick fix proved eternally elusive. All of these methods had their problems, and people's reproductive needs, desires, and circumstances were just too complicated to be answered by any one method. Whether or not one could use a given method to meet their needs was also profoundly shaped by larger structural issues: fluctuations in international contraceptive markets, the fickle nature of state policies, the lack of public health infrastructure to support those with side effects, and the social and cultural norms of the community, to name a few. Sometimes, something as seemingly small as a gentle hand, a warm speculum, or an extra ten minutes to discuss side effects could profoundly shape the wider meaning of any given method. Often, the ability to listen and adapt to the needs of those being targeted proved more important to the success of any program than the importation of newer and better technology.

Looking at the sources of those who put population policy into practice also allows us to see how actors at multiple points along the line resisted the more aggressive tactics of state programs: doctors who fudged the numbers, nurses who grounded their work in community well-being regardless of state directives, and women who gave fake addresses to researchers so they could not be traced home. Sometimes, these efforts increased the space for liberation within a program, or even led to internal or larger structural change. But the degrees of agency one could exercise in this field were fundamentally shaped by multiple inequalities: of race, class, and gender, but also of mobility and access to education. Intermediary actors like doctors and nurses could play a crucial role in either taking up the concerns of their patients or keeping them in their place, acting in solidarity with them or demeaning them and pressuring them to adopt one method or another. Certain women were listened to more than others, based on how they fit both within power hierarchies and within practitioners' ideas of what made a good patient. Those who did not have these cultural, social, and economic resources often relied on grassroots knowledge networks to find out the good and bad of these movements: though often disparaged by family planning advocates as "rumors," these networks could be crucial in both helping women learn about opportunities and protecting them from abuse.

The sources here also illustrate how the exchange of information among women within and across borders—how the ordinary act of talking and comparing experiences—came to form the foundation of the transnational reproductive rights movement that arose in the second half of the twentieth century and fueled the paradigm shift at the ICPD in Cairo. This movement began with a number of women in very distant locations witnessing pain and abuse, seeing the limits of contraceptive distribution without wider empowerment, and realizing that something was fundamentally wrong with the population control approach. This included women who had operated largely *within* the family planning, population, and development nexus, as well as those who came from outside, whose activism had started with feminism and women's health movements. When they found each other, they began to see the global backstory behind these local experiences, and the need for an equally global effort to overturn the population control paradigm. They built their conceptualization of reproductive rights by in turn talking to more women: sending letters to local women's organizations to hear their experiences and bringing women together in meetings and conferences to debate the intricacies of their concerns and points of contention. Importantly, these activities brought women from the regions most targeted by international population control policies—in Asia, Africa, Latin America, and the Caribbean—into contact with women of color targeted by similar state policies within the Global North. As a result, both the American-born "reproductive justice" movement and sections of the transnational "reproductive rights" movement developed a vision attentive to the intersections between global racism, imperialism, and structural inequality, embedded in broader understandings of human rights and social justice.

The sophisticated, multilayered analysis these women brought to these spaces, however, also means that most were left not entirely convinced that the international population movement had been "redeemed" in the aftermath of the ICPD conference in Cairo in 1994. In oral histories, they recounted their continuing concerns about the limits of the Program of Action and the troubling politics of reproduction around the globe today. In order to appreciate the full complexity of this present moment, however, we need to first understand the more nuanced dynamics of the family planning movement that came before: not only the ideological contradictions, but also the practical difficulties faced by those who operated on the ground. Through intimate social history, we can get a sense of the many more obstacles that need to be faced to realize reproductive rights and justice in the future.

Structure

The chapters that follow seek to tell the history of the global family planning movement by both looking broadly at networks of actors and zooming in on particularly rich sources. Chapter one, "Prophets," traces the trajectories and discourse of the first wave of family planning advocates who arose in the 1930s–1960s. The focus is primarily on those who formed the first family planning associations and clinics around the world, as well as those who became actively involved in transnational organizations like the International Planned Parenthood Federation (IPPF) and Pathfinder Fund. However, I also draw attention to the work of those who promoted the cause in subtler ways: incorporating it quietly into their medical practice or health promotion work, referring people to clinics, sharing information through informal networks. In doing so, I seek to expand our understanding of who counted as an "advocate" and illustrate how many layers of activism it took to propel this movement forward in this period. I also illustrate both the commonalities shaping this cohort—including the narratives of conversion and missionary work that linked them to humanitarian discourse—as well as the wide diversity that makes it impossible to characterize the cause as definitively one thing or another. This chapter also highlights the friction that shaped transnational relationships in the context of colonialism, decolonization, and cross-cultural divisions.

Chapter two, "Practice," explores early efforts (again from roughly the 1930s to 1960s) to translate prophecy into practice through the opening of clinics, distribution of contraceptives, personal visits to mothers in their homes, group discussions, and the use of pamphlets, radio, and film. At the core of this chapter is a micro-historical analysis of nine letters exchanged between the Jamaica Birth Control League and a Jamaican woman seeking support, stretching over a two-and-a-half-year period from 1939 to 1941. The letters are not used here because they are seen as representative of women's experiences. In fact, they are quite exceptional: in the length of correspondence, the level of detail, and the woman's willingness to continue engaging with the clinic despite several setbacks. Rather, the letters are used here because of their richness, the way that nearly every word and phrase hints at a larger global backstory that shaped the work of this individual clinic. Using sources from other clinics and associations as well as local histories from other areas of the world, I situate these letters within this broader context and highlight the hope, suspicion, emotion, pain, frustration, and disappointment that shaped family planning in this period.

Chapter three, "Crisis of Faith," focuses on the period from the 1960s to 1980s, when international organizations, foundations, foreign aid agencies, and states began to invest on a much heavier scale in the cause, fueling the creation of state programs that distributed new methods like IUDs, the birth control pill, Depo-Provera, and Norplant on an unprecedented scale. This chapter is also centered around a micro-historical analysis of a particularly rich and unique source: the over-two-thousand-page diary of Adaline Pendleton Satterthwaite, a consultant to the Population Council who traveled to two dozen countries from 1964 to 1974. Satterthwaite's diary provides a vivid account of the abuses perpetuated by some of these programs and the fundamental incongruency between efforts to promote the IUD as a universal method in the context of reproductive complexity. Her own crisis of faith—evident in an oral history conducted in 1974—mimics the larger questioning of the population establishment by a range of actors at the time, and ultimately pushed her to endorse the reproductive rights movement in the 1990s. However, this chapter also shows the many subtler limits to family planning programs beyond direct coercion, including a *lack* of state support, the high costs of the pill, the vagaries of international contraceptive markets, and intimate questions of tone and touch.

Chapter four, "Redemption?," expands outward again, this time to explore a particular network of women who would come to play a key role in advocating for reproductive rights on the international stage in the

1980s–1990s. By exploring their trajectories, we can see how critiques of population control and the fundamental principles of the reproductive rights framework arose from diverse locations, and how these women's backgrounds and experiences helped orient them toward a particular critique while also providing access to spaces of power. We can see the intersections between this movement and the emerging reproductive justice movement in the United States, the ways these movements pushed each other to expand their understanding of reproduction and root it more firmly in a critique of local and global economies. This chapter also reflects on the narratives women tell about their movement, one that sees the rise of reproductive rights and the meeting at Cairo as an important moment, but also as incomplete: hence, redemption (?) with a question mark.

Indeed, this story is not finished: neither in practice nor in its historical retelling. In lieu of a "conclusion," I therefore end the book with an "epilogue," considering how different starting points, and different routes through the archives, can take us in different places. I hope my particular approach has expanded our understanding of twentieth-century family planning, of what it looked like in practice, in the many intimate spaces in which this movement was made.

[CHAPTER ONE]

Prophets

We could start here with the first United Nations World Population conference, held in Rome in 1954. The conference building, headquarters to the UN's Food and Agricultural Organization (FAO), included two large blocks; it was modern, attractive, comfortable, and well appointed, with air-conditioned conference rooms equipped with individual earphones to allow for translation.[1] This was a conference of demographers, economists, physicians, bureaucrats, philanthropists, politicians: nearly all men. Their concern was "population": the perceived imbalance between resources and consumption, between food and people, between East and West, North and South, between "eugenic" and "dysgenic" bodies. Family planning—the conscious spacing/limitation of births at the individual level—was discussed vaguely and indirectly (if at all) as a means to a much bigger end, a way to contain population growth in the name of national development and world order. This was partly a political decision, an effort to avoid attracting too much ire from the Catholic Church and other conservative bodies. But it also reflected the general orientation of these men, who preferred dealing in statistics and projections, in "mathematics uncomplicated by sex."[2] These were authoritative experts, who "looked at human beings not as individuals but as a population that could be shaped through the combined force of faith and science."[3]

But then, there were other people, meeting in other spaces in these same years. We could look, for example, to the home of Sylvia Fernando, a teacher in Sri Lanka (then Ceylon). Although a member of the local elite, educated in sociology and economics, Fernando saw the trials of frequent childbearing faced by poor women through her community service work in health clinics and prisons. These very practical, material experiences inspired her to become one of the island's leading family planning advocates in the mid-twentieth century, starting the first clinic and serving as general secretary of the Family Planning Association (FPA) of Ceylon from 1953 to 1970. Her home became a meeting place in these decades for a diverse group of local doctors and practitioners who gathered for tea parties and dinners to discuss the practicalities of the movement. Family planning at the individual level, in the local context, sat at the core of these discussions. But this was still an international space, hosting family planning advocates who passed through from around the world. Fernando became close friends, in particular, with American advocate Dorothy Brush and Indian advocate Lady Rama Rau. As Fernando's daughter later recalled:

> Our house was the FPA office for all the years it didn't exist elsewhere . . . We'd always be falling over visiting family planners or researchers . . .
> We children used to have to turn envelopes. The FPA couldn't afford to buy envelopes, so my classmates and I would come home for lunch and be given enormous stacks of old envelopes. For hours, we turned enveloped [*sic*] [inside out, in order to repurpose them] for the FPA correspondence. We were bribed with lunch and ice-cream.[4]

Fernando's daughter stressed how her mother's Protestant religion influenced her activism. As she recalled: "She recognized that she was in a fortunate situation and wanted to say thank you to God." Those who worked with her described her charisma, her humor, her kindness: she was articulate, dynamic, loveable. As her successor at the FPA noted: "When you heard her you wanted to get up and do something. It was almost like taking a vow."[5]

This was the world of family planning advocates: forming local associations and leagues, hanging posters, running clinics, meeting in village squares, knocking on doors, organizing tea parties, sealing envelopes. With the exception of a coterie of male doctors and community leaders, women dominated these spaces: as doctors, nurses, social workers, charity ladies, volunteers, and fieldworkers. Most often, they described themselves as having been converted to the family planning cause by practical experiences, by the need to relieve the suffering of ailing mothers and overburdened families they came across in their work or in their own lives. They mobilized a maternalist, humanitarian, missionary discourse, suffused with emotion and spiritual reference, that stands in stark contrast to the dry statistical language adopted at population conferences. Those doing the intimate labor of the family planning movement smiled, cried, saw pain, felt joy, and spoke openly about love and compassion as critical to the success of the movement.

These worlds seem hard to reconcile with one another, but they were not as distant as they may seem at first glance. Some local family planning advocates were equally concerned about population growth, eugenics, and world peace. Some actors straddled both spaces. Dorothy Brush, for example, lingered in the hallways at the Rome conference, taking notes for the International Planned Parenthood Federation's (IPPF) *Around the World* newsletter, which she would bring to the homes of women like Fernando in her travels for the cause. The population cohort was also not quite as "rational" as they liked to claim. They slipped between mathematical calculations of overpopulation and ephemeral descriptions of "felt" pressure, based on a vague "sense of crowding."[6] The language of compassion and unity employed by practitioners for the cause, moreover, did not erase very real inequalities. If the racism, classism, and sexism underlying the cause were fairly obvious in the world of population politics, they could also infuse family planning practice, shaping intimate interactions between advocates from different countries, as well as between practitioners and communities. Finally, these worlds were directly connected through flows of money, particularly from the mid-1960s onward, when foreign aid agencies and philanthropic organizations poured millions of dollars into state population policies, many of which relied on the groundwork laid by early associations and already well-recognized local leaders to build their programs.

I will focus more on the transformations this influx of money and state intervention brought in chapter four, but here I want to chart the basic landscape of the early volunteer-based activism that preceded it in most countries. I start by tracing the trajectories of key actors who formed the first associations, ran the first clinics, and became the first advocates of the cause on the local and global scale from the 1930s to early 1960s. I found these actors both in local/national-level historical studies and in the papers of international organizations like the Pathfinder Fund and IPPF, whose fieldworkers were primarily tasked with tracking down and linking up with local enthusiasts. They collected material from local organizations, wrote descriptive lists of those doing ad hoc work in the field, and maintained correspondence with local advocates, allowing us to get a broad, bird's-eye perspective of the movement to complement that captured in local studies. I have cast a wide net in defining a family planning "advocate," including the elite doctors and charity ladies who often headed associations, but also a variety of freelance enthusiasts: midwives, taxi drivers, gas station attendants, grandmothers, nuns, and clinic patients who took it upon themselves to preach the cause to their communities. In doing so, I identify some common characteristics of this cohort, but also highlight the wide diversity of characters who became involved in this eclectic, decentralized movement during its early years.

After presenting the basic demographics of family planning advocates, I delve deeper into some of the core narratives and points of conflict that emerge from looking at this level of the movement. I start by exploring the "conversion stories" that appear in the literature, internal correspondence, autobiographical accounts, and oral histories of family planning advocates. In these stories, advocates describe their activism as being rooted in a practical response to the demand of communities they worked with and as a natural response to human suffering, rooted in core principles of medical care, religious ethics, and social service. I thus situate the global family planning movement as not only a question of feminism, eugenics, and neo-Malthusianism, but also a part of the history of maternalism, humanitarianism, and medical missionary work. I then explore how organizations like the Pathfinder Fund and IPPF attempted to build an international emotional community of family planning advocate practitioners, mobilizing a language of care, compassion, and kinship while valorizing the intimate, daily labor of family planning activism. Finally, I examine the tensions inherent in this approach: the international, local, political, and personal fractures that made these bonds tenuous and at times destructive. If faith and friendship could be powerful mobilizing forces, they were complicated by the reality of sex, race, and class inequality, destabilizing the practice of movement building and limiting the ability of these prophets to act in solidarity. Exploring the experiences of those who did this daily work—the prophecies they told, the bonds they built, and the ties that ruptured—allows us to see transnationalism as intimate practice.

Prophets

To get a broad understanding of the early decades of the family planning movement, historians have often started with a basic timeline of key events oriented around the formation of early birth control leagues and associations in the late nineteenth/early twentieth centuries. Most recognize the British Malthusian League as the first such organization, formed in 1877 after the trial of Annie Besant and Charles Bradlaugh for publishing a book explaining methods of birth control. A year later, Dutch peace and women's rights activist Aletta Jacobs began distributing diaphragms to working-class women out of a room provided by the Dutch General Trade Union in Amsterdam, providing the first model of the "birth control clinic" that would come to form a hallmark of family planning activism. Similar clinics opened by Margaret Sanger in the United States in 1916 and Marie Stopes in London in 1921 would attract international attention and lead to some of the first efforts to mobilize across borders. Both Stopes and Sanger went on lecture tours to promote the cause, traveling from Japan to Egypt to South Africa and beyond. Sanger also joined together with British activist Edith How-Martyn to form the London-based Birth Control International Information Centre (BCIIC) in 1935. Conceived as a network to disseminate knowledge around contraception, the Centre was composed primarily of women physicians, social workers, and birth control activists. From 1935 to 1936, Sanger and How-Martyn visited India, Burma, Malay, China, the Philippines, Japan, Hawaii, and Canada on a BCIIC "World Tour" to promote the cause internationally, followed by visits to India, Jamaica, and East and South Africa in 1938–1939.[7]

Starting with this traditional timeline, however, gives a somewhat misleading impression of family planning activism as something that arose in Europe and the United States and then flowed outward to the rest of the world. In fact, if we look more closely at local histories—and at Sanger's and Stopes's own records—we can see a much broader and more organic history of family planning activism, one that arose first through the initiative of local actors. Indeed, many of these early lecture tours were prompted by invitations from local activists already embedded in debates over birth control, who reached out to Stopes, Sanger, or How-Martyn in hopes that their growing international clout would help support local advocacy. Sanger's trip to China was preceded by the endorsement of birth control by the New Culture Movement among Chinese intellectuals;[8] Edith How-Martyn's trip to Jamaica was spurred by an invitation from Afro-Jamaican activist Amy Bailey, following a yearlong public debate over birth control on the island.[9] Sanger similarly found a thriving local movement when she arrived in Japan in 1922, led by intellectuals, socialists, and revolutionaries. In fact, some Japanese commentators were reportedly let down by her visit, seeing her as not nearly as radical as they had expected.[10] Vietnamese birth control advocates looked instead to countries like China and Japan for leadership in the 1920s and 1930s.[11] India was also an early leader in birth control activism, with a clinic opened in 1923 in Madras and a range of activities headed by neo-Malthusians, radical anti-caste, atheist, self-respect movements, and erotic entrepreneurs marketing contraceptive appliances alongside sex books.[12] Bombay was home to the journal *Marriage Hygiene* in the 1930s, run by Dr. A. P. Pillay and read by birth control advocates around the world.[13] Sanger herself recognized that many governments abroad were also further ahead than the United States in this field, like Russia, which legalized abortion and distributed contraception in health services from 1920 to 1936.[14]

What Sanger, Stopes, and others brought, then, was not the *idea* of birth control itself, but rather a particular *model* of birth control activism, centered around the formation of associations and the opening of clinics along the lines of their own.[15] These models spread quickly, and by 1939, birth control services were being offered by associations or government medical centers in the UK, Australia, Holland, Germany, Belgium, China, India, Austria, Japan, Denmark, Norway, Russia, Sweden, Mexico, Canada, Switzerland, Ceylon, Iceland, New Zealand, South Africa, Bermuda, Hong Kong, Puerto Rico, and Jamaica.[16] This effort was disrupted by the Second World War, with clinics in several countries closing their doors, struggling to maintain supplies, or facing drastic regulations against birth control; local advocates in Nazi-occupied areas found themselves imprisoned or forced to flee, sometimes relying on transnational birth control networks to facilitate their escape. The genocidal euthanasia and coerced sterilization policies of the Nazi regime also cast a dark shadow on the eugenics movement, and on the birth control movement by association.[17]

With the end of the war, however, activists moved to revitalize international networks, under a new and presumably more benign rubric of "family planning" or "planned parenthood." Norwegian-born Elise Ottesen-Jensen, founder of the Swedish National League for Sex Education (RFSU), invited a semi-retired Sanger and other international actors to a conference in Stockholm in 1946 to jump-start these efforts. Their collaboration led to the launch in Bombay, India, in 1952 of the International Planned Parenthood Federation (IPPF), with associations from England, the Netherlands, Hong Kong, India, Singapore, Sweden, the United States, and West Germany as its eight founding members. The IPPF's constitution outlined its central goals: to bring about acceptance of "voluntary responsible parenthood," to assist in the formation of Family Planning Associations (FPAs) around the world, to stimulate and disseminate scientific research, to provide training and support quality standards in contraceptives, and to organize international conferences.[18]

Inquiries came quickly, illustrating the truly broad nature of interest in family planning. In its 1952 report, the IPPF noted that requests for information and services had been received from the Gold Coast, Kenya, Nigeria, Nyasaland, Rhodesia, Sierra Leone, Tanganyika, Uganda, the Union of South Africa, Australia, Belgium, British Guiana, Canada, Ceylon, Cypress, Egypt, France, Germany, Greece, Holland, Hong Kong, India, Iran, Iraq, Italy, Malaya, Malta, New Zealand, Norway, Pakistan, Portugal, the Persian Gulf, St. Helena, Singapore, Tonga (South Pacific), Trieste, and

Turkey. Government representatives, family planning advocates, doctors, and social workers from Austria, Burma, Canada, Ceylon, Germany, Hong Kong, India, Indonesia, Jamaica, Japan, Mauritius, Pakistan, Singapore, the South Pacific Islands, Switzerland, Turkey, the Union of South Africa, and the United States also made personal visits to the IPPF headquarters in London. The IPPF provided these actors with information and advice on the setting up of clinics, family planning propaganda, supplies, and training in "modern contraceptive technique."[19] In 1956, the association reported receiving around 1,700 letters of inquiry and 100 overseas visitors.[20] The IPPF also began a "modest" fieldwork program in 1957,[21] and started giving out small grants to local associations for travel and conference expenses, free medical supplies, and visual aids.[22] Annual IPPF conferences also played an important role both in bringing together like-minded advocates from around the world and in providing publicity for the family planning movement in the host country. Both German and Jamaican family planning advocates, for example, noted a sharp increase in publicity and inquiries following regional conferences held in their countries in 1957 and 1958, respectively.[23]

The IPPF would be joined in this internationalist endeavor in 1957 by the Pathfinder Fund, headed by prominent American birth control advocate Dr. Clarence Gamble. Gamble had first become interested in birth control as a doctor in the United States in the 1920s, and began to actively promote contraceptive advice within a network of maternal health clinics. His work was deeply influenced by eugenic theories that contended that differential fertility rates between the "fit" and "unfit" would lead to social degeneration if not controlled.[24] To this end, he helped establish the Human Betterment League of North Carolina in 1947, aimed at promoting eugenic steriliza-tion of the so-called "unfit" while also encouraging reproduction among elite Americans (he and his wife Sarah had five children themselves). He became involved in the IPPF in its early years, but felt the organization was too timid and needed to adopt a more assertive approach to stimulate in-terest and activism in birth control abroad. The Pathfinder Fund adopted a "rapid intervention style," searching out potentially interested local doc-tors, nurses, social workers, and prominent individuals in a given country and trying to encourage them to form a formal association and open a pilot clinic. The Fund would then provide one- or two-year renewable grants for salaries, supplies, or materials to get the pilot project going, with the hope that it would grow into a larger program.[25] As Necochea López notes, they essentially "put field-workers on the ground and let them find whatever means they could to provide people with contraceptives, availing them-selves of whatever allies they could."[26]

Both the IPPF and the Pathfinder Fund relied on fieldworkers to help establish and maintain links with local actors working on family planning. The Pathfinder Fund sent out Edith Gates, Margaret Roots, and Edna Rankin McKinnon, three North American women in their late fifties/early sixties with an interest in social issues and travel abroad. These actors had no medical training, but were skilled in intercultural relations and organization: Gates had prior experience working for the Young Women's Christian Association (YWCA) and American Christian Committee for Refugees, while McKinnon had headed the Chicago chapter of the Planned Parenthood Federation of America. By 1955, the three women had collectively traveled to Ceylon, Pakistan, Greece, Egypt, Jordan, Lebanon, Syria, Iraq, Iran, Turkey, Cyprus, Sudan, Ethiopia, Kenya, Zanzibar, Tanganyika, Uganda, and Southern Rhodesia on behalf of the Pathfinder Fund.[27] The IPPF relied more on medical professionals, including American doctor Abraham Stone and British women doctors like Helena Wright and Cecily Mure, who traveled internationally to provide practical advice to local associations and clinics.[28] Wealthy volunteers also played a key role in supporting international organizing efforts. Dorothy Hamilton Brush, for example, became a close friend of Sanger's and a major donor to the IPPF through her late husband's family philanthropic organization, the Brush Foundation. Brush described her role as "an observer, reporter and hopefully friend-maker... my position is chiefly to advise persons already interested in beginning work and that advise [sic] consists largely in telling them the necessary sources for practical information."[29]

Brush was also the first editor of *Around the World: News of Population and Birth Control* (hereafter *ATW*), the IPPF's monthly bulletin, which covered the development of family planning movements around the world. Started in January 1952, the paper targeted fieldworkers and local advocates "already interested in BC [birth control] who like to know what is going on elsewhere."[30] *ATW* provided brief updates on scientific conferences, research, new books, and the work of family planning associations around the world, based on published news articles, fieldworkers' reports, and correspondence with local advocates. The paper was intentionally small and "newsy," meant for busy "workers," cheap to mail out, and relatively easy to translate into foreign languages.[31] At the end of its first year, *ATW* was reportedly reaching 6,700 people each month, in about 100 countries and colonies; by its second anniversary, this number had nearly doubled to 12,000 readers.[32] By January 1956, volunteers were regularly translating the paper into German, Spanish, Japanese, Italian, and French, with occasional issues in Chinese, Flemish, and Hausa.[33] Beyond an informative bulletin, the paper aimed to create a sense of community among family planning advocates around the world; Sanger described it as "the glue which holds our far-flung workers together."[34]

While early fieldworkers for the IPPF and Pathfinder were predominantly British and American women, the demographic profile expanded over the course of the 1950s and 1960s, particularly as the IPPF established regional offices. Women like Aziza Hussein of Egypt, Beth Jacobs of Jamaica, and Goh Kok Kee of Singapore came to serve as vice presidents of regional offices, developing multiple cross-cutting networks. Goh Kok Kee traveled around the Southeast Asia region promoting the cause, and Singapore became an important hub for family planning activity, providing materials and training to advocates from Burma, Korea, Siam, India, Pakistan, Malaya, Sarawak, and Indonesia in the early 1950s.[35] Ofelia Mendoza led fieldwork efforts in the Western Hemisphere Region (WHR), traveling across Latin America in the 1950s and 1960s opening and assisting organizations in different areas.[36] Family planning advocates also formed bilateral bonds with associations in other countries outside of the mechanisms provided by the IPPF. Jamaican advocates Lenworth and Beth Jacobs, for example, visited the Ceylon FPA in 1959 to learn more about their association,[37] while the honorary secretary of the FPA of India, Avabai Wadia, visited Uganda and Peru to support family planning work.[38] Lady Rama Rau of India also traveled widely, including a trip to Toronto in 1964 that reportedly "infused much strength into the Canadian movement, probably one of the weakest of her IPPF family, and the one which needed her help, so generously given, the most."[39]

Indeed, if population circles in the Global North had begun to shift attention to the Global South as the key site of intervention following World War II,[40] much of the IPPF's work in the 1950s and '60s continued to focus on so-called "backward" countries and regions within Europe and North America. Sometimes this categorization was based on sweeping generalizations about cultural patterns; after receiving a letter from one Greek reader, for example, Dorothy Brush concluded that "so far as we can discover, Greece knows nothing of family planning."[41] Most of the countries in this category were considered backward, however, on the basis of hostile governments or the influence of the Catholic Church. A report issued in the early 1950s noted that laws prohibiting birth control were still on the books in Austria, Germany, Spain, and Italy;[42] France did not open its first family planning center until 1961.[43] The *ATW* newsletter also lamented the slow progress in the United States: although most large cities had private family planning clinics by 1952, only eight states incorporated it into public health services and contraceptives remained banned in the two "backward states" of Massachusetts and Connecticut.[44] In family planning circles in the 1950s/60s, countries like Sweden, India, Ceylon, Pakistan, Egypt, Singapore, and Hong Kong were often seen as more "advanced," judged on the extent of family planning services and level of support from governments.[45]

In any case, as before WWII, fieldworkers found that in most places they traveled there was already a longer history of decentralized, spontaneous local family planning work underway. In her report on a trip to Borneo, Kuching, Sibu, Sungai Teku, Kapit, and Nanga Mujong in 1957, for example, the regional chair of the IPPF's Far East and Australasian Region noted that "in all these places rudimentary family planning facilities have been available for some time."[46] Indeed, fieldworkers regularly identified long lists of local actors who were either already distributing contraceptives or were interested in receiving supplies and information.[47] This included many private doctors, nurses, and women's health organizations who incorporated it into their regular services without necessarily seeing themselves as part of an international family planning movement. There was Dr. Mrs. Abeyratne, in Ceylon, who provided free birth control services in her home every Friday afternoon;[48] nurse Maria de R. Meza of Mexico, who gave advice to women through her Child Welfare Committee in Tijuana;[49] midwife Gladys George of Ghana, who gave talks on sex and contraception during her town's Christian Home Week;[50] and Mrs. Agnes Wu-Kung in Rangoon, Burma, who had no training but learned from books and articles and supplied appliances herself.[51] In Peru, midwives and doctors promoted family planning through their private practices, often struggling to make ends meet.[52] Even in places where there were laws against importation or manufacture of contraceptives, Pathfinder fieldworker Edith Gates noted that many doctors "pay little heed to these laws."[53] In Germany, a group of eighteen women physicians gave contraceptive information for free in their offices in Hamburg in 1953 despite legal restrictions.[54] Dr. Nghiem Thi Thuan, a female doctor who headed the nursing school in Saigon, talked to her graduates about family planning despite a ban on contraceptives in Vietnam inherited from French colonial rule.[55]

Family planning was also promoted by an eclectic group of sympathizers, including school principals and welfare workers who gave talks on family planning; a petrol dealer in Pakistan who gave out contraceptives to his customers; an independent publisher from Mexico who put out paperbacks on sex education; and a trilingual taxi driver in Ceylon who translated literature for the fieldworker he carted around and helped set up meetings with revenue officers, mayors, or anyone else he came into contact with along the way.[56] Networks of "bible women" in Singapore, who canvassed areas urging people to come to church, added news about the family planning clinic opened by the Singapore FPA to their repertoire.[57] In Puerto Rico, a peer-to-peer network recruited 1,371 volunteers to spread the word around their villages, composed primarily of housewives but also including some thirty firemen, seven policemen, a judge, carpenters, merchants, shoemakers, secretaries, and teachers.[58] These "fellow-travelers," as one report from the FPA of Ceylon put it, were particularly crucial in helping "spread the gospel" of family planning.[59]

Protestant religious leaders, organizations, and groups were notably active in spreading this new gospel. By the mid-twentieth century, most Protestant denominations had officially mandated the use of contraception within married couples,[60] creating space for activism by church organizations and leaders. In the Philippines, for example, leadership on family planning in the late 1960s largely fell under the auspices of the Philippine Federation of Christian Churches, in association with the United Council of Church Women and the Study Commission on Rapid Social Change. As IPPF fieldworker Barbara Cadbury noted in a trip to the Philippines in 1960, one reverend for the Federation was particularly enthusiastic: he and his wife had been combining family planning advice with their marital counseling work for at least seven years.[61] In Ghana, the first group to set up family planning information and services was the Christian Council; in Korea, the first clinics were set up in the late 1950s by a Methodist Church mothers' association.[62] In Peru, Methodist Reverend Elton Watlington worked with Edith Gates of the Pathfinder Fund to set up South America's first voluntary family planning committee in 1958.[63]

Family planning was also supported by many Catholic doctors, nurses, and nuns, despite the explicit prohibition of artificial contraceptive methods by the Church's hierarchy. On a trip to Brazil, Gates found that "the most progressive single doctor was a young Catholic" who had already started giving advice to couples preceding marriage.[64] In an oral history, Filipino demographer Mercedes Concepcion recalled the story of one Jesuit priest that she worked with:

> He said that he was always traveling with condoms in his briefcase, and when they would open it at the airports they would wonder why there was this priest in a soutane carrying condoms. And he would say, "Well, I use this as"—oh, what do you call this?—"caps for the battery of my car," he said, "because it makes [it run] very [well]"—you know, what is this—(laughter) or else he would say, "I give it to the children as balloons to play with." But he always carried these condoms.[65]

The Belgium Society for Sexual Advice similarly noted how Catholic doctors would quietly send patients to the Society's clinics, if not providing services themselves.[66] Religious leaders of other denominations were also found among the ranks of family planning prophets. A Shinto priest in Tokyo advised all the couples he married to visit the Japan Birth Control Institute before going on their honeymoon,[67] and Islamic leaders in several countries advised their followers of the acceptability of family planning. A fatwa issued by Shaykh 'Abd al-Majid Salim in Egypt in 1937, for example, sanctioned the prevention of pregnancy in marriage by either a man or a woman.[68] When traveling to predominantly Muslim countries, Pathfinder Fund employees came armed with a leaflet with excerpts from Dr. A. Ramali's book *Regulations on Health According to Islamic Law*, which claimed that family planning was not forbidden if agreed upon by both husband and wife for hygienic, social, or economic reasons.[69]

Organizing such sympathizers into official family planning associations and building/sustaining clinics could be a decades-long process, however. In Ceylon, for example, the Women's Political Union first started a campaign to teach birth control at the Medical College in 1931. This was dropped quickly due to opposition from the Catholic hierarchy, although an interested nurse managed to operate a small clinic in her house during WWII. It wasn't until 1949, however, that the All-Ceylon Women's Conference sponsored the formation of the Family Planning Association, which was not officially launched until 1953.[70] In Malaysia, Dr. A. E. Doraisamy, a government obstetrician in Kuala Lumpur, attempted to organize an association in 1938, but the first FPA was not founded until 1953.[71] Efforts to form official associations of this sort were often a combined effort of individual doctors, prominent personalities, and local women's organizations. The Marriage Guidance Association in Nigeria, for example, was spearheaded by Mrs. Abimbola Abayomi, the first female obstetrician-gynecologist, and several prominent wives of aristocrats, together with Dr. Adeniyi-Jones, medical officer at the Ministry of Health.[72] In Uganda, the Indian Women's Association and Moslem Women's Association took the lead in organizing a meeting of interested parties to form the Family Planning Committee of Kampala.[73] Expatriate doctors could also play a key role in initiating local associations. British doctor Beric Wright (son of IPPF fieldworker Dr. Helena Wright), for example, opened the first clinic in Trinidad in 1956 while working as an employee for Shell Oil. In 1959, American nurse Cevilla Knick ("Nicky") McBride helped bring together local doctors interested in family planning work to form the FPA of Trinidad and Tobago.[74]

Pathfinder and IPPF fieldworkers supported these efforts, providing guidance on how to publicize the work of an association, keep client cards for clinics, and produce monthly/yearly reports.[75] The *ATW* newsletter also printed practical guides for associations, stressing, for example, the need for lay committees (to arrange finance, housing, and staffing) and medical committees (to decide on medical policies and procedures) of "unquestioned reputation." They also provided a list of suggested names, including "Family Planning Center, Planned Parenthood Center, Birth Control Clinic, Maternal Health Clinic."[76] By 1959, some eighteen additional groups had joined the IPPF, for a total of twenty-four associations listed as full members and two public health departments (Bermuda and Vaud, Switzerland) as associate members.[77] This list, however, underestimates the full reach of family planning activism in these years. The IPPF directory of 1959, for example, listed a total of fifty-six countries offering services through public health or independent clinics, well beyond the twenty-six official members.[78]

The organization's annual report for 1959, represented in table 1.1, gives some indication of both the convergence and diversity in identity among these organizations. Half of the organizations had existed before the formation of the IPPF in 1952. Thirteen associations had adopted the increasingly standardized name of "family planning association" or "planned parenthood federation," but eleven kept or created their own variations: for example, the Belgian Society for Sexual Advice, the Polish Conscious Motherhood Society, and the Puerto Rican Association for the Well-Being of the Family.[79] Beyond contraception, at least ten out of twenty-six members provided services to treat infertility, and eleven provided marital counseling and/or specific support for those with "sexual disturbances." Some of these organizations, like the FPAs of India, Pakistan, Ceylon, Barbados, and Singapore, already had government support for their work and an expansive network of clinics, while others, like the New Zealand FPA and the Belgian Society for Sexual Advice, relied exclusively on correspondence and mailed material.[80]

The records of international organizations and fieldworkers also give us an indication of the general demographics of these groups. Most of the associations' officials included a mix of doctors, nurses, social workers, and prominent elites. Of those FPAs listed in the IPPF report of 1959, some 58 percent of officers are identifiable as women. Although 60 percent of these associations had male presidents (often a more or less honorary position), 65 percent of the doctors involved were women. Moreover, most of the general secretaries were women, doing the day-to-day work of maintaining the clinics, fundraising, and lobbying politicians.[81] The Family Planning Association of Ceylon, for example, was headed by a male president in 1959—Professor C. C. E. Silva—at the insistence of Sylvia Fernando, who saw this as strategically important. But the association and clinic were really led by a two-woman team, with Fernando doing the motivational and organizing work and Dr. Siva Chinnatamby doing the medical work.[82] The FPA of China (Taiwan) was headed by Dr. Hsu Shih-Chu, who ran the clinical program, but all of the organizational work fell on Mrs. Tze-kuan Shu Kan, the executive director.[83]

TABLE 1.1 IPPF members, 1959

Name	Founding	Services
Family Planning Association of Australia	1926	Birth control, marital counseling services
Barbados Family Planning Association	1955	Birth control, sex education, infertility services
Belgium Society For Sexual Advice	1949	Referrals to doctors, consciousness raising
Bermuda Medical and Health Department	First clinic 1934	Birth control, maternal and child welfare services
Family Planning Association of Ceylon	1953	Not listed
Family Planning Association of Denmark	1956	Not listed
Finnish Family Welfare League	1941	Birth control, marital counseling, sexual disturbance, infertility services
La Maternité Heureuse (France)	1956	Consciousness raising
Profamilia (German Society for Marriage and Family)	1952	Birth control, marital counseling, sex education, training, infertility services
Family Planning Association of Hong Kong	1950	Birth control, marital counseling, infertility services
Family Planning Association of India	1949	Birth control, training, marital counseling, sex education, infertility services, consciousness raising
Italian Association for Demographic Education	1953	Consciousness raising, training
Jamaican Family Planning Association	1957	Birth control, maternal and child welfare services, youth support, training, consciousness raising
Family Planning Federation of Japan	1954	Not listed
Mauritius Family Welfare Association	1957	Birth control, consciousness raising
Netherlands Society for Sexual Reform	1946	Birth control, marital counseling, sex education services, training
New Zealand Family Planning Association	1939	Birth control, marital counseling, sex education, infertility services, training
Family Planning Association of Pakistan	1953	Not listed

Name	Founding	Services
Society for Conscious Motherhood (Poland)	1957	Birth control, marital counseling, sexual disturbances, sex education, infertility services
Puerto Rican Association for Family Wellbeing	1954	Birth control, infertility services, consciousness raising
Singapore Family Planning Association	1949	Not listed
South African National Council for Maternity and Family Welfare	1935	Birth control, marital counseling, youth support
National Association for Sex Education (Sweden)	1933	Birth control, sex education services
Vaud Medical and Health Department (Switzerland)	N/A	Not listed
Family Planning Association of the UK	1930	Birth control, marital counseling, infertility services, training, consciousness raising
Planned Parenthood Federation of America (US)	1941	Birth control, marital counseling, infertility services

Source: IPPF "Fourth Report," London, England, 1957/01/01–1959/05/31. F10, B6, Dorothy Hamilton Brush Papers, Smith College Special Collections.

In some associations, the domination of women was even more pronounced. In the 1959 IPPF report, 80–90 percent of officers were women in the FPA of Hong Kong, FPA of India, South African National Council for Maternity and Welfare, and FPA of the UK. La Maternité Heureuse in France was composed entirely of women, from its president down to its treasurers.[84]

If anything, however, these numbers underestimate the number of women involved, since officers made up only a small part of the work of these associations, which were generally supported by an army of female staff and volunteers. For example, although only 17 percent of the officers of the Mauritius Family Planning Association were female, all of the regional supervisors were women.[85] The seven clinics run by the FPA of Hong Kong in 1956 relied on eighteen doctors and some forty-four other women giving voluntary service, as well as part-time paid clerical helpers and nurses.[86] Volunteers in these and other associations hung posters, contacted patients, filed records, answered correspondence, and reached out to potential members. They organized fundraising campaigns—tea parties, dances, lectures, Christmas cards, raffles, cooking classes, bridge games, mahjong drives, and thrift shops—and gathered old newspapers and clothes to be sold to support the clinic.[87] Constance Goh Kok Kee of Singapore recalled events where they would charge women a dollar to come to a fancy house, have tea, and listen to a speaker on "how to take care of your skin or how to lose weight."[88] As she recalled, "I worked out thirty-four ways to make money!"[89] In Washington, DC, African American social worker Ophelia Egypt and her women colleagues from the local Planned Parenthood branch held house parties to gain the support of key community leaders, from school

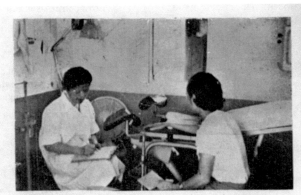

This is an inside view of our mobile clinic.

Mrs. Narciso Ramos, wife of Philippine Embassador, advosor of this Association, gave guidance to our worker.

FIGURE 1.1. "Family Planning Association of China Report, 1965." Copyright Family Planning Association of Taiwan. Source: Margaret Sanger Papers, Smith College Special Collections.

Posing before our mobile clinic are (left to right) Dr. S. C. Hsu of JCRR, Mrs. Tze-Kuan Shu Kan of this Association and Miss Julia Lieo of JCRR.

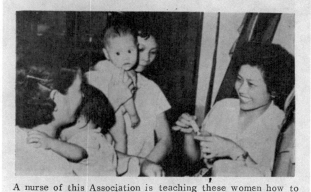

A nurse of this Association is teaching these women how to apply this contraceptive.

FIGURE 1.2. "Family Planning Association of China Report, 1965." Copyright: Family Planning Association of Taiwan. Source: Margaret Sanger Papers, Smith College Special Collections.

principals to beauty salon owners, while also putting up posters for the clinic in stores, in churches, and on bulletin boards.[90]

The high representation of women in these activities in part reflects the connections between early family planning activism and longer traditions of women's charity and social welfare work. By the 1940s/50s, many countries had a network of maternal health, child welfare, and charity organizations, which brought elite women into closer contact with working-class families and poor women, providing a natural gateway into family planning activism targeting these populations. Wives of colonial officials,

FIGURE 1.3. Edna McKinnon with a group of Indonesian doctors and midwives. Singapore, 1962. Source: Edna Rankin McKinnon Papers, Schlesinger Library, Harvard Radcliffe Institute.

FIGURE 1.4. "Informal portrait of Edna Rankin McKinnon with [unnamed] Nigerian public health nurse." Nigeria, 1964. Source: Edna Rankin McKinnon Papers, Schlesinger Library, Harvard Radcliffe Institute.

European settlers, and Christian missionaries featured heavily in many of these organizations in areas still under—or recently liberated from— European colonial rule. In Kulai, for example, two English missionary ladies incorporated family planning services into the maternity clinics they worked at, while a family planning scheme on the Tebrau Estate in Malaysia was run by the European manager's wife, who had received training on diaphragms in Singapore.[91] But women's clinics and social welfare work were also informed by longer traditions of indigenous charity and the social activism that accompanied emerging nationalist movements. In India, for example, women's advocates fit family planning within a historical tradition of social service inflected by Gandhian principles,[92] while Jamaican advocates incorporated it into a range of new women's organizations that incorporated practical services for working-class women alongside nationalist activism.[93] In Ceylon, the prime minister's wife Sirimavo Bandaranaike—who would later go on to become the world's first female prime minister—was an early volunteer at the FPA.[94]

The involvement of women doctors in the family planning movement was also connected in part to their increasing representation within medical professions more broadly. In some countries, like Pakistan, women's health issues were treated almost exclusively by female doctors, who reportedly made up roughly one-quarter of graduates from medical school by the 1960s.[95] In other places, the women were pioneers. Ceylon's Dr. Chinnatamby, for example, was of only five female medical students in her intake in the early 1940s;[96] family planning advocates Dr. Tewhida Ben Sheikh of Tunisia and Dr. Andrea Evangelina Rodriguez of the Dominican Republic were the first women doctors in their respective countries.[97] As Caroline Rusterholz points out, the fact that many of these pioneering doctors found themselves in the field of family planning likely reflected both their personal interest in helping women and their general assignment to "feminine" fields of medicine such as obstetrics and gynecology due to the belief that they were more suited for this type of work. Women doctors were also often relegated to more precarious positions within the medical hierarchy, working predominantly in welfare provision, public health, and community health.[98] These positions put them in more regular contact with working-class women in need of birth control, providing them with more practical experience in a field not taught in medical school or considered particularly respectable. As Rusterholz argues, these women essentially "capitalized on the fact that they were assigned to a low-status, feminine field of medicine and turned their practical experience into an asset at both national and international levels."[99]

This was, however, demanding and frequently unrecognized work. Doctors and nurses often contributed their labor to family planning clinics for free, outside of their normal working hours, or accepted lower pay than they would have made in hospitals or other clinics at the time. Dr. Edris Rice-Wray reported working "60 hours a week" at Mexico's first clinic, opened in 1959,[100] while Marie-Andrée Lagroua Weill-Hallé, the head of La Maternité Heureuse in France, worked herself ragged to support both the cause and her three young children.[101] Mrs. O. Djoewari of the Indonesia FPA described the headaches caused by the emotional and mental labor of family planning: the "unrelenting activities in lobbying—in smiling and scolding (only in mind) in laughing and crying—in smiling and frowning—in conforming and deviating—in accepting and bargening [sic]." She also expressed her guilt in neglecting her own family for "the cause of Family Planning."[102] Dr. Siva Chinnatamby was clear that she did not marry because of her work, noting that "with a bad case I didn't get home for three days, working day and night. So if I had a family of my own, it would have been difficult, to say the least."[103] Indeed, the Ceylon Family Planning Association noted the difficulty of maintaining paid workers due to the arduous demands of family planning work. Frequently, a clinic would close down if the main doctor or nurse switched jobs or retired from the field.[104]

Family planning work was also controversial. In spite of the active involvement of laymen in the movement, religious opposition continued among certain sections of the Protestant and Muslim hierarchies, illustrating the lack of total consensus within these bodies. The Catholic Church hierarchy and leaders of Catholic countries also denounced the global family planning movement in international forums throughout the twentieth century. The Vatican newspaper *Osservatore Romano* specifically attacked the IPPF's *ATW* newsletter in November 1959 on the grounds that it promoted "propagandistic licentiousness" and offended religion.[105] This opposition had very real consequences for local actors who found themselves targeted for repercussions. As Edris Rice-Wray, the organizer of the first clinic in Mexico, noted in September 1962: "We have our first martyr of this cause in México." Four days after becoming head of the local Mexican association, Dr. Arturo Aldama had been transferred by the government to a less desirable health center miles away from the clinic.[106] In his oral history, Dr. Mario Jaramillo of Colombia recalled several transfers and lost jobs resulting from Church opposition to his work on family planning.[107] Members of the AIED in Italy similarly found their positions terminated due to Catholic opposition.[108] Catholic nurses in Singapore were forbidden to work at the family planning clinic by their superiors, and Goh Kok Kee—although herself a Protestant—heard from friends that the Catholic priest regularly condemned her to hell for her work in family planning.[109]

Beyond religious conflicts, discussions of contraception were also simply too risqué for many respectable circles, even if discussed under the seemingly benign rhetoric of "family planning." Indeed, if some charity and humanitarian organizations embraced family planning in this period, others took pains to distance themselves from it, worrying it would embroil them in controversy and draw away from their broader agendas.[110] Those who took up the work sometimes found themselves facing considerable social ostracism. Dr. Evangelina Rodriguez of the Dominican Republic, for example, was attacked on multiple grounds: for her Afro-Caribbean heritage, her lower-class background, her plain clothing, and her lack of a husband, which led to accusations that she was a lesbian.[111] Even the class and social position of elite women failed to protect them from gendered, racialized, and sexualized dismissals by their peers in elite social circles, including "snide laughter," and "stale jokes" that followed them throughout their work.[112] Sylvia Fernando's home in Ceylon—the location where this chapter started—again provides an illustrative example. Her daughter recalled that over the years the walls of their garden were covered in insults from Sinhalese nationalists calling her a "traitor to the race" and accusing her of violating God's laws and nature's laws.[113] Despite the efforts of elite ladies to make birth control "not only permissible but fashionable,"[114] as Constance Goh Kok Kee of Singapore noted in a letter, the work of family planning was decidedly "unglamorous."[115]

Conversion Stories

What drove advocates to proselytize for this cause in spite of these attacks, and how did they find community with one another? The sources I explored revealed many of the same imperatives discussed by other scholars, as reviewed in the introduction to this book. As we might expect, fears of overpopulation loomed large, highlighted in the pamphlets of local family planning associations and articles in the IPPF's *ATW* newsletter.[116] In the newsletter's first number, for example, editor Dorothy Brush quoted ecologist William Vogt's assertion that "World overpopulation represents more of a threat to peace than the atom bomb."[117] Nearly every edition of the paper included a review of a new book or report documenting the rise of world population, a testament to the sheer explosion of literature on the subject during this period. In some countries, this was combined with an emerging environmentalism; in Costa Rica, for example, the first clinics were set up by actors concerned with deforestation.[118] IPPF and Pathfinder leaders like C. P. Blacker and Clarence Gamble, among others, retained their interest in eugenic principles, described in *ATW* through a new language of "hereditary counselling" to distance the movement from Nazi-era racial genocide.[119]

If overpopulation and eugenic discourses were visible in many spaces after WWII, however, family planning continued to draw in prominent feminist and sex reform advocates from around the world. Indian activist Kamaladevi Chattopadhyay opened the 1952 IPPF conference with a speech that challenged neo-Malthusian arguments and argued in favor of an anti-racist, anti-imperial, and feminist vision of birth control as a right.[120] Dr. Evangelina Rodriguez of the Dominican Republic situated her work within a larger agenda of feminist activism, including work on behalf of prostitutes.[121] Funmilayo Ransome-Kuti of Nigeria, a nationalist leader and founder of the Nigerian Women's Union, reportedly told an IPPF fieldworker in 1959 that she saw family planning as "a basic right of women."[122] A report in *ATW* described Dr. Lin Yutang, vice chancellor of Nanyang University in Singapore, as saying that "all emancipation of women is a mask and an illusion unless they are given the knowledge whereby they can plan their families wisely."[123] Dr. Zarina Fazelbhoy, president of the Karachi branch of the FPA of Pakistan, highlighted the importance of sex education at a conference in 1962, stressing that "if the children are to regard sex as something clean, good and natural they must be told about it in a good, clean and natural manner."[124] That same conference also hosted a roundtable discussion on the need for men and women to contribute equally to marriage and the upbringing of children.[125] Several advocates from around the world cited their interest in "the Swedish model," which focused on contraception as a means to discover and develop one's sexual self, an approach embedded in the country's pioneering sex education program from 1956 onward.[126]

The most consistent narrative I found in sources produced by those who did the day-to-day labor of family planning activism, however, eschewed a political or ideological agenda altogether, describing their work as driven by a pragmatic or humanitarian urge to answer the demands of those they encountered in their work. Doctors, nurses, social workers, and charity ladies alike described themselves as having been "converted" to the cause by "obvious patient demand."[127] A pediatrician in Bangkok, for example, explained that they had been pushed to offer services by mothers attending a weekly preschool clinic who expressed interest in family planning.[128] A doctor in Mexico began holding sex education classes at the request of mothers.[129] The Maadi Child Welfare Association and Cairo Women's Club in Egypt started offering birth control in their clinics due to "the spontaneous requests for help received from women who had suffered from repeated pregnancies."[130] Dr. Tewhida Ben Sheikh of Tunisia recalled that her private gynecological practice quickly became a space where women consulted her about "just about any problem they might have"—family disputes, relationships, child care—and inevitably "the subject of the number of children they desired would arise." As soon as contraception became legal in 1963, she began a family planning service at her hospital.[131]

Advocates also described the medical complications and emotional turmoil faced by multiparous women as a key motivating factor, regardless of whether the women asked for family planning directly. Dr. Mario Jaramillo of Colombia described seeing how repeated pregnancies, deliveries, and self-induced abortions "destroyed the bodies and minds"[132] of women who came into his hospital. As he recalled: "What those women said was very tragic and dramatic, month after month of practices. I was convinced I had to do something."[133] Dr. Siva Chinnatamby saw her experiences at the De Sousa Hospital for Women in Ceylon as a driving impetus for her family planning work. As she described: "As a consultant in charge of the emergency cases, I had many cases admitted, day and night, for complications of child birth; hemorrhage, ruptured uterus, infection . . . I realized that 95 per cent of the women had more than 10 children and that these complications were preventable. One woman I cared for had 26 children. With the 26th baby she came to the hospital dying."[134] FPA of Trinidad and Tobago clinic volunteer Dr. Elizabeth Quamina told a similar story: "I used to see mothers coming in pregnant and when we spoke to them we realized this was their fifth or sixth pregnancy, and these women were all around the age of 22. I saw the women die from anemia, I saw them die from ruptured uterus and I realized that even though family planning services existed, no one knew."[135] Social workers at the Singapore Family Planning Association related how they were "constantly meeting women worn out by frequent and innumerable pregnancies, to whom motherhood brought no joy but only fear, worry and ill-health."[136]

Many family planning advocates described themselves as having been "shocked into action"[137] by the incomplete and septic abortion cases that reportedly made up around one-third to one-half of maternity ward admissions—from Indonesia,[138] to Iran,[139] to Venezuela,[140] to Mexico,[141] to Turkey.[142] The safety of abortion had increased dramatically in the mid-twentieth century with new techniques and the use of antibiotics, but in most places it remained illegal and/or shrouded in taboo, leading many women to seek out untrained practitioners or induce it themselves. When these attempts failed or led to complications, women ended up in gynecological departments of hospitals, often in dire condition.[143] A nurse in

Venezuela, for example, described how her intense belief in family planning was rooted in the disturbing details of incomplete abortions she saw, including one where a woman arrived at the hospital with a wire in her uterus, developed gangrene, and ended up with bilateral amputation of her lower extremities.[144] Nurses from the infamous "Ward 15" in Trinidad—where women suffering complications from self-induced abortions were taken—served as early volunteers for the FPA of Trinidad and Tobago, splitting their shifts at the hospital to work at the clinic.[145] As Dr. Augustus A. Armar of Ghana similarly recalled:

> I developed an interest in family planning originally due to the incidence of infertility and attempted abortions. As a gynecologist and obstetrician I was sent to be at Kumasi. Home-made abortions were frequent. In many cases it consisted of drastic attempts to initiate the abortion process, to start the bleeding. Then the women could come to qualified medical personnel to complete the evacuation. Those who went to back street abortionists almost inevitably developed post-abortal pelvic infections due to lack of antibiotics. Since abortion was a very serious crime, we didn't see the cases until the women were in a very bad state. Terribly sad.[146]

Armar began to offer family planning services quietly due to a lack of government approval in the early 1960s, feeling that no "self-respecting gynecologist obstetrician" could do otherwise.[147]

Family planning advocates also cited the experiences of family and friends as key drivers behind their activism. Jamaican advocate Amy Bailey, for example, noted that her mother was a laundress who had a very large number of children; even as a small girl, she remembered being conscious of the difficulties this brought. Her mother also inspired her by talking openly about bodies; as Bailey recalled, "she did not leave questions unanswered."[148] Elise Ottesen-Jensen of Norway was the seventeenth of eighteen children, and was also marked by her sister's tragic life, as she was sent away due to a pregnancy outside of marriage.[149] Dr. Siva Chinnatamby lost two sisters to complications following childbirth, driving her broader interest in maternal and child well-being.[150] Sidi Coulibaly of Mali described how a "near tragedy" while he was studying in Paris influenced his advocacy for family planning. A close friend's fiancée became pregnant before their marriage; in an effort to avoid scandal, she had an abortion performed in Coulibaly's university dorm room. She hemorrhaged and nearly died, saved only by medical students at the university. As Coulibaly recalled, "This, to me, was a cruel form of social injustice . . . the next day I went out and joined the French family planning movement."[151]

An oral history conducted with Nigerian nurse-midwife Grace Ebun Delano in 2003 is emblematic of the mixing of professional and personal experiences evident in many of the auto-narratives of conversion to family planning. Born to a modest family in Lagos, Delano described herself as wanting to become a midwife because of "the reproductive history of my family,"[152] particularly that of her mother, who experienced agonizing periods of infertility, lost pregnancies, and "a succession of infant mortality."[153] While training in England, Delano saw the health complications and risky childbirths brought on by frequent pregnancies and, after attending a lecture on family planning, began to teach local women how to use the diaphragm.[154] Upon returning to work in a labor ward in Ibadan, Nigeria, Delano recalled the high number of women who ended up in the maternity ward due to complications from attempted abortions, including student midwives and nurses.[155] She described a variety of "horrible methods" used both in the UK and in her home country of Ghana to provoke early contractions, including the swallowing of caustic sodas and herbal teas, tying of binders around the woman's abdomen, the use of lime and blue laundry detergents to wash out the vagina, and the insertion of a variety of objects— from knitting pins to candles—to puncture the cervix.[156] With a fellow female staff member in Ibadan, she began talking to women in the ward about family planning, unofficially and after hours. As she described: "We were doing it because we were just interested."[157]

With these narratives, family planning advocates situated their work within a maternalist, humanitarian discourse, rooted in practical experience and principles of social and medical ethics. Dr. Ko Ko, the head of a large government health unit in Burma, reportedly described family planning as simply "basic to health."[158] Dr. Mahmud Husain, chairman of the Reception Committee of the First Indian Ocean Regional Conference of the IPPF, argued that the movement was "primarily humanitarian," concerned first and foremost with the "mother of 16" who had "exhausted her capacity to derive any enjoyment from life."[159] Zahia Marzouk of Alexandria described herself as "born with a humanitarian side."[160] Dr. Chou Ngo-Fen of China similarly argued that his experience as an obstetrician had allowed him to see that family planning was "in the highest interests of humanity."[161] Others mixed this humanitarian narrative with an emerging language of human rights. The All India Institute of Hygiene and Public Health claimed that adults had "the right for their own sake to separate the twofold functions of the sexual union," and that "children have an even better right to be brought into being . . . only if and when their births are whole-heartedly desired and conscientiously provided for."[162] The FPA of Ceylon similarly argued in its annual report that planned parenthood was, above all, "a humanitarian program serving individual people," noting that "doctors, sociologists, philosophers, humanitarians and religious leaders agree that it is the basic right of parents to have babies only when they want them. A child's first birth right is to be wanted."[163]

A number of family planning advocates also merged this narrative of health, humanitarianism, and rights with a discourse of spiritual, religious calling. Articles in *ATW* described family planning advocates as "birth control missionaries," spreading "the good news" around the world.[164] Colombian advocate Dr. Jaramillo argued that he was driven by "devotion," by "a special inclination to weak people, to people who suffer."[165] Constance Goh Kok Kee of Singapore recalled the foundational influence of the book *Ecce Homo*, which she read as part of a Christian ethics course at Shanghai Baptist College. As she recalled: "The theme of the book was 'Enthusiasm for Humanity' and this got stuck in my mind: *I* was going to be enthusiastic for humanity. I read the book when I was twenty years old and that saying became my guiding star."[166] Indeed, Goh Kok Kee situated her family planning activism within a longer trajectory of Christian social service, including previous work with the YWCA and the Church of Singapore.[167] Pathfinder Fund fieldworkers also referred to family planning as "the Great Cause,"[168] located within a narrative of Christian ethics and duty. Edith Gates argued that the ultimate goal was a "richer Christian Family Life,"[169] and Edna McKinnon, a Christian Scientist, described the family planning movement as having a "spiritual significance."[170] Margaret Roots saw her efforts for the Pathfinder Fund as "the work the Lord had wanted for me and it is wonderful that he chose the Gambles as his earthly agents."[171] Roots was so convinced of the spiritual nature of the cause that she was actually surprised her travels abroad did not qualify as "missionary work" under the eyes of the Canadian government, thus limiting her access to the state old-age security plan on her return.[172]

Many Catholic family planning advocates also portrayed their work as compatible with their faith, despite the strict position of the Church hierarchy. Exercising a degree of interpretive flexibility, they claimed that the Creator had said "to go forth and multiply," but not irresponsibly,[173] or situated family planning within principles of liberation theology that foregrounded social justice, poverty, and human rights as core to Catholic practice.[174] Some argued that the Church's approval of the rhythm method (periodic abstinence) in 1951 indicated a tacit approval of sex without reproduction, which could be used to justify the use of artificial contraception even if it remained officially prohibited. Others saw the Church as on the cusp of reform in the 1950s/60s, with the approval of artificial contraception only a matter of time. Indeed, the 1968 encyclical *Humanae Vitae*, which reaffirmed the prohibition on contraception, came as a surprise to many and provoked considerable debate, with some arguing that the encyclical could be fallible, and that personal conscience was the final authority on the subject.[175] Others simply compartmentalized their work and their faith. A Catholic doctor in the Philippines, for example, reportedly laughed when Edna McKinnon questioned him about his Catholic faith, replying: "Well, you know we are a very practical people."[176] In Manila, McKinnon noted that many Catholics would start by saying, "'I am a Catholic <u>but</u>'—and go on to explain why they do not follow *all* the teachings, or that they 'wear their Catholicism lightly.'"[177]

Some family planning fieldworkers offered up romanticized descriptions of the movement as a cross-denominational cause. In a report on her fieldwork in Ceylon, for example, Roots noted that: "With my co-worker, a Tamil Hindu, our driver a Singhalese Buddhist, and me a Western Christian, we represented all religious minorities in Ceylon."[178] Sarah Gamble (wife of the founder of the Pathfinder Fund) described the dedication of the first clinic of the FPA in Thailand thusly:

> Nine priests in saffron robes sat around the room chanting until it vibrated and the strange harmony seemed to come from everywhere and nowhere. A string was wound around the figure of Buddha on the little scarlet and gold altar, then around the bowl of holy water and then passed through the praying hands of all the priests—symbol of unity. After a feast, they chanted the second part of the ceremony leading up to a procession through all the rooms. During this, the eldest priest sprinkled both rooms and us with holy water from leaves signifying earth, silver and gold. The committee then asked Clarence as "father of the clinic" (a planned child may I add) to present gifts of bright orange bath towels to each priest. It was quite good exercise as he knelt and bowed to each one. But for us the crowning touch was that someone out of thoughtful deference to us Christians had popped a statuette of the Virgin Mary, rosary and all, on the altar beside Buddha. So now this figure also is presiding over the birth control clinic.[179]

More than a practical aid to families in need, family planning had become a site of religious practice.

Family planning advocates also frequently eschewed the dry language of statistics centered in population conferences, mobilizing a humanistic discourse of love and compassion instead. Swedish advocate Elise Ottesen-Jensen, who took over the presidency of the IPPF in 1959, for example, continually reminded people that "'statistics' referred to living human beings who could rejoice and suffer."[180] Pathfinder Fund fieldworkers described the importance of sincerity and warmth as the key to family planning advocacy;[181] the most important thing was "a good heart."[182] Indeed, Margaret Sanger attributed the success of the *ATW* newsletter primarily to the warmth of Brush as editor, "whose love for this work pulsates throughout each issue."[183] Reports on IPPF conferences in the newsletter mixed coverage of scientific papers with emotional appeals. One account, for example, described how Japanese nurse Chimo Mashima broke down into tears recounting the desperate situation of women facing multiple abortions; Elise Ottesen-Jensen embraced her, and attendees left "with the plea ringing in their hearts."[184] At a regional conference in Puerto Rico, a Spanish woman sang "soft songs of love and suffering" that "echoed the unspoken message of our movement—human love should not be penalized by human suffering."[185]

ATW also promoted a narrative of strong, dynamic, yet sensitive and caring female leadership, described through a "narrative of heroics" common to humanitarian propaganda.[186] The founders of the IPPF received much of this praise. Reporting on a trip to Japan in 1952, the paper described Margaret Sanger as being met with "unrestrained enthusiasm" by admirers and autograph hunters. Women "clad in kimonos, many with babies on their backs," gave her "their personal and affectionate welcome";[187] one woman "knelt in the street to kiss her hands."[188] Swedish activist Elise Ottesen-Jensen was described as a "human dynamo" with "boundless energy," and even as "something of a prophet, who speaks this gospel [of family planning] in six foreign tongues."[189] As *ATW* marveled, Ottesen-Jensen worked over ten hours a day, sleeping in peasant huts in isolated sections of Sweden and Lapland while on tour; despite her physical frailty, all could witness that her "vital spirit flames forth" when she spoke.[190] Indian activist Dhanvanthi Rama Rau was described as possessing "the ability to command with all the charm so necessary for success in a woman. Tall, noble in appearance, always exquisitely dressed, she has a warm deep voice which communicates as directly to an audience as if but to one person . . . Perhaps no comment was more generally heard at the Conference than this: 'How can Lady Rama Rau do all she does and yet remain so serene and poised?'"[191] Indeed, as Mytheli Sreenivas notes, these women often embraced their gendered identities, making the case for family planning *as women* uniquely able to understand and relate maternal suffering to larger political and social agendas.[192]

Beyond these leaders, local birth control pioneers and the daily labor of family planning advocacy were also regularly idolized in *ATW* and the reports of international fieldworkers. The paper highlighted the work of

FIGURE 1.5. "Six great women of international family planning movement." *Around the World: News of Population and Birth Control* 40 (December 1955): 4. Copyright IPPF. Source: Dorothy Hamilton Brush Papers, Smith College Special Collections.

"the indefatigable Dr Chinnatamby" in Ceylon; Mrs. Violet Chan, known as "Auntie Vi" by everyone interested in family planning in Hong Kong; Dr. Hameda Malik, the "Mother of Family Planning in Dacca," known for her "real love for each parent and child"; "dynamo of energy" Dr. Celestina Zalduondo in Puerto Rico; "cheerful, enthusiastic Dr Lotte Fink," who escaped Nazi Germany for Australia; and Dr. Sonia Donetz, who fled the Nazis, finished her medical studies in Italy, and worked as a laundress in Palestine until she could set up her own practice.[193] There was "petite" Rosalind Foo of Kuala Lumpur, mother of six with an amazing capacity for hard work, who had managed to secure a grant of seven cents per planted acre from a number of rubber estates in Perak to fund the local FPA.[194] Perhaps the most inspiring tale was that of Dr. Hoon Pierra Vejjabul, who left Thailand for Paris as a young woman against her parents' wishes, washing dishes in hotels to pay for medical school. Upon returning to Bangkok, she advocated for family planning while also running an institute that housed forty abandoned children she had legally adopted.[195] Brush noted that she wished they could afford more pictures in the newsletter of these local advocates in order to "make these people seem much more real."[196] As *ATW* argued, the "practical, down-to-earth pioneering work" of these women was "of more value to the movement than all the exhortatory speeches in the world."[197]

The language of love and kinship also carried through into private correspondence between advocates. Dorothy Brush called Tze-kuan Shu Khan, Taiwan's leading FPA advocate, her "dear adopted daughter," writing to her: "I shall never forget the welcome sight of you with your arms full of roses on Easter Sunday when I descended for the first time onto a foreign country where I had not been before and where I knew no one. When I left I felt as if I had known you all my life . . ."[198] Brush also reportedly "fell in love" with Ma Mya Thein of Burma and her husband during a visit to India.[199] These women also regularly exchanged gifts and holiday cards as an expression of their friendship and gratitude toward one another. Brush received dresses and paintings from Italian advocate Vittoria Olivetti and added two hearts to her charm bracelet to represent Olivetti's twins, her "adopted grandchildren."[200] She sent a raincoat to Purai na Bangxang of Thailand, who in turn sent her jewels, silk, and a sapphire, while appealing to Brush to help her son settle in the United States.[201] Brush described Goh Kok Kee as "the greatest present giver I ever knew."[202] Edna McKinnon of the Pathfinder Fund also regularly brought gifts from one country to another, giving fans from Tonga to family planning advocates in Indonesia.[203]

Through these narratives and relationships, family planning advocates constructed a world of activism that looked distinctly different from that at population conferences: centered around women and suffused with emotion, compassion, sacrifice, and care, deeply concerned with the individual over the "population." In doing so, they helped create an "emotional community"[204] of advocates, bound together by shared feeling across borders and ideologies that provided a valuable means of support. That these bonds were concrete and important is evident in the lengthy, intimate correspondence between advocates around the world. Letters written to Brush, the editor of *ATW*, also attest to the value of the newsletter in providing emotional support to those doing the daily labor of family planning activism. Dr. Marui Rouhunkoski of Finland, for example, wrote that the newsletter meant a great deal "to people like myself who work in comparative isolation. Its regular arrival gives us contact with others who have the same interests and we no longer feel alone."[205] Although the majority of letters to the newsletter came from the United States, the UK, and India, letters from Malaysia, Chile, Italy, Haiti, France, Kenya, Pretoria, Belgium, Canada, Japan, Switzerland, Puerto Rico, and Australia suggest the vision held broader appeal.[206]

Discourses of humanitarianism, maternalism, and missionary work could, of course, be strategic: a way to provide cover for either the more conservative objectives of eugenics and population control or the more radical objectives of feminism and sex reform.[207] Indeed, as Susanne Klausen notes in her study of South Africa, advocates often drew on arguments in favor of family planning in a "haphazard, unsystematic fashion,"[208] shifting their narrative for different audiences and contexts. As Pathfinder fieldworker Edna McKinnon explained in a later interview reflecting on her life's work:

> There was, of course, a great deal of concern about over-population in some of the countries. Then, in other countries, they felt that they didn't have enough people and that they needed more people to carry on the work in their land. In each country we had to adapt our "sales talk" to the situation at hand. But in every instance, we could emphasize the fact that we were trying to help individual families with their own individual problems, that if they could have the knowledge and understanding of how and when to space their children, they could bring greater happiness to their own lives and greater health and education to their children. As a result we found that men became interested in the program when they really understood the purpose and objectives of the family planning movement.[209]

McKinnon's colleague Edith Gates likewise noted that while countries had different views of "the population problem"—or whether there even was one—all could agree that high rates of maternal and infant mortality, abortion, and sterility were problems that needed attention.[210]

To dismiss these narratives as solely strategic, however, risks overestimating the power of international/elite discourses and denying the way that lived experiences can inform activism. Family planning advocates did not need to read a feminist pamphlet or attend a population conference to see the potential value of contraception to their communities. Conversion to the cause could arise organically and be felt passionately. The understanding of family planning as a matter of maternal, child, and family well-being also clearly aligned more closely with the backgrounds in social service, health, and family welfare that dominated among those involved in the day-to-day labor of the movement. Taking these narratives seriously allows us to see the power of affect in binding together transnational communities, as well as the tensions and fault lines shaping humanitarianism, missionary, and maternalist work in their own right. Indeed, in spite of—or perhaps precisely because of—these actors' claims to be part of a higher cause, family planning advocacy driven by compassion could fuel political conflict and reinforce inequalities as much as more explicitly divisive ideologies. The united community of believers imagined in local FPA brochures and the *ATW* newsletter struggled to deal with the reality of global division in the mid-twentieth century, a reality that set limits to the promise of transnational solidarity.

Friction

As noted in the introduction, the family planning movement arose in a period of widespread political conflict, shaped critically by anti-imperial struggles. The fact that family planning workers viewed themselves as missionaries, maternalists, and humanitarians did not insulate them from these political developments. On the contrary, the history of missionary entanglement with colonial rule made their work immediately suspect. The need to "enlighten" the "Other" and spread the "good news" of Christianity had served as an ideological justification for imperialism, and many church leaders and organizations had actively supported colonial rule. White women had also long been implicated in the imperial project. Indeed, several colonial governments in the early twentieth century had actively recruited European women to educate and domesticate local women; historians have described their work as a form of "maternalist imperialism," undergirded by notions of European superiority and a desire to maintain imperial rule.[211]

A number of mid-twentieth-century family planning advocates recognized these fraught politics and attempted to distance themselves from charges of colonialism or neo-imperialism. As Brush wrote in her coverage leading up to the IPPF conference in India in 1952: "We of the West are going to the conference to offer our 'know-how' but also to learn. We are not going to impose it. . . . The West needs to learn as well as the East." She quoted Indian philosopher Sir Sarvepalli Radhakrishnan as saying: "None of us has been appointed to educate humanity."[212] Brush echoed these sentiments in her field reports and correspondence with local advocates. She recognized that local leaders were "high caliber, well-educated," and capable of organizing their work themselves.[213] As she wrote to Professor St. Clair Drake in Ghana: "Times have changed entirely and it is a very good change. The International Planned Parenthood Federation does not impose its ideas on anyone, I assure you. As a rule we do not go into any country except on initiation or where we have reasons to believe that different individuals would welcome us."[214] After a world tour on behalf of family planning in 1959, she concluded that "the old days of lady bountiful are dead. Everywhere the people want our advice and our money but they certainly want to do the work themselves and that is all to the good."[215]

Pathfinder fieldworkers also continually commented on the "outstanding leadership, lay and professional,"[216] that they encountered across the globe. McKinnon, Gates, and Roots argued that their goal was to support rather than lead these organizations, which was in part why they preferred to stay for only limited periods of time in any given country. Sometimes, the North American heritage of fieldworkers could serve as an advantage, distancing fieldworkers from direct colonial legacies. Gates claimed, for example, that she was treated with less suspicion than Europeans in former colonies.[217] In Jordan, on the other hand, McKinnon noted that local actors "made very clear that they didn't want foreigners there in person trying to work with them in family planning."[218] In particular, she stressed that they resented interventions from the United Kingdom and the United States as a result of the ongoing conflict in Palestine. McKinnon apparently sympathized with these sentiments, noting in a report that: "Its [*sic*] like our deliberately beating them and then we try to make up for our bad behavior by offering to bandage the wounds we've caused."[219] Roots likewise stressed the importance of cultural sensitivity, noting that "much more harm than good would evolve if religious or local habits were stepped on or were ignored, even with the best Western intentions."[220]

If international family planning organizations ascribed to values of political sovereignty and cultural sensitivity, however, their records also reveal the continued legacy of colonial hierarchies and assumptions of national and racial superiority. In the IPPF's *ATW* newsletter, voodoo religious ceremonies in Haiti were described as "barbaric" and articles on the "primitive" beliefs in areas of Africa clearly situated the populations of these countries on a racist civilizational scale.[221] Internal correspondence also reveals racial tensions between European and American IPPF staff and advocates from other countries. Goh Kok Kee, for example, wrote to Brush in the mid-1950s that one particular IPPF director for the Southeast Asia region held "warped" attitudes toward Asian people and would do "a great deal of harm to our cause" if not removed (he was).[222] Several local actors—including Sylvia Fernando of Ceylon and Beth Jacobs of Jamaica—complained about statements made by IPPF leader C. P. Blacker that they saw as marginalizing their role in the movement or creating double standards between countries. Blacker responded defensively in a letter to Brush, complaining that "I will be afraid soon to say anything at all!"[223] While Brush generally defended local advocates in these affairs, she did so in ways that revealed her own sense of racial superiority. In one letter, for example, she described her efforts to seek solutions "whenever I think my little brown brothers may get brushed off either accidentally or on purpose."[224] Echoing Blacker's sense of white fragility, she warned her American colleagues of the rising tide of "racism" against *white people* in decolonizing countries.[225]

Locally based advocates also sometimes chafed at efforts by IPPF headquarters or fieldworkers to standardize practices across associations in ways that created political problems locally. Dr. Edris Rice-Wray, an American doctor working in Mexico, expressed her frustration with certain staff at the IPPF who pressured her to change the local clinic's name from Association Pro-Welfare of the Mexican Family to something with "family planning" or "planned parenthood" in the title, to facilitate integration with the IPPF and guarantee further funding. As she wrote to Brush: "They seemed to have the notion that whatever was done in the United States or other parts of the world could be picked up as a package and repeated here. I can assure you that nothing would be more disastrous . . . For unless we direct our program in accordance with the needs of the people and their particular desires, and what they think is important, we fail before we start."[226] Rice-Wray also noted the importance of acknowledging that the "history of relations between México and The United States has, in many occasions, not put the United States in a good light,"[227] and that "the most important quality which international public health workers must have is flexibility and willingness to adapt."[228] She expressed further exasperation in later letters, asking: "Is the important thing to have an official connection with the IPPF published for the world to see or is the important thing to give contraceptive services to the mothers in Mexico who need it?"[229] Eventually, she chose to disassociate the clinic from the IPPF altogether.[230]

While Brush sympathized with Rice-Wray in the latter case,[231] she was less flexible in dealing with Tze-kuan Shu Kan when the FPA of China (located in Taiwan) refused the IPPF's recommendation to change its name to the "FPA of Nationalist China" to avoid confusion with Communist China. Writing to "my dear adopted daughter," Brush quickly added: "Perhaps I shouldn't call you that anymore!" She expressed her shock that there had been no change in the name since their last meeting, and implored Tze-kuan: "for the sake of our friendship, won't you at least write and explain."[232] Tze-kuan responded by noting that although "Nationalist China" was used in foreign newspapers, the Taiwanese government had ruled that "The Republic of China" or simply "China" should be used. She held firm that the association would not change the name "merely for facilitating our admission to IPPF," and felt that it was "entirely unjustified for IPPF to take its present attitude toward our Association."[233] Although the two appear to have reconciled in later years, the dispute illustrates the very personal tensions that could form due to international fieldworkers' ignorance surrounding the finer points of local politics, accompanied by a sense of entitlement to determine the direction of the movement from abroad.[234]

Records of Pathfinder fieldworkers also provide glimpses of disjuncture and conflict between fieldworkers and advocates in the countries they worked with, often referred to elusively as "trouble."[235] McKinnon described her frustration at being repeatedly brushed off by a doctor she had been working with in Iran, confiding that the woman seemed to see her as "a slightly irritating nuisance."[236] Gates had a protracted conflict with Egyptian activist Hanna Rizk, who complained about Gates's aggressiveness in pushing for one person from Egypt to go to the upcoming IPPF conference over the candidate preferred by the local community.[237] There was also reportedly some resentment because she had "scolded" the secretary for a delay in opening clinics.[238] As Clarence Gamble wrote to Gates: "He says that Egypt doesn't want any more field workers until they ask for them. So perhaps there's one error for the team of pitching the ball too hard, but such things are difficult to estimate—and even with the irritation you may have accelerated."[239] In doing so, Gamble implied that the progress of the cause was more important than the maintenance of these relationships. Pathfinder fieldworkers also sometimes faced explicit critiques of their positionality within the movement. McKinnon recalled a doctor in Indonesia, for example, who accused her of promoting a cause "to control the dark-skinned races." As she recalled: "I denied this as gently as I could and explained that I'd worked for 25 years among white people in America. We parted amicably, with neither convincing the other."[240]

Pathfinder fieldworkers vacillated between a vision of colorblindness and shared humanity mixed with tired stereotypes of the countries they went to. Roots, for example, expressed her surprise at the racist attitudes of some of the white women she met at clubs and embassies around the world (who still held "the old Colonial idea that 'blacks' are inferior!"[241]) and wrote in letters to friends and families that "we are all sisters—or brothers—under the skin."[242] At the same time, she spoke of villagers in exoticized ways, describing groups of "closely-packed, white-clad brown bodies" listening raptly to her speech in a village hut.[243] She also complained of "exasperating 'Asian Inertia'"[244] in ways that plainly fell back on stereotypes, finishing one account with a sarcastic report labeled "Summary of What It Takes to Get 3 Film Reels Released from Customs in Dacca."[245] Roots argued that the key difference between East and West was that "only Westerners asked 'Why?,'"[246] implying a lack of intellectual curiosity and capacity among an entire region of people. Gates similarly adopted a hierarchical modernist narrative in her understanding of social change, noting that countries started at different "points of development," with those having the most contact with Western societies generally further along this scale.[247]

The competing impulses in the records of these women tap into a larger tension between "saving" and solidarity evident in humanitarian, missionary, and maternalist movements of the period. While fieldworkers shed the most blatant forms of racism and full-blown aspirations of control often evident in the population sphere, many still imagined themselves in a hierarchical role, as educators and protectors of the less sophisticated "Other." These contradictions reflected both their socialization and the particular positioning of these women within the global system. Although within the IPPF and larger international population community, women volunteers, fieldworkers, and advocates were often disparaged as "amateurs" due to their lack of political clout or official credentials,[248] they could find themselves quickly catapulted to the top of the local social hierarchy in the countries they visited. As Edna McKinnon noted, she was generally afforded a "privileged position"[249] during her fieldwork, and soon after arrival would be "more or less thrown with the leaders in each community."[250] This was at times based on connections with local US embassies or diplomats in the country, who would help organize her stay and invite her to dinner parties and other events where she would mingle with key interlocutors. The social capital of local family planning advocates, who themselves were often members of the middle or upper class, also helped. In Malaysia, for example, McKinnon connected with the sultana of Johore over their shared interest in family planning, becoming a featured guest at many elaborate functions at the sultana's residence.[251] In Saudi Arabia, she obtained an exclusive meeting with Her Majesty Queen Iffat.[252] Gates described talking to the mother of the president of Bolivia in her home in La Paz,[253] and Roots claimed to have convinced the deputy prime minister of Burma to go from opposed to in favor of family planning in five minutes.[254] Some local advocates reportedly acknowledged the strategic value of these foreign women, whose novelty and boldness could provide inroads into official circles that local advocates were otherwise excluded from.[255] This boldness, of course, reflected the privilege of departure: international fieldworkers could leave after stimulating controversy without experiencing the social repercussions faced by local women.[256]

If fieldworkers expressed a biased or imperialist logic and occupied a privileged position, however, we should not overestimate their power. As noted above, the work of Pathfinder and IPPF in the early years of the movement consisted primarily of responding to requests for information, trying to stimulate local efforts, providing technical and organizational support, and either paying for or helping arrange shipments of contraceptive methods. Grants in these years were often small; in some places, they were only a tiny contribution to the overall budget of an association. While these organizations occasionally checked in on the progress of clinics they were funding, they required nothing like the detailed "monitoring and evaluation" reports required by international development funders today. The decentralized organization of the IPPF and the sporadic nature of Pathfinder interventions left considerable leeway for local actors to take what was valuable to them and ignore the rest, or abandon the cause altogether. In follow-up trips to Nigeria and Zanzibar in 1959, for example, Gates noted that little had been done with the foam tablets she had provided on a previous trip and work was essentially at a standstill.[257] In Liberia, Gates's initial visit in 1956 had been followed by the formation of a family planning association in 1959, but when McKinnon visited in 1964 she observed only a few sparsely attended meetings and little activity, with no actual clinic services having been offered for years.[258] Other meetings or attempts to form federations fizzled out, and some local "associations" existed in name only.[259]

Charges of imperialism in the family planning movement could also be used as a means to suppress local family planning activism and dismiss the cause altogether. Many of the doctors, nurses, social workers, and other local family planning advocates who formed the first associations and opened the first clinics found themselves, at some point or another, accused of being pawns of colonial officials or American neo-imperialists. Afro-Jamaican advocate Amy Bailey was called a "traitor" to her race and her country;[260] Ghanaian Dr. Fred Sai was called an "Uncle Tom . . . bought by the Americans and the white people to preach their message of genocide to kill off the black races."[261] These attacks at times highlighted very real power inequalities within the movement, while also drawing attention to the social distance between some advocates and the populations they targeted (as discussed further in the next chapter). But they could also dissolve into disingenuous political attacks, used to discredit activism by those with more conservative agendas.[262] In this context, local advocates walked a tightrope when they engaged with international actors, attempting to balance their desire for moral, financial, and material support with the imperialist attitudes of some of their international "peers" and the risk of jeopardizing their local authenticity merely by reaching out beyond borders. Transnational activism was emotional and mental labor on all sides, fundamentally shaped by politics even when done in the name of faith and care.

Conclusion

When looking at the world of population conferences and high-level political debates, the family planning cause is made visible primarily as an attempt by elite men to reshape the world order by controlling the fertility of certain populations. Looking at the records of local advocates and international fieldworkers, however, suggests a more diverse, decentralized, and grounded movement, rooted in concerns for the future of the world but also survival in the present. Vague, dehumanizing population statistics sit alongside dramatic stories of maternal tragedy; political jockeying is contrasted with gift-giving and intimate personal relationships; armchair philosophizing is seen as secondary to the practicalities of clinic management and fieldwork. Local and transnational family planning activism is made visible as daily physical, mental, spiritual, and emotional labor, conducted primarily by women.

In a way, these narratives play into stereotypes of women's activism as sentimental and emotional, used by some at the time to undermine or trivialize their work. But we do not have to repeat this marginalization: we can recognize the importance of this type of labor in spreading the cause beyond high-level political forums, in making local movements and transnational connections concrete and practical, lived and personal. We can also recognize this labor without romanticizing it, without masking the ideas of racial and class superiority that frequently undergirded aspirations to "help" others in this period. Seeing this movement as a humanitarian, maternalist, and missionary endeavor allows us to dig deeper into the contradictions of these fields. Indeed, in spite of the claims of many advocates, family planning work was not "apolitical": the legacies of colonialism and contemporary national and international political struggles were always there, whether made visible or lurking in the background.

If historical memory and continuing inequalities could drive friction between family planning advocates operating in different contexts, however, the more fundamental gap in many cases would prove to be that between prophets and their congregations: the men and women who were meant to accept "the good news" and become responsible contraceptive users, to protect them from their own suffering and poverty. As advocates came into contact with these communities through their practical labor for the cause, their sympathy, faith, and sense of conviction were tested, and could even prove counterproductive, blinding them to the complexity of reproductive experience. It is to these intimate encounters in the clinic and field that we turn next.

[CHAPTER TWO]

Practice

What was it like to actually practice family planning in the early to mid-twentieth century? To answer this question, I want to start here by immersing us in a set of nine letters exchanged between May Farquharson, the honorary secretary of Jamaica's first Birth Control League, and a woman—let's call her "Mrs. Allen"—seeking services.[1] I first encountered these letters while writing my first book on reproductive politics and practice in the Caribbean; they were part of a larger collection of letters written from women to the League in response to a small advertisement placed in the *Daily Gleaner* newspaper advertising the opening of the island's first clinic. But Mrs. Allen's letters were unique in the length and depth of the exchange, stretching over a period of one and a half years, from October 1939 to February 1941. The letters provide us with a rare extended glimpse into the interaction between family planning associations and women. Here, rather than seeing them as one point in a larger data set, as I do in that book,[2] I want to give them a deeper look. In the excerpts below, we get a better sense of the complexity of family planning practice in this period.

Dear Miss Farquharson,

Having seen in the Gleaner that there is a Birth Control Clinic and your aim is to help mothers in the safe methods of birth control and that they may have a resonable [*sic*] amount of children.

I would like to attend the clinic but the distance makes it impossible, so I am respectfully asking you if you could send me the necessary information by post. I am now married four years and have three children . . . .

I would like to care for my children in the best possible way I can and to give them a good education but I can not possibly do so with many children . . .

Mrs. Allen, 18 October 1939

63

Dear Mrs. Allen,

. . . I enclose you such information as it is possible to send by post. Of course it is difficult for these things to be explained by writing, but at least it will give you some idea of how Birth Control works. Probably you already know that there is a rubber sheath or condom which can be worn by a man? And which some couples find satisfactory, but so often it is found that the man does not want to be bothered to take the trouble to take such a precaution . . .

May Farquharson, 19 October 1939

Dear Miss Farquharson,

I have to thank you, very much . . . I have got the Sponge and Foam Powder and in doing same according to instructions.

Again I have to thank you for your kind service and to wish you much success in your work.

Mrs. Allen, 24 November 1939

Dear Mrs. Allen,

Thank you for your letter . . .

I want to correct a possible misunderstanding in the Confidential Advice I sent you. Referring to Method (3) (the cottonwool and vinegar) a "pint" in Jamaica is generally taken to mean a pint bottle. The right amount of vinegar for this is 5 teasponnfuls [*sic*] (five). If however, a pint measure is used, then the right amount of vinegar is two tablespoonfuls. (A pint bottle holds twelve ounces of water, and a pint measure holds twenty ounces.) As you are using the Foam Powder, this won't affect you, but in case you should be telling any other mothers about the methods, please be sure they understand. The easiest way is to mix up a bottle of the potion, (either five teaspoonfuls of white vinegar to the pint bottle or two tablespoonfuls to the pint measure) with clean, pure water, keep it in a carefully corked bottle, and then pour enough of it into a cup on each occasion, to saturate the cotton wool, which must then be squeezed out, as given in the directions. If the woman gets into a squatting position, it makes it easier for her to insert, and later to take out, the cotton wool. It may be as well to mention [*sic*] that she need have no fear of the cotton wool getting lost inside her, as that portion of the body is shut off from the rest, and there is little difficulty in taking out the sponge or cotton wool or whatever is used. It must not be left in longer than overnight, say eight or ten hours.

I Wish you every success, I enclose a couple of pamphlets. They do not deal with methods, only with the reasons for birth control . . .

May Farquharson, 29 November 1939

Dear Miss Farquharson,

Again I have to ask your kind advice. My baby is now six months old and I am still nursing her, I believe there are some mothers that do not menstruate during the entire period of nursing, but I am not of that type as soon as my baby is two months old I started to menstruate and do so during the whole nursing period. The case is this now since I am using the "foam-powder" I haven't menstruated. . . . Please say if you think it is the "foam-powder" that act upon same and cause it to stop coming until after the nursing period, or if you think it is conception, as there is not any symptoms otherwise to make me believe it is conception . . .

Mrs. Allen, 19 January 1940

Dear Mrs. Allen,

I wrote to the Foam Powder people in New York. and have also talked to our Clinic doctor. There does not seem to be experience that Foam Powder could stop menstruation, and I am afraid that you must be one of the women who would have to be personally advised as to a method of Birth Control. The makers of the Foam Powder write that it is successful in all but a small number among a very large group of women, but of course no method of Birth Control, even those advised by docotrs [*sic*] for individual, succeeds with everybody. . . .

. . . Don't lose hope with Birth Control, whatever you do. You can look around for yourself and see how few of the better-off people nowadays have large families, and that is just because they are using Birth Control methods. It is of course hard to get one suitable for yourself unless you can see a doctor and get individual advice.

May Farquharson, 2 March 1940

Dear Miss Farquharson,

I have not been successful with the using of the Foam Powder, as I am really pregnant, but I am not discouraged, as soon as the baby comes, and I am able to get out, I will come to Kingston and visit the Clinic . . .

Mrs. Allen, 13 March 1940

Dear Miss Farquharson,

You will remember I wrote you some time ago and was adviced [*sic*] to use sponge and Foam Powder but unfortunately that method failed to help me.

I am now mother of four children . . .

You can imagine what it is, having them so quickly and would like very much to be helped with the spacing of them.

Kindly advice me just what to do if I am to come to the Clinic, or I can see an experienced Doctor . . .

Mrs. Allen, 3 February 1941

Dear Mrs. Allen,

We were glad to get your letter. You are a long way from Kingston, and I dont know whether it is difficult for you to get up. [List of doctors in her area that might provide advice] . . .

If however, you can get to Kingston, the lady doctor is at the Clinic each second and each fourth Friday in the month, at 4 p.m., that is, next week Friday. If people cannot come then, we can send them to one of the doctors who are Directors of the League . . . but in that case they have to go early to the Clinic on one of the days it is open (Monday, Wednesday, Friday, 10 to 12, Wednesday 3 to 5) and get a note to the doctor, and a case card filled out, and then they have to go back to Nurse to fetch the apparatus the doctor orders, and be taught by the nurse how to use it.

As to charges, the diaphragm and jelly cost 5/-. If people can pay, the Clinic charges 10/-6d, but if we know that people are poor, then this charge is not made, but as a great number of our patients are too poor even to pay for their apparatus, it is very important to us that everybody who possibly can do so, should pay . . .

Please let us hear what you decide to do.

May Farquharson, 4 February 1941

The correspondence ends there. It is not clear what happened to Mrs. Allen: whether she got to the clinic and had a diaphragm inserted, whether the diaphragm worked, whether she completed her family, or whether she changed her mind and decided she wanted another child. But her letters—and the responses from Farquharson—tell us already a great deal about early twentieth-century family planning: about the aspirations of women and advocates, about the practical difficulties of mixing contraceptive potions at home and trying to get to a clinic to see a doctor, about the fundamental insecurity of reproduction in this period. Beyond prophetic visions of population control as global security, or planned parenthood as humanitarian salvation, we see family planning as practice: a complicated, inconsistent, and messy affair.

In this chapter, I situate the experiences of May Farquharson and Mrs. Allen within both the local context of early twentieth-century Jamaica and studies of clinics in other areas of the world. My claim is not that Mrs. Allen can represent all women, or even all Jamaican women. Rather, I want to use this particularly rich exchange to unpack some of the underlying assumptions, the taken-for-granted facts, and the language that at first seemed unclear to me in order to explore the multiple factors that shaped the practice of family planning from the 1930s to late 1950s. I start below by exploring the relationship between these two women and the conditions under which they encountered one another. The very fact that the Jamaican Family Planning League existed, and existed in the form that it did, was influenced both by local concerns and by Farquharson's connections with the global family planning community. The particular set of options that Farquharson offered to Mrs. Allen also drew on international models and were informed by international networks, adjusted to fit with local realities. This very intimate, local encounter has a global backstory.

I then move on to explore some of the emotional and sensorial subtext of the letters, and of the movement more broadly: the discourses of hope, triumph, and certainty, but also the suspicion, doubt, and failure that colored both the experiences of women who attended these clinics and the narratives of those who created and promoted them. As I argued in the previous chapter, many advocates believed strongly that family planning was the answer to maternal suffering, high abortion rates, and broader questions of poverty and inequality. Some women who came to early clinics or engaged with early fieldworkers shared this sense of hope for a better future but, like Mrs. Allen, found the reality of family planning less inspiring than the promise. Others viewed family planning advocates with suspicion or doubt from the outset, and rebuffed their efforts to proselytize in their communities. This could create conflict between those who wanted to help and those who were meant to be helped, revealing some of the deeper tensions underlying humanitarian, medical, and missionary-style interventions in this period. Zooming in on these interactions is thus crucial to understanding the movement as a whole.

Service

To really see what is going on in the exchange between May Farquharson and Mrs. Allen, we need to first think about the two actors it involved: how they were positioned in Jamaican society at the time, and how that positioning shaped both their experiences and the historical record they left behind. Or maybe we need to start the other way around. The very fact that Mrs. Allen comes to us through *May Farquharson*'s personal papers, held at the National Archives of Jamaica, already tells us something about their relative positioning in society. One actor (Farquharson) left behind a dozen boxes of materials, intentionally preserved in a national institution to record her impact on Jamaican society. The other, Mrs. Allen, left behind five letters.

As a result, we know much more about May Farquharson than we do about Mrs. Allen. Farquharson was a member of the small white elite on the island of Jamaica, at the time still a British colony, with a population composed primarily of descendants of enslaved Africans brought over to work on brutal slave plantations from the fifteenth century onward. After emancipation in 1834, free laborers found themselves constrained by deep race and class inequality, made worse by the Great Depression in the interwar years. Farquharson was insulated from much of this as the daughter of a wealthy sugar planter, Sir Arthur Farquharson, living on an estate just outside the main city of Kingston. However, she took an early interest in charity and social work, and after attending school in London and serving as a nurse in World War I, returned home to advocate for a number of causes, including an old-age insurance program for laborers. In many ways, she was a pretty standard white elite woman philanthropist, privileged by financial security and a social position that allowed her to dedicate her time to these causes. But she also saw herself as different from other "charity ladies" who, she complained, "yap round Committee tables . . . too many cocktail parties, and too much bridge, and time is limited!"[3] She described herself as a "respectable spinster"[4] and, unlike most other elite white islanders, supported the burgeoning Jamaican nationalist movement in the 1940s and 1950s. She was also one of few white women who collaborated with Afro-Jamaican women activists at a time when most spaces on the island remained (unofficially) racially segregated. Still, her personal correspondence vacillates between, on the one hand, thoughtful critiques of the conditions in the colony, and on the other, blatantly racist comments about the "backwardness" of Jamaicans.[5] These competing impulses comprise a subtle subtext of her letters to Mrs. Allen, and her interactions with Jamaican women more broadly.

Farquharson's collection also tells us a great deal about the Jamaican Birth Control League, which renamed itself the Jamaica Family Planning League in 1941. The League was created in March 1939, at the end of a lecture tour of the island by British birth control advocate Edith How-Martyn. As mentioned briefly in the previous chapter, How-Martyn came to Jamaica on the invitation of Amy Bailey, a middle-class Afro-Jamaican nationalist, feminist activist engaged in a variety of causes. Together with social worker Alma LaBadie and pan-Africanist activist Maymie (Madame de Mena) Aiken, Bailey argued that birth control was a critical resource for women suffering the physical and financial burden of repeated pregnancies, and a broader aid to efforts of social uplift on the island as it pushed for independence from British rule. Birth control was further promoted by several doctors on the island in the late 1930s, who wrote articles in the press and published pamphlets touting the medical, social, and economic benefits of the cause. Perhaps unsurprisingly, birth control found vocal support among members of the white elite, who mobilized a eugenic, neo-Malthusian discourse blaming islanders' poverty on their fertility rates. In a reflection of her social positioning and political orientation, Farquharson's views on family planning mixed all of the above, vacillating between a social service–oriented desire to relieve poor women of their suffering and an elitist, eugenic fear of social degeneration.[6]

Farquharson at first sat in the backdrop of this movement, writing the occasional letter to the editor of the *Gleaner* on the subject, using a pseudonym. But when the League was formed, she agreed to serve as honorary secretary and provided the financial backing to open the first birth control clinic at 24 East Race Course Drive in Kingston in 1939. In the following decades, she acted as the de facto head of the clinic, overseeing daily operations, exchanging with nurses and doctors who delivered the actual services, answering letters, producing material, and advocating for the cause among her networks on the island. The clinic was the sole dedicated birth control center on the island until 1953, when a second clinic was opened by Dr. Lenworth and Beth Jacobs, a middle-class, mixed-race couple located on the other side of the island in St. Ann's Bay. In 1957, the two endeavors joined together to form the Jamaica Family Planning Association.[7]

Of Mrs. Allen, we know much less. From her letters, we can see that she is literate, which might indicate a middle-class position, but not necessarily: the island had relatively high literacy rates compared to other British colonies, with some 75 percent of the adult population having obtained primary school education by 1943.[8] She writes in deferential terms to Farquharson, perhaps indicating her awareness of a lower social position.

Claims of wanting to give children a good education and raise them "in the best possible way" speak to family values shared by both middle-class and working-class families in Jamaica in this period,[9] and fed directly into the discourses of family planners who touted the small family as an exhibition of responsibility and social advance. We cannot know whether Mrs. Allen really ascribed to this belief or was simply mobilizing it to get relief from constant childbearing; either way, through her practice, she situated herself as a "deserving subject" of aid.[10] Mrs. Allen's letters illustrate how personal situations could shift over time. While her first letter takes an aspirational tone ("I would like to care for my children in the best possible way I can and to give them a good education"), as the fourth child arrives things become more urgent ("You can imagine what it is, having them so quickly . . ."). But Mrs. Allen also wishes Farquharson "much success in your work"; here, she subtly shifts from being an appreciative or desperate object of the movement to a more active position, in which she expresses solidarity with Farquharson and with the larger cause. She is not only a patient, a target, a birth control "acceptor," but also a birth control supporter herself.

The Jamaica Family Planning League (JFPL) was not alone in receiving these kinds of letters upon the opening of a clinic. Family planning associations reported to the IPPF's *ATW* newsletter that an onslaught of letters usually followed the opening of a clinic. The Polish Society for Conscientious Motherhood received some 10,820 letters asking for advice within its first eleven months;[11] the National FPA of the UK's ninety-four branches responded to nearly 9,000 letters in 1951;[12] and the Planned Parenthood Federation of America received 14,741 letters in 1954.[13] That the JFPL received even 500 in its first year is fairly remarkable considering the clinic advertised itself with only a very small notice in the *Daily Gleaner* newspaper, buried in the "Wanted" section. Perhaps Mrs. Allen saw the ad while searching for a job or for food or other items to purchase. But it is also equally likely that someone else brought the advertisement to her attention. Women were known to share newspapers and read them aloud to one another, along with other materials like the birth control pamphlets Farquharson sent.[14] Indeed, Farquharson acknowledges this in her follow-up letter of November 29, 1939, when she writes, "in case you should be telling any other mothers about the methods, please be sure they understand." Clinics around the world, from Singapore to South Africa to Mexico, likewise noted that the highest percentage of their patients were referred by other women, speaking to the power of women's networks in spreading information about family planning services.[15] Like Mrs. Allen, these women should be counted as important family planning advocates in their own right, critical to the expansion of the cause in these years.

The letters also hint at the existence of prior knowledge of birth control techniques, including a range of low-tech methods passed on from woman to woman through generations. Mrs. Allen notes that "there are some mothers that do not menstruate during the entire period of nursing," suggesting an awareness that breastfeeding could provoke amenorrhea and delay childbearing. Although—as evident in the case of Mrs. Allen—this method was not entirely reliable, it was widely practiced across the globe as a means of child spacing. Taboos surrounding sex with a nursing mother in many cultures could also help protect women from another pregnancy for a year or two.[16] In Jamaica, as elsewhere, other women reported engaging in post-coital douching to rid their bodies of sperm. Men practiced withdrawal; as Linda Gordon points out, this was "the single most common contraceptive method in history."[17] Others practiced periodic abstinence or "the rhythm method," counting the days between periods and trying to avoid sex during ovulation.[18] Family planning advocates from India to Egypt to Canada also recorded a range of herbal methods and improvised physical barriers used by their patients, including coconut shells, cocoa butter, and lemon peels to block the cervix and the use of rags dipped in different concoctions believed to have spermicidal properties.[19]

Records of family planning advocates and associations also attest to the fact that pharmacies and other retail establishments in many countries stocked a range of birth control methods in the first half of the twentieth century. Farquharson acknowledges this in her first letter when she writes that "probably you already know that there is a rubber sheath or condom which can be worn by a man?" Indeed, an analysis of the first 1,000 patients at the Kingston clinic showed that 23 percent of married patients and 4.8 percent of unmarried had previously used birth control, particularly condoms and "Rendell's," a brand of soluble quinine pessaries that was advertised in the *Gleaner* and could be ordered by mail.[20] A survey in Florida in 1932 showed that condoms were sold at 376 places other than drugstores, including gas stations, garages, restaurants, and barber shops.[21] In Peru in 1941, the government felt that the sale of condoms on the street had reached such "alarming proportions" that they began to enforce a ban.[22] Fieldworkers for the IPPF and Pathfinder Fund often made a point of stopping in at local pharmacies to see what was available in the different countries they visited. In Mandalay, Burma, Margaret Roots found a variety of chemical spermicidal methods, including Speton, Gynomin, Ortho, and Sampoon tablets, as well as some Czechoslovakian brands.[23] Edris Rice-Wray found Preceptin, Orthogynol, and Lorophyn vaginal jellies in pharmacies in El Salvador and Honduras.[24] In a feature on Canada in 1952, *ATW* argued that the drugstore sale of contraceptives "prove that birth control is widely practiced," even in places with restrictions.[25]

Clinics and associations around the world further recorded a variety of traditional methods used to end a pregnancy that had already begun. In a report produced at the request of the IPPF, Farquharson described a range of local methods, including ram goat rose, pennyroyal, pepper elder, rice bitters, or boiled rusty nails.[26] Other family planning associations around the world told stories of mothers in France who passed down homemade recipes to their daughters;[27] Native Americans who soaked the roots of the desert herb leptospermum ruderal in cold water and drank them;[28] women in Barbados who described themselves as having a "slip," meaning either that something was slipped into the uterus to provoke an abortion, or that a miscarriage was produced by falling.[29] A practice acknowledged from Chile to South Africa to the United States in the mid-twentieth century involved the injection of soapy or chemical solutions into women's uteri.[30] As Linda Gordon points out, many of these methods worked indirectly, by essentially irritating the uterus or poisoning the body to the point that it would cause rejection of the fetus as a side effect.[31]

While much of the knowledge-sharing around these methods took place quietly, among women, others were advertised in newspapers and pharmacies under names like "Portuguese Female Pills" or "woman's tonic" to treat menstrual "irregularity."[32] While the language of treating period "irregularity" might seem disingenuous, we should remember that home pregnancy tests were only developed in the 1970s; throughout most of history, pregnancy was a more fluid experience, often not entirely confirmed until the "quickening" (the moment around sixteen to twenty weeks when the mother would have begun to feel the fetus move inside her). Mrs. Allen's letter of January 19, 1940, speaks to this uncertainty, as she notes that her menstruation has not come, but "there is not any symptoms otherwise to make me believe it is conception." It is only in March, when she would have been about four months along, that she expresses certainty about her pregnancy.

These records remind us that the concept of contraception was not entirely new to many of the people targeted by family planning missionaries. But advocates argued that many of the traditional methods—breastfeeding, withdrawal, douching, periodic abstinence, homemade pessaries—were not reliable enough to provide for secure family planning. They also noted that many of the methods stocked in pharmacies had not been tested for efficacy or were sold well past their best-buy date. Some advertisements were blatantly misleading. A contraceptive sold in Sibu, on the island of Borneo, in 1955, for example, was advertised as "Birtab No. 1, The World's Finest Birth Control, The Only Birth Control That Does Not Fail. Two Doses for One Year."[33] Condoms were more effective in principle, but could be used incorrectly or lose efficacy if stored incorrectly, and the method remained stigmatized in many places, associated more with protection against diseases than with use within "respectable" families.[34] Diaphragms sold over the counter were also often ineffective since they had to be fitted to a woman's cervix size to work.[35] As noted in the previous chapter, family planning advocates had also seen firsthand the potentially devastating results of women's efforts to provoke their own abortions. Indeed, although the clandestine nature of the practice in most places makes it difficult to determine how effective or dangerous, on average, these methods really were, the cases that did end up in hospitals were usually dire.[36]

The goal of the family planning movement, as Dorothy Brush of the IPPF wrote, was thus to spread awareness about contraceptive methods and replace dangerous and "unreliable" methods with "harmless yet hygienic techniques."[37] The favored method among many advocates in the 1920s–1950s was the female diaphragm. Margaret Sanger and Marie Stopes promoted competing diaphragms: the Dutch Cap versus the "ProRace" cap, respectively, which were estimated at around 90 percent efficacy if fitted properly to the cervix by a trained person and inserted correctly by the woman before sex.[38] The IPPF likewise promoted the diaphragm as the best method, as well as condoms, several chemical methods—spermicidal powders and foaming tablets—their team had tested in their lab, and some early IUDs, including the German Grafenberg ring and Japanese Ota ring. Fieldworkers for the Pathfinder Fund carried foaming tablets and powders with them on trips but also actively promoted the use of the "cottonwool and oil" or cotton and salt method, which could be made at home by soaking a piece of cotton in oil, salt, or vinegar (as described in May Farquharson's letter of November 29, 1939 above). The cottonwool method served as a point of conflict between Pathfinder and leading figures within the IPPF like Dr. Helena Wright and Lady Rama Rau, who saw the method as deeply unreliable and likely to undermine or discredit the cause.[39] The IPPF also critiqued some producers of contraceptive methods for false advertising or overly aggressive marketing techniques. When the Sunnen Foundation offered a supply of their Emko spermicidal solution for free to the Family Planning Association of Trinidad and Tobago, for example, Brush warned that "Mr. Sunnan [sic] is a millionaire self-made who did not go past the third grade and has very little respect for such matters as testing products. Unless I am mistaken he has refused to have Enko [sic] tested since he himself is certain it is so good. The reason it has been widely used in Puerto Rico is because he gave $300,000 to Puerto Rico for its distribution and for the aid of Family Planning."[40] Brush stressed that the IPPF needed to actively link family planning associations with different manufacturers that used more "reliable" techniques to protect them from relying on experimental methods.[41]

Local advocates positioned themselves differently within this international debate. Some felt that the diaphragm was too impractical, especially in areas where health clinics were few and far between; the cottonwool or sponge and salt method, though less reliable, could spread much further and more quickly.[42] Others were insistent on the need to stick with the diaphragm or cervical cap. Dr. Jorge Sarmiento of Lima, for example, was adamant in his preference for diaphragms over salt and sponge methods, even after facing pressure from a Pathfinder Fund fieldworker to adopt the latter.[43] Formal associations that affiliated to the IPPF tended to adopt the methods approved by the Federation. A survey of thirteen national associations with clinics in the early 1950s conducted by the IPPF, for example, showed that all thirteen offered the cap with chemicals, ten offered condoms with chemicals, five offered sponges with chemicals, nine offered chemicals alone, and four advised on the rhythm method.[44] But organizations and individual doctors alike were often forced to work with what they had, which could be limited due to lack of supply or explicit bans on contraceptives. The FPA of Indonesia, for example, did not advertise its services in its early years openly because they had so few supplies to actually offer. Visiting the country in 1961, Pathfinder fieldworker Edna McKinnon noted that one clinic had only sponges and foam powder on offer, despite the interest of many women in the cervical cap.[45] Pathfinder agreed to send 300 tubes of Contab foaming tablets each month for one year to the association, which enhanced the supply but did not address the issue of choice.[46] In places that contraceptives were banned, organizations like Pathfinder would find creative ways to get methods to local doctors, as when the Fund slipped foaming tablets into a supply of medical goods being shipped to Peru by the Church World Service, or when one fieldworker arrived at the airport with twelve hundred Durafoam tablets hidden in her lingerie.[47]

In Jamaica, too, the list of methods on offer was influenced by a mix of international standards, global supply chains, and local priorities. The Marie Stopes clinic, for example, sent Farquharson samples of "racial caps" and clinic caps, while Edith How-Martyn linked Farquharson with the company Holland-Rantos, which provided Sanger-approved diaphragms.[48] Although Farquharson indicated an interest in the cottonwool method, How-Martyn warned Farquharson that it was "just little removed from quackery & will fail much too often to make much impression on the pop.n [population]."[49] One of the clinic's main medical advisors, Dr. Jai Lal Varma, agreed, arguing that: "The cheap method is very liable to fail in many cases with the result that Contraception will get a bad name. Once the public has lost confidence in the method advised it will be hard to persuade them afterwards to try a better method. With the expensive method we will not be able to reach a very large number of patients but whatever's done will be more thorough."[50] However, Farquharson also reached out beyond her existing networks in her search for contraceptive methods, writing to clinics and programs around the world to see what they were using. In 1938, for example, she wrote to the Society of Cultural Relations in Soviet Russia to inquire about metal pessaries a friend of hers saw at a Mother and Child Exhibition in Moscow a few years earlier.[51] Farquharson also contacted manufacturers directly, like Durex and Holland-Rantos ("the Foam Powder people in New York," as she calls them in her letter to Mrs. Allen) to get special rates for their contraceptives and get guidance on their use.[52] By the mid-1950s, the clinic in Kingston stocked Holland-Rantos diaphragms in sizes 70, 75, 80, and 85 as well as foam powder, sponges, douche equipment, condoms (both disposable and a heat-treated "washable" version), Koromex jelly, and Prentabs, a vaginal suppository.[53]

What this meant practically for women seeking family planning in this period can be illustrated in the pamphlet Farquharson sent to Mrs. Allen, entitled "The Confidential Advice for Mothers." The pamphlet began with the disclaimer that although no method was absolutely sure, "96% of women using doctors' methods do not conceive."[54] It then proceeded to explain the "doctors' method"—the diaphragm—with an image of the vagina and womb to illustrate how it worked. In her letters to Mrs. Allen, Farquharson stresses that this is the best option, noting that "it is of course hard to get one suitable for yourself unless you can see a doctor and get individual advice." But in both her letter and the pamphlet, Farquharson recognizes that this would be difficult to do, and explains a variety of other methods as well. There was the "foam powder and sponge" method, which Mrs. Allen opts for at first: this could be purchased, apparently, at chemist shops across the island for 3/6d per sponge. To use this method, Mrs. Allen would have had to sprinkle the foam powder on the sponge, work it into a slight lather, and insert it as high as possible into the vagina, well in advance of intercourse. The sponge could also be used with paste or, as a last resort, soaked in household products like olive oil, coconut oil, household vinegar, white soap, or Castile soap. She would have needed to make sure to leave it in all night, then wash it with soap or hot water and hang it to dry somewhere not exposed to dirt or dust. The pamphlet explained that she could attach a cord to it to make it easier to pull out. The pamphlet also described the cottonwool method, which required one to cut a piece of cottonwool or a silk handkerchief—about the size of a large hen's egg or half the size of a clenched fist—and soak it in oil or vinegar, then fit it around the neck of the womb. This would be left in all night, then taken out the next morning and burned or thrown away. If nothing else was available, smearing a thick coat of Vaseline over the cervix with a finger was better than nothing. The pamphlet advised women to also douche the next morning, either with vinegar, soap, or lime juice. Finally, it noted the availability of disposable condoms—the sheath or "French letter"—for 3/- per dozen at chemist shops in Kingston, which should particularly be used "if there is the least suspicion of gonorrhea or any venereal complaint."[55]

If Mrs. Allen did manage to make it to the clinic in the end, her experience would have been remarkably similar to that of women in many other areas of the world. This was not a coincidence: many clinics in the 1930s and 1940s were deliberately modeled after those promoted by Sanger and Stopes.[56] The IPPF's *ATW* newsletter also provided a "general guide" in 1952, based largely on American doctor Abraham Stone's pamphlet "How to Establish a Birth Control Clinic." It suggested a staff of one director, a physician, a trained nurse, and clerical help, as well as adjunct social workers, who could be partially or entirely volunteers "but must be adequately trained, responsible and sympathetic human beings." The guide encouraged small-scale endeavors, noting that "even a single, weekly, 2–3hr clinical session could give adequate care for 10–15 patients," and advised clinic operators to collect fees from patients who could pay to offset the costs of supplies, while providing clinical services for free when needed. The clinic should have a minimum of two rooms (one waiting room and one exam room), although preferably with a third room for reviewing case histories. The exam room would need gynecological equipment for physical and pelvic exams as well as materials to illustrate how to use the contraceptive method. Other services could include diagnosis and treatment of sterility, marriage guidance, research, and training. Records, the guide stressed, "must be scrupulously kept." These measures were of course partly about good management of the clinic, but also about establishing family planning as a clean, efficient, respectable aspect of medical care. Indeed, the article noted that incorporating clinics at teaching hospitals was key to granting contraception "its justifiable position as a scientific health measure."[57]

The clinic in Jamaica followed these models as closely as possible. Although they had only one room available, it was divided into three cubicles and two other sections, with two couches for examinations and fitting, an adjustable enamel bed for medical treatments, and a trolley with specula, sterilization materials, and rubber gloves.[58] As indicated in Farquharson's letter above, the clinic was open three days a week in the early 1940s, including Monday, Wednesday, and Friday mornings and Wednesday afternoons. On certain Fridays, women could see Dr. Hyacinth Lightbourne—the "lady doctor" referenced in Farquharson's letter—a white Jamaican woman who had attended medical school in London and received training in the diaphragm at a British family planning clinic.[59] Otherwise, they would have to first go to another doctor in the Kingston area associated with the League to be fitted for the diaphragm, then return to the clinic to have the nurse explain its use. As Farquharson wrote, the clinic encouraged "everybody who possibly can do so" to pay, but also provided both services and diaphragms for free to those who could not.

Clinics in other areas of the world had similarly limited hours, often working around the day jobs of clinic staff. In Kuala Lumpur in 1952, for example, four municipal clinics provided two birth control sessions a month each;[60] by 1960, the headquarters were open daily from 9:30 to 12:30 and from 2 to 4:30 on Monday, Wednesday, and Thursday.[61] In Egypt, clinics were open at first for three afternoons a week, after regular clinic hours, with physicians providing services on an overtime basis.[62] In Singapore, four out of twenty-seven FPA clinics were open daily, while others were open once or twice a month.[63] Perhaps the most impressive center in the mid-century family planning world was the headquarters of the FPA of Hong Kong, opened in October 1956. This "large modern clinic" included a waiting room seating fifty, a registration office, a preliminary instruction room, three consulting rooms, a clinic supervisor's room, and a nursery on the ground floor; a lecture room, office, stockroom, lab, restroom, and sub-fertility clinic on the first floor; and a library and three-roomed all-purpose apartment on the third floor.[64] This was upgraded in 1960 to a four-story building with parking facilities, covered playground, and accommodation for a doctor and two nurses.[65]

These clinics often blended the international and the intimate. Many received visitors from abroad: Mexico's first clinic, for example, hosted some forty-seven doctors from different countries in one year.[66] As Deborah A. Cohen argues, these clinics were "conscious and constructed space[s]," aimed at freeing birth control from negative associations and linking it to respectability. Marie Stopes's clinics in the 1920s/30s UK were decorated with framed pictures of mothers and babies; women were given tea and biscuits, and receptionists played with the children while women were being seen.[67] In Japan, Shidzue Ishimoto modeled her clinic along the lines of her friend Margaret Sanger's, but also used Japanese décor to make it feel more familiar for the women who came.[68] Dr. Zarina Fazelbhoy of the FPA of Pakistan stressed the importance of "the congenial atmosphere of the clinic."[69] The Mexican Association of Family Welfare claimed that although many patients entered "with timidity and apprehension," they were soon "set at ease by the cordial and pleasant surroundings" and the "well-trained and sympathetic persons to whom they can confide their emotional and family problems and seek the solution. They go out smiling and radiant with

Shown here is the Central Clinic and Headquarters of The Family Planning Association of Hong Kong, 152, Hennessy Road, Wanchai, Hong Kong which was opened by Lady Grantham on October 29th., 1956.

FIGURE 2.1. "Family Planning Association of Hong Kong, Sixth Annual Report, 1956." Copyright: Family Planning Association of Hong Kong. Source: Margaret Sanger Papers, Smith College Special Collections.

hope."[70] Some noted that the existence of "lady doctors" was particularly key to creating this atmosphere,[71] as evident in Farquharson's specific mention of the days on which Mrs. Allen could see the female doctor at the Kingston clinic. A midwife working for the FPA of China (in Taiwan) noted that when visiting women, she "repeatedly emphasized that our doctor is a lady," adding that "the proficiency and kind heart of our Dr. Peng has won confidence from people and number of applications has increased."[72] A clinic in Taipei likewise found that patients deliberately waited until the female doctor—Dr. Gao—was at the clinic.[73]

Reports from family planning associations and fieldworker correspondence also give us some sense of the daily rhythm of these clinics. Sarah Gamble, for example, described a session of the birth control clinic at the Nathan Strauss Health Center in Israel, which ran from 7 to 10 p.m.: "Dr Esther Ernhorn had 5 cases marriage guidance, and Dr. Sonia Donetz had 25 for birth control; watched the nurse give a demonstration to a group of 8 or 9, with a pelvic model, diaphragm, plastic coil, suppository (Glovan) and Volpar (foam tablet); many of the group seeing for first time, many questions asked."[74] In any of the eight clinics established in Cairo in 1955, patients were examined by a doctor (usually a woman) first. A social worker would then take precise case histories of each patient, including marital history, number of children, family resources, and general health of the parents and family. The patient was then advised on either family planning methods or treatment for infertility.[75] Indeed, many clinics combined contraceptive advice with treatment or referrals for infertility. In the FPA of Ceylon in the mid-1960s, for example, about one out of seven cases were inquiries about subfertility by couples with no children.[76]

Other early clinics went well beyond contraceptive and infertility services, situating their services within a broader program of reproductive and sexual health care and support for women and children. "Marriage Guidance" clinics of the Finnish Family Welfare League in 1958, for example, provided birth control, pregnancy tests, subfertility advice, advice on sexual disturbances and "maladjustment in marriage," references for abortions, and a heredity guidance clinic.[77] The Institute of Family Welfare in Indonesia, formed by a small circle of "medically oriented women," provided family planning alongside consultations with expectant mothers and babies, and a kindergarten and creche for children of women laborers.[78] In Egypt, early family planners adopted a "social approach," integrating contraceptives into community development projects.[79] In Taiwan, the FPA of China provided adoption/child placement services and temporary care for children in addition to contraceptives.[80] The Singapore FPA developed a "welfare section," conducting visits and providing assistance in the form of powdered milk for babies, clothing, access to creche spaces for young children, and connections to the Social Welfare Department.[81]

Some associations noted that they were prompted to provide these more expansive services due to demand from their patients. The Central Agency for Marital Advice in Zurich, for example, was established in 1933 as a birth control center but found that there was more demand for psychological and legal advice on "marital discord."[82] In Lusaka, Northern Rhodesia, patients at the family planning clinic kept asking for advice on infant welfare, prompting the clinic to incorporate family planning into a larger maternal and child health service.[83] Indeed, the FPA of Ceylon noted that although their clinics were "run on the same lines and as efficiently as any in the U.K. or U.S.," they found that women were "not sufficiently motivated to attend clinics run exclusively for family planning." As a result, they incorporated well-baby, preschool, and antenatal clinics.[84] The Mexican Association for Family Welfare provided birth control services for about 75 percent of patients, but also responded to a variety of demands for guidance on sterility, gynecology, menopause, abortion, prenatal care, adoption services, cancer detection, and psychotherapy for children and adults, among others. The association also provided help for one pregnant girl with her wedding, contributing to the cost of the wedding gown, purchasing the rings, and finding a priest to perform the service without charge.[85]

The clinic in Kingston, Jamaica, was more circumscribed, limited for the most part to providing fittings, advice, and general gynecological exams (although even those were a rarity for most women on the island). As indicated in Farquharson's letters to Mrs. Allen, the League also provided a referral service, producing lists of local doctors who were known to provide birth control advice to pass on to women in their area. In some countries, particularly those where openly distributing birth control was illegal, this was the largest component of their service. The Canadian Federation of Societies for Population Planning, for example, had six member societies in 1964 but only one clinic; the rest of the societies were confined to distributing literature and instructions while also referring inquiries to sympathetic doctors and "the semi-secret birth control services of hospitals."[86] The New Zealand FPA operated for fourteen years before opening its first clinic, focusing instead on linking women with local doctors who provided family planning advice.[87] Even in places where there were some clinics, FPAs recognized that they could only ever reach a very small portion of the population interested in family planning. Looking at the letters between Farquharson and Mrs. Allen, for example, one can easily see the difficulty of asking Mrs. Allen to travel across the island to see a doctor on a specific afternoon or conduct three trips to and from clinics to see one of the other doctors, with four children in tow. Indeed, many family planning advocates saw the clinics themselves as something of a "demonstration" space, there to exhibit what birth control services *could* look like, rather than an actual functional answer to the needs of the broader population.

If she had lived a bit closer, Mrs. Allen might also have been privy to a visit, in either her village or her home, by a fieldworker sent out by the Jamaica Family Planning League. As Manon Parry notes, the early global family planning movement had two central components: "the clinic" and "the field."[88] Most associations in the 1940s–1960s combined both of these

FIGURE 2.2. "Family Planning works of FPA Thailand." Pah-Pai Village, Thailand, 1967. Source: Dorothy Hamilton Brush Papers, Smith College Special Collections.

elements. The JFPL, for example, sent its two nurses out to the countryside periodically in the 1940s, to explain the concept of family planning and the work of the clinic to small gatherings or individual mothers, while also handing out pamphlets of the type sent to Mrs. Allen.[89] In the late 1950s, the newly consolidated Jamaica Family Planning Association pioneered in the use of a mobile clinic.[90] Others hired social workers or specific staff to do fieldwork. A social worker in India, for example, reported giving over 150 meetings and film shows in one year.[91] Another set up a tent at a weekly market, with four orators who spoke to three to five men each, and twenty social workers who signed men up for vasectomies or sold men and women contraceptives.[92] In Hong Kong, over the course of eight months a social worker visited twenty-six blocks of the Wong Tai Sin Resettlement Estates and spoke to 4,961 mothers; in the last three months of 1960, a social worker visited 1,306 women in their homes or as they came to their work stations.[93]

Through these activities, mid-century family planning advocates came into contact with a larger body of people, beyond those like Mrs. Allen who proactively sought out their services. They used these opportunities not only to distribute contraceptive methods, but also to proselytize: to sell the broader vision of family planning and the concept of the small family, to those who were already interested, to those who were curious, and to those who were otherwise opposed. In this larger mission, letters like that written by Farquharson and Allen were used both as evidence of the inevitable success of the movement and as a means to transmit the values deemed necessary to the proper practice of family planning. In doing so,

FIGURE 2.3. "Two healthcare workers, or nurses, standing outdoors, discussing birth control methods with a group of mothers with young children." Korea, c. 1965. Source: Schlesinger Library, Harvard Radcliffe Institute.

advocates engaged not only in the very practical work of distributing tablets and fitting diaphragms, but also in the ephemeral work of selling hope and modernity, one demonstration at a time.

Hope and Faith

Mid-century family planning advocates saw letters like that written by Mrs. Allen as clear evidence of their core belief: that the women of the world wanted family planning, and would seize on the opportunities created by clinics. As Farquharson's friend Violet Allwood wrote in a letter to the *Gleaner* in 1940, the response to the clinic showed that lower-class women were equally anxious "to avail themselves of the knowledge to plan the number of their children according to means. Only those with this experience can appreciate that these poor women want to do the best for their children, and get a chance for themselves too."[94] The IPPF's *ATW* newsletter and fieldworker reports told stories of clinics "besieged by eager patients."[95] When a hospital in Rangoon, Burma, opened a clinic two days a week, for example, the demand was apparently so great that some women had to wait for eight sessions before being seen.[96] In Trinidad, fears of opposition on the opening day of the first clinic were assuaged when "in fact all that happened was that the interested ladies, some of whom had come from Port of Spain, queued up to be photographed as the first patient!"[97] According to *ATW*, the reactions of women to family planning advocacy were "nearly always favorable."[98] Fieldworkers likewise claimed that "the need for family planning . . . was almost universally accepted,"[99] and that "there is probably no country in the world that does not need Family Planning."[100]

Local and international family planning newsletters regularly published "desperate letters from hard-pressed parents"[101] to support these claims of universal contraceptive need and desire. A feature in *ATW*, for example, included the following excerpts from letters written to the AIED in Italy:

"Four years ago I had my child from a man I later discovered had tuberculosis. I have fought desperately to stop it in the baby's body: but from his limbs to his glandules and bones, the sickness is constantly migrating and never won. I cannot stand the fear of another unwanted child like this."

A workman's wife: "I am 20 and have four children. I married at 16, because of an unwanted pregnancy. When my husband touches me, I get mad, I cry and insult him. I realize later he is not responsible but I shall commit suicide if I become pregnant again. You are my only hope."

A blind man from Pisa: "I suffer from acute hereditary retinitis. All my children would be blind. My wife became pregnant once and we agreed on an abortion. But we cannot go on like that."

Happier letters to answer arrive from young couples desiring first to make a home and then to space welcome children—"in order to raise them better."[102]

A letter from a "Nicaraguan mother" published in the newsletter read: "I am badly in need of your help. I am thirty two years and have six children under 12. My privation is very great. My husband is but a humble carpenter, wages low. Please assist me!"[103] A mother from Mexico noted that she had seven children before age thirty-two and had been "a slave to Child Bearing all this 11 years." She was two months pregnant at the time of writing and noted that "it almost drives me wild if I shall think of having another child."[104]

Family planning newsletters and annual reports for associations also recorded case histories of women who came to the clinics, highlighting particularly desperate situations. A feature on Ceylon in *ATW* noted: "For the most part, case histories reveal a record of constant pregnancy—one woman, who confessed to having intercourse with her husband only once a month, had had ten children in ten years, and said she was only 28 years old. Another whose eighth child was only eight weeks old, was found to be pregnant once again during the examination."[105] The Family Planning Association of Winnipeg in Canada described troubled families and young parents suffering from "nervous breakdown" in its annual report.[106] The Singapore Family Planning Association recorded a case of a thirty-six-year-old woman who had a total of twenty-five pregnancies, resulting in ten living children, one spontaneous miscarriage, and fourteen induced abortions.[107] Sometimes the facts themselves were deemed damning enough, without much embellishment. The Cape Town Mothers Clinic in South Africa, for example, provided the following list of current cases in 1954:

> Age 33. 11 pregnancies in 15 years, 9 alive. Suffers from hypertension. 1 room. Husband earns £3.15 per week.

> Age 43. 20 pregnancies in 27 years, 12 alive. Blood pressure. Married 15 years.

> Age 33. 8 pregnancies, 6 alive. Husband blind, earns £18 per month working for Civilian Blind Society.[108]

In their coverage of the Mothers Clinic, *ATW* praised the association for using images of female clients in its materials, which were, it related, "more telling than all the statistics. (Other family planning agencies take notice!)"[109]

Family planning advocates also mobilized tales from the field to illustrate the supposedly universal appeal of birth control, challenging the "myth" that "illiterate villagers are uninterested in birth control, and would not take the trouble to practice it."[110] A social worker in a village in Mysore, India, described a story of two peasant men who "walked eighty miles to consult her on how to limit their families."[111] Celestina Zalduondo of Puerto Rico told the story of a man who had walked for an hour through the mountains with a flashlight to attend an information session, "because the people of his village needed f.p. [family planning] so much."[112] A report on Indonesia described how a group of women, after hearing a lecture on family planning, "literally mobbed" the fieldworkers "trying to get the few tablets they had brought with them."[113] Fieldworkers claimed that, for these people, birth control was a matter of common sense. A story in *ATW* titled "The Old Man" described discussions between an anonymous family planning worker in India and "the old man of the village" who reportedly compared family planning to the pruning of his lime tree:

> It is "spacing" that does the trick. He said . . . with a twinkle in his eye, that it was true also in the animal and human world . . . Had he planned likewise his family? Yes, he had . . .
>
> The old man had given full expression to the modern ideas of birth control and family planning. Had anybody taught him these things? No, they had come to him with the passing of years and the things he had seen in the human, animal and plant world during his lifetime.
>
> The old man had done what I intended to do that day in the village. He made my work easy. There was nothing for me to do but to make a list of all the persons willing to learn . . . family planning the right way.[114]

Miss Fung Hsien-mei, a midwife working for the FPA of China in Taiwan, similarly described a sixty-year-old woman as her chief ally in one community, accompanying her to visit families in their homes and taking a pile of posters to distribute to her friends. As she recalled: "Since then, I have never hesitated in contacting aged women who I now believe will transmit my message to proper persons."[115]

While some of these tales may have been embellished or allegorical, surviving letters written to clinics around the world and surveys of patients who came to clinics do illustrate that, for many, childbearing in the mid-twentieth century was a fraught process that could spur very real interest in family planning. Mrs. Allen's peers in Jamaica spoke of the economic, physical, and psychological stress of having children "too quickly," one after another, without any end in sight.[116] In their letters to early family planning associations in Canada, women spoke of having lived their entire married lives either pregnant or nursing young children; they documented the anxiety of becoming pregnant, their desire to restore sexual pleasure to marriage, and their inability to fulfill their ideal roles of wife and mother under the pressure of uncontrolled reproduction.[117] Women in Chile surveyed by doctors noted the heavy weight of childbearing on their lives and the challenges of controlling reproduction without easy access to contraceptives: some reported having multiple illegal abortions in their lifetime.[118] These letters were not necessarily representative of the average woman's experience in any given country: often, it was the most desperate and long-suffering cases who took the step to reach out to clinics. Trent MacNamara points out that many letters written to Margaret Sanger in the early twentieth-century United States took on a more brief, matter-of-fact tone, with the writer seemingly interested in being brought "up to date" on the latest methods, rather than desperately seeking contraception for the first time.[119] Some women in early twentieth-century South Africa reached out on behalf of their daughters, hoping to provide them with sex education early in their lives.[120] Either way, as Deborah Cohen argues, working-class women appear in these sources not as "pawns" of the family planning movement, but rather as active birth control seekers, as "people who wanted to change their lives."[121]

Advocates frequently portrayed their cause as simply a matter of fulfilling this already existing demand, providing guidance and materials to the desperate parents around the world already eager to learn more. But advocates also noted that there were many people who had not heard of family planning; moreover, a broad or abstract interest in family planning did not always translate into sustained contraceptive practice. Even women like Mrs. Allen could become discouraged when family planning proved more complicated than it seemed at first glance. As a result, family planning advocates were engaged in a constant process of both affirming that everyone already wanted family planning and proselytizing the importance of family planning to those who presumably already wanted it or needed it. In her second letter to Mrs. Allen on November 29, 1939, for example, Farquharson sends her a pamphlet outlining the "reasons for birth control": a curious choice, at first glance, for someone who was seemingly already convinced enough to contact the clinic in the first place. But as I saw the correspondence unfold, and Mrs. Allen's struggles and eventual failure with the foam powder and sponge method, it made more sense. Farquharson had likely already seen many women abandon the cause when it failed to fulfill its promise, and worried that Allen would do the same. In her letter of March 2, 1940, she reinforces the need for diligence, writing: "Don't lose hope with Birth Control, whatever you do. You can look around for yourself and see how few of the better-off people nowadays have large families, and that is just because they are using Birth Control methods." Embodying family planning, Farquharson argued, would require more than just the initial demand documented in letters and inquiries to clinics.

Farquharson's reference to "the better-off people" taps into one of the dominant narratives employed by advocates to try to either sell or reinforce faith in family planning, by portraying it as a tool of social advance. A Jamaican pamphlet produced in 1956 entitled "Which One?," for example, illustrated the fate of two friends, both mechanics, named Tom and Harry. Tom marries Joyce, and resists the pressure from "Grannie" to have as many children "as God says": as a result, they have a neat, small family, with three children, well fed and nicely dressed. Harry and Mary, on the other hand, keep having children. Mary's fate is classic: she is always tired, the house is never tidy, the kids are not able to go to school; in the end, after nine children, Mary dies at a young age.[122] A report in *ATW* in 1957 on an exhibition at a community center in Shanghai, China, illustrates a similar motif: "Large posters showed a harried father unable to work because of many children milling around him and the worn-out mother likewise sitting helplessly in the midst of crawling, climbing off-spring. Next came a contrast, all peace and orderliness; the father happily engaged at his desk, the mother, all smiles, attending to the needs of two healthy children. Immediately adjacent were many carefully detailed pictures of appliances and their usage."[123] In Ghana, a story of two brothers likewise linked individual family prosperity to the use of contraceptives.[124] *ATW* reported the popularity of this trope across the material mediums of family planning proselytization: the posters, pamphlets, flip charts, flannel boards, and contraceptive advertisements that nurses used in demonstrations and fieldworkers brought on their journeys.[125] This imagery—of the small, nuclear, "modern" heterosexual family with two children (usually one boy and one girl)—was replicated across a variety of divergent contexts, presumed to be universally relevant, achievable, and desirable.[126]

FIGURE 2.4. "A Small Family is a Happy Family poster." India, 1964. Source: Ford Foundation Papers, Rockefeller Archive Center.

These images also carried into other forms of media. Indeed, the family planning cause was a visual, sonic, and cinematic experience. In 1954, the Jamaican Family Planning League released its first radio spots. As *ATW* described, the spot began with the sound of a baby crying, followed by "a Jamaican woman's warm (important detail) voice" announcing the date and time of the family planning clinics, where a mother could "get sound advice and all the help you need for modern and intelligent family planning." Since radios were left on all day in shops in Kingston, this method was seen as particularly effective.[127] In 1950s Puerto Rico, spot announcements ran every morning on the radio around breakfast time;[128] in Singapore, five-minute talks ran on Radio Malaya; in Bermuda, fifteen-minute broadcasts on "Bermuda's Future and Yours" tackled different aspects of family planning;[129] and in Taiwan, programs on family planning ran every Monday, Wednesday, and Friday on the radio.[130] Family planners also came up with songs like this one, written on a paper found in Farquharson's collection:

> Gone are the days when parents did not know
> And mothers wept in poverty and woe,
> Now we can choose how many babes we'll bear
> The Family Planning Clinic will its knowledge share
> CHORUS: I'm coming, I'm coming, for the Clinic is the place
> Where I can learn to plan my life and children space.
> Gone are the days when life was full of care
> Gone are the days of not enough to share
> Gone are they all for a better way we find
> To plan and space our families and ease our mind.[131]

ATW also covered early experiments in film. The Jamaican film *Too Late*, for example, told the story of two families—one planned and the other unplanned—and directed the audience to "the appropriate one."[132] An Indian film produced by the Welfare and Family Planning Society of Dehra Dun told the "true story" of a village which, "by a wholesale adoption of family planning," improved its standard of living.[133]

The high degree of similarity among these materials was, again, not a coincidence: rather, it speaks to the active exchange of strategies, materials, and techniques across borders in these years. *ATW* contributed to this process at the most basic level through its coverage of the work of different associations, highlighting different methods that could be adopted by those in other places. The newsletter also advertised colorful, "eye-catching" IPPF pamphlets like "Do You Know?," "Family Benefits from Family Planning," "Family Planning Is No Secret," and "A Child Should Be Born When?" that could be ordered for a shilling per dozen from the IPPF in London.[134] Internal correspondence illustrates that these were indeed actively translated into local languages by FPAs in Ceylon, France, Germany, Poland, and East Africa.[135] While many of these were British or American pamphlets sent abroad, material also circulated in other directions. Kenyan advocates sought out films produced in Jamaica and India,[136] the FPA of Thailand got materials from the FPA of China,[137] and a Planned Parenthood Center in Cleveland released an American version of a pamphlet called "The Happy Family" created by the FPA of Hong Kong.[138] The FPA of the UK also showed films from India (*In Your Hands*) and Kenya (*Planned Parenthood Is Happy Parenthood*).[139] *ATW* promoted films made in Japan, like *Kagiri-Aru-Kodakura* (The Limited Children), a thirty-five-millimeter film "uncensored in accordance with Japanese candor."[140] This mixing and matching of materials could lead to some remarkably international moments, even in the most local of spaces. At a monthly meeting of municipal midwives in Jakarta, Indonesia, in 1962, for example, the audience was shown an African film explained in the local language afterward, followed by a Malayan-language family planning film made in Singapore.[141]

A "Family Planning Handbook for Speakers and Lay Workers" issued by the Singapore FPA circa 1960 provides a further illustration of the message being sold to communities. The pamphlet described family planning as "a discipline, an enlightened way of life," and the task of the fieldworker to "AROUSE public interest and MOTIVATE married people to adopt this new attitude towards richer, healthier and happier living."[142] The pamphlet claimed that while most people agreed that large families are a burden, the vast majority saw family size as something beyond their control. It was the lay worker's "mission" to "show them the way."[143] Rather than talking about "the impending population explosion," the pamphlet encouraged workers to try to appeal to maternal instincts by stressing the importance that children be wanted, loved, and properly cared for. The pamphlet also noted that improvements to the mother's health would allow "more time for rest, leisure, going out, seeing friends etc. Improve their status as women, and play their part in a modern State."[144] They stressed that the total number of children should be determined by the people themselves, but suggested the ideal number was three to four, on the basis of the increased maternal and infant mortality rates beyond the five-child mark.[145] Lay workers were instructed to stress that "Family Planning is THE SOLUTION for EVERY FAMILY, and NOT for just a few."[146]

Indeed, beneath the language of free choice in many family planning materials was an underlying assumption that families would make the "societally correct decisions" once informed,[147] acting in a responsible, "rational" way.[148] Clearly, the ideal promoted here was the small nuclear family, presented as the pinnacle of modernity and development, an "index of civilization," and a bulwark of stability, happiness, and order.[149] Some associations also explicitly wove religious language into their materials. The cover of a pamphlet from the Philippines, for example, read:

Parents are Partners with God
. . . In the creation of His Children
. . . Their love for their children expresses God's love
. . . Their care for their children expresses God's care
. . . They are to make God real to their children
. . . They are to make a home in which God's Spirit dwells
. . . They are to rear children worthy of their Heavenly Father
. . . They are to rear children to be responsible members of society.
Christians are called by God to Responsible Parenthood.[150]

Inside, the pamphlet noted that "every child has the right to be wanted" and to be provided with love and care, adequate food, proper clothing, a decent home, the opportunity for good education, and "enough time for character training and spiritual upbringing."[151]

As Sandra Whitworth argues, this portrayal of the happy nuclear family frequently remained mute on women's subordination within families: it was thus "gendered as much through its silences as through explicit statements concerning women and men."[152] Many advocates saw this as a strategic move, a way to sanitize the movement and increase its popular acceptance: the very term "family planning" had a gentler appeal than "birth control."[153] Still, the more radical feminist and sex reformist premises of the early family planning movement were not entirely erased in these years. Caroline Rusterholz, for example, notes some of the progressive discussions of sexual pleasure and anatomy that took place in English FPA clinics, some of which included guidance on the clitoris and how to caress it. As she notes, if the aim of many of these advocates—the maintenance of family life—was "traditional," the methods and ideas they promoted in their sexual counseling services could be quite radical.[154] Eunjoo Cho likewise illustrates how the reports, leaflets, and training materials published by the Planned Parenthood Federation of Korea in the mid-twentieth century stressed the importance of sexual pleasure (particularly of women), providing detailed discussions on foreplay and the value of sex to healthy relationships. Although the ultimate goal of the movement was, again, the strengthening of the heterosexual family, the materials promoted a disruptive, positive vision of sex.[155] As Manon Parry points out, even the seemingly tamest of materials could be deemed controversial at the time, provoking outrage and censorship for simply daring to break the silence on contraception, however carefully.[156] Indeed, many of these publications "skirted the boundaries of respectable and non-respectable sexualities—suggestive at once of a titillating 'pornography' and of 'serious guidance' for married couples."[157]

In any case, we cannot assume that the ideals promoted by family planning propaganda were swallowed whole by those they targeted; rather, we need to explore how "such imagery is produced and consumed by a broad range of people who may resist, negotiate, or accommodate encoded meanings."[158] As Trent MacNamara illustrates, appeals to "modernity" by American family planning advocates could be powerful, tapping into individuals' own desires to be "forward-thinking" or "progressive"; for others, however, modernity was associated with decadence or irreligiosity, something to be rejected rather than embraced.[159] Indeed, some audiences in India, when presented with the classic "impoverished large family and modern small family" scenario, actually sympathized with the large family and felt sorry for the small one, understanding "prosperity" in ways that fundamentally differed from those of family planners.[160] As Leslie Dwyer points out, even the most static and homogenizing imagery could come to life in the context of discussions: women might embrace them, poke fun, ask questions that went far beyond their intention, or simply leave.[161] Indeed, family planning workers themselves often recognized the posters, films, and pamphlets as conversation starters rather than authoritative mechanisms of social influence. As one health education officer in Pakistan noted, the goal of family planning materials was to evoke "an emotional response" and launch a discussion.[162] In Bermuda, likewise, fieldworkers noted that "it was the question period afterwards that is of most value."[163] It was in these personal, intimate discussions that the hopes and fears of both advocates and communities were expressed, challenged, and reshaped.

Intimate Encounters

The certainty and self-assertion with which advocates recounted the universal desire for family planning in some spaces is tempered by evidence of more fraught relationships between advocates and communities in others. Indeed, beneath the narratives of hope and faith that dominate in family planning material—both local and global—lies a distinct undercurrent of suspicion. This suspicion runs two ways. On the one hand, the communities targeted by outreach activities at times appear suspicious of the motivations and approaches of family planning missionaries. On the other hand, family planners could be suspicious of their target communities, doubtful of their ability to really comprehend and practice contraception in a sustained way. These suspicions led to tension within the practice of family planning, as advocates and communities struggled to assert their own understandings of what was needed, and how each should behave in these intimate interactions.

In their correspondence and internal reports, family planning advocates swapped stories of local resistance to their efforts. Nurses in Jamaica, for example, were sometimes invited and welcomed to communities they visited, but at other times women were reportedly "rude" and gave them "only abuse."[164] Home visitors in Hong Kong had doors slammed in their faces.[165] Some communities cut family planning advocates down to size through humor; the Singapore FPA, for example, noted how quickly the subject could turn into "a target of ribald jokes and ridicule."[166] A team of family planning outreach workers in Indonesia found that their work was derailed in one division by a woman who, having found herself disappointed with the supplies on offer, "endeavored to turn our explanations into a joke."[167] But communities could also be more assertive in their rejection of family planning proselytizing, throwing rocks at advocates or forcing them to leave. Some families in Japan doused outreach workers in water and threw the contraceptives they handed out back at them.[168] All of this could lead to a general "climate of suspicion" around clinics in some areas.[169] Maria Luisi de Marchi, one of Italy's earliest advocates, noted that there had been "many weeks of tension" during her outreach activities in working-class communities, such that "you feel sometimes that the border between friendship and lynching is very thin."[170]

This climate of suspicion was likely enhanced in some cases by the overly aggressive methods used by some family planning advocates. A creche matron in Jamaica, for example, complained about nurses "creeping" around, handing out "Christmassy Cards" to mothers with information about the family planning clinic.[171] In a report on the Jamaican FPA's mobile clinic, *ATW* acknowledged that, "as has been found in other countries," women were not always receptive to "a suddenly appearing clinic held in a large truck."[172] It probably didn't help that the driver of this particular truck accidentally hit and killed a man en route to one community.[173] In Barbados, family planners similarly found that a "bombastic" approach including loudspeakers, films, and speeches was rarely as successful as personal visits to households.[174] Although these experiences were often attributed to the "shyness" of women, this report did note that perhaps it might be better if the mobile clinic was preceded by "community education, conducted by a convert already resident in and accepted by the neighborhood."[175] But even home visitors who took a more private or individual approach could be seen as intrusive. Some were accused of being door-to-door salesmen for birth control firms, prompting one experimental program in Malaysia to encourage family planning nurses to dress in white and state that they were coming from the hospital to be distinguished from those seeking to make a profit.[176]

Family planning advocates sometimes dismissed these forms of resistance as evidence of the ignorance or lethargy of communities being targeted. The Singapore FPA's tenth annual report in 1960, for example, lamented "the apathy—or even antipathy—of the very people they were trying to help."[177] Pathfinder Fund fieldworker Edna McKinnon recognized that some resistance was due to legitimate practical issues but argued that in other cases it was simply "apathy, ignorance, or laziness which is universal."[178] Some distinguished between the "cooperative" communities who accepted family planning and "uncooperative" communities who resisted.[179] But even those who accepted methods could be suspect: fieldworkers noted that some people took contraceptives or even made an appointment to go to the clinic "either out of politeness or just to get rid of the motivator," but made no actual effort to follow up.[180] Dr. Simon Frazer, a British doctor living in Bermuda, noted that it was "very unusual indeed to find an unwilling response" when he discussed the subject with women who came to his clinic, but added that Bermudians "are generally polite, and tend to give the answers they think the questioner wants."[181] Some feared in private that the universal demand for family planning was, in practice, a façade to appease family planners.

Family planning advocates also complained about women who came once to a clinic but never returned, or abandoned their contraceptive practice after only a few months. Indeed, mid-century clinics around the world noted low rates of continuation and follow-up. A report on the first 4,000 clinics at Farquharson's clinic in 1955 showed that 50 percent never returned, and a further 13–16 percent returned only once.[182] Similar numbers were recorded at early clinics in South Africa, the United States, Ceylon, and Malaysia.[183] A clinic in Zanzibar operating in the late 1950s had almost no return visits at all.[184] Staff of the Barbados FPA concluded that the major problem was "not attracting clients, but retaining them."[185] As Sylvia Fernando aptly summarized in 1962: "Ceylon is not alone in finding that sustained use of a contraceptive method is an exception rather than the rule."[186] Indeed, an article on "The Return Visit" in *ATW* claimed that the difficulty of getting women to continue with a method or return to a clinic was a universal struggle among family planning associations.[187]

Family planning advocates and contraceptive manufacturers could be quick to blame these low rates of continuance on women's presumed lack of discipline. Advocates described women who failed to use a method as "apathetic" and even "stupid."[188] A report from Hong Kong in 1956 claimed that those who conceived while using one of their methods had done so "chiefly through careless neglect."[189] A pamphlet of the FPA of Ceylon put it frankly in a Q&A section, responding to the question "Suppose the contraceptive we choose fails?" with the response that "Method failure is rare. Failures, if any, are due to your own fault."[190] After Mrs. Allen's failure with the sponge and foam powder method, as noted in the letters above, Farquharson wrote to the manufacturer to ask whether the size of the sponge might be the problem. The reply was curt:

> A report of failure in an isolated instance on the part of a woman who had not even been examined in the clinic can scarcely serve as an indictment of a method. I assume that you have no way of knowing whether or not the use of the material was regular or intermittent, or if it was so stated whether or not the statement was to be trusted. The great difficulty in accumulating information about the success of any method is the fact that every person having a method fail is prepared to swear that it has been used faithfully and in complete accord with the instructions. The great weakness of obtaining an entirely successful birth control method is the fact that its use or non-use is completely under the control of the patient, and there is no way, except an admission, to determine what the facts may be. There is, therefore, no foolproof method since all methods are used by "fools" and the entire responsibility is on the shoulders of the patient.[191]

Farquharson's response to Mrs. Allen is relatively gentle in comparison, noting that "no Birth Control method . . . succeeds with <u>everybody</u>" and suggesting she would need to visit a clinic to get a diaphragm. But in private correspondence to the League's nurse, Farquharson complained that "in theory, women want birth control, but in practice, when they find it means trouble, they won't keep up the good work!"[192] Racist and classist ideas clearly underlay these frustrations. She claimed to a friend that "the very poor, who need b.c. [birth control] most, can't be bothered to take the trouble, or exercise the self-control and lead the orderly life that is the sine qua non of successful b.c.," in part because they were content to live "an almost animal existence."[193]

If family planning advocates could be suspicious of women's determination and ability, they often had even less faith in men. Farquharson expresses this in her first letter to Mrs. Allen, when she mentions the condom but notes that "so often it is found that the man does not want to be bothered to take the trouble to take such a precaution." Both local advocates and international family planning fieldworkers exhibited similar attitudes. A clinic in Berlin lamented how women's efforts could be undermined by "undisciplined husbands";[194] fieldworkers in Latin America blamed the slow progress of the movement on "male dominance of the wife";[195] and a Singapore FPA pamphlet for fieldworkers warned that while "husbands generally love and care for their wives," others could be "beastly and cruel," treating their wives like "mute slaves."[196] These statements sometimes descended into crude racist and classist stereotypes of marginalized men that failed to recognize the interest of many men in family planning, and their experiences as active contraceptive users themselves. Indeed, recent scholarship has pointed to the critical role of male methods like withdrawal and the condom in the twentieth century, and the active efforts of men to draw on family planning services.[197] But family planners' concerns about men could also draw attention to very real constraints imposed by patriarchal cultures and gender inequalities, as women around the world reported on their difficulty of using methods in the face of opposition from their partners. In Trinidad, for example, the family planning association created policies to help women conceal their identities from partners who objected; still, one of their patients ended up in the hospital, a victim of domestic abuse after her husband discovered she was obtaining contraceptives.[198] In other places, family planners officially insisted that women obtain their husband's consent to use contraceptives, but made no efforts to follow up with women who came, essentially allowing them to act independently.[199] Some family planners openly argued that the movement's success would require a larger transformation, including an expansion of opportunities for women and an increase in their social status.[200]

If some family planning advocates in this period sought to ally themselves with women against these patriarchal structures by helping keep their contraceptive practice secret, more often they tried to work within the system and convert men to the cause. Already by the mid-1950s, FPAs and individual doctors in India, Barbados, the United States, Japan, Ceylon, and beyond had begun stressing the importance of reaching out to men.[201] Pathfinder Fund representative Edna Rankin McKinnon put it bluntly, arguing that: "It will help if men are made to feel that they have initiated the 'idea' of child spacing."[202] To that end, an enterprising nurse in Japan, Miyoshi Oba, started a "Mandarin Duck Club" aimed at bringing husbands and wives together to talk about family planning.[203] Dr. Edris Rice-Wray conducted a project with male prisoners in Mexico since—as *ATW* reported—"the prisoners had nothing better to do. Thirty fathers did listen—and with great interest. Since then she has conducted successful group meetings—out of jail—with both fathers and mothers."[204] IPPF fieldworker Dorothy Brush shared the Mexico story with Dr. Adeniyi-Jones, pioneer of family planning in Nigeria, noting that where men see themselves as "supreme ruler" of their wives, "deferring to the husband as the real boss has made an enormous difference."[205] Some began to promote vasectomy or condom use more actively in their clinics and campaigns.[206] For the most part, in the mid-twentieth century, however, these efforts focused on getting men to *allow* women to use contraceptives, rather than getting the men to use contraceptives themselves. Indeed, when Hong Kong opened a male clinic in 1960, it was described by IPPF fieldworkers as an "unusual pioneer feature"[207] in a field still focused primarily on female methods.

Regardless of whether they worked with men, women, or both, family planning advocates' daily experience of promoting the cause could sometimes lead them to an increased recognition of the practical issues that limited their reach, beyond people's supposed "apathy." Farquharson's letters indicate her tacit awareness of the difficulty for Mrs. Allen of getting to the clinic in Kingston, due to its distance and the limited hours. Clinics in other areas also reported the problem of transportation as significant or at times insurmountable.[208] The FPA of Winnipeg, in Canada, noted that attending a clinic regularly was also made difficult for low-income families due to the general instability of their lives, which led them to be constantly on the move in their search for employment and affordable housing.[209] Some fieldworkers recognized that their visits were simply an additional burden for already overworked people. Describing a session aimed at laborers, for example, one team of fieldworkers in Indonesia noted that "they are tired after a long day and our enquiries are a tedious business."[210] Many women visited in their homes were likewise tied up with domestic tasks and struggled to pay attention to a family planning sermon while trying to prepare a meal and tend to multiple children at once.[211] Language could also be a considerable barrier: one FPA clinic relied on a roster of voluntary interpreters to make it possible for patients to converse in their own tongue.[212]

This led some family planning advocates to stress the need for more sensitive and respectful approaches. A project in Puerto Rico, for example, argued that the most important thing was that volunteers had "the respect of the group they are to serve and that they have a spirit of service."[213] Singapore's FPA stressed that lay workers needed to be "pleasing in manner and sympathetic in approach at all times," well informed, tolerant, not prone to showing off knowledge or ridiculing another's ignorance, and "a dedicated person who knows that his is a humanitarian commission."[214] Mohammad Moizuddin, a health education officer in East Pakistan, noted that "education like this cannot be given in wordy lectures, dry slogans, nor boring rules or irksome restrictions. It can only be the result of a teaching which is alive to everyday problems, adapted to the various needs of the individual and social groups."[215] The key was sympathy and sincerity; Moizuddin advised fieldworkers to "BE kind and tolerant," "Identify yourself with them as far as possible," and "Always work with the people and never work for them."[216] The goal of discussion was not to "convince or defeat" opponents, but rather to "give them the opportunity and freedom to discuss their problems and find out the solutions."[217] Mr. E. L. Fernando, speaking from Ceylon, argued that social workers need to have the "capacity for identification with the needs, sufferings and problems of their fellowmen," exhibit a "prophetic vision," and exercise "love in its most unselfish form."[218] Indeed, many FPAs attributed the success they did have to the personal qualities of particular nurses, social workers, and home visitors. One clinic in Ceylon noted that the rate of checkup and follow-up visits were satisfactory "due almost entirely to conscientious and tactful home visiting on the part of the clinic worker, who belongs to the same socio-economic group as the people who patronize the Clinic."[219] Family planning advocacy, as Dorothy Brush put it, relied on "the human touch."[220]

This could be hard to achieve in places where clinics were understaffed and trying to see as many patients as possible. But even if properly instructed, some advocates recognized, contraceptive practice in the early to mid-twentieth century was simply difficult. As evident in the pamphlet and letters sent to Mrs. Allen by Farquharson, most methods required a significant amount of advance planning and privacy: one had to prepare foam powders and diaphragms in advance of the sex act, then wash and hang everything to dry afterward, which could be awkward in places where people lived in crowded housing conditions, slept all in one room, or had to stand in long queues at municipal taps for water.[221] Dr. Siva Chinnatamby in Ceylon noted that families struggled to keep their diaphragms in private places and out of the reach of children; one hung it out to dry on the line and had a crow fly away with it.[222] Condom use was also difficult to conceal in housing units with common bathrooms.[223] Diaphragms could be hard to insert, especially for women not used to touching their genitals.[224] One fieldworker, for example, reported on a patient trying to use a diaphragm with a coil spring: "Every time she tried to insert it, it sprang apart until she was practically in tears."[225] Other family planners noted that many women had cervical infections that made the diaphragm difficult to use, or they struggled to pause the sexual act to insert the diaphragm in a situation of unequal gendered power balance.[226] Even the supposedly "simple" method using cottonwool and vinegar was relatively complex. Indeed, Farquharson's description in her letter of November 29, 1939, to Mrs. Allen of the different amounts of vinegar to mix and the preparation of the "potion" reads like instructions for a laboratory science experiment.

The many chemical spermicidal methods devised in the 1940s and 1950s also proved disappointing, and directly contradicted advocates' belief that what worked in one place could be transferred to another. Chemical contraceptives with a low melting point deteriorated quickly in heat and humidity; as Farquharson noted, the label "Store in a cool dry place" on the container was unrealistic for most of the people seeking contraceptives in tropical climates.[227] Rendell tablets melted, while other pastes would expand in the tube and burst out of the end.[228] As early as 1950, British Drug Houses Ltd. came to the conclusion that it was "impossible" to manufacture a gel that would melt readily at vaginal temperature but retain its form when stored in a hot climate.[229] Volpar foam tablets were withdrawn in India in the 1960s due to their poor storage quality and poor foaming quality; many were found discolored, and stocks were returned to manufacturers.[230] Bermudian doctors noted that patients did not like the medical smell of Volpar tablets; they also expressed (understandable) concern that the Volpar tubes were marked "poison" on the label.[231] Indeed, some brands of foaming powders and tablets contained mercury, a potentially toxic element, or chemicals like hydroquinone, which had not been proven safe at the time.[232] As one report on an experimental program with foam tablets in Johore, Indonesia, summarized: "For some they are too hot; others find them awkward to use at a psychologically inopportune time; for some it's too messy; The tablets disintegrate in tropical countries; The packaging is not very satisfactory. Also the tablets have not been sufficiently researched for effectiveness and acceptability with the result that workers lack the confidence to offer them to patients as a fool proof method."[233] The Johore FPA argued that in light of these realities, the tablets "can hardly be called a simple method."[234] In a presentation in 1957, the Medical Committee of the IPPF concluded that all existing spermicidal methods were "more or less unsatisfactory."[235] Dr. A. S. Parkes of the Medical Research Council of the UK further described the landscape of both chemical and mechanical methods of birth control in 1961 as "a disgrace to science in this age of spectacular technical achievement."[236]

This could be incredibly frustrating for advocates like Farquharson, who eventually acknowledged that "all known methods of birth control are troublesome and too expensive, and require privacy which our women have not got."[237] Writing to the British Family Planning Association in 1952, Farquharson outlined the problems with each method and implored the organization to "tell us if there is any good news at any time about a simple method, or about defining a period during which contraceptives are essential, making the use of birth control less onerous."[238] Vera Houghton of the IPPF responded by noting that "believe me, we do appreciate the desperate need for a simple contraceptive, and we have now got a number of scientists at least interested in the problem."[239] Indeed, *ATW* tracked a variety of research projects in the 1950s exploring the physiology of reproduction and conducting early trials of steroids.[240] This included early trials of what would come to be the birth control pill, conducted by American researcher Gregory Pincus with funding from Katharine McCormick, a wealthy philanthropist and friend of Margaret Sanger. Drawing on Mexican research that extracted progestin from the barbasco root (a traditional Andean contraceptive), Pincus worked with the Searle company to produce a hormonal contraceptive pill and began trials on the US mainland and in Puerto Rico. Already in 1955, headlines had begun reporting that "the 'pill' was here," although the IPPF warned that there was need for much more research to test safety and efficacy before it could be released to a broader public.[241]

In the meantime, women who found "modern" methods of contraception wanting were left with few options: they could return to the less reliable methods they had previously used (withdrawal, douching, etc.), or they could try to get a sterilization. Some FPA clinics did offer sterilizations in the mid-twentieth century, although only for mothers who met certain conditions. The Singapore FPA stressed, for example, that "this method of treatment is never recommended lightly, but only when another pregnancy would endanger the mother's life or health"; this usually included women with heart disease, tuberculosis, eight or more pregnancies, or where a physical handicap like anterior poliomyelitis and leprosy made it difficult to care for babies.[242] In Hong Kong FPA clinics, a majority of physicians reportedly opposed sterilization except for cases of insanity, disease, or for women over thirty-five with at least six living children.[243] Other places required joint consent, on the part of both the woman and her partner.[244] In most places, however, FPA clinics did not conduct sterilizations but rather referred women to hospitals, where they might face similar restrictions, high fees, and long waiting lists. In Kuala Lumpur in 1959, for example, there was reportedly a waiting list of as long as nine months to be sterilized, as obstetrical departments could not keep up with demand.[245]

If sterilization was difficult to access in many contexts, it was aggressively promoted in others. Many eugenic sterilization policies remained on the books well into the 1950s, used to coercively sterilize thousands of men and women around the world, from Japan to the United States to Scandinavia. People with disabilities, marginalized communities, people living in institutions, and those dependent on state support were particularly vulnerable to these policies. But even in places where there was no official policy, doctors took liberties through their own initiative, pressuring women to undergo the procedure or simply conducting it without their knowledge during childbirth or a caesarean section. In Peru, for example, where restrictions were particularly tight, a doctor bragged about having "sterilized thousands of women without their husbands' permission, nor theirs."[246] Jamaica had no eugenic sterilization law: attempts to initiate one in the early 1940s had been quickly stymied by public protest.[247] But individual doctors indicated their support for more aggressive policies in ways that suggest that patient consent was not their priority. As one doctor wrote to Farquharson in 1944: "Of course, I am able to get sterilization done by cutting the Fallopian Tubes whenever we do a Caesarean Section and at some operations when it is indicated. I wish we could get the public to believe that a girl who has a second illegitimate child is feeble minded and should be sterilized by the cauterization of the internal Fallopian openings when examination is made after delivery before they leave the hospital etc."[248] A broader program of sterilization, according to this doctor, was the only way to "control the population."[249]

This doctor recorded these thoughts in a private letter to Farquharson, a letter among friends, fellow members of the white elite who could speak freely about their frustrations and desires for the family planning movement. But the doctor in question also appears in the correspondence between Farquharson and Mrs. Allen, as one of the local doctors Farquharson suggests she might get in touch with to be fitted for a diaphragm, adding another element to our speculation about Mrs. Allen's fate. If she did make it to a doctor's office in her area, did she get a diaphragm after all, or did she end up with a sterilization? Did she want one? Would she have been happy to put an end to the onslaught of pregnancies that brought her to write to Farquharson in the first place? Or would she have felt pressured by the authority of the doctor and acquiesced in the moment to a procedure that could not be reversed? What did Mrs. Allen ultimately get out of the mid-century family planning movement?

As with most women at the receiving end of family planning advocacy, we can only guess Mrs. Allen's fate. As for Farquharson: by the mid-1950s, she had nearly given up on the cause, which she described as "this rather depressing B.C. movement, which seems to make such slow headway."[250] In June 1955 she threatened to resign, on account of the "crescendo of disillusionment" and "hopelessness" she felt over the lack of suitable methods and motivation.[251] When criticized by IPPF fieldworker Barbara Cadbury for her negative attitude, Farquharson replied sarcastically that she had forgotten that "one must never put these thoughts into words, when family planners are about!"[252] For Farquharson, the discourses of hope and faith that glued the movement together had become a charade, a façade. She began to sign her letters as "W.B." or "Wet Blanket."[253] In May 1956 she made a final "Plea from a Pioneer" in *ATW*, asking:

> Why is it that the world must wait so long for the most crying need of today—the invention of a simple cheap acceptable contraceptive? After nearly 20 years, we workers here in Jamaica give way at times to utter despair! . . . True, we hear occasional rumors of contraceptive research but always hedged with cautious reservations: don't get your hopes up; too soon to tell; years away. Where is the scientist to devote all his powers to it? Where the philanthropist or the foundation to support such research with total funds instead of dribbles? Just the achievement of this one longed-for boon to mankind would do more to bring about a happy healthy world than all the current palliative stop-gaps put together.[254]

And with that, she resigned.[255]

Conclusion

The letters between Farquharson and Allen—and the records of early family planning associations more broadly—provide us with a general sense of the complexity of family planning practice in the early to mid-twentieth century. We can see how local advocates drew on and adapted international models to create clinics that at times went well beyond the mandate of contraception, becoming centers that offered broader reproductive health, sexual well-being, and social welfare services. We can observe how the promises of the family planning movement intersected with the aspirations of men and women around the world, drawing advocates and patients together into a set of intimate encounters. But we can also see the resistance of local communities, contradicting the assumption of family planning advocates that contraception was "always already desirable for rational and autonomous individuals."[256] We can get a glimpse into the practical difficulty of family planning in these years even for those who *did* want it: of inserting vinegar-soaked cotton balls, foaming tablets, and rubber diaphragms, of battling with reusable condoms and spermicidal powders that quickly deteriorated or went bad in hot climates. We can see the many conflicting impulses that shaped the relationships between family planning advocates and those they sought to convert: of hope, love, and compassion, but also fear, suspicion, and the darkest aspirations for control over others. The deep faith in family planning that served as such a powerful motivator for advocates to overcome the political constraints of the cause could also serve as a barrier to true connection with the communities they sought to "save," making it difficult to handle objections, critique, wavering commitment, and outright failure.

But even for those who *were* able to recognize the practical constraints shaping family planning practice and try to adapt their programs to better fit people's lives, the reach of the cause in the 1930s to 1950s remained limited. Most advocates recognized that the small scale of voluntary-based organizations or the scattered efforts of individual doctors would never be enough to spread the cause beyond "a privileged few."[257] The ultimate goal, as the IPPF reported in 1963, was government support, so that "one day family planning will be an integral part of health services everywhere."[258] From the 1960s onward, this objective would be realized in many parts of the world, as governments began to commit more proactively to family planning, supported by large influxes of money from foreign aid agencies and international organizations. Dreams of more reliable methods would also come true with the introduction of the birth control pill and a variety of new intra-uterine devices (IUDs), contraceptive shots, and implants. But these developments would bring their own set of problems: with greater investment came greater possibility for control over others. It is to the peak of the population control movement that we turn next.

[CHAPTER THREE]

Crisis of Faith

Let's begin here with excerpts from the work diary of Dr. Adaline Pendleton—"Penny"—Satterthwaite: obstetrician-gynecologist, medical missionary, technical advisor to the Population Council, and believer in the transformative potential of the modern IUD, also known as "the loop" or, in Spanish-speaking countries, "the aparatico" (apparatus).

03/12/66—Taiwan
[Miss T. M. Lee] took us to visit a family near the Health Station and we talked with Mrs. Wang who is an enthusiastic loop-wearer. Miss Lee told us that she has the cooperation of the Township Registry clerk who talks with the new fathers and suggests they should encourage their wives to visit the Family Planning clinics.[1]

3/14/66—Hong Kong
I was very impressed by the excellent organization of the clinic, the use of auxiliary personnel and nurses so that the doctor's time for insertion is maximized . . . I found that the women had considerable confidence in the woman physician; but it seemed to me that her own confidence in the method was wavering since she tended to remove the device for what appeared to be trivial complaints judging from what could be observed on examination.[2]

3/31/66—Thailand
In the Taupoon clinic there were only 4 out of 20 patients who came for Family Planning. This is one clinic where a bad rumor got started about IUD and all the new patients come asking for pills. A school-teacher in the area has been buying the pills for more than a year, having had a loop failure (abortion) with 27.5 mm. device in utero.[3]

103

10/12/66—Singapore
There was some discussion as to whether or not women should be warned of the possibility of translocation of the loop. It was finally agreed that this should not be done since it was a rare complication and in medicine one cannot discuss all the possible complications of any procedure.[4]

5/30/68—Pakistan
Both of us feel rather cynical today. It almost seems as though all the figures are a fraud—with infertile women getting insertions and unsuspecting men getting pressed into vasectomy. Barry inadvertently visited a vasectomy "camp" in Karachi and the only client was an old man who had no family and who didn't know what was about to happen to him! There have been two or three articles in the paper recently along the same vein.[5]

07/31/68—Pakistan
Rumors, rumors, rumors! Gwen said that yesterday one of our LHVs [Lady Health Visitors] went home visiting on the Megesterol Acetate project and had trouble and she is afraid to go out alone now—so Gwen went visiting with her in the Ford Car instead of the NRIFP [National Research Institute of Family Planning] microbus. They had no trouble, but five out of the six homes they visited talked about the rumors.[6]

10/1/71—Venezuela
Went to the Abortion ward with one of the motivators. In many of the 5 bedrooms there were two women in a bed. We made about 20 interviews and gave 15 appointments. In the course of the interviews we turned up 3 women who had used IUD—one for 5 years who had been hospitalized for D&C because of menorrhagia; another who had a full-term stillbirth after IUD and a third with an ectopic pregnancy. Two other women talked about a case of perforation they had heard of, so it's evident that the number of complications is growing as the numbers of IUD cases increase. Most women said they wanted FP [Family Planning] but not the "aparatico."[7]

Penny's diary comes to us in a period of transformation in the family planning movement, when the cause expanded beyond a handful of small associations and clinics to become a part of widescale government programs offering new, more highly effective contraceptives, supported by a dramatic increase in funding from international donors. For some, the decades of the 1960s–1980s are seen as a period of "quiet revolution," in which the dreams of widespread access to effective contraception came true and millions of families were able to plan and space their children, contributing to dramatic declines in birth rates around the world.[8] For others, this was a period of heightened control and coercion, when aggressive state programs headed by male elites prioritized population control over human well-being, fueling a range of unethical and directly abusive practices.[9] We can see both of these stories in the excerpts above: there are tales both of enthusiastic loop-wearers and of unsuspecting men being coerced into vasectomies. But there is also something more here: physicians debating the finer points of medical ethics, schoolteachers buying pills to distribute on their own, "trouble" with communities, and women refusing the IUD but demanding family planning all the same. Between the black and white, there is a lot of gray.

Penny's work diary provides a particularly unique source through which to delve into the black, white, and gray zones of the high period of population control. The diary covers her work as a technical advisor to the Population Council from 1965 to 1974, a decade she spent traveling to over two dozen countries to observe population programs and provide advice on contraceptive research trials. She was a vigilant documenter: her personal collection includes a wide range of correspondence and reports, and the diary itself runs over 2,000 pages long, with entries made nearly every day. Of course, it provides us with only a partial perspective: namely, that of an American woman from a middle-class background whose time in these countries ranged from a few days to several years. Penny's diary was also produced for a particular audience, sent back in installments to her superiors in the Population Council's New York office; it is likely that she censored herself to some extent. Still, the remarkably frank and comprehensive nature of the diary, its broad transnational scope, and its attention to the daily work of population programs make it an undoubtedly rich source. By coupling it with local-level studies, it allows us to move beyond the global geopolitics of the IUD and population control movements, to see what all of this meant in the day-to-day world of reproductive practice.

This chapter begins by exploring the shifting landscape of population and family planning internationally in the 1960s and 1970s. I illustrate how Penny's personal trajectory mimicked these shifts, as she transitioned from a medical missionary to contraceptive researcher working on the birth control pill field trials in Puerto Rico in the 1950s/early 1960s. Exploring her work on the trials illustrates the continued role played by women in the population field, even as male population experts consolidated their position in the higher echelons of the movement. I then follow Penny to her first posting for the Population Council in Thailand in 1966–1967. Penny's time in Asia illustrates the fragility of the movement even in this period of dramatic international expansion: if some countries were launching widespread, aggressive programs, others continued to work discreetly, engaging in quiet, ad hoc studies. Indeed, the general sense that comes from these records—coupled with reports from family planning associations—is of a broadly unregulated and decentralized landscape of contraceptive testing far beyond that conducted under the purview of state population control programs. The introduction of the IUD in this region also shows both the hope and fear that surrounded the method. As evident in the excerpts above, population control advocates were not the only actors excited about the IUD: it attracted a range of practitioners and women who saw the potential value of the method to their lives. But this hope faded quickly in many places, as "rumors" spread about uterine perforations, expulsions, ectopic pregnancies, bleeding, and a range of other complications. I put "rumors" in quotation marks because it generally has a negative connotation, but we might rather see these stories as a form of knowledge-sharing that provided a crucial means of self-protection for targeted communities.

The chapter then follows Penny to her posting in Pakistan (1967–1971), where she was confronted more directly with the power and coercive potential of a state-led population control program. Her diary bears direct witness to the ways that aggressive targets for IUD insertions and fertility rate declines could translate into abusive practices on the ground: of elderly men being pressured into vasectomies, of women having IUDs inserted, removed, and then reinserted again to hit insertion targets. It also illustrates the power of some intermediary actors and of communities to ultimately overturn a program, whether through quiet withdrawal or direct resistance. Following Penny to Latin America (1971–1973), however, illustrates that even a lack of incentives and a commitment to quality care were not necessarily enough to ensure reproductive freedom. Other issues fundamentally shaped the ability to match people's needs to programs: from structural issues like dependencies on foreign aid and fluctuating international contraceptive markets, to small things like shifts in tone and the element of human touch during an intimate discussion in a clinic. Penny's later years—including an oral history conducted in 1974—also illustrate how experiences in the field could lead practitioners to become early critics of the population movement, and of the international aid apparatus more generally. Indeed, if Penny begins at the Population Council as an enthusiastic believer, she ends with a crisis of faith, one that reflected a larger questioning of the movement already evident in the mid-1970s. Following her journey allows us to see both the depths and the unraveling of the population control movement in practice.

CRISIS OF FAITH ⟩ 107

A New Hope

How can we explain the dramatic expansion of the population movement in the 1960s–1970s? We could start by following the money. As Matthew Connelly notes, early transnational organizations like the Pathfinder Fund and IPPF had focused more in the 1950s on networking rather than grant-making: in 1958, the IPPF provided a mere $100,000 in grants.[10] However, major American philanthropic foundations like the Ford and Rockefeller foundations dramatically increased their spending in the 1960s. The Ford Foundation, for example, spent $10.7 million for population projects in 1962 alone, more than all of its support over the previous decade.[11] The Population Council also became an increasingly powerful player in this period. Created by the Rockefeller Foundation and headed by a committee of prominent elites and demographers (including John D. Rockefeller III, Frank Notestein, and Frederick Osborn), the organization committed itself explicitly to the management of "over-population" internationally, pouring millions into the cause.[12] The entry of foreign aid agencies onto the scene also radically transformed the funding landscape. The Swedish International Development Agency (SIDA) was the first to commit explicitly to family planning internationally, but the US Agency for International Development (USAID) was "the biggest prize."[13] After decades of lobbying by population advocates, the US government endorsed aid for family planning in 1963; by 1967, $37 million of the agency's budget was earmarked for family planning, some of which went directly abroad and some of which was used to support organizations like the Pathfinder Fund and IPPF.[14] The UN General Assembly also endorsed technical assistance for family planning in 1965, leading to new funds for local programs from the WHO and the newly created United Nations Fund for Population Activities (UNFPA), as well as the World Bank.[15] By 1968, international population programming had become a $77.6 million industry.[16]

This money funded a range of activities and programs. Governments around the world were given money for censuses and fertility studies to track population dynamics in their countries, as well as scholarships to train demographers and other researchers at new "population centers" in American universities. Investments in health education and communication led to the production of a range of materials aimed at a mass audience. The Population Council, for example, collaborated with the Walt Disney Company in 1968 to produce a film called *Family Planning*, in which Donald Duck explained the dangers of population growth and made the case for small families. The film was translated into twenty-three languages and aired

FIGURE 3.1. Film clip from the movie *Family Planning*, Disney and the Population Council, 1968.

throughout Asia, Africa, and Latin America.[17] Donors also invested heavily in contraceptive research. By the late 1950s/early 1960s, institutions like the Population Council had begun to pour millions into widescale international testing of the pill as well as a new generation of plastic and copper IUDs.[18]

This influx of money also contributed to the increasing professionalization of the movement. The amateur volunteer fieldworkers of the 1950s like Dorothy Brush and Edna McKinnon were replaced by communication specialists, foreign advisors, and technical consultants. Connelly describes this cohort as a "jet set" group of elites, mostly men: indeed, the Population Council had only a small handful of professional women on its staff in the 1960s and 1970s. As Connelly argues, the new network of consultants promoted a remarkably uniform vision of population policy featuring a set of progressive steps: a government declaration on the need to reduce population growth, followed by the setting up of a national Family Planning Council, the gathering of surveys and statistics, the setting of targets, and the creation of a brigade of family planning visitors to promote contraceptives, particularly the IUD.[19] Even the IPPF, which had long provided a space for female leadership in the movement, began to draw in more professional men, including demographers, physicians, and bureaucrats who spoke the language of statistics, "target groups," and "acceptors," blurring the lines further between the two worlds I presented at the beginning of chapter two.[20] This was embraced by some family planning pioneers: Margaret Sanger, for example, advocated explicitly for the need to pull more men into the organization to enhance its prestige.[21] Others were more hesitant. Dorothy Brush expressed her hope in the late 1950s/early 1960s that "our increasing size will not so constrict the heart of the IPPF with red tape, so that the personal touch is lost."[22]

Moving beyond international agencies to look at the local level suggests that this ambivalence was shared by many of the early family planning advocates discussed in chapters one and two. On the one hand, these actors had often explicitly lobbied for state and international support. Indeed, attributing too much credit to international donors in spurring the expansion of population programs ignores the day-to-day work of local advocacy required to actually get political leaders to commit to a state program. As Mytheli Sreenivas argues, women activists like Dhanvanthi Rama Rau, Avabai Wadia, and Lakshmibai Rajwade played a critical role in pushing the Indian government to incorporate family planning into its First Five-Year Plan in 1952.[23] Beth and Lenworth Jacobs of Jamaica likewise actively pushed for state support, driving from their home base in St. Ann's to Kingston on Sundays in the 1960s to meet with key politicians.[24] Some of these actors were also directly incorporated into the new state apparatuses created to direct family planning programs, facilitating direct links between state and nonstate activism. When the Jamaican government committed to a program in 1967, for example, Lenworth Jacobs became the first executive director of the National Family Planning Board. When the government of Singapore decided to endorse family planning and launch a publicity campaign, they likewise recruited the medical director of the Singapore FPA, Dr. M. Lim, to get things started.[25] However, many early advocates found themselves marginalized within state apparatuses over time. Aziza Hussein, initiator of the Cairo Women's Club's contraceptive program in Egypt, for example, had actively sought out international support and became the chair of the Joint Committee on Family Planning in Egypt in 1964,[26] but was replaced in 1966.[27] Constance Goh Kok Kee of Singapore complained that the state program quickly became "top-heavy," weighed down by bureaucracy, waste, and "so many meetings!" She lamented the decline of the early zeal that shaped the movement and its shifting demographics. As she summarized: "Women started the family planning movement at the ground level and then when it became respectable the men jumped in."[28]

Penny's background and personal trajectory provide something of a microcosm of this broader shift in the family planning movement and the opportunities and tensions it could bring. Like many of the practitioners explored in chapter one, Penny came from a medical missionary background. Born Adaline Pendleton in California in 1917, she rooted her pursuit of a medical career in an early passion for social service driven in part by her "ecumenical" Christian faith. She completed medical school at the University of California, followed by surgical training in San Juan, Puerto Rico (1944–1946). In Puerto Rico, she met and married William Satterthwaite, a nurse who worked in artificial limb construction, although she continued to use her maiden name Pendleton professionally (shortened almost universally in the records to "Penny"). In 1947, Penny and William moved to China with their five-month-old son David to work as medical missionaries under the Congregational Christian Mission Board.[29] The Satterthwaites' time in China, however, proved politically and personally tumultuous. In November 1947, the American Consulate left Peking in the face of Mao Tse-Tung's advancing revolutionary army; in the spring of 1949, Bill died suddenly of a pulmonary embolism, leaving Penny alone with their now two-year-old son.[30] After another two years in China, Penny decided to return to the United States with her son, and in 1952 she took a position as the only ob-gyn at the Ryder Memorial Missionary Hospital in Humacao, Puerto Rico.[31]

It was in Puerto Rico that Penny first became involved in family planning work. Like other practitioners, she rooted her interest in the field in her experiences as a physician and missionary. In correspondence and reports, she noted that her work was driven first and foremost by "the problems of my patients and their families"[32] and stressed the "almost sacred relationship between a woman and her physician."[33] She also recalled being particularly driven to respond to the high rate of sterilizations on the island in the 1950s. As she recalled: "I had a number of women come to me at the Ryder

FIGURE 3.2. "Dr Adaline Pendleton Satterthwaite." Puerto Rico, c. 1960–1965. Source: Adaline Pendleton Satterthwaite Papers, Smith College Special Collections.

CRISIS OF FAITH > 111

who had been operated on, sterilized by others, and had lost a child, or had remarried, and were very unhappy that they had had an operation. In fact, this was one of the reasons that made me anxious to find some other acceptable reversible method."[34] Penny also remembered her earlier frustration as a medical intern at a Catholic hospital on the US mainland, where most of the staff had refused to do sterilizations or teach birth control methods. As she remembered: "It was to me very, very wrong . . . women with heart disease, obvious medical complications, were being hospitalized almost the entire pregnancy, in order to . . . make them produce a baby, when they obviously needed some type of advice."[35] Penny began teaching women how to use diaphragms in the mid-1950s, challenging popular views at the time that Puerto Rican women could not learn how to use the method.[36]

If Penny defended her patients' capacity, however, her work was also colored by an underlying sense of difference between herself and her patients. As Kathryn Lankford illustrates in her in-depth analysis of Penny's time in Puerto Rico, Penny believed Puerto Ricans lacked discipline, self-control, and a planning ethic; she was particularly suspicious of Puerto Rican men, repeatedly noting in letters to her friends how they failed to live up to their role as family heads and breadwinners. She saw contraception as key to stabilizing and modernizing the Puerto Rican family.[37] This concern led her to attend an IPPF meeting in San Juan in 1955, where she recalled learning about "the problems of population growth in Puerto Rico."[38] In that same year, she was approached by Clarence Gamble, head of the Pathfinder Fund, who had helped organize the first trials of the Enovid oral contraceptive pill in Río Piedras, Puerto Rico, with the collaboration of American doctor Edris Rice-Wray and the Puerto Rican FPA Profamilia. The trials had led to the approval of Enovid as a menstrual disorder corrective by the US Federal Drug Administration (FDA) in 1957, but the pill's advocates hoped to further show the efficacy as a contraceptive method and relevance to a broader population. Gamble scoped Ryder as a second location for clinical trials of the pill and solicited Penny's collaboration.[39]

The trials at Humacao would turn out to be foundational, leading to approval of Enovid as a contraceptive in 1960. Within a year, one million American women were on the pill, which quickly became an icon of sexual liberation and youth cultural revolution in the United States.[40] If revolutionary in many senses, however, the pill trials left a more complicated legacy in Puerto Rico. As Laura Briggs argues, the selection of Puerto Rico as the trial site was deeply embedded in the colonial relationship between the American mainland and the island, which had been seized from the Spanish in 1898. American commentators portrayed Puerto Rico as overpopulated, underdeveloped, and unruly, justifying a host of interventions in the private

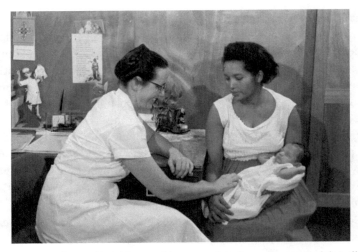

FIGURE 3.3. "Dr Penny with one of the research patients who stopped the pills after 3 years to have a baby." Puerto Rico, c. 1960–1965. Source: Adaline Pendleton Satterthwaite Papers, Smith College Special Collections.

lives of Puerto Rican subjects that sparked resistance from an emerging nationalist movement in the early twentieth century.[41] Indeed, the pill trials were immediately controversial, described in Puerto Rican newspapers in 1956 as a neo-Malthusian, colonialist plot by mainland Americans to reduce the Puerto Rican population.[42] The conduct of the trials also raised the question of informed consent, an ethical mandate that was still under development in the 1950s. While there is little evidence that women were actively forced to participate in the trials, it is unclear whether they knew that the methods were experimental.[43] Accusations that the trials had exploited Puerto Rican women as "guinea pigs" became a dominant narrative in the following decades among leftist and anti-colonial groups both in Puerto Rico and on the US mainland. These claims found a wide public audience with the 1999 documentary *The Pill*, released just after the 100-year anniversary of the American occupation of Puerto Rico.[44]

These critiques draw our attention to the powerful legacy of colonialism on the island and the potential for exploitation inherent in medical research. As Johanna Schoen points out, however, to dismiss the trials entirely as exploitative "is to fail to explain the appeal they held for the many women who decided to participate in them."[45] Indeed, Penny was struck by the high demand for the pill she encountered in Puerto Rico. One of the project's central difficulties, she recalled, was that "we always had more people wanting to participate in our studies than we had drugs to supply."[46] While some women were recruited by social workers, others came on their own account, explicitly requesting the pill.[47] It is hard to really understand the experiences of these women through the existing records, many of which reduce them to abstract figures. Based on her careful analysis of the trials, however, Lankford argues that the women's experiences ranged considerably, including instances of collaboration, service, and exploitation, sometimes in the same interaction.[48] Revisiting the interview transcripts used for *The Pill* documentary, for example, Lankford illustrates how some women pushed back against the narrative of "guinea pigs," portraying themselves as purposeful and self-driven actors who made "decisions, if not choices."[49] While some undoubtedly felt duped by the trials and suffered through their engagement, others claimed they knew the trials were experimental and described the pill as "fabulous."[50] Women also spoke of their positive relationships with Penny and other doctors, illustrating the importance of these intimate interactions in shaping the ultimate meaning of the trials for participants.[51]

Turning our attention to these intimate spaces of the trials also contests the portrayal of the trials—and of the pill more broadly—as a simple story of increasing male medical control over women's bodies. In fact, the trials relied heavily on women, including doctors like Edris Rice-Wray and Penny, American missionary social worker Betty MacDonald, and professional Puerto Rican health educators and social workers like Iris Rodríguez and Noemí Rodríguez. As Lankford notes, social workers appear only sporadically in the records—hidden in the "acknowledgements" section of scientific papers or referred to vaguely as "the social workers"—but played a foundational role as "ground-level architects of the trials."[52] They visited women in their homes and at clinics to explain the methods, conducted medical surveys, obtained their participation, distributed the pills, and followed up with participants to track their progress. While medical histories tend to privilege narratives of singular men who authored publications, initiated trials, and publicized their results, this daily labor made the trials— and continued contraceptive use beyond the trials—possible. As Lankford notes, this was hardly a "utopian experience of sisterhood": hierarchies of race, class, and nationality divided the women who worked on these trials.[53] Still, Penny and others clearly saw the importance of those on the front lines, arguing that "the degree of acceptability and satisfaction in continued use is directly related to the confidence which the women have in the medical personnel with whom they come in contact."[54]

The practical experiences of social workers and practitioners could also fuel an increasing concern over the risks and problems created by the pill. Early versions contained nearly ten times the amount of progesterone and four times the amount of estrogen as contemporary pills, contributing to a host of side effects that ranged "from the unpleasant to the life-altering."[55] Women experienced dizziness, chronic headaches, vomiting, abdominal pain, weakness, and chloasma (discoloration of the skin).[56] Some women described years of sporadic pain and bleeding that lasted for months at a time.[57] Women voted with their feet: of the 838 women who took Enovid in the 1957 trials, for example, by 1965 only 150—about 12 percent—were still using the pill.[58] Those involved in field trials on the ground warned the designers of the pill that it was not the panacea they had dreamed of. Rice-Wray concluded as early as 1956 that the pill had "too many side reactions to be acceptable generally,"[59] and Penny came to see the pill as useful in some situations, but not universally appropriate.[60] These concerns were shared by other advocate practitioners of the early family planning movement. At an IPPF regional conference in Warsaw in 1962, for example, British doctor Margaret Jackson noted that the clinical and laboratory work to establish the full efficacy and safety of the pill was still incomplete, and the method should be approached with continuing caution; others at the conference opposed its use altogether.[61] Indeed, although the risks of the pill were not studied in detail until 1969, already by the early 1960s a range of issues had been reported, including the first pill-related deaths from pulmonary embolisms (blood clots).[62]

Contraceptive researchers reacted in a variety of ways to these developments. Pioneers of the pill frequently denied the side effects or argued that these were rare events, incomparable to the toll of pregnancy.[63] Others argued that the pill could be refined and adapted, calling for more testing internationally. Many turned their attention to different methods instead, including a new generation of plastic, nylon, and copper IUDs. This was a period of extensive experimentation: by the 1970s, at least forty different experimental models of IUDs were being tested.[64] The most widely used included the plastic Lippes loop and Margulies spiral, the nylon Zipper ring, and the Copper T, a T-shaped plastic ring wrapped in copper coil. The new IUDs built on the general concept of the earlier Grafenberg and Ota rings, which presumably prevented conception by creating an inhospitable environment in the uterus. But the different promoters argued that the new materials and shapes would allow them to act more effectively and with fewer side effects and complications, allowing for much broader applicability and acceptability.[65] Penny was intrigued, and in November 1961 she obtained a $10,000 grant from the Population Council to provide plastic Margulies spiral and Lippes loop IUDs to her patients.[66]

As scholars have noted, the IUD quickly became the favored method of international donors like the Population Council. Unlike other methods available at the time, the IUD was cheap, could presumably be inserted once and left in for years (maybe even decades), and provided high levels of efficacy, giving it much higher potential reach. As Chikako Takeshita illustrates, the method fit perfectly within the ideology of population control embraced by these donors, touted as a "method for the masses," or "birth control for a nation."[67] Indeed, in a progress report in 1963, Penny noted that "it may prove a highly satisfactory method for widespread population control in over-populated countries and would lend itself to a mobile-unit type of distribution."[68] However, Penny's records also show that the turn to the IUD was influenced by more practical concerns of practitioners like herself, driven by their increasing disillusionment with the pill. The IUD trials in Puerto Rico also illustrate the method's potential appeal for women. Indeed, Penny found that the IUD trials required no active recruitment by social workers: aspiring participants sought out the clinic themselves to obtain the new method.[69] Penny wrote in letters to her family that she would regularly arrive at the clinic in the early hours of the morning to find patients already waiting for her at the front door.[70] As other outpost clinics were set up across the island, the numbers increased dramatically, with women traveling from far distances to obtain IUDs and doctors observing around thirty new cases and forty rechecks per day.[71]

Penny's work on the IUD trials would ultimately solidify her transition from medical missionary doctor to professional contraceptive researcher/ "expert." In 1964, the Population Council decided to recruit her to a position as technical advisor, describing her internally as "somewhat of a missionary type but an able and likeable person who we think is doing a terrific job in the birth control field."[72] Although originally intended to do occasional short consultancies abroad, in December 1965 she resigned from her position in Puerto Rico and prepared for a posting in Thailand that lasted for a year. Her time in Thailand would be followed by longer postings in Pakistan and Venezuela, as well as dozens of shorter trips to different countries. Her work at first focused on medical oversight of international studies of Lippes loop and Margulies spiral IUDs,[73] but she soon became involved in a variety of aspects of family planning programs internationally. She strategized with government officials, reviewed training manuals, listened to the concerns of doctors and other practitioners, conducted trainings, and attended conferences and workshops. As a doctor who liked to be involved in "the action as well as in the desk work,"[74] Penny also spent a good portion of time following nurses on their trips to the field, visiting clinics, speaking to patients, and occasionally even conducting IUD insertions and sterilizations herself. As a result, her work diary allows us to see some of the finer details of international "technical advising," an intimate look into a transnational journey that stretched over ten years and two dozen countries (table 3.1).

TABLE 3.1 Adaline Pendleton Satterthwaite's work timeline with the Population Council

	Primary posting	Short trips for Population Council	Outside consultancies
12/1965–03/1966	Puerto Rico and New York	Korea, Thailand, Honduras	
03/1966–06/1967	Thailand	Taiwan, Hong Kong, Iran, Pakistan (2x), Singapore (2x), Indonesia, Chile	
06/1967–08/1971	Pakistan	Italy, Singapore, Egypt, Colombia, Venezuela, Thailand, Malaysia, Philippines	Mauritius (World Bank)
09/1971–11/1973	Venezuela	Mexico, Geneva (2x), Washington, Dominican Republic (6x), Brazil (3x), Peru, Egypt, Puerto Rico, Bangladesh	
11/1973–10/1974	N/A (short-term consultancies only)	Dominican Republic, Mexico (2x)	

Source: Compiled by the author.

Carloads of Women

When Penny arrived at her first posting in Thailand in 1966, the local government was officially opposed to family planning. Still, as in other places, Penny found a range of ad hoc work being conducted by interested doctors, nurses, and social workers. Dr. Winich Asavasena, the director of the "Family Health" division of the Department of Medical and Health Services, was engaged in a range of contraceptive research trials, regularly trained physicians and nurses in the methods, and had quietly opened family planning clinics in a number of hospitals and health centers. As Penny noted: "He says that as long as the cabinet does not make birth control illegal he sees no reason why this program should not go ahead."[75] Still, government nurses were cautious, using flip books and other materials they could take with them to illustrate how to use different methods, rather than handing out leaflets that could fall into the hands of politicians.[76] Dr. M. L. Kashetra Snidvongs conducted research at Chulalongkorn University, working through the wives of governors and members of the Red Cross to get villages enrolled in research programs without involving the central government.[77] Loops were also inserted at a range of voluntary associations, including the FPA of Thailand as well as the Chinese Beneficent Society and Church of Christ in Thailand.[78] The Thai Medical Women's Association incorporated IUDs into their broader maternal health service, which included pap smears and mental health services.[79] Individual doctors and nurses also took it upon themselves to run their own small-scale clinics. Dr. Chatr, working at a hospital in Bangkok, brought back a stack of Lippes loops to insert following a trip to the United States in November 1965; an unnamed "nurse-midwife" in Soi Fa ran a family clinic out of her home; and a doctor in Roi Et gave out pills that he bought with his own money.[80]

Indeed, Penny's diaries from this period, combined with other sources, point to a heterogeneous, decentralized, and unregulated landscape of contraceptive research in many countries in the 1960s. Penny observed trials of the Lippes loop, Margulies spiral, Zipper ring, various brands of the pill, and the Depo-Provera injection in dozens of countries; she noted that clinics around the world also continued to test the Japanese Ota ring and Oppenheimer ring, while others made their own rings out of silkworm gut or nylon.[81] While many of these were initiated and funded by organizations like the Population Council, local advocates and FPAs also collaborated directly with contraceptive inventors and manufacturers. For example, Dr. Jack Lippes visited the FPA China (Taiwan) in May 1964 to obtain their support for a research trial of his "Lippes loops"; Penny noted that the FPA had quickly enrolled 100 volunteers.[82] In Egypt, IUDs were first introduced by the network of clinics initiated by Aziza Hussein and the Cairo Women's Club.[83] Dr. Siva Chinnatamby of Ceylon made it clear that pill and IUD trials had come to the country through her own initiative; in fact, she had to convince Gregory Pincus to make Ceylon a test site.[84] By 1966, an estimated 628 physicians in eighty-two countries were testing Lippes loop and Margulies spirals.[85] Even in countries like Mexico, where propaganda for contraception was prohibited until 1973, private organizations and pharmaceutical companies conducted experiments with a range of mechanical devices and chemical preparations, while public hospitals quietly ran postpartum family planning programs with Population Council support.[86]

The difficulty of accessing new contraceptive methods in many parts of the world—due to a combination of legal restraints, lack of availability, and high costs—led many local organizations and doctors to become involved in research trials as a means to stock their clinics. The family planning clinic in Mexico, for example, relied almost entirely on grants from three pharmaceutical companies, which enabled them to distribute oral contraception in the early 1960s in exchange for data; by 1964, they had carried out thirteen projects testing pills from nine different countries.[87] Medical director Dr. Edris Rice-Wray justified this by noting: "The important thing is that we are receiving grants from <u>several</u> differenc [*sic*] sources so that in no way could it be said that we are a front for any pharmaceutical house. We are completely independent and publish the facts as we find them."[88] Still, one can imagine that these situations of dependency created a range of potential conflicts of interest. They could also lead to a narrowing of choice for women: Penny observed that although many clinics committed officially to a "cafeteria choice of methods"—offering advice and access to all methods and letting the patient decide—in practice, they only had one or two methods available, usually the IUD or other experimental methods provided for free by pharmaceutical companies for research trials.[89] Birth control pills were particularly hard to come across if not provided by a research trial, as they were expensive in many countries. Women in Iran, for example, were given only one cycle at a time to try to manage costs, which created an additional burden of regular trips to the clinic for women on the method.[90] In Thailand, Dr. Asavasena noted to Penny in 1966 that the Department of Health did not have the budget to buy birth control pills, which cost eighteen or twenty baht per month; as a result, "the program must be based on the loops, only offering pills where the loops have been tried and cannot be used."[91]

International organizations also contributed to limiting choice by actively investing in and promoting some methods over others. The Population Council, for example, spent millions of dollars to promote the Lippes loop worldwide in the 1960s, and recommended it as the best option for the different state and non-state programs they advised.[92] Technical advisors like Penny, however, did not always transmit this advice directly or consistently. In a letter to Honduras on behalf of the Council in January 1966, she wrote that "in areas where there is no knowledge of contraceptive practice, the emphasis should be placed on the IUD, although it is understood that all methods should be available on demand."[93] However, only a few months later she informed doctors in the field that they were "just as interested in pill users as IUD acceptors" and that postpartum clinics should offer family planning more generally rather than being tied to any particular method. This recommendation apparently came as a surprise to her interlocutors, who had assumed the program was meant to be solely focused on the IUD.[94] Later that year, she also explained to a doctor working on a Population Council–funded postpartum program in Singapore that it was not an IUD program, but rather should include a cafeteria choice of methods.[95] In spite of these recommendations, however, the very fact that the Council more actively supported, funded, and distributed the IUD in a situation of scarcity meant it was likely to be pushed as the first—or only—choice in practice.

Local-level studies and records of FPAs, doctors, and fieldworkers suggest that the Population Council's enthusiasm for the IUD was shared—at least initially—by many women around the world in the 1960s. Women in India reportedly traveled great distances to obtain the loop,[96] and clinics in Egypt had long IUD waiting lists.[97] Workers at the FPA of China (Taiwan) noted that "for years, women have expressed their demand for a kind of simple, non-injurious, and long-effective contraceptive,"[98] and were eager to get hold of the IUD. Sai Poh of the Philippines wrote that the IUD was "the rage" in her country, the demand "remarkable" considering the strong opposition of the Catholic Church.[99] Clinics in Shiraz, Iran, started in 1964, had more demands for enrollment in the IUD program than they could handle,[100] while a clinic in Tehran had to restrict the program to women who already had four children to keep things manageable.[101] Penny noted that many of these women came on the advice of friends, relatives, and fellow "users."[102] Some women apparently became active loop proselytizers in their own communities. Penny described, for example, an "intelligent but unlettered" thirty-nine-year-old woman in Mauritius with nine pregnancies who took it upon herself to recruit other women and volunteered to assist an IUD clinic whenever it visited her village.[103]

This grassroots activism could be incredibly effective, as illustrated in a 1966 IUD project funded in part by the Population Council and run at Chulalongkorn hospital in urban Bangkok and the rural district of Potharam, Thailand. As the final report—contained in Penny's papers on the country—noted, the project had managed to attract ten times the number of women directly informed of the program, a number they attributed entirely to the strength of word-of-mouth communication.[104] These women came from fifty-four out of seventy-one of Thailand's provinces, with some traveling over 200 kilometers to attend a clinic.[105] The report emphasized that most of the women were: "not urban, not well educated, not in middle or upper income brackets, and not of excessive parity (according to the standards of the culture). Rather, the typical woman who comes to the Chulalongkorn clinic from the provinces is the wife of a farmer, has four or fewer years of education (as does her husband), has a family income of less than US $30.00 per month, and has three or four living children."[106] Penny spoke to Thai doctors who reported "carloads of women" arriving at the clinic in Potharam;[107] indeed, the initial demand exceeded the materials available and the capacity of the staff. By August, there were some 2,000 women on the waiting list; most had to wait four to six weeks from the date of registration to obtain the IUD.[108] One doctor working at Chulalongkorn, Dr. Nikorn

Dusitin, recalled that they had been given 300 IUDs and expected them to last six months, but ran out within a few weeks. Women would come at four or five in the morning, waiting for the clinic to open at one or two o'clock in the afternoon. The clinic apparently became so popular that it fell prey to a scam, with tour operators selling a trip to Bangkok that would purportedly include visits to the palace in the morning and IUD insertion at the clinic in the afternoon.[109] Although Dusitin noted that accurate recordkeeping soon became difficult because of the pressure on the clinic,[110] Chulalongkorn was reportedly one of the largest IUD clinics in the world at the time, with some 66,000 clients between 1965 and 1971.[111]

If the Thai project provided evidence of the appeal of the IUD and power of word-of-mouth communication between women, however, the euphoria was short-lived. Researchers saw a sharp drop-off in attendance at the Potharam project after a "spate of anti-IUD publicity," including newspaper articles and radio reports linking the IUD with cancer.[112] There was a sharp rise in requests for removals, and eighteen months into the project a follow-up study showed that only 50 percent of women were still using the method.[113] Similar figures were recorded in places as distant as Mauritius, Taiwan, Egypt, and Morocco, where some 50–60 percent of women dropped out and/or had the loops removed within one to two years.[114] In India, a clinic trial in 1964 let to the insertion of over one million IUDs, but by 1972, only a negligible percentage of women still had them in,[115] in part as a result of the circulation of "atrocity stories" of bleeding and pain among patients.[116] Indeed, researchers found that the very networks and communication that had brought women to IUD projects could quickly turn on them. Sometimes, just a single complication could lead to a wave of bad rumors and a decline in patients,[117] or even bring a program to an end. Rumors of an abnormally high rate of perforations at a Singapore hospital in 1966, for example, ultimately led to the discontinuation of a postpartum IUD program.[118] As Penny stated frankly: "The situation being what it is, the women of Singapore (and the profession also) have lost confidence in the IUD."[119]

Penny's diaries provide us with a vivid illustration of the many complications and bodily experiences that led women to turn against the IUD. The most prevalent and often troubling side effect was prolonged or sporadic bleeding, a condition made worse for anemic women, women living in cultures where bleeding was taboo, and women without access to medications or sanitary napkins to manage it.[120] Several hours of bed rest and iron pills or vitamins could help reduce the severity of post-insertion bleeding, but was not always possible, and in other cases the bleeding continued to be heavy/sporadic for months afterward.[121] In addition to being difficult to manage, excessive bleeding undermined the privacy of the IUD, exposing women to their husbands and families. In other cases, a *lack* of bleeding—due to the cessation of the monthly period—could also be troubling, whether due to cultural beliefs that menstruation was healthy and cleansing or because it took away the reassurance of knowing each month that one was not pregnant.[122] In addition, women experienced expulsions of the IUD, vaginal discharge, pelvic inflammatory disease, and abdominal pain. A prior history of menometrorrhagia, early pregnancy, fibroids, cervical lesions, liver dysfunction, hypoproteinemia, hepatomegaly, and anemia were all potential contraindications. If women did become pregnant with an IUD, there was a higher incidence of early miscarriage or a dangerous or fatal ectopic pregnancy (a fertilized egg located outside the uterus).[123]

Like many doctors at the time, Penny saw these issues as partly a technical question. Loop size mattered: researchers found over time that the smaller Lippes loops A (25 mm) and B (27.5 mm) were less effective, and by the mid-1960s were largely using the Lippes loop C (30 mm) and D (31 mm).[124] However, the larger IUDs prompted more disturbances and thus expulsions, pain, and bleeding, leading others to turn to the smaller Copper T.[125] In any case, it became apparent that there was no "one size fits all" solution: the size and shape of a woman's uterus, the number of children they had, and their pre-existing conditions all influenced how effective and/or acceptable the method was.[126] Penny also noted the importance of proper technique during the insertion of the IUD. If not inserted at the right plane, the IUD could perforate the uterus; since this was silent, women might not discover until much later, requiring a laparotomy or other invasive procedure.[127] Some nurses and health visitors were very skillful at insertions, but lacked sufficient sterile equipment or a way to re-sterilize equipment in the field, increasing the risk of infection.[128] Penny's willingness to get out in the field and actually insert IUDs herself also drew her attention to problems with inserters, some of which became soft after only a few procedures, increasing the risk of complications.[129] Beyond these technical issues, however, Penny also stressed the importance of the more personal and subjective elements of the experience: the care taken by the doctor or nurse to properly pre-screen patients and rule out contraindications, to explain the possible side effects, and to provide the appropriate level of reassurance and support before and after insertion. In fact, she argued that this individualized, personal attention was in many cases "the most important factor."[130]

The experiences of those working in the field thus challenged the faith among population controllers that the IUD could provide a "quick fix," or a "universal method." There was no universal body, but rather a set of local reproductive physiologies shaped by socio-economic conditions and culture.[131] As a result, the IUD in fact required considerable personal attention and long-term tracking to make sure it was an appropriate method and that side effects were properly managed and addressed.[132] Lippes himself had argued that the loop needed to be observed with regular exams, at five weeks, three months, six months, and a year,[133] but few IUD programs in the 1960s did this, whether by design or due to a lack of resources. The FPA of China (Taiwan), for example, admitted in 1968 that although 7,568 loops had been inserted in the previous four years: "Just as many other loop programs, we have not planned to have follow-up visits for our loop acceptors. We did not even have an opportunity to plan for a periodic follow-up study of limited sample size. We really do not know what has happened to those who have been inserted with loops by our doctors in the past few years."[134] When the FPA did manage to track down 425 women to be interviewed, they found that less than 20 percent still had the IUD in place.[135] A study in Trinidad likewise found that of 724 women inserted with IUDs, 20–30 percent had experienced serious side effects including pain, expulsion, bleeding, and discharge, made worse by the lack of effective treatment or follow-up campaigns to address women's concerns.[136] The lack of continued care also led to skewed results for research studies. As Penny noted, many doctors seemed to assume that women who did not return were satisfied users, such that "data" on the success of the IUD in some places consisted primarily of "general impressions."[137] Indeed, one of her colleagues in Thailand, Dr. Tuanpark, questioned the excellent results claimed by her colleagues, noting that the failures and dissatisfied women simply came to her rather than going back to the original clinic.[138]

Moreover, while many doctors and nurses involved in these projects had been trained to insert IUDs, few had been trained to remove them, which could lead to further complications even when women did seek follow-up care. This is evident in an "unfortunate case" in Chanthaburi, Thailand, recorded by Penny in September 1966. As she wrote in her diary:

> As we were able to piece the story together, it is as follows. A 31 year old Para 6 [woman with 6 prior pregnancies] had an insertion of a Lippes "C" two months post-partum on August 8, 1966. She returned for the regular check-up visit on Sept. 19, 1966 and because of some pain and persistent bleeding asked for removal. [The doctor] was in Bangkok and the person (his wife, the nurse) who was attending the clinic could not find the thread. Instead of telling the woman that she could not remove the loop and ask her to return when her husband was in the clinic, she proceeded with vain attempts at intrauterine manipulation to try and remove the device. This was about 1:30 p.m. on Sept. 19, 1966. She sent the patient home without further treatment and at 2.15 a.m. Sept. 20 (about 12 hours

after the manipulation) the patient presented at the Emergency Room with anxiety and severe epigastric pain. She was admitted to the Medical Ward with incomplete history and examination as a case of "neurosis." About 9 a.m. (7 hours after admission) it was evident that she had some evidence of peritoneal disease and fever and she was transferred to the Gynecological Service where a pelvic examination revealed acute lower abdominal tenderness and rigidity. She was started on massive antibiotic therapy. Flat plate of the abdomen was taken at this time and revealed an extra-uterine Lippes loop and evidence of paralytic ileus. The following day Sept. 21, she became septic and quite confused and walked out of the hospital. She was brought back comatose by a relative on Sept. 23 and was dead on arrival in the OPD.[139]

As Penny noted, the case led to "a great deal of suspicion and fear around the IUD": a "tragic outcome" that, she argued, "could have been avoided by proper management at the first follow-up visit."[140]

The lack of care given to women in IUD projects and trials cannot be reduced, however, to individual error or poor planning. As Takeshita argues, it also reflects the larger denigration of women by many IUD researchers and their funders, who envisioned patients as a means to an end, as empty vessels to achieve population control objectives. This is evident in the language they used in their studies, which reduced women to "acceptors" or referred to a woman's body as a disembodied "IUD-holding uterus."[141] Takeshita, for example, cites Robert Wilson, the chair of ob-gyn at Temple University in 1962, asking: "How serious is [an intrauterine infection that ends up with a hysterectomy and surgical removal of both ovaries]? Not very. Perhaps we have to stop thinking in terms of individual patients and change our direction a bit."[142] Researchers often compared the risks of any contraceptive method to the risks of pregnancy, which were nearly always higher, thus providing a grounds to justify a whole range of side effects as acceptable.[143] Others were "blatantly sexist," dismissing the pain women were experiencing as "a psychological reaction to a normal side effect" and refusing to remove the devices.[144] Indeed, in the case described above, the woman's life-threatening pain is initially dismissed as a case of "neurosis," a misdiagnosis that in this case contributed directly to her death.

But the lived experience of witnessing women's pain and suffering could also lead some of those working on the front lines to question the emphasis on the IUD. Penny noted an increasing division within the medical profession: doctors at one hospital in Thailand, for example, were reportedly split into "those pro and those contra IUD."[145] In other places, doctors and nurses simply returned to promoting the diaphragm or condom, even when it meant giving up the higher bonuses they would get from promoting IUDs.[146] Penny herself also began to question the unregulated, sometimes reckless nature of contraceptive testing in this period. She expressed particular concern over a comparative study of Depo-Provera injections and Ovulen birth control pills being conducted by American doctor Edwin B. McDaniel in Ban Pong, Thailand, with free supplies from Upjohn and Searle. Penny noted with obvious disapproval that "Mr. McDaniel has had no experience with the use of pills and has not instructed the staff what to tell the patients about difficulties such as breakthrough bleeding or amenorrhea."[147] She continued to critique the program over the following months, feeling that McDaniel was taking on too many cases of Depo-Provera, which "should be limited and more intensively studied rather than trying to start a mass program"; she also warned against the "haphazard way" he provided estrogen to women to control bleeding.[148] In spite of Penny's concerns, by March 1967 McDaniel had enrolled 782 women to test Depo-Provera in the village and another 200 in outlying clinics.[149]

These concerns were shared by her local Thai colleagues, who also began to push back against foreign intervention in the population field more broadly. Indeed, a public controversy erupted in spring 1967 when the American actor Marlon Brando, visiting Bangkok on behalf of UNICEF, reportedly called for the country to adopt birth control to stymie rapid population growth.[150] The comment led to a series of newspaper articles on the question of population growth, including a long discourse by Dr. Erb Na Bangxang, the president of the Thai FPA. Dr. Erb explicitly argued against a government program, claiming that birth control was/could be made widely accessible through other means and that a state program could lead to coercion. He also questioned the value of "experts" from "great power countries where the governments do not treat birth control as an important policy matter . . . Why then do they come and put pressure on the Thai government regarding birth control?"[151] Penny noted in private letters an increasing sense of mistrust among her local colleagues, who seemed to "resent outside advisers."[152]

These tensions, as well as the Population Council's frustration with the continued lack of commitment from the government, ultimately led to Penny's transfer from Thailand to Pakistan in May 1967. As the Council wrote to Penny's key collaborators in Thailand: "Pakistan has a definite population policy, and is energetically implementing a national family planning program."[153] Indeed, by the time Penny arrived in Karachi in June 1967, Pakistan's state family planning program was in full swing. It was here that Penny would bear witness to the coercive potential of state population control.

Targetitis

Pakistan's government had been an early convert to the population cause, announcing a national policy to control population growth in 1957, ten years after obtaining independence from British colonial rule. However, the program remained limited in its early years: the country's Second "Five-Year Plan" for development (1960–1964) provided only a modest sum for the promotion of family planning through the Ministry of Health, with technical assistance from Ford, the Population Council, and SIDA. In 1965, population policy became a priority, leading to the creation of a National Family Planning Board with an explicit target of reducing fertility by 20 percent by 1970. Supported by USAID and a range of other international donors, the program expanded dramatically in the following decade, with the establishment of district-level family planning officers (FPOs) to reach all corners of the country. It adopted a "supply-oriented" approach, focused on the mass distribution of contraceptives (including condoms and foam tablets as well as IUDs and oral contraceptives) in a vertical program relatively disconnected from the broader health system.[154] Internal reports estimated that by August 1, 1967, some 903,039 IUDs had been inserted across the country, with 145,000,000 units of conventional contraceptives sold and some 68,652 sterilizations performed.[155] Family planning was also promoted through mass media and became an integral part of the visual landscape of the country. Indeed, if Thai doctors could barely hang a poster without fear of repercussions, by the mid-1960s Pakistan was plastered with advertisements for family planning. Upon her arrival, Penny expressed her amazement at seeing pro–family planning messages displayed in public exhibitions, in slides shown before movies at the theater, and on "signboards and lighted advertisements on the lamp posts competing with 'Salkia' sewing machines and METRO cigarettes."[156]

Pakistan was one of many countries to adopt targets and rapidly expand their program along these lines in the mid-1960s. India provides an emblematic example: although the government had been the first to announce state support for family planning in 1952, the program ramped up considerably in the mid-1960s, setting targets and offering cash incentives to doctors and nurses to fit women with IUDs and conduct vasectomies on men. "Loop squads" and vasectomy camps were created to spread the method en masse. Within two years, some two million women had been fitted with an IUD;[157] one vasectomy camp reportedly set a world record with 221,933 vasectomies in two months.[158] In addition to bonuses for practitioners, the state program offered cash, free meals, radios, and other incentives to those

FIGURE 3.4. "Four men installing an advertisement outdoors for Planned Parenthood Clinics in India." India, 1953. Source: Sarah Bradley Gamble Papers, Schlesinger Library, Harvard Radcliffe Institute.

willing to undergo the procedure, accompanied by disciplinary action in some cases for those who refused.[159] In Indonesia, family planning "safaris" arrived in rural villages in the 1960s accompanied by military or police escorts to enforce the power of the state; in some places, loans, access to high-yield rice varieties, and school scholarships were made available only to those who accepted family planning.[160] In Egypt in the late 1960s, the government adopted a set of cash incentives for doctors and patients to promote the IUD.[161] Singapore's state program featured a mix of incentives and disincentives, including restrictions on maternity leave, progressively higher delivery charges for later births, restricted income tax relief, priority for public apartments to families with fewer children, priority for registering children in school, and paid leave for civil servants who would undergo sterilization, among others.[162] Even Sri Lanka (formerly Ceylon), which had focused on freedom of choice in the early years of its program, began to set targets for numbers of acceptors of the IUD and sterilization in the 1970s, while also providing bonuses to doctors.[163] Sometimes, targets were explicitly pushed by donors. For example, USAID provided support to Jamaica on the premise that it would achieve at least a level of 34,000 new family planning acceptors annually.[164]

Penny's diaries capture the initial enthusiasm that prevailed among many early family planning pioneers over these expansive state programs.

In Pakistan, Penny bonded in particular with Dr. Nafis Sadik, a local doctor who described having come to the cause through her experiences treating legions of "malnourished, anemic" pregnant women, already with several children, trapped in an endless cycle of childbearing.[165] As Sadik noted in a later oral history, she became frustrated with the limits of trying to help patients "one at a time," and saw state public health programs as a means to have a greater impact.[166] Like Penny, her transition into this world was supported by the rise of the international population establishment: she attended a course on health planning at Johns Hopkins University financed by USAID before returning home to help Pakistan's Planning Commission draft the Five-Year Plan.[167] When the new program was created, she became director of planning and training. In her oral history, Sadik recalled the enthusiasm and optimism of the 1960s, a time when the Pakistani economy was doing well and "everyone was very gung-ho and doing something."[168] The state family planning program also pulled in a number of other doctors, including many women; Penny estimated in 1967 that about 25 percent of graduates from medical schools in Pakistan were women.[169]

Penny also observed with interest the widespread involvement and enthusiasm of paramedical or auxiliary forces in the family planning program, most of whom were women. Indeed, as in other areas of the world, middle-class and upper-working-class women nurses, social workers, and public health workers became crucial mediators between the state and the population.[170] In Pakistan, the core forces on the ground were the "Lady Health Visitors" (LHVs; public health workers who incorporated family planning into their work) and "Lady Family Planning Visitors" (LFPVs; women recruited specifically for the family planning program, without broader medical training). In part a response to the lack of sufficient medical personnel in the state health system, LFPVs did most of the groundwork of the program: establishing clinics, reaching out to families in their homes and through village meetings, providing information, distributing conventional contraceptives (condoms, chemical methods), and even doing IUD insertions for less complicated cases.[171] The LFPVs also worked with local *dais*, the traditional midwives who still delivered the majority of children in most areas of the country. Penny argued that these cadres of women were uniquely situated to support the program because they had "the confidence of the community."[172] Their labor was also seen as contributing to efficiency, since it could free up doctors to handle more complicated cases. Indeed, the broad, decentralized approach adopted by the Pakistani government in these years was seen as a "model program," attracting a range of visitors from other countries.[173]

If Penny's diaries capture the enthusiasm that shaped Pakistan's program, however, they also provide direct, compelling evidence of the way incentives and targets fueled unethical and coercive practices on the ground.

In addition to broad country-level targets, district-level FPOs were given specific targets on numbers of IUD insertions each month, which were then passed down to doctors and LFPVs in the area. Although officially the program adopted a "cafeteria approach"—discussing all methods—in practice, in many places, the IUD was promoted to the exclusion of any other methods. One internal study, for example, found that on average 90 percent of women who accepted the IUD knew of no other contraceptive method, suggesting not even a minimal concern for contraceptive choice.[174] Penny witnessed the insertion of IUDs on women over the age of forty, with contraindications, in rapid succession without any discussion of side effects, and using poor techniques that led to perforations of the uterus and other complications.[175] One LFPV reported to Penny that some fieldworkers were removing loops at the end of the year, reinserting a new loop, and counting it as a "new case" to hit their targets;[176] some women were reportedly given milk and medication in return for accepting an IUD.[177] Vasectomy campaigns adopted a similarly aggressive approach. In one district where vasectomy camps were conducted, an estimated 93 percent of those interviewed knew of no other method of family planning.[178] In other places, as noted in the diary excerpts that opened this chapter, "unsuspecting men" were pressed into vasectomies with little understanding of the procedure or motivated by promises of food or cash.[179]

These practices were directly related to pressure from above. As one Pakistani doctor reported to Penny in 1967: "Targets which were intended as guidelines had become rigid directives. A threat was always present at the district level and this was transmitted to the FPO."[180] Indeed, a letter from the secretary of the Family Planning Council, Enver Adil, to provincial secretaries in 1967 stressed that district heads "need have no hesitation in replacing inefficient or inept staff placed under them" if they were not reaching their targets after three months of employment.[181] Penny reported on one internal meeting where Adil stressed the need "to get the job done . . . with the clenched fist (which he illustrated)."[182] Doctors described the IUD targets as "unrealistically high"[183] and in a constant state of flux, sometimes tripling in number from one year to the next.[184] LHVs reported feeling powerless to stand up to their superiors,[185] and one doctor told Penny that the whole campaign had been "completely demoralizing."[186]

But Penny's diaries also illustrate the consistent and sometimes powerful resistance of local actors to these practices, even at the pinnacle of the movement. Penny was struck, for example, when Begum Ra'ana Liaquat Ali Khan, a leader in women's rights and widow of the Pakistan's first prime minister, was openly critical in a meeting with the government program for their authoritarian approach to family planning.[187] The Pakistan Medical

Association refused to cooperate with the state's program throughout Penny's tenure in the country,[188] citing the wrath of complications they had seen firsthand as a result of the frantic nature of IUD insertions.[189] FPOs complained that "lady doctors" were hurting targets by being too selective with clients and eliminating those with contraindications,[190] suggesting that some continued to follow best practices despite the pressure from above. Penny also recorded multiple cases of passionate and compassionate LFPVs and LHVs who continued to take the time to explain the method and side effects properly, provide reassurance, and persist with follow-up in spite of the pressures coming from the government.[191] Some doctors started refusing to send out staff for IUD camps;[192] others simply wrote down false numbers. One doctor in Pakistan, for example, admitted to Penny that while he'd recorded 108 vasectomies, in reality he had done only eight.[193] Indeed, several doctors estimated that as many as 20–25 percent of reported IUD cases in some areas were "bogus."[194]

The program also faced increasing resistance from its target population. As elsewhere, rumors of side effects and negative experiences with the IUD spread quickly around Pakistan, leading many women to abandon the program or start demanding pills instead. Among women attending a rural health center in Rajshahi in 1969, for example, Penny recorded that "the most emphatic statement was <u>not coil</u> because of stories of neighbors or relatives who had bleeding and other complications; [the women] asked for pills instead."[195] Some had the IUD removed by a village *dai* (midwife);[196] others even removed the loops themselves.[197] Pakistani women also appear to have adopted a variety of passive tactics to resist the state program more broadly. Reports noted over and over again the difficulty of doing follow-up studies since addresses turned out to be false or non-existent.[198] Some "accepted" birth control pills and then left them to sit on the shelf or fed them to the family chickens.[199] Local communities were also relatively unimpressed by the high-production Disney/Population Council film described earlier. As Penny recorded: "Apparently the idea of animals talking and painting pictures, etc. . . . is completely foreign."[200]

By July 1968, the aggressiveness of Pakistan's family planning program combined with a general wave of backlash against the state and international community fueled a crisis situation. A rumor that one man had died and another suffered serious infection following a vasectomy apparently created such a reaction that the local district officer was attacked in his jeep and stoned by villagers.[201] In December 1968, a brick was heaved through the back window of a UNICEF Volkswagen carrying Penny and colleagues; the brick shattered the glass, although they managed to get away unscathed.[202] Participants in Pakistan's International Family Planning Conference in

January 1969 in Dacca had a picnic lunch interrupted when a group of students carrying black flags walked by them and proceeded to tear down the "Family Planning" sign in front of the local health center.[203] Some Pakistani officials dismissed the unrest, blaming it on radical students or political interests.[204] Follow-up investigations on specific cases did seem to confirm that at least some of the supposed deaths from IUDs or vasectomies were actually from unrelated causes,[205] leading Penny herself to dismiss the rumors as "a hysterical reaction which finds fallow-ground among the ignorant."[206] At other times, however, Penny recognized that "unfortunately there is undoubtedly some truth in these oft-repeated rumors."[207] Her own diaries attest to the fact that these "rumors" were grounded in a very real craze that made individual bodies sacrificial to the population control cause.

In any case, the resistance was so strong that several trials were forced to close down,[208] and in February 1969 officials got word to relax pressure to achieve targets.[209] By May, Secretary Adil had been replaced by a Mr. Ali K. M. Ahsan, who opened his first meeting by condemning the "targetitis" that had plagued the previous program.[210] He called for a broader program offering multiple methods and more comprehensive training for paramedical staff.[211] Although Penny observed that many of the old practices persisted into 1970,[212] some clinics did begin to offer a wider selection of methods and better-quality care. In some cases, this led to an increase in new cases;[213] in others, Penny noted that "not as large a volume of work was being done, but it was genuine."[214] Still, Penny noted that for many Pakistanis, "the words 'family planning' are 'loaded' and mean only IUD and there are many people who have personally had bad experiences with IUD or know other women who have had difficulties. Even when MCH [Maternal and Child Health] is emphasized it is said to be just a camouflage. This was especially reactivated when offering immunizations (DPT) for the child—these were said to be injections which would make the children permanently sterile!"[215] Beyond the family planning program itself, the aggressive tactics had potentially discredited public health measures altogether.

Penny's annual report on Pakistan for the Population Council in 1969–1970 laid out her concerns. It was evident, she reported, that although the Pakistan program had succeeded in spreading awareness of family planning: "It had been equated with governmental pressure to adopt the principal program methods, IUD and vasectomy—with a resulting negative response from the public. It was evident that acceptance of family planning had not been based on genuine understanding of the benefits to the family which could produce behavioral change, not by understanding of the various methods, but by target pressure and monetary incentives to workers and acceptors resulting in abuses."[216] In a later report, she was more explicit, calling the approach of the Pakistan program "little short of coercion" and arguing that "the practice of family planning cannot be bought by monetary incentives and program efficiency ensured by targets. Corruption and abuses often result."[217] Penny was joined in sounding the alarm by her Pakistani colleague Dr. Sadik. In 1971, Penny related how Sadik frankly outlined the problems of the program to her superiors: inadequate training, moving too actively into service without a climate for acceptance, too many rushed procedures, too-rapid clinical expansion without technical supervision, poor evaluation and feedback, the use of monetary incentives to buy acceptance, and a general lack of a critical approach.[218]

The decline of the program and changing political dynamics in Pakistan would ultimate lead both women to leave the country shortly after voicing these complaints. The outbreak of the 1971 Indo-Pakistani War and Bangladesh Liberation War brought an abrupt halt to plans for Penny to transfer from Karachi to the Dacca office. Instead, the Population Council decided to send her to Latin America to establish a regional office in Venezuela.[219] The unrest also prompted Sadik to accept a position with the UNFPA in New York.[220] If both women escaped the challenges of government bureaucracy, however, they would soon find that the problems with the population movement were broader and deeper than any one aggressive state program.

A Parade of Short-Term Experts

Penny's arrival in Caracas, Venezuela, in 1971 was seen as a significant intervention for the Council in a region often perceived by advocates as a family planning "dead zone" due to the strong influence of the Catholic Church and lack of support among many Latin American governments.[221] Opposition came from both right- and left-wing leaders: the right portrayed family planning as a threat to Catholic faith and family values, while the left argued that it was a tool of American imperialism and/or a false panacea, diverting attention from the reality of capitalist inequality.[222] A 1969 Bolivian film claiming the US Peace Corps had sterilized indigenous Quechua women without their consent prompted a wave of activism against population "controlistas,"[223] particularly when connected to American funding. Some governments, like Argentina, explicitly prohibited birth control activities in the 1970s,[224] while in other areas the political atmosphere created a chilling effect. In Guatemala, for example, efforts of the family planning association and Ministry of Health to promote contraceptives were effectively quashed by political pressure from pro-natalist groups and backlash against USAID funding from the leftist university.[225]

Still, as Necochea López has illustrated, a range of "vast, complex and fragile local family planning establishments" managed to operate in many Latin American countries in the 1960s–1970s.[226] In Peru, this included government officers in the Ministry of Health who promoted family planning, as well as Catholic programs that combined distribution of pills with health exams, sex education, and parenthood training for couples in poor urban areas.[227] In Chile, trials of the nylon "Zipper ring," invented by local physician Dr. Jaime Zipper, ran throughout the 1960s, and in 1967 the Chilean Association for Protection of the Family (APROFA) hosted the eighth International Conference of the IPPF.[228] In Costa Rica, distribution of contraceptives was illegal but doctors within the Ministry of Health and major hospitals quietly promoted the IUD and pill.[229] The most active program in Latin America in the 1960s–1970s was run by the voluntary organization Profamilia in Colombia, which had the support of presidents and physicians, universities, labor unions, and women's organizations despite the fact that Colombia was known to have one of the most powerful and least progressive church hierarchies in Latin America.[230] By 1974, Profamilia had forty urban family planning clinics as well as several joint programs with Coffee Growers' Associations.[231] In several countries, the pill was also available in pharmacies and could be purchased over the counter without a prescription, allowing it to spread to some extent even without state support.[232]

In Penny's new home of Venezuela, a lack of official government approval meant that most family planning activities were done quietly, on the initiative of an interested doctor or clinic with financial support from external funders like the Population Council. As elsewhere, Penny found that many local advocates rooted their concern in individual family welfare and women's health rather than the "population" question, which some argued was not relevant in the sparsely populated country of Venezuela.[233] Dr. Liendo Coll, for example, argued that a country should provide family planning services regardless of its population or economic situation, as it was "uno de los derechos fundamentales de la mujer [one of women's fundamental human rights]."[234] Penny also befriended several pioneering women doctors like Dr. Ela Bacalao, who was apparently so convincing that she was able to "convert" a fellow doctor who had been "violently opposed" to family planning through just one seminar.[235] Penny documented a range of other ad hoc, grassroots activities: doctors who organized sex education sessions for mothers and teenage daughters at the request of patients,[236] nurses who snuck condoms to women even when the doctor on call refused to provide advice,[237] and even Catholic nuns and priests who directed women to clinics. Indeed, although the *Humanae Vitae* released by the pope in 1968 reinforced the Catholic Church's opposition to all but natural family planning methods, believers found ways to interpret the edict that allowed some breathing room for family planning practice. For example, Penny recorded a conversation with Padre Arrusa, the Jesuit vice rector at the Catholic University of Andres Bello, in which he apparently explained "that the Pope intended to proscribe Government programs which involved <u>coercion</u> but that there was opportunity for the exercise of the individual conscience in voluntary programs."[238]

As in other areas of the world, Penny bore witness to the demand for family planning among women. She described arriving at the maternity hospital in Caracas at 7:45 a.m. to find all eighty-two chairs in the waiting room already filled with women hoping to get a family planning appointment; several would have to wait until their third visit before they were successful. Penny noted that "this was especially tragic for those women who had had an expulsion of IUD or who only needed to get refills on pills and were ready to restart the next day."[239] Women could be insistent in their demands. Penny described the case of a thirty-six-year-old woman in Mérida thusly:

> She had an IUD insertion several weeks ago and then went to Caracas because of the death of her father and was taken to MCP [Maternidad Concepcion Palacios hospital] with a hemorrhage. A D&C [Dilation and Curettage] was done and the IUD was removed (and not reinserted). She has not had a menstrual period since and she was adamant that the doctor should insert another IUD immediately. He gave her medication to induce menses and told her to return for reinsertion at that time. She could hardly be convinced to leave the clinic without the IUD.[240]

Still, as elsewhere, Penny saw many issues with the IUD. In the last excerpt of diary entries that started this chapter, for example, Penny observes that as the number of IUD cases grew, so did reports of complications—menorrhagia, ectopic pregnancy, stillbirth, perforations—leading women to increasingly demand any method but the "aparatico."[241] Other women asked for the "new" IUD, referring to the Copper T, rather than the Lippes loop, or for birth control pills instead.[242]

Penny noted the careful way that some doctors tried to respond to these concerns and support their patients. Bacalao, for example, gave talks to women in the waiting room at clinics, covering everything from attitudes toward sex to "deftly countering the rumors and fears which the women had expressed about the various family planning methods." Her only fault, according to Penny, was perhaps going on *too* long.[243] The ability of doctors and nurses to respond to these needs, however, was fundamentally constrained by the high cost of the birth control pill and unreliable nature of the international contraceptive market. As in Thailand, doctors in Venezuela and in other Latin American countries Penny visited noted that they simply struggled to get hold of enough pills for their patients, or that they were too expensive to distribute widely. A clinic in Brazil, for example, could not maintain sufficient stock of the pills to give out long-term supplies, and so women had to wait in line each month to get a new batch.[244] A lack of government support for family planning compounded these supply chain issues. In Venezuela, for example, a number of women using the pill had to switch to IUDs when a shipment of pills was held up by customs officials.[245] Women who could not afford to purchase the pills themselves and so relied on free or low-cost packages from clinics were particularly vulnerable to these fluctuations. As one Venezuelan doctor noted in a Seminar on Health Education and Family Life Education: "In the absence of public family planning services . . . the poor were automatically being discriminated since the rich could afford private service."[246]

The lack of state support also meant that Venezuelan practitioners relied heavily on international donors to support their work, which made them particularly vulnerable to attack from local critics. Indeed, family planning became a site of political controversy in November 1972, when a Dr. Armando Diaz Lovera accused the IPPF, Population Council, and US-AID of promoting "population <u>control</u>" in a local newspaper article. Diaz Lovera specifically called out the work of "una llamada Dra. Satterthwaite [one called Dr. Satterthwaite]" on a postpartum IUD insertion program as "evidence of coercion."[247] At an evening forum shortly after, Diaz Lovera again accused the Population Council and Penny in particular of "coercing Venezuelans to practice FP," apparently unaware that Penny was in the audience.[248] Penny's local colleagues jumped to her defense and told her not to take the attacks seriously.[249] A friend did, however, suggest that in light of the controversy she might want to reconsider using her nickname, Penny: since "pene" was Spanish for "penis," Penny wrote, "it would be literally foreign penetration in the family planning movement!"[250] Penny also recognized the difficulties American interventions created for local partners, who had to "bend over backwards not to be accused of being 'controlers' [sic] and pawns of the CIA."[251]

If Penny and her local colleagues allied with each other in public spaces, however, her diaries also illustrate the private frictions that continued to shape international collaboration in these years. Dr. Liendo Coll, for example, complained to Penny that "PC [Population Council] was always talking about increasing the number of acceptors and he did not think that was an important criterion of the service," which, he argued, should focus instead on quality of care and continuation rates.[252] Dr. Merchán, the head of the main maternity hospital in Venezuela, also vetoed the PC's suggestion that they offer incentives for IUD insertions, out of fear that doctors might put the financial payout ahead of their patients' best interest.[253] Penny noted that Merchán was "a clinician concerned about the quality of the service" who "judges the service by the level of medical care which the women receive" rather than the number of acceptors.[254] Dr. Bacalao also complained to Penny about the lack of coordination among different donors, asking whether it might be possible for the IPPF, Population Council, and Ford Foundation to join forces "so that there would be <u>one</u> source of money supporting the MCP—so that it would not be necessary to negotiate a new grant and new budget with four entities every year."[255]

Penny sometimes privately scoffed at these critiques of international donors, seeing them as politically driven.[256] At other times, however, she recognized that American advisors could be damaging to a program, especially when they did not work with locals as "counterparts."[257] Indeed, over the years Penny became increasingly critical of the structure of development aid, complaining about the excessive time spent on grant and report writing,[258] the inability of different organizations to work together effectively,[259] and the inherent limits of a system built on a "parade of short-term experts."[260] She criticized the great number of consultants who "come through in all sorts of fields writing reports and going away without any apparent intent of becoming involved in application or implementation."[261] In a tour of the Dominican Republic in 1972, she noted the frustration felt by local researchers over the number of studies "conducted by outsiders who take the data abroad for analysis and report writing and the Dominicans are not learning by the experience nor are they receiving the reports which could be helpful in program development."[262]

By late 1973, the relationship between foreign donors and local critics in Venezuela had become so fractured that the Population Council decided to close the office and move its regional headquarters to Bogotá, Colombia.[263] Recognizing her future was uncertain, Penny accepted a request from her old friend, Pakistani doctor Nafis Sadik, to go to Bangladesh and advise on a new UNFPA project.[264] In June 1974, however, before heading to Bangladesh, Penny conducted an oral history interview with historian James Reed that provides a vivid illustration of her increasing ambivalence within the movement. She recalled the corrupt and damaging practices of the Pakistani program but also noted that overall "we were a little overenthusiastic about the IUD. I think we thought it was going to be more of a panacea than it was, and we probably over-pushed it."[265] She repeatedly noted that "no single method will be suitable for all women in all cultures,"[266] and stressed the importance of personalized care by physicians. She also questioned the very nature of international consulting, arguing that "you couldn't translate the experience of Puerto Rico to Thailand or Pakistan,"[267] even though this was, in essence, her job description. She argued that the tying of international aid to population control and the intervention of foreigners in local family planning programs could in fact be counterproductive, particularly in places like Latin America, where it undermined and discredited local activism.[268] When asked about the links between population growth and resources, Penny responded: "I think that the decisions that have to be made must be made by countries themselves. I don't think that we as outsiders have any . . . I mean, we can offer a response to requests . . . but I think that the policy decisions have to be made by the nationals themselves."[269] When Reed pressed her further on the continued fear that rapid population growth would lead to global collapse, Penny replied simply: "Well, it may well come . . . But still, I don't see how we can do anything about it."[270] Ten years in the field had, evidently, transformed Penny from an enthusiastic missionary into a more cautious critic.

Crisis

The concerns Penny expressed in her diaries and June 1974 oral history were shared by an increasing number of actors within the international aid community, including within the Population Council itself. Perhaps most vocal among these was Joan Dunlop, an adviser to John D. Rockefeller III. Moving to New York from the UK in the 1950s, Dunlop had been recruited by Rockefeller in the early 1970s to handle his interests in population. As she later described in an oral history, Rockefeller told her there was "something wrong with the population field" and asked her to "take a year and go around and go to meetings and listen to people and tell me what you think is wrong."[271] Dunlop described her shock at listening in on conversations among demographers and Population Council staffers where populations were treated as a monolithic block and women in particular as mere "vehicles" for meeting demographic goals.[272] Dunlop began to meet with the few other women in the field and found a kindred spirit in Adrienne Germain, a staffer at the Ford Foundation who shared her critical lens on population policies. Dunlop described returning from a dinner with Germain and telling Rockefeller that the "problem" with the population field was that it was "shot through with unintended sexism and racism, and there was a stranglehold on money and ideas."[273] As she wrote in a memorandum to Rockefeller in February 1974, the dominant framework was also too focused on population growth in the developing world and failed to recognize the role of developed countries as resource consumers and contributors to the problems of the developing world, including through the "public policy ineptness in international aid organizations."[274] As she summarized it, there were "no new faces; no new ideas, no sensitivity or intellectual honesty about addressing this population issue within a broader framework."[275] She posed a "broader philosophical question" to Rockefeller: Did he want to "continue that view or open up and move into something new and different"?[276]

Dunlop's call would be echoed on an international stage mere months later, at the International Conference on Population and Development (ICPD) held in Bucharest in August 1974. Attended by government delegates from 133 countries as well as hundreds of representatives of NGOs, youth activists, and journalists, the conference exposed a number of critical fault lines in the international movement. A "Non-Malthusian Coalition" including a mix of activists and practitioners hosted a press conference publicizing abuses in state family planning programs, calling for attention to social inequality and more resources for broader public health rather than a narrow focus on contraceptives. Critics accused the population movement of being little more than colonialism in a new form, employing former colonial servicemen as new "experts" to embark on a demographic civilizing mission in their former colonies. Delegates and activists alike further portrayed family planning as a false panacea for the problems facing their countries, calling for alternative development models and a "New International Economic Order" (NIEO) that would include a global redistribution of resources. Feminists attacked the fact that the "World Population Plan of Action" had only one paragraph on women and that 127 out of 130 national delegations were headed by men, despite the fact that women were the primary targets of family planning programs.[277] Perhaps the biggest shocker, however, was the speech given by Rockefeller. Written primarily by Dunlop and Germain, the speech called for a radical reappraisal of the field to focus it on the basic needs and role of women.[278] While not all of these critiques were embodied in the World Population Plan of Action (WPPA), it did expand to include six paragraphs on women, and stipulated clearly that population policies should be constituent elements of broader socio-economic development policies, rather than substitutes for them.[279]

These critiques did not lead to an immediate collapse of the population movement or of the kind of abusive practices noted above. Some of the most infamous examples of coercive population control would come in the years following Bucharest, including the mass sterilizations of millions of people during the Emergency Period in India from 1975 to 1977 and the launch of China's One Child Policy in 1979.[280] But the Bucharest conference did prompt a number of changes within core organizations of the population establishment. The Population Council, for example, went through a period of inner turmoil following the conference, shaped by a deep split between those who wanted to maintain the population control focus and those who wanted to reform. Dunlop helped promote the latter, pushing for the election of a new president in 1976, George Zeidenstein, who worked to refocus the Council's work more firmly in human welfare.[281] Under the new leadership of African American businessman Franklin A. Thomas, the Ford Foundation also began to shift focus from state population programs to small-scale grassroots women's health organizations.[282] The IPPF launched a new "Planned Parenthood and Women's Development" program to focus on women's health, pulling increasing numbers of women into the organization who clashed with the more conservative family planning and population control stalwarts.[283] Other women left the traditional population organizations to join explicitly feminist organizations. In 1984, Dunlop took over as executive director of the International Women's Health Coalition (IWHC), an organization formed in the 1970s primarily to distribute menstrual regulation (abortion) kits internationally. Dunlop brought Germain into the fold and reoriented the organization to adopt a broader approach to reproductive health, investing in grassroots women's health clinics around the world.[284]

Penny observed these changes from an increasingly distant position. Although her records are sparser after she left the Council, she appears to have become a more critically engaged and selective international advocate in the following years, choosing short-term consultancies with agencies that were committed to maternal-infant health more broadly rather than a narrow vertical approach to family planning.[285] She also mobilized her networks to ensure that projects she engaged with were responsive to local needs. Before agreeing to a position in Nepal in 1981, for example, she wrote to a Nepalese colleague to make sure the project was not "simply being imposed on Nepal by USAID as a <u>condition</u> of their assistance."[286] Penny also appears to have become increasingly aligned with the emerging women's health movement. Although in her oral history with Reed in 1974 Penny claimed that she did not see herself as a "feminist,"[287] she did find her way onto the mailing list of the feminist IWHC. As a result, in 1993 Dunlop sent her a copy of the "Women's Declaration on Population Policies," a foundational critique of population programs that called for a paradigm shift to a women-centered, reproductive rights approach.[288] This document is at the core of the next chapter, but suffice it to say here that many of the critiques raised in the document undoubtedly resonated with Penny. Long before the language of reproductive rights was developed, practitioners like her had seen firsthand the need for a woman-centered approach, and the many layers of local, national, and international complications that shaped the possibility of such a program. Penny, aged seventy-seven, added her name to the list of signatories.[289]

Conclusion

Penny's diary vividly illustrates the underlying tensions of the post-WWII development agenda, the inherent contradiction between "a stated commitment to universal health, welfare and democratization on the one hand and the exigencies of a top-down and antidemocratic drive to control population growth on the other."[290] We can see how the enthusiasm over the IUD as a "method for the masses," when promoted without sufficient care and follow-up, damaged women's bodies and ultimately backfired, prompting resistance not only to the method but to family planning programs more broadly. We can see how targets and aggressive policies created by state programs could filter down into everyday ethical violations and coercive practices.

At the same time, Penny's diaries also illustrate a broader range of issues shaping the movement in these years, beyond neo-Malthusian ideologies and state aggression. The lack of independent access to new contraceptives and the high cost of the birth control pill left many programs reliant on international organizations and contraceptive manufacturers, helping facilitate unregulated clinical trials and constraining choice for women in practice. We can see the powerful role played by practitioners, whether in resisting dictates from above or acting as powerful "method gatekeepers"[291] themselves, influenced by patriarchal and hierarchical medical traditions that existed above and beyond the neo-Malthusian mandate. Even for practitioners more invested in patient well-being and quality of care, the lack of a broader health infrastructure in many countries made it difficult to provide the physical supplies needed for IUD programs, to manage the side effects they provoked, and/or to offer a broader range of options. In many places, access to contraceptives remained erratic and conditioned by a number of indignities that hit those with the fewest resources the most.[292] At the same time as we condemn the abuses of aggressive state programs, then, we must also recognize that a *lack* of state intervention could enforce inequalities of its own.

Critiques like those raised in Bucharest were crucial to challenging the momentum behind population control and revealing the illiberal logics underlying neo-Malthusianism. However, they did little to address the other structural issues that prevented people from exercising full reproductive freedom. Indeed, actors like Dunlop and Germain recognized the need not only for a critique, but for an alternative framework to drive state and international action in the field.[293] Around the same time, Penny's former colleague, Dr. Nafis Sadik, would take over as director of the UNFPA, becoming the first female director of a UN body and beginning a process of internal reform within the organization to move it away from population targets and incentives and toward health-focused approaches.[294] But it would take more than a handful of women to overturn the population control paradigm. It would take a new transnational movement, one driven equally by a concern for suffering but grounded more firmly in a feminist analysis of injustice, unequal gender relations, and political economy. This movement, too, would rely on women's labor.

[CHAPTER FOUR]

Redemption?

I opened chapter one with a description of two seemingly separate worlds: the male-dominated world of population experts represented at the United Nations' World Conference on Population in Rome of 1954, and the world of voluntary family planning associations, centered in women's labor and networks. Chapter three traced how these worlds became more directly entangled with one another, as women's labor was mobilized toward large-scale population control programs, provoking both collaboration and resistance. But it was at the 1994 International Conference on Population and Development (ICPD) in Cairo, some forty years after Rome, that the many worlds of family planning and population would collide most openly and publicly. As researcher and activist T. K. Sundari Ravindran recalled to me in an interview in 2021:[1]

> I remember that in ICPD [at Cairo], when they [the demographers] came, a lot of them were stunned that—this was like a women's conference. This was supposed to be a population conference. And it had been their territory, till 1984. But in 1994, suddenly, there were like 5000-plus women from various women's groups, all over the place, taking the whole scene over like it was a women's conference. So that left quite an impression. They were wondering, I mean, what happened to all these women? How come they have this much ownership on this? Never seen them, they're not demographers. And we were saying: what do these guys know about reproductive health and rights? They've only been calculating numbers so far, you know, what's the fertility rate and mortality and migration. Now you're champions of women's reproductive rights?[1]

Ravindran's reflections perfectly capture the turbulent nature of the conference which, indeed, departed significantly from its predecessors. Women engaged actively with the process from the start, attending and leading different forums of the Preparatory Committee ("PrepCom") meetings that took place from 1992 to 1994 and drafting much of the language of the Program of Action that would be discussed, edited, and ultimately adopted at Cairo. They had infiltrated several government delegations, allowing them a direct seat at the negotiating table. The mass onslaught of women that Ravindran described was also a reflection of the decision of the UNFPA executive director, Nafis Sadik (the Pakistani doctor we met in the last chapter), to open up Cairo beyond government delegations and population experts, and welcome women's organizations. With these women's organizations came a different, more expansive vision of the future. Beyond family planning to save mothers, or population control to protect nations, they called for "reproductive rights": a woman-centered agenda based in the basic right of individuals to decide the number, spacing, and timing of their children, the information and freedom to do so, the right to the highest standard of sexual and reproductive health, and the right to make decisions free of discrimination, coercion, and violence.[2]

If the appearance of all these women—and the language of reproductive rights—seemed surprising to some of the demographers at Cairo, it was anything but sudden. Rather, it reflected decades of women's mobilization at the local, national, and international level. In this chapter, I begin by tracing the trajectory of this new generation of reproductive rights activists from the 1970s to 1990s, starting with a basic timeline of international reproductive rights activism, as it has been told to date. I then focus in on a particular network of twenty-seven women from seventeen countries who played a key role in organizing women in the buildup to Cairo, using their backgrounds to expand our understanding of the different social, geographic, and activist locations from which the movement emerged. I then use a set of oral histories conducted by the Population and Reproduction Oral History Project, the Women's Learning Partnership, and my own Reproductive Rights Oral History Project to explore the narratives these actors tell about their engagement with the movement.[3] Like the family planning advocates of the early twentieth century, many of these women came from middle-class backgrounds and described their activism as linked to their experiences with working-class or impoverished communities that they encountered in their work. However, many of their narratives stress a sense of injustice rather than sympathy, informed by engagement with anti-colonial, feminist, and anti-racist movements in the 1970s to 1990s. Stories of maternal suffering are replaced by stories of gender inequality; stories of "conversion" with stories of rising consciousness; stories of hope and progress with stories of material inequality and structural limitations; stories of "spreading the gospel" with stories of listening to women and trying to build up a framework based on their lived experiences. In some ways, we might see this as a trajectory that flows naturally from the lessons learned by earlier movements: in the previous chapters, we have seen examples of early family planning advocates who become increasingly sensitive to the needs of communities and population consultants who became critical of the top-down approach of international development. But this generation of reproductive rights activists also layered this experiential learning with an analysis of the broader structural inequalities that shaped the lives of women in the Global South. In doing so, they connected powerfully with women of color in the Global North, whose emerging vision of "reproductive justice" both drew on and fed into the transnational reproductive rights movement.

The chapter then moves on to explore the many forms of daily labor that went into building these frameworks and transnational communities. This was the work of building networks, of collecting experiences, of pressuring key decision makers, of consensus-building. It was mental, emotional, and physical work, but could also be joyful work, embedded in tight transnational relationships that at times invoke the emotional language of bonding and reciprocity we saw among family planning advocates in chapter one. As in chapter one, these networks were strained by hierarchies within the community, set across the backdrop of larger geopolitical tensions. However, in the end, the larger division within the movement was ideological and strategic: Was "rights" the best language for this cause, and could something as intimate as reproductive freedom ever really be implemented by a patriarchal state and unequal international system? Was it even worth trying? While women were able to agree on enough principles to present a united front at Cairo, these larger questions remain unresolved.

For historians, Cairo has often been seen as an endpoint: the moment when the population movement was finally "redeemed."[4] For others, it is a starting point: the beginning of a profound paradigm shift established by the Program of Action, which officially adopted the language and several core principles of reproductive rights.[5] In this chapter, instead, I want to situate Cairo as one of hundreds, if not thousands, of conversations about the intersections of population, reproduction, women's rights, and social justice that had taken place before and continue to take place after. Cairo was an important moment in this history, a moment where these conversations and the language of reproductive rights found a much broader platform than ever before. But the tensions that shaped this process are both bigger and smaller than Cairo, and worth revisiting as we think about the past, present, and future of reproductive rights and justice.

Visionaries

To trace the path to and through Cairo, we could start with a timeline of key UN conferences. In the last chapter, I discussed the rocky political landscape of the ICPD in Bucharest in 1974; these conflicts persisted at the next ICPD, held in Mexico City in 1984. Critics continued to challenge the population control paradigm and its instrumentalization of women, while also drawing attention to the coercive practices that persisted in many countries. However, the Mexico City conference is probably most remembered for the profound shift in the policy of the USAID, the largest single donor to population programs internationally at the time. Under the conservative government of Ronald Reagan, the United States allied itself with the Vatican and announced a new policy—known thereafter as "the Mexico City Policy"—to cut off funding to all international and non-governmental organizations that provided abortions. While some organizations complied, others refused, and lost a major source of funding for family planning more broadly. The International Planned Parenthood Federation, for example, was forced to lay off sixty of its 217 staff members and canceled the opening of five field offices in response. The shift in US policy also corresponded with and helped fuel a larger rise in pro-natalist politics in the international sphere, pushing back against the reign of population control in the previous decades but also against feminist demands for bodily autonomy.[6]

Conversations about population and reproduction also took place at other UN conferences in these years. The International Conference on Human Rights, held in Tehran in 1968, established the basic human right of parents "to determine freely and responsibly the number and spacing of children."[7] In 1975, the UN hosted its first World Conference on the Status of Women in Mexico City, followed by a second Women's Conference in Copenhagen in 1980 and a third in Nairobi in 1985. In Mexico City, women from the Global South and women of color from the Global North pushed for the "World Plan of Action" produced by the conference to explicitly acknowledge the history of violations of reproductive bodies in the context of slavery, colonialism, and neo-colonialism. According to scholars, it was in a meeting at the conference between the US National Committee of Negro Women and a group of non-governmental organizations from Africa, the Caribbean, and Latin America that the term "reproductive rights" was first used.[8] In Nairobi, women pushed back against anti-abortion advocates who disrupted sessions on reproductive health at the NGO forum to denounce abortion and birth control as "genocidal." On the last day of the forum, seventy-three women from twenty-six Global South countries joined with ninety-six "Friends of Third World Women" to produce a declaration condemning these advocates for attempting to "co-opt" women by using their legitimate critiques of population control programs against them. They called for "quality reproductive health care" and "safe and accessible methods of family planning to protect our health, control our fertility and our ability to participate in social, economic and political activities."[9] The document was submitted to the US government delegation by Joan French of Jamaica, Srilatha Batliwala of India, Mercedes Sayagues of Uruguay, and Grace Ebun Delano of Nigeria (the midwife we first met in chapter one).[10]

Family planning also became a subject of debate within the UN Commission on the Status of Women, which became increasingly critical of the population rhetoric and assertive in its demand for family planning to be addressed within a framework of maternal and child health and women's rights. The Committee on the Elimination of all Forms of Discrimination Against Women (CEDAW), formed in 1979, called on states "to ensure, on a basis of equality of men and women, access to health care services, including those related to family planning," and to provide "access to the information, education, and means to exercise these rights."[11] The expanding language of rights at the UN, however, continued to sit alongside neo-Malthusian discourses of control, creating points of deep friction. At the United Nations Conference on Environment and Development (UNCED) in Rio de Janeiro in 1992, for example, women protested narratives that blamed women's fertility for environmental destruction, calling instead for a woman-centered approach to sustainable development.[12]

Women also mobilized internationally outside of the UN world. We could look, for example, to a series of "International Woman and Health Meetings" (IWHMs), organized by the International Contraception, Abortion and Sterilization Campaign (ICAS) in Italy in 1974, Hanover in 1980, and Geneva in 1981. While initially dominated by North American and European women and focused on access to contraception and abortion, the agenda expanded considerably at a fourth meeting in Amsterdam in 1984, attended by some 400 women from sixty-five countries. Women from the Global South and women of color within the North drew attention to the coercive practices of population control programs targeting their bodies, prompting the conference slogan of "No to Population Control: Women Decide." They also called for better maternal health care and access to resources to allow them to *have* children safely. Following the conference, the more broadly conceived Women's Global Network for Reproductive Rights (WGNRR) was formed and took over the hosting of IWHMs in the 1990s and beyond.[13]

Scholars have also recognized the important role played by the International Women's Health Coalition (IWHC), introduced in the previous chapter, alongside Development Alternatives with Women for a New Era (DAWN), an organization of women from the Global South. Founded in

Bangalore in 1984, DAWN brought together researchers, policymakers, and activists who had grown increasingly critical of dominant development paradigms. In 1985, DAWN released the book *Development, Crises, and Alternative Perspectives: Third World Women's Perspectives*, which documented the devastating impact of debt and structural adjustment programs (SAPs) imposed by organizations like the World Bank and International Monetary Fund, which had slashed government services and support systems in countries across Africa, Latin America, the Caribbean, and Asia. The book called for a fundamental reorganization of the "development" concept to privilege the basic needs of poor women and other marginalized communities.[14] In the early 1990s, the organization began to focus more specifically on the question of reproductive rights. Key figures from DAWN met with IWHC and other allies at a meeting in London in 1992 to draft the "Women's Declaration on Population Policies," aimed at inserting a feminist perspective into the population discussion in the buildup to the 1994 ICPD conference in Cairo.[15] These women then joined together with Citizenship, Studies, Research, Information, Action (CEPIA), a Brazilian organization, to organize a "Reproductive Health and Justice: International Women's Health Conference" in Rio de Janeiro from January 24 to 28, 1994, that brought together 215 women from seventy-nine countries to debate population policies, reproductive rights, and feminist strategy. The outcome—known as the "Rio Statement on Reproductive Health and Justice"—outlined a more critical and expansive platform to guide women engaging in the Cairo process in the months to follow.[16] Women from this network further elaborated their vision in a number of core publications, including the edited volume *Population Policies Reconsidered: Health, Empowerment and Rights* and DAWN's *Population and Reproductive Rights: Feminist Perspectives from the South.*[17]

Working through this timeline of key conferences and documents allows us to get a broad sense of the evolution of reproductive rights on the international level. However, it tells us little about the broader origins of the movement and the daily labor that went into constructing networks, building consensus at conferences, and elaborating a framework that could be shared across a vast array of contexts. While most scholars recognize that the movement was built by women from across the world and influenced by prior local activism, in most studies we see only a handful of figures who were most visible in the international sphere (or whose archives happen to be preserved), like Sadik, Dunlop, and Germain.[18] There is also an assumption that the movement originated with concerns of women in the West and then flowed outward from there.[19] As Maud Bracke argues, this obscures the role that women's organizations and individual women from the Global South played in developing and pushing for the reproductive rights framework.[20]

FIGURE 4.1. "Rio 1994 Women's Platform Steering Committee." Source: Adrienne Germain Papers, Smith College Special Collections.

Starting with the Women's Declaration/Rio Conference organizers and working backward to explore who they were and how they came together provides one potential entry point into the larger story, one way to decenter the analysis, trace the broader roots of the movement, and capture some of its dynamism. As indicated in table 4.1, the twenty-seven women in this network were located in seventeen different countries at the time of the Women's Declaration/Rio Conference. For most, these countries corresponded to their nationality, with the exceptions of Peggy Antrobus (originally from Grenada), Noeleen Heyzer (Singapore), Marge Berer (US), Claudia García-Moreno (Mexico), and Kanwaljit Soin (Pakistan). Their affiliations also indicate a range of organizational ties. International women's organizations are represented by women from IWHC, WGNRR, DAWN, and ISIS International. There are also regional feminist alliances, namely Women Living Under Muslim Laws (WLUML) and the Latin American and Caribbean Women's Health Network (LACWHN). There are women's medical associations: the Kenya Medical Women's Association (KMWA) and Medical Women's International Association (MWIA). Traditional development and humanitarian organizations also appear, including the World Bank and Oxfam, as well as new "gender and development" centers like the Women and Development Unit in Barbados and the Gender and Development Program at the Asian and Pacific Development Center in Kuala Lumpur.

TABLE 4.1 Initiators of the Women's Declaration (WD) and organizers of the Rio Conference

WD initiator and/or Rio organizer	Country (at time of WD/Rio)	Last name	First name	Organization (at time of declaration)
WD	Bangladesh	Kabir	Sandra	Bangladesh Women's Health Center (BWHC)
WD and Rio	Barbados	Antrobus	Peggy	Women and Development Unit (WAND), UWI St Michaels
WD and Rio	Brazil	Corrêa	Sonia	National Feminist Health and Reproductive Rights Network (NFHRR)
WD and Rio	Brazil	Pitanguy	Jacqueline	Citizenship, Studies, Research, Information, Action (CEPIA), Rio
WD and Rio	Chile	Claro	Amparo	Latin American and Caribbean Women's Health Network (LACWHN), ISIS International
Rio	Egypt	Zulficar	Mona	Women's Health Improvement Association (WHIA), Egypt
WD and Rio	France/ Algeria	Helie Lucas	Marieme	Women Living Under Muslim Laws International Solidarity Network (WLUML)
WD	India	Ravindran	T. K. Sundari	Rural Women's Social Education Center (RUWSEC), Tamil Nadu
Rio	India	Sen	Gita	Development Alternatives for Women in a New Era (DAWN)

WD initiator and/or Rio organizer	Country (at time of WD/Rio)	Last name	First name	Organization (at time of declaration)
WD and Rio	Kenya	Manguyu	Florence W.	Medical Women's International Association (MWIA), Nairobi
WD	Kenya	Njenga	Eva	Kenya Medical Women's Association (KMWA), Nairobi
WD and Rio	Malaysia	Heyzer	Noeleen	Gender and Development Programme, Asian and Pacific Development Center (APDC), Kuala Lumpur
WD	Morocco	Mernissi	Fetima	No affiliation
WD and Rio	Netherlands	Keysers	Loes	Women's Global Network for Reproductive rights (WGNRR)
WD	Nigeria	Ilumoka	Adetoun	Empowerment and Action Research Center (EMPARC), Lagos
WD and Rio	Nigeria	Madunagu	Bene E.	Women in Nigeria (WIN)
WD and Rio	Philippines	Marcelo	Alexandrina	Institute for Social Studies and Action, Women and Health (for WD); WomanHealth (for Rio)
WD	Singapore	Soin	Kanwaljit	Association of Women for Action and Research (AWARE)
WD	Uganda	Kasolo	Josephine	Safe Motherhood Office, World Bank, Kampala
WD	Uganda	Neykon	Florence	Uganda National Council of Women (UNCW)

(continued)

TABLE 4.1 (Cont.)

WD initiator and/or Rio organizer	Country (at time of WD/Rio)	Last name	First name	Organization (at time of declaration)
WD	UK	Berer	Marge	Reproductive Health Matters (RHM)
WD	Mexico and UK	García-Moreno	Claudia	OXFAM
WD	US	Dunlop	Joan	IWHC, New York
WD and Rio	US	Germain	Adrienne	IWHC, New York
WD	US	Kissling	Frances	Catholics for Free Choice (CFC), Washington
WD and Rio	US	Petchesky	Rosalind	International Reproductive Rights Research Action Group (IRRRAG)
WD and Rio	US	Scott	Julia	Public Education and Policy Office, National Black Women's Health Project (NBWHP), DC

Source: Compiled by the author.

The majority of affiliations, however, fall under the realm of national activism. This includes a number of women's health organizations and feminist organizations: the Bangladesh Women's Health Center (BWHC), the National Feminist Health and Reproductive Rights Network (NFHRR) in Brazil, the Women's Health Improvement Association (WHIA) in Egypt, the Rural Women's Social Education Center (RUWSEC) in India, Women in Nigeria (WIN), the Uganda National Council of Women (UNCW) in Uganda, and Catholics for Free Choice (CFC) and the National Black Women's Health Project (NBWHP) in the United States. There are also a number of national "action research" or policy research centers, including CEPIA in Brazil, the Empowerment and Action Research Center (EMPARC) in Nigeria, the Institute for Social Studies and Action (ISSA) in the Philippines, the Association of Women for Action and Research (AWARE) in Singapore, and the International Reproductive Rights Research Action Group (IRRRAG), which consisted of seven research teams located in Brazil, Egypt, Malaysia, Mexico, Nigeria, the Philippines, and the United States.

That was a lot of organizations and acronyms. But I think it is important in illustrating already the broader landscape of work being done, in many places, at many levels, and in many fields, beyond the most visible international organizations. Looking at the founding dates of these different groups also allows us to extend the timeline of activism further back. Four of the organizations listed above were formed in the 1970s, and nine others were created between 1980 and 1985, with three more joining the scene in the early 1990s. Indeed, the 1980s appear as a key period in women's health activism, undertaken both by explicit women's health organizations and by feminist organizations more generally, in Asia, Africa, Latin America, the Caribbean, and North America. Two organizations also date back much further: the Medical Women's International Association, formed in 1919, and the Women's Health Improvement Association of Egypt, formed in 1939. Their appearance reminds us of the much longer history of work in women's health, and the connections between more recent reproductive rights activism and the early family planning activism explored in chapter one.

These links came out even more clearly when I began investigating the trajectories of the individual women listed in table 4.1, based on published biographies, their own writing, and oral histories. Adetoun Ilumoka of Nigeria, for example, told me that her mother, Ayoola Ilumoka, had been a prominent nurse-midwife and one of the pioneers of the Family Planning Council of Nigeria, with connections to Pathfinder Fund representatives like Edna McKinnon.[21] This sent me back to my records on McKinnon, who indeed described Ayoola Ilumoka as a key force in the movement (while also noting how charmed she was by Ayoola's four daughters, one of whom was Adetoun).[22] Peggy Antrobus's husband, Dr. Kenneth Antrobus, had also played a foundational role in the creation of the St. Vincent Family Planning Association (FPA) during the couple's stay on the island in the mid-1960s. Peggy distinguished the St. Vincent FPA from the international population control policies we had met to discuss, noting to me: "I suppose, from the work you've done before, you will know that people come to family planning from many different disciplines and from many different positions, motivations, right?"[23] She rooted his family planning advocacy within the couple's broader work in maternal and child health: Kenneth was primarily based at the children's ward of the local hospital, while Peggy worked as a social worker, doing home visits and health education. While this was a retrospective reflection on motivation many decades after the fact, it fits quite neatly with the maternalist, humanitarian narratives prevalent in local FPAs headed by doctors, social workers, and volunteers, as discussed in chapter one.

Many of these women had direct experience working within the family planning/population world. While Germain and Dunlop were at Ford and the Population Council in the 1970s, Antrobus was serving on the Pathfinder Fund board, Mona Zulficar was doing various consultancies with the WHO and UN in Cairo, and Sandra Kabir was working for Family Planning International Assistance (FPIA) in Bangladesh. At the time, they would have been among only a handful of women working at higher levels of the core organizations of the population world. However, as noted in the previous chapter, the demographics of these organizations began to shift from the mid-1970s onward. Indeed, two of the women on my list had connections to the IPPF in the 1990s: Marge Berer as a member of the IPPF board from 1993 to 1998 and Alexandrina Marcelo of the IPPF South Asia Regional Office (1993–1995). Women had also begun to enter traditional academic population centers. T. K. Sundari Ravindran taught at the Population and Development program in Trivandrum, India, in the 1980s–1990s, while Gita Sen was specifically recruited as a visiting professor at the Harvard School of Public Health to work on gender and population.

The appearance of a number of action/policy research centers on the list of affiliations for this network is also intriguing. On the one hand, this is a continuation of a longer history of entanglements between advocacy and research in the population world. As discussed in previous chapters, the population movement pulled in—and was propelled forward by—a wide variety of researchers: from those who sought to illustrate the links between population growth and resources to those who developed the contraceptives mobilized by family planning programs. The academic discipline of demography, in particular, essentially developed in tandem with the population movement, both providing the data and theories to fuel the movement and receiving funding and legitimization from the movement.[24] But the action/policy research centers listed above were different in their demographics—headed and staffed primarily by women—and their focus on social justice, women-centered, and/or explicitly feminist research. Their existence reflects the infiltration of women into a broader range of academic disciplines in these years, including those traditionally associated with the population and development world.[25] Indeed, beyond the doctors, nurses, and social workers who formed the core of the family planning movement, the reproductive rights network included a number of highly educated women—several with MAs and PhDs—in a much wider range of fields: math, philosophy, literature, communications, sociology, natural sciences, political science, law, and economics.

Many of the women in this network held a variety of positions in their lives and went in and out of different spaces. Claudia García-Moreno, for example, started out as a doctor in Mexico before doing an MSc in community medicine/public health in London that led to a position in Africa with Oxfam.[26] T. K. Sundari Ravindran formed the Rural Women's Social Education Center (RUWSEC) with a group of Dalit women in Tamil Nadu while she was working on her PhD in economics. She then held a number of positions in the development and global health world before joining together with Marge Berer to create *Reproductive Health Matters*, a journal dedicated to feminist, evidence-based research on reproductive health.[27] Amparo Claro, in contrast, had no university education, surviving on odd jobs as a single mother of two in Chile before becoming the coordinator of the Latin American and Caribbean Women's Health Network in 1984.[28] Kanwaljit Soin had perhaps the most eclectic life/career path. Born in Pakistan (then part of British India), Soin had fled to Singapore with her family following independence/Partition. In Singapore, she trained as an orthopedic surgeon before founding the Association of Women for Action and Research (AWARE) and becoming the first female nominated member of Parliament. As one tribute to her summarized: "Kanwaljit Soin is probably the only woman in Singapore who can speak Punjabi, perform surgery on your hand, deliver a passionate speech in Parliament on women's rights, and tell you where to find the best dosai on Race Course Road."[29]

How did an Oxfam staffer, an economist from India, and a Pakistani-Singaporean parliamentarian end up in the same network, with a shared vision of reproductive rights? By combining the documentary record with oral histories, we can get a better sense of the experiences that brought these women together and led them to develop a particular understanding of reproduction that went well beyond concepts of family planning and population control.

Consciousness

Like family planning advocates before them, women in this reproductive rights network came primarily from a middle-class or elite background, with a father employed in a professional career (doctor, engineer, lawyer, civil servant, etc.). Still, most women rooted their activist work primarily in experiences they had as children witnessing suffering and inequality. T. K. Sundari Ravindran described living next to an informal settlement in Mumbai and having her father regularly challenge her to think about why some people were disadvantaged, and to question the naturalization of this inequality. She noted that this gave her "a very strong sense of rights and wrong and things being unfair, even by the time I finished high school."[30]

Claudia García-Moreno described the powerful experience of seeing her father giving food and blankets to rural migrants who rang their doorbell in Mexico City.[31] Rosalind Petchesky was appalled by segregation and racism—both in the United States and in a trip she took as a teenager to Israel—and became involved in civil rights activism in her hometown of Tulsa by the time she was fourteen.[32] Two of the women in the network, Frances Kissling and Noeleen Heyzer, had grown up in working-class families and experienced this inequality more directly.[33] Heyzer described how her social consciousness arose out of her "sense of outrage" at the daily indignities experienced by her community in a low-income neighborhood in Singapore.[34]

With the exception of French/Algerian activist Marieme Helie Lucas—who grew up in "a family of feminists"[35]—most women noted that organized feminism came to their lives much later. However, nearly all described something of a latent feminist consciousness while growing up, centered around a general frustration with the status quo of gender relations. García-Moreno, for example, described the unfair division of labor within her home growing up in Mexico, which left her taking on household work and care of her siblings while her brothers roamed freely.[36] Several women also remembered having a generally rebellious nature. Jacqueline Pitanguy started a revolt at her all-girl Catholic school in Brazil around age thirteen that led to the expulsion of herself and fifteen other girls, but also taught her "that we were able to resist, to rebel, and to achieve a goal."[37] Ravindran described having a "healthy skepticism about authority figures" that led her to challenge the increasing restrictions placed on her as a girl when the family moved from liberal Mumbai to more conservative Chennai.[38] As she noted, although she did not have the words to describe "gender-based inequality" at the time, she knew that "I wouldn't take any unequal treatment from anybody."[39] Heyzer likewise described observing the many "sisterhoods" of unmarried women in her neighborhood in Singapore. As she recalled: "Even before we knew the name feminism, they were feminists, of the best kind because they felt they could transform their own lives, but they also did it in solidarity."[40]

Interviewees also spoke of struggles in their personal lives around the subjects of sex, marriage, and childbearing that influenced their understanding of gender and reproduction. Several described developing an increasing frustration within their marriages over time, whether due to the prioritization of their husbands' careers, conflicting political ideologies, or violence.[41] Sandra Kabir married in Bangladesh at age eighteen and had her first child at age twenty, with another following a year and a half after; she experienced domestic violence at the hands of her husband and conservative in-laws, leading to a divorce after nine years.[42] American Frances Kissling described seeing her single mother struggle with her children and thinking that she would have had a better life if she had not become pregnant.[43] At least two women (Dunlop and Berer) had obtained an abortion in their lifetime and described how it fed directly into their activist sensibilities. As Berer described:

> I mean, the law changed here [in the UK] in 1967. So it was still quite a new thing. It wasn't totally accepted. The doctor said to me: "If you were married, I wouldn't agree to this." That kind of attitude was still very much around. Probably still is. But yes, it just—and it happened at a point where the anti-abortion movement in this country realized that they were going to have to organize themselves to try and reverse the 1967 law that made abortions legal, well, sort of legal. And so they were very active, and that meant people like me were moved to get active to respond to them.[44]

Women also spoke of how their experiences of pregnancy and childbirth shaped their understanding of gender. Pitanguy described pregnancy as giving her an "extraordinary sense of being a woman," and an awareness of how her experience differed from that of men, even those in the Marxist community.[45] In contrast, Heyzer and Antrobus described difficulties becoming pregnant.[46] Others witnessed the complex landscape of inequality and reproduction through their work. García-Moreno, for example, recalled her first clinical rotation in a maternity ward while a medical student in Mexico, where she saw women treated "horribly" by the staff, including both physical and verbal abuse.[47] Florence Manguyu of Kenya stressed the importance of her experience as a pediatrician, which led her to see children's health and women's rights as inseparable.[48]

Most women described their years at university from the 1960s and 1970s as a key period that allowed them to connect the dots between these different underlying sentiments. García-Moreno described joining a feminist women's group while doing her master's degree in public health in London that allowed her to "understand a lot of what my life experience had been till then."[49] It was also at university where many were exposed to a broader range of activism around race, class, and international power dynamics. Heyzer described Singapore University as a "hotbed of contestation," where movements around anti-colonialism, communism, and the Non-Aligned Movement (NAM) raged during her time, shaping her transformation into a self-identified "democratic socialist."[50] At the University of Kent, Adetoun Ilumoka was exposed to student groups debating African Marxism, anti-apartheid struggles, and feminism.[51] Ravindran recalled being profoundly influenced by critical approaches to education based on Paulo Freire's philosophy, as well as the general student radicalism and Maoist and Dalit movements spreading through universities in 1970s India.[52] All of the Americans interviewed described getting involved in leftist, anti-Vietnam, and civil rights protests during their time at university.[53] Women from the Global South who attended university in Europe or North America also described experiencing racism firsthand, both subtle and overt, sometimes for the first time in their lives, enhancing their understanding of racial discrimination.[54] Sen further recalled how her experience as a student in the United States complicated her understanding of gender equality. While in a sense she felt liberated by the freedom from restrictions on her mobility that she had faced back in India, she also was surprised to see how gendered the field of economics was in the United States, something that had not been the case back home. It allowed her to see gender inequality as something contextually specific, taking different forms in different places, some more visible than others.[55]

The women in this cohort followed different paths to reproductive rights activism. Berer and Kissling started their activist careers in the abortion movement (in the UK and United States, respectively), and then branched out from there to think more broadly about reproductive rights. Petchesky's involvement started with concerns over the Hyde Amendment (which denied Medicaid funding for abortions) and sterilization abuse. In the 1970s, she joined together with other socialist and Marxist women to found the Committee for Abortion Rights and Against Sterilization Abuse (CARASA).[56] The organization's pamphlets outlined a vision of "reproductive freedom" that included abortion services, safe birth control, sex education in schools, pre- and post-natal maternal health rights, and sexual freedom, situating this within a call for a "radical transformation of society and quality of life."[57] After realizing that she was not a particularly good organizer, Petchesky decided to devote her career as a political scientist to the elaboration of a theory for the movement.[58] For others, reproductive rights were one part of a broader engagement with feminist activism, rather than the primary focus. Amparo Claro, for example, had been actively involved in the feminist "Circle of Studies of the Women's Condition" created in Chile in 1978, as well as La Morada, a woman's house, and Radio Tierra, a feminist radio station, in the mid-1980s.[59] She recalled that her primary interest was actually in sexuality; she ended up working in reproductive health since it was one of the few spaces at the time where one could broach this field. She described her awe at a women's health meeting in Colombia in 1984 where women talked openly about sexuality and looked at their vaginas; it was, she noted, "very, very extraordinary" for the time. When women at the meeting asked her to coordinate the newly formed LACWN, she agreed.[60]

As noted earlier, several women started out in more traditional philanthropic organizations and programs engaged primarily in development work, like Dunlop at the Population Council, Germain at the Ford Foundation, and García-Moreno at Oxfam. However, the critical lens they had inherited from their personal experiences and engagement with leftist movements led them to question the approaches these organizations took, particularly to their work with women. As noted in the previous chapter, Dunlop found herself disgusted with the blatant racism and sexism in the movement, the way that women were "treated as objects and a means to an end."[61] Germain likewise described how her colleagues at Ford "never referred to women as real people" but only as "contraceptive acceptors or users or postpartum cases."[62] In the field, she witnessed the horrible treatment of women in some population programs and recalled feeling strongly that "you could not treat any human beings in this way."[63] García-Moreno described herself as becoming increasingly aware of the ways women were made invisible within the development and global health field while working at Oxfam. She noted, for example, how the AIDS crisis was understood as a disease exclusive to homosexual men well into the late 1980s, even though it was already apparent that in Africa women made up a nearly equal number of those infected.[64] She also recalled being shocked by the "colonial" attitudes of some prominent Oxfam board members, including "a real Malthusian guy who strongly believed that you need to control the number of people."[65] In response, she drafted an internal memo on population policy that both provoked debate within the organization and put her on the radar of Dunlop and Germain, pulling her into the reproductive rights network.[66]

Sandra Kabir likewise described a path from population to reproductive rights rooted in her practical experiences. She had first obtained a position with Family Planning International Assistance (FPIA), a USAID-funded organization, while trying to support her two young children as a recent divorcée in Bangladesh. She described herself as initially being "brainwashed" by the population movement,[67] but became disenchanted when she saw the impact of USAID's Mexico City Policy on FPIA's work. She could not believe the organization would agree to principles that were so clearly harmful to women. As she recalled: "When this happened I decided that there's no way that I can continue to work in this organization. Because I knew the importance of safe abortion for women."[68] She left FPIA and founded the Bangladesh Women's Health Coalition (BWHC), opening up a clinic across the street to provide safe abortions, using "menstrual regulation" kits the

FPIA wanted to get rid of before auditors from USAID arrived.[69] But Kabir soon found herself pushed by women clients to include further services. As she described:

> So I said, "Well, I'll show USAID that we can overcome your trying to stop us providing safe abortion services . . ." Then women obviously said, Well, what's the point of having a safe menstrual regulation service when you've got no family planning backup . . . And then the women were telling us, Look, you're providing us safe menstrual regulation services, you're providing us family planning. What about basic health of our children? We want our children to be immunized . . . And then women started telling us that, Look, it's so degrading for us that whenever we have to sign a document we have to use our thumbprint. We'd like to learn to read and write. So, then we started adult literacy classes for women. And that's how the Bangladesh Women's Health Coalition progressed. It was, I would say, very, very much dominated by the demands of the women we were serving.[70]

Although Kabir acknowledged that they did not use the terms at the time, this was essentially a "sexual and reproductive health"[71] approach. Indeed, when Dunlop and Germain took over the IWHC, they saw the BWHC as a perfect example of the kind of broader approach they wanted to support, and began providing financial aid for the organization.[72] On a visit to the clinic in 1984, Dunlop described the atmosphere of deep equality, care, and respect among both staff and patients, describing it as "clearly outstanding. One senses it immediately upon walking in the door."[73]

This approach was also embedded in the work of RUWSEC in India, formed by Sundari Ravindran and a group of Dalit women. Like Kabir, Ravindran described herself as being pushed into the reproductive health field by women she encountered while doing adult education in India. She recalled how the women kept asking her about family planning and contraception, sharing their experiences of repeated unwanted pregnancies and sexual violence in the home.[74] At the same time, she saw how the state's answer to this need could become a form of violence in itself. She described how women were essentially "caught between families and husbands who absolutely prohibited use of contraception and health workers who were literally, you know, hunting prey. Who can I get as a target? . . . Nobody was giving them information that they wanted, so that they could make their choices, and everybody was pushing them in one way or another."[75] Ravindran came to see the need for a feminist approach, leading her to invest in a copy of *Our Bodies, Ourselves*, the classic woman's health book created by the Boston Women's Health Collective in 1970. RUWSEC decided to create a pamphlet of images based on the book, using it to guide group discussions with women covering multiple aspects of reproductive health.[76] It was only years later, when she met Marge Berer and connected to the WGNRR, that she was introduced to the term "reproductive rights" and "understood that all the things that we were doing—just quite nebulous, saying, 'My body is mine'—that this was the term to call it by."[77]

In their travels in the 1980s, Germain, Dunlop, and other IWHC staffers encountered many other organizations around the world mobilizing organically along the same lines. In the Philippines, the Women's Health Care Foundation ran two clinics in Manila, with support from Alexandrina Marcello of ISSA (another Women's Declaration initiator). Marcello reportedly stressed at clinic meetings that "women are to be treated with respect, and that it is the 'whole woman' coming to the clinic, not just a person with health needs."[78] At the SI-MUJER clinic in Colombia, Dunlop observed how the clinic staff—a mix of women and "men who share the feminist philosophy"[79]—embedded the women-centered approach in practice through attention to every detail: choosing cervical forceps that were more comfortable for women (rather than the ones preferred by doctors), asking women how they felt every step of the way, giving out handmade colored cotton smocks instead of paper clothes, and "endless touches of this kind that give a quality to the place quite different from the 'medical' model."[80] Clinics in Indonesia, Brazil, Peru, Chile, Nigeria, and Cameroon likewise found ways to center the particular needs of women in their own local contexts.[81]

Organizations like the National Black Women's Health Project (NBWHP), directed in the early 1990s by Women's Declaration initiator Julia Scott, sought to bring this kind of localized, nuanced care to women of color in the United States as well. Like women in the Global South, African American, Asian American, Latina, and Native American women found themselves caught between a health system that either neglected them entirely or targeted them aggressively with sterilization programs aimed primarily at curtailing their fertility, undergirded by racist and classist assumptions about who "deserved" to have children.[82] In addition to speaking out against these coercive practices in the 1970s and 1980s, women of color began to produce their own alternatives. The NBWHP, founded in 1984 by activists Byllye Avery and Lillie Allen, adopted a broad, holistic approach to reproductive health care. They offered self-help workshops focused on addressing the physical, spiritual, emotional, and psychological health needs of women, published a newsletter addressing questions of reproductive health for women of color, and established the Center for

Black Women's Wellness in Atlanta, which provided coordinated health services, social services, referrals, education, and advocacy skill training. This holistic approach distinguished these organizations from mainstream white-dominated "reproductive rights" organizations in the United States at the time, which were focused primarily on the subject of abortion and a framework of "choice" that failed to capture the needs of women in marginalized communities.[83]

Indeed, the initiators of the Women's Declaration network shared a core belief that analysis of reproduction needed to recognize that gender power relations were deeply embedded in race and class inequalities. Several argued that their feminism had always been "intersectional," even before the term became popularized.[84] For some, this arose out of their own lived experiences as racialized women and disenchantment with social movements that tried to separate out and rank their different identities.[85] Sen, for example, remembered her frustration with traditional leftists in both the United States and India who saw discussions of race and gender as divisive, spouting the "usual nonsense" about how "once we have the revolution . . . we'll come to the woman question." As she recalled: "It seems sort of quaint and strange how this could possibly have been the case. I lived it in my lifetime. We had to fight and argue for it."[86] This was also the key rationale behind the formation of DAWN, which sought to bring an intersectional sensibility to multiple spaces. As Peggy Antrobus noted, at DAWN, "we don't separate class and race and gender and international relations. Our feminism is grounded in all of those realities."[87] The strength of the organization, she argued, lay in their ability to see the big picture and the larger power structures, while also remaining connected to those working on the ground.[88]

The various action/policy research centers listed in table 4.1 proved to be critical spaces in which to develop these kinds of connections between experiential knowledge and academic analysis. Their existence reflects the perceived need for alternative models of research. Many of the women with MA or PhD degrees described feeling disconnected from mainstream academia in the 1980s, which seemed blind to the realities of people's lives. Peggy Antrobus, for example, noted that her time working in Jamaica on development projects for women under the government of Michael Manley—a Jamaican politician who promoted a "third way" of democratic socialism—made her aware of the limits of her university education. As she recalled: "I learned more economics in the '70s in Jamaica than I ever learned at university. That's when I realized that the economics I learned at university really does not help you understand Caribbean economies or economies anywhere."[89] Gita Sen likewise noted her disenchantment with mainstream neoclassical economics; it was not until she found—or rather, helped found—the field of feminist political economy that she became comfortable within academia.[90] Rosalind Petchesky described her sense of isolation as a lone feminist within the "sea of men in suits"[91] at American political science conferences in the late 1970s/early 1980s. She found her "home" with the formation of the International Reproductive Rights Research and Action Group (IRRRAG) in 1992. The group included seven teams in seven different countries, each of which was composed of a mix of researchers and activists, providing a foundational model of participatory research.[92] Marge Berer and T. K. Sundari Ravindran likewise created the journal *Reproductive Health Matters* as a space where they could bridge the priorities of the women's movement with evidence-based research.[93]

Indeed, if there is one essential characteristic that unites the women in these cohorts, it is their in-betweenness, their ability to straddle multiple worlds: academic and grassroots, political and practical. Unlike many family planning advocates who tried to separate the clinic from the political world and portray their work as neutral, reproductive rights activists saw these worlds as essentially, necessarily connected. They sought to blend arguments based on experience with those rooted in other forms of evidence and academic analysis.[94] Illustrating these connections and building a framework that integrated them, however, would require multiple conversations in multiple spaces, both building common ground and recognizing conflict along the way.

Labor

As one might expect, many of the women interviewed cited the importance of UN conferences and the IWHMs as spaces where women came together to share experiences and begin to build a framework for reproductive rights. Germain described the excitement of meeting other feminists at the first World Conference on Women in Mexico City,[95] while several others saw the first meeting of DAWN in Bangalore in 1984 and the Nairobi women's conference in 1985 as particularly formative.[96] These meetings were valued for bringing women together, allowing them to see their shared concerns and struggles. Women of color activists from the United States, for example, described these conferences as critical in helping them situate their issues within a larger framework of global racism and imperialism, forge solidarity with women from the Global South, and understand the broader scope of human rights frameworks.[97] But the meetings also provided spaces for conflict that could prove equally productive. When women from the Global South disrupted the IWHMs in Geneva and Amsterdam in the 1980s to draw attention to the lack of serious discussion of race and population control, they forced white women from Europe and North America to confront their own biases and paradigms. Loes Keysers of WGNRR, for example, circulated a paper after the Amsterdam conference entitled "Does Family Planning Liberate Women?," in which she described how these confrontations led her to fundamentally reconsider her understanding of reproductive rights, recognizing how contraception could be a force of both liberation and coercion.[98]

Others pointed to smaller meetings in more confined spaces as key to building networks and expanding the framework of reproductive rights. Petchesky hosted a meeting at Hunter College in the early 1990s, for example, that brought together forty women from nineteen different countries.[99] A number of the initiators of the Women's Declaration met each other for the first time at this meeting and began to see the connections between their work. Ravindran recalled presenting with Marge Berer a paper outlining a feminist perspective to population policies; she was approached by Dunlop afterward, who assured her that "there are many others who think like this."[100] The meeting also highlighted the particular concerns of women of color. African American activist Dázon Dixon Diallo spoke on the limitations of the "choice" framework, stressing the interconnectedness of multiple issues and calling for the right not only to contraception, but "to have healthy children and manage our families well."[101] Edna Roland of GELEDES, a black women's organization in Brazil, likewise stressed the need for reproductive rights to be embedded in the broader framework of struggles against poverty and racism, stressing the similarities between the conditions of women in the Global South and black women in the United States.[102] The summary of the conference outcomes noted the continuing divisions among attendees—over whether feminists should engage with population policy and international human rights instruments, over the question of technology—but also the shared desire for "international solidarity" in developing a conceptualization of reproductive rights that recognized the impact of poverty and economic crisis on a global and local scale.[103]

The meeting in London in November 1992 that led to the drafting of the Women's Declaration brought together nineteen of the women who would later serve as initiators.[104] As Germain noted, the impetus for the meeting came in large part from conversations with IWHC's colleagues in the Global South. Following the UNCED conference in Rio, she recalled: "We got these calls from some of the women that I most respect in the world—Peggy Antrobus, Jacqueline Pitanguy, Gita Sen, Sonia Corrêa—saying basically, 'We have to do something about this. Cairo is coming up in '94.'"[105] Dunlop, too, remembered talking to Nigerian activist Bene Madunagu, who argued that they needed a feminist vision to counter both pro-natalist and anti-natalist forces. Dunlop started making calls, and within a week had assembled a few dozen women for the first "brainstorming session" in London.[106] García-Moreno remembered her excitement at joining the meeting, feeling "wowed by all these women" and excited to have finally found "like-minded people" outside her organization.[107] Dunlop provided a vivid description of the meeting in her interview: "I can see Peggy Antrobus now, typing away at her—she was one of the first people to have a laptop computer—and Adrienne dictating it to her. There was about six people working on it. If we could agree—the twenty of us around the table—then all of us would take the declaration back to our countries and begin to work our networks, and we'd give ourselves three to six months to do it."[108] In the following months, several changes were made to the initial draft, pushing it to adopt a stronger critique of existing population control programs, call out sexist, racial, and class biases more explicitly, and demand a broader overhaul of the population and development approach.[109]

The resulting Declaration outlined many of the core foundations of the reproductive rights framework. It argued that population policies needed to be attentive to the wide range of conditions that shaped the "reproductive health and rights" of women and men, and connected to broader development agendas addressing "the unequal distribution of resources and power between and within countries," including along the lines of gender, age, race, religion, social class, rural-urban residence, nationality, and other social criteria. The Declaration critiqued population policies that targeted racialized and low-income groups and the impact of structural adjustment programs and privatization on people's well-being more broadly. It called for population policies to be grounded in principles of women's rights and empowerment and argued that women needed to be subjects, not just objects of population policies, able to exercise their reproduction and sexuality free from coercion to either have or not have children. Finally, it called for balanced attention to different elements of reproductive and sexual health, including pregnancy, delivery, and postpartum care; safe and legal abortion services; safe choices among contraceptive methods; info, prevention, and treatment of STDs, AIDS, infertility, and other gynecological problems; child care services; and policies to support men's parenting and the fair distribution of household responsibilities.[110]

Within a year, the Declaration had been endorsed by 2,539 individuals and organizations from over 110 countries.[111] Still, the Declaration provoked criticism among sections of the larger women's health movement on the grounds of both process and content. Activists argued that the exclusive nature of the London meeting reflected the elitism of policy-focused groups, and was a sign of the broader "NGO-ization" of the women's movement, a turn away from the grassroots mobilizing seen as the core of feminist activism. Others argued that the Declaration's call for "population policies that are responsive to women's needs and rights" implicitly endorsed the idea of viewing reproduction through the lens of population, a framing that most women's health advocates rejected. They also felt that the Declaration was too soft on the population community, stopping short of a complete condemnation of the sexist, racist, and imperialist nature of the movement.[112] The January–March 1993 edition of the WGNRR newsletter published a number of critiques on these grounds from the Boston Women's Health Collective, the Feminist International Network of Resistance to Reproductive and Genetic Engineering (FINRRAGE), and the Committee on Women, Population and Environment.[113] Indeed, although Loes Keysers of the WGNRR served as an initiator of the Declaration, the organization itself hesitated to sign it, ultimately deciding to endorse it solely as a strategic document to be used in engagement with the population community/Cairo process.[114] Others, like FINRRAGE, rejected it completely.[115] A group of women gathering in Bangladesh in December 1993 released their own "Declaration of People's Perspectives on Population," which argued that "there cannot be any feminist population policy because it violates and contradicts the basic premise of feminism" and would only lead to the co-optation of "their language—and individual women—to legitimize population-control policies."[116]

These issues were debated at dozens of local, regional, and international meetings over the course of 1992–1994, from the LACWHN meeting in Uruguay and "Meeting on Population Policy" hosted by WLUML in France in 1992, to the International Women's Health meeting in Uganda in 1993.[117] DAWN also organized a series of regional meetings to inform their own concept paper on reproductive rights, where the research coordinator, Sonia Corrêa, took in comments from 181 different women.[118] As Antrobus recalled, the DAWN process was centered around a model of "building from below, from the experiences of people and reaching out and saying 'tell us.'"[119] Antrobus gave an example of the complexity of integrating different viewpoints:

> She [Corrêa] made all the difference in articulating a South position. I remember the tension between the Latin American women and the women from Africa. It's a good example of how DAWN resolves the differences and why the differences are so important to acknowledge. The African women were much more concerned about health services, whereas the

Latin American women, because of their own history on human rights, were much more focused on reproductive rights. It seems kind of obvious now, but at the time when these fissures first appeared it took a lot of negotiating to recognize that you couldn't separate rights from health. Reproductive health services without rights were meaningless, but similarly, rights without services were meaningless. The two things had to go together. But what I'm noting here is that it's a good example of how DAWN operated.[120]

The final document, *Population and Reproductive Rights: Feminist Perspectives from the South*, published in April 1994, provides an exceptionally rich, broader exploration of the power structures underlying reproductive health and politics. Over 112 pages, the book provides a thorough overview of the history of the population movement and addresses everything from neo-Malthusianism and neoliberalism to religious fundamentalism, social reproduction theory, the pharmaceutical industry, and cultural relativism. It argues that effectively guaranteeing women's empowerment and reproductive self-determination would require "a virtual revolution in prevailing gender systems and development models,"[121] and notes the need to intervene at "all links of the chain," from macro policies to the ground level.[122]

Even before its official publication, the draft paper of the DAWN study served as a key background document for the "Reproductive Health and Justice: International Women's Health Conference for Cairo '94" held in Rio de Janeiro in January 1994, along with the Women's Declaration and several other statements (including critiques of the Declaration by FINRRAGE and others). Organized by the Declaration initiators and additional allies, the Rio Conference brought together 215 women from seventy-nine different countries to develop tools and strategies to influence Cairo and to strengthen the women's health movement beyond the ICPD.[123] The conference organizers deliberately sought out diversity in terms of nationality but also religion, culture, age, sexual orientation, income level, profession, and philosophy.[124] Eighty percent of the attendees came from the Global South; the conference report also explicitly mentioned "the strong presence" of women of color from the United States, including Julia Scott and Cece Modupé Fadopé of the NBWHP, Luz Alvarez Martinez of the National Latina Health Organization (NLHO), and Charon Asetoyer of the Native American Women's Health Education Resource Center (NAWHERC).[125] The diversity of positions and philosophies was also evident; as Ravindran recalled, there were "people inside the system, totally opposed to the system, those who were inside and out, those who were in academia: all groups were there."[126] There were actors who saw all family planning as a colonial imposition and those who thought it was women's liberation.[127] The goal of the conference, as outlined in the report, was to "search for and identify common ground and universalities in women's perspectives on reproductive health and justice, while recognizing and respecting the diversity that exists in the women's movement."[128]

Identifying common ground among this group of "highly opinionated, very articulate, and very feisty women"[129] proved laborious. Each day the conference hosted panel discussions followed by unstructured free periods where anyone was able to speak and express their views on the different issues. Participants could also submit language and edits to the statement throughout the day and evening. Claudia García-Moreno and Gita Sen, the two rapporteurs for the meeting, remembered staying up late every night trying to draft language that would be acceptable to the floor: women would go out for dinner after the panels and then "the bits of paper would come trickling in at 9 o'clock, 10 o'clock, 11 o'clock, midnight."[130] As Germain recalled: "Even with all that careful preparation, Gita Sen had to stand up for six hours, I think it was, in the plenary on Friday and negotiate every single word of that policy statement. I've never seen such an action. Gita is extraordinary. She's one of our strongest leaders, really. And it was amazing how she handled it, because the hostility from certain quarters at that time was enormous. And it required every ounce of wisdom and

FIGURE 4.2. "Rio 1994 Participants." Source: Adrienne Germain Papers, Smith College Special Collections.

sort of personal centeredness and leadership, really, that she had. I mean, it was extraordinary."[131] Sen described herself as essentially going into a "Zen" state, embracing people's right to object and trying to be as flexible as possible while still moving the program along. She saw it as "uncomfortable, undoubtedly," but also "intellectually stimulating and exciting" and "emotionally satisfying."[132]

The resulting "Rio Statement" maintained many of the elements of the Women's Declaration but took a more critical position on a number of issues, a reflection of the diverse opinions present at the conference. The statement started by noting that participants "strongly voiced their opposition to population policies intended to control the fertility of women," adding that "a significant number of participants opposed population policies as being inherently coercive."[133] It recorded "unanimous opposition to designing fertility control measures or population policies specifically targeted at Southern countries, indigenous people, or marginalized groups within both Southern and Northern countries, whether by race, class, ethnicity, religion, or other basis."[134] The statement moved on to provide an analysis of the underlying causes of poverty and marginalization of women, stressing the impact of inequitable development models, structural adjustment programs, external debt, government corruption, and violence and calling for "alternative development strategies." The statement explicitly located the causes of environmental degradation in exploitative profit-driven economic systems, unsustainable elite consumption patterns, and militarism, arguing that "focusing on women's fertility as a major cause of the current environmental crisis diverts attention from root causes."[135] Instead, social development policies should be designed to "start from the concerns and priorities of women."[136] As in the Declaration, the Rio Statement outlined the need for a broad spectrum of women-centered and women-controlled reproductive health services beyond family planning.[137] The statement also called for more expansive understandings of the family and women's right to experience sexuality with pleasure, while recognizing diverging opinions within the movement over the role of contraceptive technology.[138]

In doing so, the statement outlined a more expansive vision of reproductive rights than previous iterations, one that also pulled in the question of *justice* more directly. The importance of justice is highlighted already in the name of the conference: the pairing of "reproductive health and justice" also appears a number of times throughout the conference report. The Rio Statement stressed the need to "redistribute resources" and "address reproductive health and rights needs and concerns (including the right to free and informed choice) within the context of social and economic justice."[139] As Petchesky noted in her presentation at the conference, this point had been continually raised over the years by both women from the Global South and women of color organizations from the North, including many of those present in Rio.[140] Indeed, only a few months after the Rio Conference, a group of twelve black women gathered in Chicago would coin the term "reproductive justice" to merge the reproductive rights and social justice frameworks together more explicitly.[141] They stressed that the right to have, to not have, and to raise children safely needed to be supported by "specific, community-based resources including high-quality health care, housing and education, a living wage, a healthy environment, and a safety net for times when these resources fail."[142] As Loretta Ross (one of the founders of the movement) argued, the reproductive justice framework drew on both the experiences of women of color in the United States and their conversations with women from the Global South over the years in international spaces.[143] The reproductive justice movement would expand rapidly in the following years, coming to encompass issues as diverse as the right to assisted fertility services for low-income women and the maternal health care of incarcerated women.[144]

In the meantime, the Rio Statement and other documents/discussions provided guidance for women engaging directly with the Preparatory Committees (PrepComs) leading up to Cairo, a series of four meetings where the Program of Action for the conference was drafted. Germain described the initial document prepared by the UNFPA as "a disaster from word one," filled with neo-Malthusian language and calling for the kind of fertility and contraceptive distribution targets that had been roundly criticized by the women's movement.[145] Women attempted to influence the process through a variety of strategies: lobbying delegates, drafting policy documents and recommendations to give to them, and getting sympathetic women onto the government delegations.[146] The Women's Environment and Development Organization (WEDO), a group headed by Bella Abzug of the United States with extensive experience in the UN system, helped coordinate these activities, organizing a "Women's Caucus" to produce critiques and draft new language for the Program.[147] By the time of the third and fourth PrepComs, feminists had effectively moved from the external NGO forum into the main debates.[148] As Antrobus recalled: "Basically we wrote that draft program of action for Cairo, we had to literally take apart what the UN had prepared with the governments, take it apart and reconstruct it. A lot of intellectual and political analysis went into that."[149] Indeed, inside observers noted the effectiveness of the Women's Caucus and their allies within government delegations, which led to the removal of demographic targets, significant reduction of population language, and new chapters on women's empowerment and reproductive rights drawn directly from publications of the women's movement.[150] Still, at the end of the fourth PrepCom, a document had not been agreed on, due largely to repeated opposition by the Vatican which eventually broke out into a direct confrontation. As Germain recalled:

> God, I'll never forget it. I'm sitting with Tim Wirth in the U.S. delegation, you know, desk. Joan and our colleagues from southern countries come streaming down out of the gallery. You know, Joan is very tall and very noticeable. And she goes storming up to the Holy See and basically, short of grabbing the guy by his dog collar, I mean, really, just clearly was reading the riot act. (laughs) Just—I'll never forget the image as long as I live. And she's totally surrounded and buttressed by all these feminists, you know, Amparo Claro and just everybody from all over. And Nafis still up on the podium sort of looking down on us . . . And in that moment, I know for a fact Nafis saw that if she was going to win in Cairo, the women had to lead. And she, from that day forward, she sent a clear signal not just to her staff but to her coterie of family planning organizations and donors that, Look, women are out front on this. These are women's issues. They have the moral high ground. You fall into line and support them.[151]

However, several of the core paragraphs on abortion, reproductive health, the family, and individual rights remained bracketed: in other words, up for debate at the conference.[152]

The labor of women's activists thus continued at Cairo in September. Women who managed to make it onto the government delegations described the intensity of debates that went on for hours, sometimes over the phrasing of a single sentence.[153] Jacqueline Pitanguy, in the Brazil delegation, recalled "endless discussions" and being afraid to go to the bathroom in case important language might be changed while she was away.[154] Claudia García-Moreno, in the UK delegation, noted that many of the negotiations took place in the basement of the UN building and at times went from seven in the morning to 4 a.m. the next day. As she recalled: "You literally started to feel like a mole. You go in the morning and then you emerge, kind of like the crack of dawn of the next day. It is very bizarre."[155] Germain and two other women in the US delegation stayed glued to the sides of representative Tim Wirth to make sure he stayed on message.[156] Women who were not in the delegations would try to influence them through whatever means necessary. Sandra Kabir noted that "we'd lobby anywhere—in the coffee shop, in the toilets, in the corridors." They would try to sneak into meetings by turning their "NGO" badges backward so security guards could not see who they were. Sometimes, they would get thrown out: it was, she recalled, "great fun."[157] Women inside and outside the conference also met every morning at 6 a.m. to recap the existing situation and plan for the day.[158] As Ravindran described to me, the women on delegations would take feedback on "any very strong feelings about what was bracketed, what they could negotiate on, what was absolutely a no-no, you know, that kind of thing . . . I don't remember any other conference like that where that kind of feedback was taken and fed actively."[159]

The interjections of the women's movement faced considerable resistance at the conference, where the Vatican joined together with Catholic and a number of Islamic countries in what observers called "The UnHoly Alliance." They distributed pamphlets claiming that "reproductive health" was a euphemism for abortion and repeatedly disrupted the proceedings of the conference.[160] As scholars have noted, a number of traditional population advocates and organizations ultimately decided to ally with the women's movement, seeing little choice in the wake of rising religious fundamentalism and declining resources from the United States since the Mexico City Policy in 1984.[161] Still, the women at the conference recalled feeling continued hostility from these quarters. García-Moreno noted that the population organizations continued to see them as "very disruptive and annoying";[162] the quote from Ravindran's interview that opened this chapter suggests this feeling was mutual. Indeed, in a later interview, Rei Ravenholt, head of the USAID population programs in the 1960s/1970s, dismissed the activists at Cairo as a "politically active lesbian faction" that diverted attention and money away from the real work of birth control and population programming.[163]

The final Program of Action—adopted by all governments at the conference (with reservations added by seventeen)—reflected these tensions. "Population" remained a central framework, but was considerably watered down compared to the final programs of previous ICPD conferences, confined primarily to the introduction and a chapter on "Population Growth and Structure." Of the 243 recommendations for action, one-third mentioned women and children explicitly, and the program retained the strong emphasis on women's empowerment that emerged from the PrepComs. Women's empowerment was understood broadly, including questions of political representation, education, employment, protection against violence and rape, legal equality, ownership rights, income distribution, and policy articulation, with attention to time and workloads, grassroots representation, family status, the needs of the "girl child," and the importance of male responsibility and participation. Reproductive health was defined as "a state of complete physical, mental and social well-being and not merely the absence of disease or infirmity, in all matters relating to the reproductive system and to its functions and processes," including the right to safe, effective, and affordable family planning methods of one's choice, the right to health care services for a safe pregnancy and childbirth, and the right to make all decisions about reproduction free of discrimination, coercion, and violence. The Program recognized unsafe abortion as a challenge and argued that it should be safe where legal, but not used as a method of family planning; it also recognized the right to a "satisfying and safe sex life."[164] The document explicitly mentioned the concerns of women of color in the Global North, something that had been particularly pushed by a delegation of black women from the United States.[165]

For a number of the women engaged in the conference, the adoption of this platform represented an incredible victory, a profound paradigm shift on the international stage brought through decades of women's labor. Adrienne Germain described the joy of the moment, the feeling when "the last gavel was brought down and the thing is through. And we all just went berserk—never mind UN procedures. We're dancing down the halls."[166] Joan Dunlop described it as "empowering,"[167] Pitanguy as "extraordinary";[168] Amparo Claro recalled the wonderful "energy" at Cairo, the sense of unity and purpose of the women's movement at that time.[169] And yet, others had more tempered reactions. Adetoun Ilumoka described having "mixed" feelings after the conference, seeing it as an opportunity to organize women and meet government officials but also feeling somewhat disenchanted with the "attitude to power" of some organizers.[170] Marge Berer likewise saw it as a "victory" in many ways but also felt somewhat alienated from the process and deeply disappointed by the outcome language on abortion.[171] Peggy Antrobus at first described the Cairo consensus to me as a "major victory," but then quickly qualified that probably it would be seen as a "partial victory" since "any victory at a UN conference is never a full victory, because whether it's successful or not depends on the extent to which governments actually take up these programs of action and implement them."[172] Indeed, most women recognized Cairo not as the endpoint of their movement, but one part of a larger process, a larger conversation over the intersections of reproduction, population, and feminism that would continue beyond.

Tension

The mixed reactions at Cairo reflected the longer tensions that had shaped these conversations, and which remained unresolved. These fault lines fell in part along the lines of race, class, and national lines. As critics have pointed out, feminists have been no more immune to racism and elitism than other activists in the twentieth century, whether maternalists, humanitarians, or population controllers. Indeed, historians have traced the long history of intersections between imperialism and feminism, in which white women from Europe and North America projected themselves as the natural leaders of the women's movement, in charge of spreading rights to women abroad. In her classic essay "Under Western Eyes" published in 1984, Chandra Talpade Mohanty highlighted the way Western feminists continued to see "The West" as "the primary referent for feminist theory and praxis," while constructing a monolithic view of the "Third World Woman" as "a group or category automatically and necessarily defined as: religious (read 'not progressive'), family-oriented (read 'traditional'), legal minors (read 'they-are-still-not-conscious-of-their-rights'), illiterate (read 'ignorant'), domestic (read 'backward') and sometimes revolutionary (read 'their-country-is-in-a-state-of-war-they-must-fight!')."[173] These views created tensions at international women's conferences in the mid-twentieth century, where women from across the so-called "Third World" repeatedly denounced the way that white feminists from Europe and North America attempted to speak for all women, while also isolating women's experiences from the broader context of colonialism, racism, and neo-colonialism. Women also critiqued the overrepresentation of elite white women in international spaces, a reflection of their greater economic resources and access to power.[174]

As noted above, by the early 1990s the reproductive rights movement had already begun to address many of these structural inequalities and to create expanded spaces for more diverse representation. Ravindran described how the pushback from women of color at the 1984 IWHM in Amsterdam not only expanded the concept of reproductive rights to reflect concerns of women in the Global South, but also led to a practical shift in the location of future IWHMs to Africa, Asia, and Latin America to make it easier for women from these countries to attend and be represented at the table. She argued that these actions, and the responsiveness of those in charge, allowed reproductive rights to become a "truly global women's health movement."[175] Gita Sen likewise challenged critiques that the "Women's Declaration" and other international reproductive rights actions were "yet another Northern liberal feminist agenda,"[176] noting the active engagement of DAWN and many individual women from the Global South in building the framework. As noted above, the Rio Conference of 1994 was also considerably diverse, in terms of the backgrounds of conference participants. Still, Ilumoka's comments about "the attitude of some of the organizers" remind us that inequalities could be reinforced in subtle ways. As she recalled in her oral history, there were times where she felt shut down in various conversations over the years, when she would ask a question and face a hostile reaction, or hear offhand comments that "the African women are being ambiguous."[177] These subtle questions of tone and reception are less easily resolved than numerical representation.

Activists and scholars have also continued to debate whether the use of "rights" terminology advances or hinders the cause. For some, concepts of "human rights" are seen as so deeply intertwined with histories of Western imperialism and individualism that they are inherently alienating. Others have argued that the concepts underlying "rights" emerged from—and speak to—a much wider range of experiences than any other global language of activism.[178] "Rights" language is also contested *within* the West: in the United States, for example, it is often associated with the mainstream "reproductive rights" movement, which, as noted above, emphasized personal autonomy and individual choice. In this context, "reproductive justice" is seen as the real paradigm shift, in its recognition of the broader racial, economic, and political structures shaping reproduction.[179] Indeed, some organizations and activists in other areas of the world have begun to take up the language of reproductive justice over reproductive rights. At the same time, Lynn Morgan notes that this shifting terminology might not be appropriate in all contexts. In her research on Argentina, for example, she found that the language of "reproductive justice" failed to resonate with contemporary Argentine activists. In part, she argues, this reflects the fact that "reproductive rights" movements in Argentina were attentive from the outset to questions of class, race, and inequality; there was therefore perhaps less need for a new framework to capture this element, as in the United States. The language of "human rights" has also been one of the most powerful and effective political discourses in Latin America since the 1980s democratic turn. Argentine feminists thus continue to prefer the language of "reproductive rights," even if they are committed to "the values espoused under the banner of reproductive justice."[180]

The much larger division within reproductive rights and justice movements, however, is arguably strategic. Nearly all observers of these conferences recalled the deep debate over whether engaging with the population movement and governments was a valuable way to try to transform the movement, or a fast road to co-optation. Amy Higler describes this as a conflict between "radical outsiders" and "pragmatic insiders,"[181] with groups like FINRRAGE on one side and the Women's Declaration/Rio Conference organizers on the other. Indeed, some of the women in the latter network, like Adrienne Germain, saw themselves as representing the "moderate voice of women";[182] Noeleen Heyzer was unapologetic about her willingness to "use any space that I can to make the changes that I want."[183] Yet other women within the network noted their ambivalence on this question. Peggy Antrobus, Ros Petchesky, Marieme Helie Lucas, and Frances Kissling all noted that they actually agreed with many of the critiques of more "radical" feminists. As Marxists and anti-imperialists, they were highly skeptical of the population and international aid system and its ability to reform.[184] Frances Kissling also recognized that there was a fundamental contradiction in advocating a "feminist" population approach. While a population perspective starts with the question of having fewer people, the feminist starts with "a basic commitment to women's well-being": thus, she argued, these two different core philosophies may not be entirely reconcilable, with one taking privilege over the other at any given point.[185]

The buildup with Cairo forced women to face directly the potential implications of this larger theoretical question. In *Population and Reproductive Rights: Feminist Perspectives from the Global South*, Corrêa and Reichmann portrayed the engagement with ICPD as a temporary, strategic move grounded in necessity, noting that DAWN "has decided to struggle to gather the forces necessary to exert power where power lies. We find that intervening to defend women's interests and rights does not mean we have abandoned a broader critique of the system's inequalities. But a decision not to intervene means leaving the control of power in the hands of others."[186] Antrobus noted that, while she was fully aware of the limits of the state, it was also the only body large/powerful enough to institute real change. As she put it: "You could put up all the women's health clinics you like, could have all the schools that you like, or daycare centers. But in the end, it is the state that has to guarantee those things, that has to establish a public health system."[187] Ravindran argued that the women's movement obviously needed both "feminists in the system" and those in the street: "So instead of, you know, fighting over which is better, we should do both."[188] Pitanguy, who came the closest to state power through her cabinet position within the Brazilian government in the 1980s, likewise noted that different institutions could be used strategically, if always with clear parameters. In fact, when the government began to limit her work on the Women's Council, she resigned with most of her staff, realizing that "from then on, to remain in power was to be coopted . . . and so there is a limit. You have to negotiate, understand that you have to make alliances, compromise, but up to a point. You do have your identity, you do have key points of your agenda that if you are a feminist, you can't let them go."[189]

This balance, however, was often easier to achieve in principle than in practice. As Sen, García-Moreno, Germain, and others who were directly involved in the Cairo delegations noted, once one entered that space of power and negotiation, compromises had to be made. The main compromises involved the language on abortion and sexuality: the Rio twenty-one-point document (along with other feminist publications from the time) had called for recognition of abortion as a right and included explicit language on "sexual rights," neither of which made it into the final Cairo Program of Action. Germain took responsibility for giving up the language of "sexual rights," noting that she did so "in exchange for the protection of forty-two para[graph]s on adolescents' sexual and reproductive health and rights." Still, she recognized that there were many who would never forgive her for it, and that the whole situation was "awful."[190] Berer noted that the limited language on abortion may have seemed like a small compromise, but proved to be an enormous setback for abortion rights movements, contributing to her sense of alienation from the international community following Cairo.[191] Indeed, numerous scholars and critics have pointed out that a lack of access and criminalization of abortion can itself be seen as a form of coercion, forcing women to bear children regardless of their personal circumstances or reproductive desires.[192] Petchesky, Corrêa, Ravindran, and other women in the network also noted that if the Program of Action recognized some of the harms of structural adjustment and other mainstream development approaches, it left out the calls for larger-scale macro-economic restructuring needed to actually make reproductive rights viable. In short, it adopted the reproductive "rights" without the "justice" advocated at the 1994 Rio Conference, seriously curtailing the ability of any program to actually provide the enabling conditions to ensure these rights.[193]

The continued coupling of the new language of "reproductive rights" with the old language of "population" in the Program has also complicated the impact of this "paradigm shift."[194] The years following Cairo did lead to a noticeable change in many international organizations, including the IPPF, Population Council, UNFPA, and WHO, which outlined new policies focused on reproductive health and brought in personnel from the women's movement to lead the change.[195] As Petchesky noted: "I don't think UNFPA would be the same today if it hadn't gone through that challenge of having to deal with all these crazy feminists and listen to their arguments."[196] In several countries, including Brazil, Nigeria, and parts of India, women's advocates noted genuine changes in the priorities and practices of state programs following Cairo.[197] In other places, however, the language of "reproductive rights" served merely as a smokescreen for policies that continued to be rooted in neo-Malthusian ideologies. A coercive sterilization campaign targeting indigenous women in Peru, for example, took place *after* the country signed the Cairo Program of Action, under a program officially dedicated to reproductive rights.[198]

Scholars have also noted a resurgence of apocalyptic population narratives in recent decades, particularly in the context of climate change.[199] Concepts like "carrying capacity" and charts illustrating the impact of different behavioral changes on emissions stress the need to have fewer children to protect against environmental destruction. As Betsy Hartmann notes, this language often repeats the same mistakes of earlier population control movements, focusing on numbers of people over consumption habits, diverting attention from the larger structural causes of climate change, and stereotyping the most vulnerable people in ways that can facilitate coercive practices.[200] The new narratives are sometimes more nuanced than in the past, acknowledging the importance of choice, presenting family planning as a "win-win" for women's rights and climate change, or even framing climate programs within a language of "reproductive rights" or "reproductive justice." As Jade Sasser argues, however, this language is fundamentally paradoxical, as "the autonomy that is described here is actually the freedom to behave in the way that development actors prefer, which is to have fewer children. And the ability to exercise so-called autonomy comes with a price: the expectation, nay *obligation*, to act as sexual stewards in the service of climate change priorities . . . women's childbearing decisions are thus never individual, never free from the weight of potential environmental catastrophe, and thus never free from a duty to reproduce (or not) responsibly."[201] The underlying desire to support only those women who make certain choices defies the essential principles of reproductive rights, while also leading to an overemphasis on family planning above the broader understanding of comprehensive reproductive health services advocated at Cairo. As scholars and activists alike have argued, reproductive rights and justice cannot simply be a new way to say "family planning": they demand "a comprehensive reformulation of an organization's analysis and organizing around reproductive issues."[202]

Even in contexts where the commitment to a reproductive rights or reproductive justice approach has been more genuine on a policy level, it can be difficult to implement in practice on a broad scale. As those who pioneered in the field of providing comprehensive sexual and reproductive health services note, making this framework real requires attention to both the broader context of women's lives and a genuine, deeply rooted shift in attitudes toward women. Kabir described how the effectiveness of groups like the Bangladesh Women's Health Coalition often came down to the most intimate of interactions between practitioners and patients: "How do they behave and react and interact with people whom they serve: Are they respectful? Are they offhand or not offhand? Do they look at people when they're talking to them?"[203] Petchesky likewise noted that a rights-based approach required "clinicians that were not racist, that were sympathetic to whoever walked in the door, that followed up and tried to make sure that [their patients were] going back to decent housing and sanitation."[204] If activists can change the paradigm on a conceptual level, only these intermediary actors and practitioners can transform it into daily clinical practice. Yet several recent studies have illustrated how practitioners across the globe continue to hold neo-Malthusian and classist biases that shape their interactions with patients.[205] As Lisa Richey argues, better training in the reproductive rights paradigm would help, but truly embodying this paradigm requires a larger shift in attitudes and relationships between actors of different backgrounds and social classes.[206] It can also be fundamentally difficult to transfer the level of sensitivity and care provided in a feminist clinic to large-scale primary health care systems in countries suffering from a lack of financial stability, riddled with staff shortages and missing basic materials. As discussed in chapter three, these programs will naturally gravitate toward the cheaper practices, the quicker methods, limiting women's choice even without a neo-Malthusian or coercive paradigm.

Indeed, as interviewees stressed, implementing this paradigm in practice requires money. Several described the 1980s and 1990s as something of a golden era for women's health movements in terms of access to financial resources. Foundations like Ford, MacArthur, Pew, and Carnegie and the foreign aid agencies of Sweden and the Netherlands hired a number of feminist and anti-racist advocates in these years, who actively redirected money away from population control programs and toward women's movements. They invested directly in local women's health organizations and provided the funding for women from around the world to attend women's health conferences in Colombia and Rio, as well as Cairo: in other words, giving them the literal tickets to the table.[207] Some of these actors were directly connected to the women's movement: as Gita Sen noted, Carmen Barroso of the MacArthur Foundation was a Brazilian feminist, reproductive rights activist, and member of DAWN before taking her position within the philanthropic organization.[208] Explicitly feminist international organizations like IWHC and ISIS also provided extended support for local and regional women's rights organizations in the buildup to Cairo, including funding for the early clinics in Bangladesh and Manila.[209] Several women described the flexible and congenial nature of funding relationships in these years. Claro highlighted the importance of quick, small grants for women's grassroots organizations—US $200 here, US $500 there—to do a workshop, run a program on the radio, and so on.[210] Antrobus recalled her tight relationship with Kristen Anderson at Carnegie, who invested in her as a leader rather than in specific projects per se. As Antrobus described: "That's amazing.

I don't know. You can't get luckier than that, to have somebody that has that kind of trust in you, and knows that's how things get done. That's how change happens, to support leadership . . . I wrote proposals . . . but I deliberately had very vague objectives, like 'providing technical assistance' or 'raising awareness.' And that was good enough."[211] Ravindran likewise described the relationship between RUWSEC and its central donors (the Unitarian Universalist Service Committee and ISIS) as embedded in the "spirit of feminist partnerships": the organization was given a flat sum each year, and evaluation focused on long-term growth rather than short-term "success stories," with open discussion of problems they encountered and how to move forward.[212]

Ravindran and others, however, noted a shift in the international scene in the years following Cairo. Somewhat ironically, the adoption of the reproductive rights agenda by traditional population and development organizations could lead to a diversion of resources back to these organizations and away from small, local, grassroots women's networks. The efforts of international organizations to open regional headquarters and country offices could also reinforce this trend: investing in "local" reproductive rights work could simply mean investing in the local branch of a major international organization.[213] Some of the women also worried about the professionalization of "gender expertise" in the international development world from the 1990s onward. As Ravindran noted, "that first crop of women in the system were from the feminist movement, they were not gender specialists from the university. So they had links. It's not to say that there shouldn't be gender specialists from the university, but they had links with everybody else and they had also done work on the ground."[214] She felt that in recent years many women had lost these linkages and developed a "disproportionate emphasis" on international policymaking.[215] As Loes Keysers put it in a reflection in the late 1990s, Cairo perhaps "distracted the [women's health] movement from broad horizontal work into a more vertical summit and lobby orientation. While advocacy per se is needed it is not all there is to the feminist health 'project.'"[216] Increasing emphasis on monitoring and evaluation in international aid programs, although meant to promote accountability, could also create challenges for sexual and reproductive health programs aimed at comprehensive, holistic care. At the end of the day, it is much easier to quantify the number of IUDs inserted per year than to show that a patient has achieved a safe and satisfying sex life.

Finally, we must remember that there is only so much that a clinic, or a program, or a state policy can do. People's reproductive lives are also made in their homes, fundamentally shaped by their relationships with their sexual partners, families, and social circles. As Iris Lopez argues, reproductive freedom involves having "the right to decide if, when, and how many children they will have without violence or coercion," as well as "the best social conditions that enable a family to have children—for example, having viable birth control options, quality prenatal and child care, and a support system that allows women and men to raise children in the most healthy environment." But, she adds: "*Optimal* reproductive freedom is something more. It necessitates that individuals and society also have reached the level of individual, educational, and cultural awareness that promotes egalitarian gender relationships, responsible parenting, and emotional and social intelligence."[217] Access to quality reproductive health services is thus "necessary but not sufficient . . . caring relationships are just as important."[218] Making reproductive rights real thus requires not only change at the international, national, or clinic level, but also changes in the bedroom, in the basic relations between partners. It is a movement that continues to rely on the most intimate of interactions to find its meaning.

Conclusion

In the 1990s, women moved from being targets and implementers of policy to becoming leaders and makers of policy.[219] As this chapter has illustrated, this process was driven by a diverse group of women from around the world who drew on their own experiential knowledge and combined it with an analysis of structural inequality to create a framework that encompassed a much broader understanding of reproductive rights and justice. This framework gave voice to many of the observations of the women who did the labor of family planning and population programs in the previous decades, accounting at the same time for the very real need/desire for contraception, the history of coercion/violence in contraceptive programs, and the broader social and economic conditions needed to ensure reproductive freedom. But unlike many of the family planning doctors and nurses discussed in previous chapters, these women did not make claims to neutrality or try to establish their position solely on the grounds of compassion or medical ethics. They made it political. As Antrobus argued, the reproductive rights movement was not just women-led, it was *feminist*.[220]

As the women involved in this movement themselves recognized, their victory was partial, limited by the many difficulties of actually ensuring a reproductive rights– or justice-based approach in a world that continues to be shaped by so many layers of inequality. The recent resurgence of conservative movements and backlash against reproductive rights on a global scale makes their framework seem all the more utopian in the twenty-first century. And yet, to dismiss it as such would be short-sighted. As Sonia Corrêa wrote in *Population and Reproductive Rights: Feminist Perspectives from the Global South* in 1994: "We are well aware of the challenges of implementing such a comprehensive constellation of services in diverse cultural and political settings. However, our blueprint for change is no more audacious than the Malthusian utopia must have appeared when social engineers drew up their plans to orchestrate the fertility decline of the entire world's women."[221] Visions of reproductive rights and justice provide powerful guiding frameworks for future policy, activism, and practice, allowing us to see so many dimensions of reproductive experience. The deep reflexivity of the women who promoted it—their awareness of its fault lines, and of their own blind spots—also reminds us that a vision need not be a gospel: it can be responsive, flexible, and able to adapt to people's needs rather than a conviction to be delivered by force.

This vision has not lost its relevance: if anything, it has only gained importance in the twenty-first century with the backlash against women's and gender rights globally, the reversal of *Roe v. Wade* in the United States, the attack on abortion rights in Poland, renewed stories of coercive sterilizations from India to Canada, and the continued lack of access to fully satisfactory contraception in most of the world. Still, many of the women I talked to expressed their enthusiasm over the newest waves of local and global feminist activism. It thus seems fitting to end here with some wise words from Peggy Antrobus, eighty-six years old when I interviewed her in fall 2021. When I asked her to reflect on the impact of Cairo, the backlash against it, and the contemporary reproductive rights climate, she stressed the importance of historical memory and her optimism for the future. As she related:

The struggle that is continuing is a struggle: the old struggle, but sharper. I find people are very discouraged, who fought for those gains, and have seen them all reversed and how easily they are reversed. I don't get discouraged, because I understand that each generation has to fight for those things for themselves...

All I can do is to share the experiences—this is where documentation is so important. We have to document how far we got so that when the next generation comes along, maybe not this one, there will be people who could pick up that again and say, this is what happened...

The reason I'm not discouraged is because I see the big picture. I always say, Nicole, that, for me, it's important to see the big picture, because if you see the big picture, and you understand how strong those forces are, you could position yourself as a dot on the periphery and find meaning in what you're doing. Because you know that what you're doing speaks to challenging that. And even if you don't succeed, it's still something that you're doing, something that's meaningful . . .

[The] new intermediate generation . . . They're ready for the fight.[222]

Epilogue

In this book I have started in different places: UN conferences, the homes of family planning workers, letters, diaries. I have followed different threads: networks, correspondence, international travels. In a world of infinite possibilities, these are essential considerations for a historian. Many of the differences we see in historical accounts are based, at core, on different starting points and different routes taken through the archives. Starting with local histories and working up to the global provides a different telling of global history than going the other way. Starting with those who worked in clinics rather than those who wrote treatises on population allows us to see the many other perspectives and concerns that shaped this movement. Starting and staying with practice, even as it connects with politics, allows us to get a sense of the social and material realities of historical phenomena, how it mattered to the actual people who lived through it.

Starting with women can be particularly narrative-shifting. Not because women are inherently or biologically different, but because most of our societies *see* women as different, and assign them different social roles and physical locations. Excluded from the higher echelons of political power throughout most of history, they have nevertheless shaped the past in different spaces: homes, clinics, doorsteps, village squares. They have not always done so in ways that we might celebrate: they have variously perpetuated inequalities, challenged them, and occupied ambivalent spaces between. But if we want to understand the meaning of any one historical phenomenon in its full complexity, we need to look for them: we need to see where they were located, and what knowledge they created from this location. The provocation of early women's historians and feminist scholars to ask "where are the women?"[1] remains as relevant in twenty-first-century historiography as it was sixty years ago. Breaking this broad category down to ask where certain women were—those marginalized by racial, class, and national hierarchies, for example—takes us even further.

The threads that we follow are also crucial. Confronted by boxes of often loosely organized materials at the archives, we gravitate toward some collections; we skim through others; we get caught up in a single folder, losing track of time. We often do this unconsciously, shaped by our questions and plans but also by emotional reactions like excitement, empathy, anger, boredom. It is also undeniable that the directions we go are shaped by our backgrounds, our own histories. The fact that I was drawn to the stories of secretaries rather than politicians seems likely to reflect the fact that my mom worked as a secretary all her life, allowing me to observe with interest how different systems rely on this gendered labor, and how unrecognized it often goes. I saw in Mrs. Allen's letters an experience that made me think of my grandmother, a Catholic mother of six in the mid-twentieth century, even while recognizing the immense differences between their lives. Of course this is not to say that we can or should only study those who fit within our own social backgrounds: that would be an intellectually limited project. But these subtle biases one way or another can fundamentally shape the final product: which parts of the story we have more material on, where the emphasis lies, whose stories we focus on, which arguments we tell first and who we give the last word.

I hope the different starting points and threads I followed here have allowed us to expand our understanding of family planning, population control, and reproductive rights and justice, to see the critical role of intermediary actors and intimate spaces in shaping each of these movements. On the one hand, this is an empowering tale, of ordinary people trying to respond to the needs of their communities, of nurses who resisted pressures from above and tried to center their patients' concerns instead, of women who refused to stay on the sidelines and took their demands all the way up to the highest echelons of power. But this is also a cautionary tale, reminding us of the frequent gaps between discourse and practice, of the multiple levels of inequality that fundamentally shape any one interaction, of the immense power that an individual doctor in a hospital room or a social worker on a doorstep can have over people's bodies and lives. While the global paradigm shift to reproductive rights is a crucial step, it will take a true commitment to this vision at all these levels to make it real.

Of course, there are also other visions, other activities that were going on outside the purview of the sources I relied on, less visible to me but perhaps even more important to those living through these movements. As one of my interviewees reminded me, even in selecting the particular network of women I focused on in chapter four, I was already making an argument, choosing a position to highlight over others, that would not be satisfying to all. If I had started with WGNRR and extended out from there, or with

FINRRAGE, I could have ended up with a different geography and timeline of this movement, perhaps a more radical one. I have also missed the work of many local actors, those that were not captured in existing local histories I read or who did not come into contact with the international actors whose archives I explored. As Mytheli Sreenivas argues, certain forms of family planning activism "traveled" more than others, based on their ability to fit with national or transnational agendas and a multitude of power inequalities (class, nation, language, etc.).[2] I hope that by capturing those that traveled in this book, I can also leave space for histories of those that did not. At the end of the day, the story I've told here is only one possible route, one possible start and end. I hope scholars will continue to take up this history, whether at the local, national, or global level. There are many more stories to be told.

Acknowledgments

This book was written over many years, shaped by the birth of my daughter Nina in 2018, the COVID-19 pandemic (remember that?), and several random injuries/medical issues. Considering the subject matter of this book, it seems fitting to start here by thanking the people who provided the daily practical and emotional support to write a book in these circumstances: my husband (Rowan Palmer), my parents (Bev and Bill Bourbonnais), my sister and brother-in-law (Michelle and Tim O'Connor), and my in-laws (Nick and Catherine Palmer). I love and appreciate you all so much. I'm also grateful for the wonderful child-care workers at Crèche La Jonction, our main babysitters (Vanessa Parada, Pokuaa Oduro-Bonsrah, Letizia Gaja Pinoja, Amanda Monroe), and the friends who jumped in to help out with child care, hospital trips, and dinners at short notice (Molly Kellogg, Christoph Hasse, Kali Taylor, Efrat Gilad, Anjela Jenkins, José Pedro Monteiro). Thank you to our wider group of friends, both in Geneva and scattered across the globe, for making life fun, and to Eva and Harrison O'Connor for being such a great little niece and nephew. Nina, you are my favorite person in the world, and the best part of my day.

A decade after finishing my PhD, I am still indebted to Alejandra Bronfman and Lara Putnam for their guidance and the University of Pittsburgh Department of History for providing a deep grounding in social history. The International History and Politics Department at the Geneva Graduate Institute of International and Development Studies has been a great academic home for me, with the best colleagues. Thanks especially to Carolyn Biltoft, Amalia Ribi Forclaz, and Aidan Russell for the comradery, and Mohamed Mahmoud Ould Mohamedou for the mentorship (even if you don't like that word). The Gender Centre at the Institute is a wonderful second home: thank you to Claire Somerville, Aditya Bharadwaj, Emmanuelle Chauvet, Shirin Heidari, and our many affiliates for the rich collaborations. Elisabeth Prügl has been a source of constant support and inspiration, beyond what I can express here. I'm also grateful to the broader Institute faculty and staff for the sense of community over these last ten years, and to my wonderful students, for all of their insights. In fact, it was a question from one of my students in a class on reproductive politics—asking what the "average" family planning advocate looked like—that in part prompted the focus of this book on intermediate actors.

I am also lucky to be part of several incredibly supportive academic networks. I have gained so much from formal and informal conversations with scholars of reproduction over the years, including Sanjam Ahluwalia, Holly Ashford, Juanita de Barros, Alison Bashford, Maud Anne Bracke, Deirdre Cooper Owens, Natasha Erlank, Martha Espinosa Tavares, Susanne Klausen, Philippa Levine, Krystale Littlejohn, Zakiya Luna, Ling Ma, Sara Matthiesen, Emily Klancher Merchant, Raúl Necochea López, Elizabeth O'Brien, Jesse Olszynko-Gryn, Manon Parry, Jadwiga Pieper Mooney, Isabel Pike, Alejandra Ramm, Cassia Roth, Caroline Rusterholz, Jade Sasser, Chelsea Schields, Christabelle Sethna, Rickie Solinger, Mytheli Sreenivas, Chikako Takeshita, and Ogechukwu Williams. I am grateful to the Pierre du Bois Foundation and Swiss National Science Foundation for financial support to bring many of these scholars to Geneva in October 2023 for the annual Pierre du Bois Conference, and to Sara Arab for the crucial support. Thank you to everyone who gave feedback on this project at other lectures and conferences over the years, in person and online, hosted by the University of Cambridge, Université Sorbonne Paris Cité, Brocher Foundation, Berkshire Conference, Institut National d'Études Démographiques, University of Basel, Wits University, University of Coimbra, University of New South Wales, University of Glasgow, American Historical Association, European Congress on World and Global History, and the Gosteli-Gespräche Talks at the University of Bern. Thanks also to ReproNetwork, which has been such a fantastic resource over the years.

My understanding of the history and politics of reproduction has also been enriched by talking to reproductive rights activists. In Geneva, Paola Salwan Daher and Carrie Shelver serve as vivid illustrations of activism informed by a sophisticated analysis of social, economic, and political structures. Loretta Ross has graciously participated in several roundtables I've organized over the years, bringing her powerful critique of the system and rich articulation of reproductive justice. I am also eternally indebted to the nine women who agreed to be interviewed by me for the book: Peggy Antrobus, Marge Berer, Amparo Claro, Adetoun Ilumoka, Claudia García-Moreno, Florence Manguyu, Rosalind Petchesky, Gita Sen, and T. K. Sundari Ravindran. Learning about your work in the field of reproductive rights, and your broader life histories, was deeply inspiring: I hope that enthusiasm comes through in the book. Thank you to the Graduate Institute for a Seed

ACKNOWLEDGMENTS › 189

Grant that allowed me to hire research assistants Urvashi Dinkar and Yunshi (Daisy) Liang to prepare the transcripts, and to my mom (again!) for helping out when the grant finished. I'm grateful to Marie de Lutz for putting together the online Graduate Institute Oral History Archive, which hosts some of the interviews and transcripts from the project. I also benefited a great deal from the interviews with activists hosted by the Women's Learning Partnership's Oral History Project and Smith College's Population and Reproductive Health Oral History Project.

My sincere thanks to the many librarians and archivists who retrieved files, directed me toward other resources, and helped me track down photographs used in the book, including the Atria Archives in the Netherlands, the National Archives and National Library in Jamaica, the University of the West Indies in Trinidad, the Wellcome Library in the UK, and the Francis A. Countway Library of Medicine, Schlesinger Library, Smith College Special Collections, and Rockefeller Archive Center in the United States. The Rockefeller Archive Center also provided a valuable travel grant to facilitate research. I am grateful to Jennifer Boittin for encouraging me to approach the University of Chicago Press with the manuscript, and to Dylan J. Montanari and Fabiola Enríquez Flores for living up to the praise, with an exceptionally responsive and smooth editorial and production process. Last but not least, I am grateful to the anonymous peer reviewers, who provided clear and constructive feedback that helped me sharpen the core arguments of the book.

Sections of chapter three were previously published as "Population Control, Family Planning, and Maternal Health Networks in the 1960s/70s: Diary of an International Consultant." *Bulletin of the History of Medicine* 93, no. 3 (2019): 335–64. © 2019 by Johns Hopkins University Press.

Sections of chapter one were previously published as "The Intimate Labor of Internationalism: Maternalist Humanitarians and the Mid-20th Century Family Planning Movement." *Journal of Global History* 17, no. 3 (November 2022): 515–38. © 2021 by the Author. Published by Cambridge University Press.

Notes

INTRODUCTION

1. See, for example, Alison Bashford, *Global Population: History, Geopolitics and Life on Earth* (New York: Colombia University Press, 2014); Alison Bashford and Phillipa Levine, eds., *The Oxford Handbook of the History of Eugenics* (Oxford: Oxford University Press, 2010); Matthew Connelly, *Fatal Misconception: The Struggle to Control World Population* (Cambridge, MA: The Belknap Press of Harvard University Press, 2008); Manon Parry, *Broadcasting Birth Control: Mass Media and Family Planning* (New Brunswick, NJ: Rutgers University Press, 2013); Emily Klancher Merchant, *Building the Population Bomb* (Oxford: Oxford University Press, 2021); Randall M. Packard, *A History of Global Health: Interventions into the Lives of Other Peoples* (Baltimore: Johns Hopkins University Press, 2016); John Sharpless, "Population Science, Private Foundations, and Development Aid: The Transformation of Demographic Knowledge in the United States, 1945–1965," in *International Development and the Social Sciences*, ed. Frederick Cooper and Randall Packard (Berkeley: University of California Press, 1997); Rickie Solinger and Mie Nakachi, eds., *Reproductive States: Global Perspectives on the Invention and Implementation of Population Policy* (Oxford: Oxford University Press, 2016); Chikako Takeshita, *The Global Biopolitics of the IUD: How Science Constructs Contraceptive Users and Women's Bodies* (Cambridge, MA: MIT Press, 2011); Jonathan Zimmerman, *Too Hot to Handle: A Global History of Sex Education* (Princeton, NJ, and Oxford: Princeton University Press, 2015).

2. Trent MacNamara, *Birth Control and American Modernity: A History of Popular Ideas* (Cambridge University Press, 2018), 14. See also Angus McLaren and Arlene T. McLaren, *The Bedroom and the State: The Changing Practices and Politics of Contraception and Abortion in Canada, 1880–1997* (Toronto: McClelland & Stewart, 1986), 22; Manon Parry, *Broadcasting Birth Control*, 2; Ilana Löwy, "Defusing the Population Bomb in the 1950s: Foam Tablets in India," *Studies in History and Philosophy of Biological and Biomedical Sciences* 43 (2012): 583.

3. Raúl Necochea López, "Gambling on the Protestants: The Pathfinder Fund and Birth Control in Peru, 1958–1965," *Bulletin of the History of Medicine* 88, no. 2 (2014): 362.

4. IPPF, "Historical Highlights of Birth Control: Malthus (1798) to Tokyo, Japan (1955)"; "IPPF: Publications, 1955–62" Folder, B40, MS Papers, SSC; Susan Fan, "Hong Kong: Evolution of the Family Planning Program," in Warren C. Robinson and

John A. Ross, eds., *The Global Family Planning Revolution: Three Decades of Population Policies and Programs* (Washington, DC: World Bank, 2007), 193.

5. On early family planning activism in different countries, see, for example, Linda Gordon, *The Moral Property of Women: A History of Birth Control Politics in America* (Chicago: University of Illinois Press, 2002); Richard A. Soloway, *Birth Control and the Population Question in England, 1877–1930* (Chapel Hill: University of North Carolina Press, 1982); Susanne Klausen, *Race, Maternity, and the Politics of Birth Control in South Africa, 1910–39* (Basingstoke, Hampshire, and New York: Palgrave Macmillan, 2004); Nicole C. Bourbonnais, *Birth Control in the Decolonizing Caribbean: Reproductive Politics and Practices on Four Islands, 1930–1970* (New York: Cambridge University Press, 2016).

6. Connelly, *Fatal Misconception*, 233.

7. Gordon, *The Moral Property of Women*, 280. For this distinction, see also Rickie Solinger and Mie Nakachi, "Reproductive States: Global Perspectives on the Invention and Implementation of Population Policy," in Solinger and Nakachi, *Reproductive States*, 1; Iris Lopez, *Matters of Choice: Puerto Rican Women's Struggle for Reproductive Freedom* (New Brunswick, NJ: Rutgers University Press, 2008), xiv.

8. On Sanger and Stopes, see Gordon, *The Moral Property of Women*; Deborah A. Cohen, "Private Lives in Public Spaces: Marie Stopes, the Mothers' Clinics and the Practice of Contraception," *History Workshop* 35, no. 1 (Spring1993): 95–116. On eugenics, see Bashford and Levine, *The Oxford Handbook of the History of Eugenics*; Chloe Campbell, *Race and Empire: Eugenics in Colonial Kenya* (Manchester and New York: Manchester University Press, 2007); Connelly, *Fatal Misconception*; Klausen, *Race, Maternity, and the Politics of Birth Control in South Africa*; Dorothy Roberts, *Killing the Black Body: Race, Reproduction, and the Meaning of Liberty* (New York: Pantheon Books, 1997).

9. Mytheli Sreenivas, *Reproductive Politics and the Making of Modern India* (Seattle: University of Washington Press, 2021), 15.

10. Bashford, *Global Population*; Connelly, *Fatal Misconception*; Karl Ittmann, *A Problem of Great Importance: Population, Race and Power in the British Empire, 1918–1973* (Berkeley: University of California Press, 2013); Sreenivas, *Reproductive Politics and the Making of Modern India*.

11. Solinger and Nakachi, "Reproductive States," 6. On the postwar population panic, see Packard, *A History of Global Health*, 181–225; Connelly, *Fatal Misconception*; Klancher Merchant, *Building the Population Bomb*. On nationalist leaders, see Sanjam Ahluwalia, *Reproductive Restraints: Birth Control in India, 1877–1947* (Urbana and Chicago: University of Illinois Press, 2008); Bourbonnais, *Birth Control in the Decolonizing Caribbean*; Raúl Necochea López, *A History of Family Planning in Twentieth-Century Peru* (Chapel Hill: University of North Carolina Press, 2014); Sreenivas, *Reproductive Politics and the Making of Modern India*. On decolonization more broadly, see Marc Philip Bradley, "Decolonization, the Global South, and the Cold War, 1919–1962," in *The Cambridge History of the Cold War Volume 1, Origins, 1945–1962*, ed. Melvyn P. Leffler and Odd Arne Westad (Cambridge: Cambridge University Press, 2012).

12. Ahluwalia, *Reproductive Restraints*, 3.

13. Bashford and Levine, *The Oxford Handbook of the History of Eugenics*, 9–11. See also the contributions to Solinger and Nakachi, *Reproductive States*.

14. Solinger and Nakachi, "Reproductive States"; Roberts, *Killing the Black Body*.

15. Connelly, *Fatal Misconception*, xi.

16. Bashford and Levine, *The Oxford Handbook of the History of Eugenics*, 3–4.

17. Faye D. Ginsburg and Rayna Rapp, "Introduction: Conceiving the New World Order," in Faye D. Ginsburg and Rayna Rapp, eds., *Conceiving the New World Order: The Global Politics of Reproduction* (Berkeley: University of California Press, 1995), 3.

18. Sanjam Ahluwalia and Daksha Pamar, "From Gandhi to Gandhi: Contraceptive Technologies and Sexual Politics in Postcolonial India, 1947–1977," in Solinger and Nakachi, *Reproductive States*, 125.

19. Betsy Hartmann, *Reproductive Rights and Wrongs: The Global Politics of Population Control* (Boston: South End Press, 1995 [1987]), 4.

20. Solinger and Nakachi, "Reproductive States," 9.

21. Solinger and Nakachi, "Reproductive States," 3.

22. See Ittmann, *A Problem of Great Importance*; Bourbonnais, *Birth Control in the Decolonizing Caribbean*; Campbell, *Race and Empire*.

23. See, for example, Frederick Cooper and Randall Packard, "Introduction," in Frederick Cooper and Randall Packard, eds., *International Development and the Social Sciences* (Berkeley: University of California Press, 1997), 1–41; Packard, *A History of Global Health*; Michael Barnett, *Empire of Humanity: A History of Humanitarianism* (Ithaca, NY, and London: Cornell University Press, 2011).

24. Connelly, *Fatal Misconception*, 17, 235.

25. Connelly, *Fatal Misconception*, 5.

26. Necochea López, *A History of Family Planning in Twentieth-Century Peru*, 86.

27. Parry, *Broadcasting Birth Control*, 81–82; Steven W. Sinding, "Overview and Perspective," in Robinson and Ross, *The Global Family Planning Revolution*, 9; Sandra Whitworth, *Feminism and International Relations: Towards a Political Economy of Gender in Interstate and Non-Governmental Institutions* (New York: St. Martin's Press, 1994), 98; Corina Dobos, "Global Challenges, Local Knowledges: Politics and Expertise at the World Population Conference in Bucharest, 1974," *East Central Europe* 45 (2018): 215–44.

28. Omnia El Shakry, "Reproducing the Family: Biopolitics in Twentieth-Century Egypt," in Solinger and Nakachi, *Reproductive States*, 180; Aiko Takeuchi-Demirci, *Contraceptive Diplomacy: Reproductive Politics and Imperial Ambitions in the United States and Japan* (Stanford, CA: Stanford University Press, 2018), 205. On the hesitance of the WHO specifically, see Marcos Cueto, Theodore M. Brown, and Elizabeth Fee, *The World Health Organization: A History* (Cambridge: Cambridge University Press, 2019), 146–69.

29. See, for example, Bourbonnais, *Birth Control in the Decolonizing Caribbean*, chap. 1; Jennifer Nelson, *Women of Color and the Reproductive Rights Movement* (New York and London: NYU Press, 2003).

30. Maud Anne Bracke, "Contesting 'Global Sisterhood': The Global Women's Health Movement, the United Nations and the Different Meanings of Reproductive Rights (1970s–80s)," *Gender & History* 35 (2023): 811–29; Amy J. Higler, "International Women's Activism and the 1994 Cairo Population Conference," in *Gender Politics in Global Governance*, ed. Mary K. Meyler and Elisabeth Prügl (Lanham, MD: Rowman & Littlefield Publishers, 1998); Jutta M. Joachim, *Agenda Setting, the UN, and NGOs: Gender Violence and Reproductive Rights* (Washington, DC: Georgetown University Press, 2007); Rosalind P. Petchesky, *Global Prescriptions: Gendering Health and Human Rights* (London: Zed Books, 2003).

31. For this vision, see in particular Sonia Corrêa and Rebecca Reichmann, *Population and Reproductive Rights: Feminist Perspectives from the South* (London: Zed Books, 1994); Gita Sen, Adrienne Germain, and Lincoln C. Chen, eds., *Population Policies Reconsidered: Health, Empowerment, and Rights* (Boston: Harvard School of Public Health, 1994); Petchesky, *Global Prescriptions*; CEPIA and IWHC, "Reproductive Health and Justice: International Women's Health Conference for Cairo '94," Conference Report (Rio de Janeiro, Brazil: CEPIA AND IWHC, 1994).

32. Nelson, *Women of Color and the Reproductive Rights Movement*; Jennifer Nelson, *More Than Medicine: A History of the Feminist Women's Health Movement* (New York and London: New York University Press, 2015); Kimala Price, "What Is Reproductive Justice? How Women of Color Activists Are Redefining the Pro-Choice Paradigm," *Meridians: feminism, race, transnationalism* 10, no. 2 (2010): 42–65; Zakiya Luna and Kristin Luker, "Reproductive Justice," *Annual Review of Law and Social Science* 9 (2013): 327–52; Loretta J. Ross and Rickie Solinger, *Reproductive Justice: An Introduction* (Berkeley: University of California Press, 2017); Zakiya Luna, *Reproductive Rights as Human Rights: Women of Color and the Fight for Reproductive Justice* (New York: New York University Press, 2020); Jael Silliman, Marlene Gerber Fried, Loretta Ross, and Elena Gutierrez, *Undivided Rights: Women of Color Organizing for Reproductive Justice* (Boston: South End Press, 2004).

33. Connelly, *Fatal Misconception*, xii.

34. Sinding, "Overview and Perspective," 9–10; Solinger and Nakachi, "Reproductive States," 24–25; Price, "What Is Reproductive Justice?," 61; Luna and Luker, "Reproductive Justice," 342–43.

35. Takeuchi-Demirci, *Contraceptive Diplomacy*.

36. Bashford, *Global Population*.

37. Takeshita, *The Global Biopolitics of the IUD*.

38. Connelly, *Fatal Misconception*.

39. Carole Joffe, *The Regulation of Sexuality: Experiences of Family Planning Workers* (Philadelphia: Temple University Press, 1986), 9.

40. See, for example, Ahluwalia, *Reproductive Restraints*; Holly Ashford, *Development and Women's Reproductive Health in Ghana, 1920–1982* (New York: Routledge, 2022); Laura Briggs, *Reproducing Empire: Race, Sex, Science, and U.S. Imperialism in Puerto Rico* (Berkeley: University of California Press, 2002); Amy Kaler, *Running after Pills: Politics, Gender, and Contraception in Colonial Zimbabwe* (Portsmouth: Heinemann, 2003); Firoozeh Kashani-Sabet, *Conceiving Citizens: Women and the Politics of Motherhood in Iran* (Oxford and New York: Oxford University

NOTES TO PAGES 14–17 › 195

Press, 2011); Klausen, *Race, Maternity, and the Politics of Birth Control in South Africa*; Necochea López, *A History of Family Planning in Twentieth-Century Peru*; Jadwiga E. Pieper Mooney, *The Politics of Motherhood: Maternity and Women's Rights in Twentieth-Century Chile* (Pittsburgh: University of Pittsburgh Press, 2009); and national chapters in Robinson and Ross, *The Global Family Planning Revolution*; Solinger and Nakachi, *Reproductive States*. For a full list of articles, dissertations, and chapters, see the bibliography.

41. Necochea López, *A History of Family Planning in Twentieth-Century Peru*, 2–5.

42. Cohen, "Private Lives in Public Spaces."

43. Roberts, *Killing the Black Body*, 76–78, 82–88; Rhonda Wells-Wilbon, "Family Planning for Low-Income African American Families: Contributions of Social Work Pioneer Ophelia Settle Egypt," *Social Work* 60, no. 4 (October 2015): 335–42.

44. Laura Briggs, "Discourses of 'Forced Sterilization' in Puerto Rico: The Problem with the Speaking Subaltern," *differences: A Journal of Feminist Cultural Studies* 10, no. 2 (1998): 56; Parry, *Broadcasting Birth Control*, 8.

45. Johanna Schoen, *Choice and Coercion: Birth Control, Sterilization, and Abortion in Public Health and Welfare* (Chapel Hill and London: University of North Carolina Press, 2005), 7.

46. Schoen, *Choice and Coercion*, 8. See also Wells-Wilbon, "Family Planning for Low-Income African American Families," 340.

47. Schoen, *Choice and Coercion*, 137.

48. Lopez, *Matters of Choice*.

49. Bourbonnais, *Birth Control in the Decolonizing Caribbean*.

50. Peter Stearns, "Social History Present and Future," *Journal of Social History* 37, no. 1 (2003): 9–19.

51. Mathew Hilton et al., "History and Humanitarianism: A Conversation," *Past and Present* 241, no. 1 (November 2018): 28.

52. Carole H. Browner and Carolyn F. Sargent, "Towards Global Anthropological Studies of Reproduction: Concepts, Methods, Theoretical Approaches," in Browner and Sargent, eds., *Reproduction, Globalization, and the State: New Theoretical and Ethnographic Perspectives* (Durham, NC: Duke University Press, 2011), 6.

53. Sigurõur Gylfi and István M. Szijártó Magnússon, *What Is Microhistory? Theory and Practice* (Oxon: Routledge, 2013), 1–12.

54. Julia Laite, "Traffickers and Pimps in the Era of White Slavery," *Past & Present* 237, no. 1 (November 2017): 246.

55. The idea of "intimate" history is also inspired by Saidiya Hartman's *Wayward Lives, Beautiful Experiments: Intimate Histories of Social Upheaval* (New York: W. W. Norton & Company, 2019), although I would not claim to offer anything as rich as that masterpiece.

56. Sreenivas, *Reproductive Politics and the Making of Modern India*, 12.

57. MacNamara, *Birth Control and American Modernity*, 5.

58. El Shakry, "Reproducing the Family," 173.

59. Takeuchi-Demirci, *Contraceptive Diplomacy*, 5. See also Sreenivas, *Reproductive Politics and the Making of Modern India*, 94.

60. Quoted in Barnett, *Empire of Humanity*, 34.

CHAPTER ONE

1. Margery K. Butcher, "Impressions of the United Nations Conference on World Population, Rome, 1954," 1955/03/24, 1 ("IPPF Minutes, 1953–1964," B40, MS Papers, SSC).

2. Matthew Connelly, "Population Control Is History: New Perspectives on the International Campaign to Limit Population Growth," *Comparative Studies in Society and History* 45, no. 1 (January 2003): 126. See also Bashford, *Global Population*, 212.

3. Connelly, *Fatal Misconception*, xii.

4. Perdita Huston, *Motherhood by Choice: Pioneers in Women's Health and Family Planning* (New York: The Feminist Press at the City University of New York, 1992), 52.

5. Huston, *Motherhood by Choice*, 46.

6. Alison Bashford, "Nation, Empire, Globe: The Spaces of Population Debate in the Interwar Years," *Comparative Studies in Society and History* 49, no. 1 (2007):181; Connelly, *Fatal Misconception*, 258.

7. Bashford, "Nation, Empire, Globe," 176; Caroline Rusterholz, "English Women Doctors, Contraception and Family Planning in Transnational Perspective (1930s–70s)," *Medical History* 63, no. 2 (April 2019): 156–57; Ahluwalia, *Reproductive Restraints*, 54–81; Takeuchi-Demirci, *Contraceptive Diplomacy*, 34. On the early history of the movement, see also Connelly, *Fatal Misconception*, 18–114.

8. IPPF, "Historical Highlights of Birth Control: Malthus (1798) to Tokyo, Japan (1955)," 9 ("IPPF: Publications, 1955–62," B40, MS Papers, SSC); Warren C. and Fatma H. El-Zanaty Robinson, "The Evolution of Population Policies and Programs in the Arab Republic of Egypt," in Robinson and Ross, *The Global Family Planning Revolution*, 15–16; El Shakry, "Reproducing the Family."

9. Bourbonnais, *Birth Control in the Decolonizing Caribbean*, 104.

10. Takeuchi-Demirci, *Contraceptive Diplomacy*, 25–26, 37, 40.

11. Thuy Linh Nguyen, "Overpopulation, Racial Degeneracy and Birth Control in French Colonial Vietnam," *Journal of Colonialism & Colonial History* 19, no. 3 (2018).

12. Sarah Hodges, *Contraception, Colonialism and Commerce: Birth Control in South India, 1920–1940* (Burlington: Ashgate Publishing Ltd., 2008).

13. Ahluwalia, *Reproductive Restraints*, 63–64.

14. Margaret Sanger, "Birth Control in Soviet Russia," n.d., 3 ("Soviet Union," B59, MS Papers, SSC).

15. As Jonathan Zimmerman notes, the voluntary association was the United States' "archetypal political mechanism." Zimmerman, *Too Hot to Handle*, 50.

16. IPPF, "Historical Highlights of Birth Control: Malthus (1798) to Tokyo, Japan (1955)" ("IPPF: Publications, 1955–62" Folder, B40, MS Papers, SSC); Susan Fan, "Hong Kong," in Robinson and Ross, *The Global Family Planning Revolution*, 193.

17. Connelly, *Fatal Misconception*, 80.

NOTES TO PAGES 30–33 > 197

18. "World Foundation," *Around the World: News of Population and Birth Control* 18, 1953/10 (F12, B6, DHB Papers, SSC), 1. See also Vicky Claeys, "Brave and Angry— The Creation and Development of the International Planned Parenthood Federation (IPPF)," *European Journal of Contraception & Reproductive Health Care* 15, no. 2 (2010): 67–76.

19. "Second Report of Our Committee," *ATW* 9, 1952/11 (B6, DHB Papers, SSC), 4.

20. "Progress Reports," *ATW* 60, 1957/12 (B7, DHB Papers, SSC), 4–5.

21. "Mrs. Sanger in London," *ATW* 57, 1957/09 (B7, DHB Papers, SSC), 2.

22. IPPF, "Fourth Report," London, England, 1957/01/01–1959/05/31 (F10, B6, DHB Papers, SSC).

23. On Germany, see IPPF, "Fourth Report," 76; on Jamaica, see Bourbonnais, *Birth Control in the Decolonizing Caribbean*, 193–94.

24. Schoen, *Choice and Coercion*, 33–34.

25. Beth Baron, "The Origins of Family Planning: Aziza Hussein, American Experts, and the Egyptian State," *Journal of Middle East Women's Studies* 4, no. 3 (Fall 2008): 68.

26. Necochea López, "Gambling on the Protestants," 368.

27. Bourbonnais, "'A Grande Causa': Missionários do Planeamento Familiar no Fim do Império [The "Great Cause": Family Planning Missionaries at the End of Empire]," *Ler História* 85 (2024).

28. Rusterholz, "English Women Doctors, Contraception and Family Planning in Transnational Perspective," 159.

29. [Dorothy Brush] to Clarence [Gamble], "Letter," 1958/06/24 (F23, B1, DHB Papers, SSC), 1.

30. Margaret Sanger to T. O. Griessemer, "Letter," 1955/01/06 (F27, B1, DHB Papers, SSC), 1.

31. Sanger to Griessemer, "Letter," 2.

32. "Our First Birthday," *ATW* 11, 1953/01 (B6, DHB Papers, SSC), 4; Margaret Sanger, "Happy Birthday," *ATW* 21, 1954/01 (B6, DHB Papers, SSC), 1.

33. "IPPF Progress," *ATW* 41, 1956/01 (B6, DHB Papers, SSC), 4.

34. "Farewell," *ATW* 50, 1956/12 (B6, DHB Papers, SSC), 4. For a more thorough examination of *ATW*, see Nicole C. Bourbonnais, "The Intimate Labor of Internationalism: Maternalist Humanitarians and the Mid-20th Century Family Planning Movement," *Journal of Global History* 17, no. 3 (November 2022): 515–38.

35. "Malaya," *ATW* 2, 1952/02 (F12, B6, DHB Papers, SSC), 2.

36. María Soledad Zárate Campos and Maricela González Moya, "Planificación Familiar En La Guerra Fría Chilena: Política Sanitaria Y Cooperación Internacional, 1960–1973," *Historia Critica* 55 (January–March 2015): 214; María Carranza, "'In the Name of Forests': Highlights of the History of Family Planning in Costa Rica," *Canadian Journal of Latin American and Caribbean Studies* 35, no. 69 (2010): 130.

37. "Annual Reports," *ATW* 79, 1959/11 (B7, DHB Papers, SSC), 2.

38. Necochea López, *A History of Family Planning in Twentieth-Century Peru*, 44; "Kampala," *ATW* 95, 1961/05 (B7, DHB Papers, SSC), 3.

39. Barbara Cadbury, "Report from the Canadian Federation of Societies for Population Planning," 1964, 1 ("Canada" file, B57, MS Papers, SSC).

40. Connelly, *Fatal Misconception*, 159.

41. "Greece," *ATW* 7, 1952/09 (B6, DHB Papers, SSC), 3.

42. "Copy," 1 ("Europe" File, B57, MS Papers, SSC).

43. Rusterholz, "English Women Doctors, Contraception and Family Planning in Transnational Perspective (1930s–70s)," 154; see Nguyen, "Overpopulation, Racial Degeneracy and Birth Control in French Colonial Vietnam," on French colonial policy.

44. "India," *ATW* 8, 1952/10 (B6, DHB Papers, SSC), 1; "United States," *ATW* 17, 1953/09 (B6, DHB Papers, SSC), 2.

45. Bourbonnais, "The Intimate Labour of Internationalism," 19–21.

46. IPPF, "Fourth Report," London, England, 1957/01/01–1959/05/31 (F10, B6, DHB Papers, SSC), 38.

47. See, for example, Edna R. McKinnon, "List of names of people in Indonesia" (F97, MC325, ERM Papers, SL).

48. "Ceylon," *ATW* 24, 1954/04 (F12, B6, DHB Papers, SSC), 3.

49. IPPF, "Fourth Report," London, England, 1957/01/01–1959/05/31 (F10, B6, DHB Papers, SSC), 89.

50. Ashford, *Development and Women's Reproductive Health in Ghana*, 159.

51. "Burma," 28/11/1958 (File "Burma," B57, MS Papers, SSC).

52. Necochea López, *A History of Family Planning in Twentieth-Century Peru*, 96.

53. Edith M. Gates, "An Exploratory Tour into South America," 1959 [c.] (F19, B7, DHB Papers, SSC), 4.

54. "Germany," *ATW* 15, 1953/05 (F12, B6, DHB Papers, SSC).

55. Pansy K. Belling to Mr. William D. Strong, "Letter," 1968/01/02 (F79, MC325, ERM Papers, SL), 2. On earlier birth control advocacy in Vietnam, see Nguyen, "Overpopulation, Racial Degeneracy and Birth Control in French Colonial Vietnam."

56. Edith M. Gates, "News from the Rhodesias," 1959/11 (F19, B7, DHB Papers, SSC), 1; Adaline Pendleton Satterthwaite, "Diary 1968 (Pakistan)," 3/8/68 (B14, APS Papers, SSC); Adaline Pendleton Satterthwaite, "Diaries, 1972 (Peru and Venezuela)," 11/23/72 (B14, APS Papers, SSC); "Pathfinding in Family Planning for Pathfinder Fund," 5–6 (F559, MC368, SMBG Papers, SL).

57. Huston, *Motherhood by Choice*, 61.

58. "Puerto Rico," *ATW* 98, 1961/10 (B7, DHB Papers, SSC), 2.

59. Family Planning Association of Ceylon, "Eleventh Annual Report 1963–1964," 1964 (F3, B8, DHB Papers, SSC), 44–45.

60. John Morgan, "Anglicanism, Family Planning and Contraception: The Development of a Moral Teaching and Its Ecumenical Implications," *Journal of Anglican Studies* 16, no. 2 (2018): 150.

61. George W. and Barbara Cadbury, "Report on Visit to Manila," 1960/12, 1 ("Philippines" file, B58, MS Papers, SSC).

62. Huston, *Motherhood by Choice*, 135; Taek and John A. Ross Kim, "The Korean Breakthrough," in Robinson and Ross, *The Global Family Planning Revolution*, 179.

63. Necochea López, "Gambling on the Protestants: The Pathfinder Fund and Birth Control in Peru, 1958–1965," 350.

64. Edith M. Gates, "An Exploratory Tour into South America," 1959 [c.] (F19, B7, DHB Papers, SSC), 3.

65. Mercedes Concepcion, interview by Rebecca Sharpless, "Transcript of audio recording, August 17–18, 2004" (PRHOHP, SSC), 22.

66. "Second Annual General Meeting," 1956 ("Belgium" Folder, B57, MS Papers, SSC).

67. "Tokyo Conference," *ATW* 40, 1955/12 (F12, B6, DHB Papers, SSC), 2.

68. El Shakry, "Reproducing the Family," 168.

69. Edna R. McKinnon, "Report of a Third Trip to Indonesia," 27/02–27/08/1963, 2 (F97, MC325, ERM Papers, SL).

70. "Ceylon," *ATW* 29, 1954/11 (F12, B6, DHB Papers, SSC), 2; Darshi Thoradeniya, "Altruism, Welfare, or Development Aid? Swedish Aid for Family Planning in Ceylon, 1958 to 1983," *East Asian Science, Technology and Society* 10, no. 4 (2016): 423–44.

71. Nai Peng Tey, "The Family Planning Program in Peninsular Malaysia," in Robinson and Ross, *The Global Family Planning Revolution*, 259–61.

72. Grace Ebun Delano, interview by Rebecca Sharpless, "Transcript of audio recording, October 7–8, 2003" (PRHOHP, SSC), 27–28.

73. "Uganda," *ATW* 58, 1957/10 (B7, DHB Papers, SSC), 4.

74. Bourbonnais, *Birth Control in the Decolonizing Caribbean*, 123–24.

75. Edith M. Gates, "Special Visit to Nairobi, Kenya," 1959/08/24–09/03 (F19, B7, DHB Papers, SSC), 1.

76. "Clinics," *ATW* 4, 1952/04 (F12, B6, DHB Papers, SSC), 2.

77. Associate members could attend IPPF meetings but were not given representation on the IPPF Council. "IPPF Meetings," *ATW* 60, 1957/12 (B7, DHB Papers, SSC), 8.

78. IPPF, "World List of Family Planning Agencies," 1959/05 (in file "IPPF: Member Lists 1952–62," B40, MS Papers, SSC).

79. The latter moniker was popular in South America, where (as Edris Rice-Wray reported after a tour in 1962) associations explicitly avoided the language of "family planning" and "planned parenthood" to slip under the radar of Catholic opposition, adopting names like "the Committee for the Protection of the Family" or "League for Family Welfare" instead. Edris Rice-Wray to Mrs. Dorothy Brush, "Letter," 1962/08/20 (F18, B2, MS 23, DHB Papers, SSC), 1–2.

80. IPPF, "Fourth Report," London, England, 1957/01/01–1959/05/31 (F10, B6, DHB Papers, SSC).

81. IPPF, "Fourth Report," London, England, 1957/01/01–1959/05/31 (F10, B6, DHB Papers, SSC).

82. Huston, *Motherhood by Choice*, 43, 45.

200 ‹ NOTES TO PAGES 37–44

83. Edna R. McKinnon, "Report for the Far East and Australasian Region of IPPF: Taipei, Taiwan," 26–30/09/1960 (F96, MC325, ERM Papers; SL). See also Sreenivas, *Reproductive Politics and the Making of Modern India*, 102, on the deliberate mobilization of male heads of associations for political purposes.

84. IPPF, "Fourth Report," London, England, 1957/01/01–1959/05/31 (F10, B6, DHB Papers, SSC), 75.

85. Adaline Pendleton Satterthwaite, "Diary, 1969 (New York–Pakistan)," 12/1/69 (B14, APS Papers, SSC).

86. Family Planning Association of Hong Kong, "Sixth Annual Report," 1956, 5 ("Hong Kong" file, B58, MS Papers, SSC).

87. See, for example, "U.S.A.," *ATW* 14, 1953/04 (F12, B6, DHB Papers, SSC), 4; "New Publications," *ATW* 57, 1957/09 (B7, DHB Papers, SSC), 4; Asociacion Mexicana Pro-Bienestar de la Familia, "Bulletin No. 1," 1960/01 (F13, B8, DHB Papers, SSC), 2; Asociacion Mexicana Pro-Bienestar de la Familia, "Annual Report," 1960/02/29 (F13, B8, DHB Papers, SSC), 5; Family Planning Association of China, "Monthly Activity Report," 1964/04 (F4, B8, DHB Papers, SSC), 1; "U.S.A.," *ATW* 14, 1953/04 (F12, B6, DHB Papers, SSC), 4; Asociacion Mexicana Pro-Bienestar de La Familia, "Bulletin No. II," 1960/07/01 (F13, B8, DHB Papers, SSC), 7; Singapore Family Planning Association, "10th Annual Report," 1960, 34 (F671, MC229, MME Papers, SL).

88. Huston, *Motherhood by Choice*, 62.

89. Huston, *Motherhood by Choice*, 62.

90. Wells-Wilbon, "Family Planning for Low-Income African American Families," 338.

91. E. R. McKinnon, "Progress Report No. 2 on the Johore Family Planning Program," 07/02/1961, 2 (F98, MC325, ERM Papers, SL); "Family Planning Scheme on Tebrau Estate," n.d. (F98, MC325, ERM Papers, SL).

92. Sreenivas, *Reproductive Politics and the Making of Modern India*, 102.

93. Bourbonnais, *Birth Control in the Decolonizing Caribbean*, chap. 1.

94. Thoradeniya, "Altruism, Welfare, or Development Aid?," 435.

95. Adaline Pendleton Satterthwaite, "Diary, 1967 (Thailand and Pakistan)," 5/5/67 (B14, APS Papers, SSC).

96. Darshi Thoradeniya, "Birth Control Pill Trials in Sri Lanka: The History and Politics of Women's Reproductive Health (1950–1980)," *Social History of Medicine* 33, no. 1 (2020): 276.

97. Huston, *Motherhood by Choice*, 96.

98. Rusterholz, "English Women Doctors, Contraception and Family Planning in Transnational Perspective (1930s–70s)," 154; Caroline Rusterholz, *Women's Medicine: Sex, Family Planning and British Female Doctors in Transnational Perspective, 1920–70* (Manchester University Press, 2020), 13–17.

99. Rusterholz, *Women's Medicine*, 4.

100. Edris Rice-Wray to Mrs. Dorothy Brush, "Letter," 1960/03/31 (F18, B2, DHB Papers, SSC), 1. For a full analysis of Edris Rice-Wray and the Mexico clinic, see Martha Liliana Espinosa Tavares, "'They Are Coming in So Fast That if We Had Publicity about

the Clinic We Would Be Swamped': Edris Rice-Wray, the First Family Planning Clinic in Mexico (1959), and the Intervention of US-Based Private Foundations," *Journal of Women's History* 34, no. 2 (2022): 76–96.

101. C. P. Blacker to Rufus S. Day Jr., "Letter," 1958/07/05 (F30, B2, MS 23, DHB Papers, SSC), 1.

102. Mrs. O. Djoewari to friends, Letter, 1968/12/31 (F109, MC325, ERM Papers, SL).

103. Huston, *Motherhood by Choice*, 49.

104. Family Planning Association, "The Fifth Annual Report," 09/1957–08/1958, 4–5 ("Ceylon" file, B57, MS Papers, SSC).

105. L. N. J., "Tut-Tut!" *ATW* 72, 1959/02 (B7, DHB Papers, SSC), 2.

106. Edris Rice-Wray to "Letter," 1961/09/29 (F18, B2, MS 23, DHB Papers, SSC), 1.

107. Mario Jaramillo, interview by Rebecca Sharpless, "Transcript of audio recording, July 22–23, 2004" (PRHOHP, SSC), 18–23.

108. Maria Luisa de Marchi, "A Report on the Rendall Gels Distribution in Vibo Valentia (Italy)," 1959/08/12 (F20, B7, DHB Papers, SSC), 23.

109. Huston, *Motherhood by Choice*, 60.

110. Takeuchi-Demirci, *Contraceptive Diplomacy*, 56, 60.

111. Huston, *Motherhood by Choice*, 16.

112. Wilma Dykeman, *Too Many People, Too Little Love: Edna Rankin McKinnon, Pioneer for Birth Control* (Austin, TX: Holt, Rinehart and Winston, 1974), 64, 4.

113. Huston, *Motherhood by Choice*, 52.

114. Dykeman, *Too Many People, Too Little Love*, 69.

115. Quoted in Margaret to Clarence, "Letter," 1958/01/03 (F2865, B182, CG Papers, FACLM).

116. Bourbonnais, "The Intimate Labour of Internationalism," 12.

117. "The World's Population," *ATW* 1, 1952/01 (B6, DHB Papers, SSC), 2.

118. Carranza, "In the Name of Forests."

119. Connelly, *Fatal Misconception*, 163; Bourbonnais, "The Intimate Labour of Internationalism," 13.

120. Sreenivas, *Reproductive Politics and the Making of Modern India*, 111.

121. Huston, *Motherhood by Choice*, 10–23.

122. Mrs. Morain, "Field Report for Mrs Brush by Mrs Morain, Africa," 1959/01–02 (F1, B8, DHB Papers, SSC), 3.

123. "Singapore," *ATW* 33, 1955/03 (B6, DHB Papers, SSC), 3.

124. Family Planning Association of Pakistan, "Report on the First Indian Ocean Regional Conference of the International Planned Parenthood Federation," Lahore, 1962 (F10, B6, DHB Papers, SSC), 97.

125. Family Planning Association of Pakistan, "Report," 141.

126. Zimmerman, *Too Hot to Handle*, 4, 65–69, 90–91. On Swedish efforts to export their vision to the rest of the world, see Annika Berg, "A Suitable Country: The

Relationship between Sweden's Interwar Population Policy and Family Planning in Postindependence India," *Berichte zur Wissenschaftsgeschichte* 33, no. 3 (2010): 297–320.

127. Adaline Pendleton Satterthwaite, "Diary, 1967 (Thailand and Pakistan)," 2/23/67 (B14, APS Papers, SSC).

128. Adaline Pendleton Satterthwaite, "Diary, 1966 (Thailand–Taipei)," 7/20/66 (B14, APS Papers, SSC).

129. Adaline Pendleton Satterthwaite, "Diaries, Jun–Dec 1971 (Pakistan)," 10/19/71 (B14, APS Papers, SSC).

130. Baron, "The Origins of Family Planning," 36.

131. Huston, *Motherhood by Choice*, 100.

132. Mario Jaramillo, interview by Rebecca Sharpless, "Transcript of audio recording, July 22–23, 2004" (PRHOHP, SSC), 5.

133. Jaramillo, interview by Sharpless, 6.

134. Hutson, *Motherhood by Choice*, 46.

135. Patricia Mohammed, "A History of the Family Planning Association of Trinidad and Tobago," 1986 ("Family Planning" File, CGD, UWI), 5.

136. Singapore Family Planning Association, "10th Annual Report," 1960, 36 (F671, MC229, MME Papers, SL).

137. Adaline Pendleton Satterthwaite, "Corr. Family & friends: 1960–64," Letter to Family, 1963/04/14 (B10, APS Papers, SSC).

138. Adaline Pendleton Satterthwaite, "Diary, 1966 (Thailand–Taipei)," 10/1/66 (B14, APS Papers, SSC).

139. Satterthwaite, "Diary, 1966 (Thailand–Taipei)," 4/20/66.

140. Adaline Pendleton Satterthwaite, "Corr. Family & friends: 1960–64," Letter to Family, 4/14/63.

141. Asociacion Mexicana Pro-Bienestar de la Familia, "Annual Report," 1960/02/29 (F13, B8, DHB Papers, SSC), 2. The importance of abortion rates as a critical motivating factor is also stressed by that national-level literature on Latin America. See, for example, Necochea López, *A History of Family Planning in Twentieth Century Peru*; Zárate Campos and González Moya, "Planificación familiar en la *Guerra Fría chilena*"; Espinosa Tavares, "'They Are Coming in So Fast That if We Had Publicity about the Clinic We Would Be Swamped.'"

142. Ayse Akin, "Emergence of the Family Planning Program in Turkey," in Robinson and Ross, *The Global Family Planning Revolution*, 89.

143. Susanne M. Klausen, *Abortion under Apartheid: Nationalism, Sexuality, and Women's Reproductive Rights in South Africa* (Oxford: Oxford University Press, 2015), 19–21.

144. Adaline Pendleton Satterthwaite, "Diaries, 1972 (Peru and Venezuela)," 10/18/72 (B14, APS Papers, SSC).

145. Bourbonnais, *Birth Control in the Decolonizing Caribbean*, 125.

146. Huston, *Motherhood by Choice*, 144.

147. Huston, *Motherhood by Choice*, 144.

148. "Amy Bailey Great Family Planning Pioneer," *JFPA News*, Col. 1I 1970, 12 (J2235, Rare Books and Pamphlets, NLJ), 8.

149. Huston, *Motherhood by Choice*, 24–38; Doris H. Linder, *Crusader for Sex Education: Elise Ottesen-Jensen (1886–1973) in Scandinavia and on the International Scene* (Lanham, MA: University Press of America, 1996).

150. Huston, *Motherhood by Choice*, 49.

151. Huston, *Motherhood by Choice*, 162.

152. Grace Ebun Delano, interview by Rebecca Sharpless, "Transcript of audio recording, October 7–8, 2003" (PRHOHP, SSC), 9.

153. Delano, interview by Sharpless, 2.

154. Delano, interview by Sharpless, 11–12.

155. Delano, interview by Sharpless, 26.

156. Delano, interview by Sharpless, 24–26.

157. Delano, interview by Sharpless, 29.

158. Margaret F. Roots, "Report to Pathfinder Fund: Burma," 1959/12 (F20, B7, DHB Papers, SSC), 2.

159. "Report on the First Indian Ocean Regional Conference of the International Planned Parenthood Federation," Lahore, Pakistan, 1962 (F10, B6, DHB Papers, SSC), 17.

160. Huston, *Motherhood by Choice*, 75.

161. "Birth Control in China," *ATW* 63, 1958/03 (B7, DHB Papers, SSC), 2.

162. "India," *ATW* 42, 1956/02 (B6, DHB Papers, SSC), 4. See also "War and Peace," *ATW* 60, 1957/12 (B7, DHB Papers, SSC), 7; "Italy," *ATW* 93, 1961/03 (B7, DHB Papers, SSC), 3.

163. Family Planning Association of Ceylon, "Eleventh Annual Report 1963–1964," 1964 (F3, B8, DHB Papers, SSC), 39.

164. See, for example, "U.S. National Committee on Maternal Health," *ATW* 39, 1955/11 (F12, B6, DHB Papers, SSC), 3.

165. Mario Jaramillo, interview by Rebecca Sharpless, "Transcript of audio recording, July 22–23, 2004" (PRHOHP, SSC), 4.

166. Huston, *Motherhood by Choice*, 58.

167. Huston, *Motherhood by Choice*, 60.

168. Margaret to Sarah, "Letter," 1965/04/13 (F559, MC368, SMBG Papers, SL).

169. Extract from report, "Written 1961 for YWCA Magazine—Not Published" (F2907, B184, MSC23, CG papers, FACLM), 4.

170. Edna McKinnon to "Pathfinding for the Pathfinder Fund in the Field of Family Planning from the Year 1960–1966," 1971 (F76, ERM Papers, SL), tape 3, 5.

171. "Pathfinding in Family Planning for Pathfinder Fund" (F559, MC368, SMBG Papers, SL), 3.

172. Margaret to Sarah, Letter, 1965/11/22 (F559, MC368, SMBG Papers, SL), 1.

173. Juan Alejandro Lopera López, "Paternidad O Procreación Responsable: Iglesia Católica, Acción Cultural Popular y Control De La Natalidad En Colombia (1964–1978)," *Historia y Sociedad* 31 (July–December 2016): 252–54.

174. Hernán Sanhueza, "Family Planning in Chile: A Tale of the Unexpected," in Robinson and Ross, *The Global Family Planning Revolution*, 113.

175. Necochea López, *A History of Family Planning in Twentieth-Century Peru*, 129–32. See, for example, SSC, Adaline Pendleton Satterthwaite, "Diary, 1967 (Thailand and Pakistan)," 10/6/67, "Diary 1968 (Pakistan)," 2/8/68, "Diary, 1969 (New York–Pakistan)," 12/3/69, "Diaries, 1972 (Peru and Venezuela)," 3/17/72 (B14, APS Papers, SSC).

176. McKinnon, "Pathfinding for the Pathfinder Fund in the Field of Family Planning from the Year 1960–1966," 1971 (F76, ERM Papers, SL), tape 2, 4.

177. Edna R. McKinnon, "Report for Manila, The Philippines," 30/09–09/10, 1960 (F96, ERM Papers, SL), 1.

178. McKinnon, "Pathfinding in Family Planning for Pathfinder Fund" (F559, SMBG Papers, SL), 6.

179. "Thailand," *ATW* 41, 1956/01 (F12, B6, DHB Papers, SSC), 2. See also Burton Benedict, "Mauritius," *ATW* 61, 1958/01 (B7, DHB Papers, SSC), 1; Huston, *Motherhood by Choice*, 61.

180. "IPPF President on BBC," *ATW* 86, 1960/06 (B7, DHB Papers, SSC), 5. See also Elise Ottesen-Jensen, "The President's Message," *ATW* 91, 1961/01 (B7, DHB Papers, SSC), 1.

181. McKinnon, "Pathfinding in Family Planning for Pathfinder Fund" (F559, MC368, SMBG Papers, SL), 4.

182. McKinnon, "Pathfinding for the Pathfinder Fund in the Field of Family Planning from the Year 1960–1966," 1971 (F76, ERM Papers, SL), tape 2, 7.

183. Margaret Sanger, "Happy Birthday," *ATW* 21, 1954/01 (B6, DHB Papers, SSC), 1.

184. "The Conference," *ATW* 18, 1953/10 (B6, DHB Papers, SSC), 4. See also Linder, *Crusader for Sex Education*, 193.

185. "Puerto Rico Conference," *ATW* 36, 1955/06 (B6, DHB Papers, SSC), 2.

186. Bernard Taithe, "Humanitarian Masculinity: Desire, Character and Heroics, 1876–2018," in Esther Möller, Johannes Paulmann, and Katharina Stornig, *Gendering Global Humanitarianism in the 20th Century: Practice, Politics and the Power of Representation* (London: Palgrave Macmillan, 2020), 55.

187. "Flags out for Margaret Sanger," *ATW* 10, 1952/12 (F12, B6, DHB Papers, SSC), 1.

188. "Margaret Sanger," *ATW* 12, 1953/02 (F12, B6, DHB Papers, SSC), 2.

189. "Sweden," *ATW* 3, 1952/03 (B6, DHB Papers, SSC), 2; "Poland," *ATW* 82, 1960/02 (B7, DHB Papers, SSC), 3; Barbara Cadbury, "Conference in the Sun," *ATW* 96, 1961/06 (B7, DHB Papers, SSC), 2.

190. "The Conference," *ATW* 18, 1953/10 (F12, B6, DHB Papers, SSC), 2.

191. "Bombay Conference," *ATW* 13, 1953/03 (F12, B6, DHB Papers, SSC), 2.

192. Sreenivas, *Reproductive Politics and the Making of Modern India*, 94.

193. "Ceylon," *ATW* 90, 1960/12 (B7, DHB Papers, SSC), 2; Margaret F. Roots to Mr. Kabir, "Letter," 1959/05/05 (F20, B7, DHB Papers, SSC), 1; Sarah [Gamble], *Letter*, ed. Dorothy (1960/02/11) (F13, B8, DHB Papers, SSC), 1; "Bombay Conference," *ATW* 13, 1953/03 (B6, DHB Papers, SSC), 2.

NOTES TO PAGES 53–56 › 205

194. Dykeman, *Too Many People, Too Little Love*, 146–47.

195. "Thailand," *ATW* 4, 1952/04 (B6, DHB Papers, SSC), 1; McKinnon, "Pathfinding for the Pathfinder Fund in the Field of Family Planning from the Year 1960–1966," 1971 (F76, ERM Papers, SL), tape 2, 9.

196. Dorothy H. Brush to Mrs. Lloyd Morain, Letter, 1959/05 (F1, B8, DHB Papers, SSC), 1.

197. "Morocco," *ATW* 98, 1961/10 (B7, DHB Papers, SSC), 2.

198. Dorothy Brush to Tze-kuan Shu Khan, "Letter," 1959/05/12 (F6, B2, DHB Papers, SSC), 1.

199. Dorothy Brush to Mrs. Shane [Ma Mya Thein], "Letter," 1959/10/06 (F27, B2, DHB Papers, SSC), 1.

200. Dorothy Brush to Vittoria [Olivetti], "Letter," 1958/02/26 (F14, B2, DHB Papers, SSC), 1; Maria Luisa de Marchi to Dr. Clarence J. Gamble, "Letter," 1959/04/06 (F23, B1, DHB Papers, SSC); [Dorothy Brush] to Rufus [Day], "Letter," 1962/01/18 (F17, B1, DHB Papers, SSC), 1.

201. Dorothy Brush to Purai, "Letter," 1960/11/18 (F10, B1, DHB Papers, SSC), 1.

202. Dorothy Brush to Sai Poh, "Letter," 1962/07/12 (F26, B1, DHB Papers, SSC), 1.

203. Dykeman, *Too Many People, Too Little Love*, 203.

204. Ilaria Scaglia, *The Emotions of Internationalism: Feeling International Cooperation in the Alps in the Interwar Period* (Oxford: Oxford University Press, 2019), 3.

205. "The Conference," *ATW* 18, 1953/10 (B6, DHB Papers, SSC), 4.

206. See, for example, "Expressions of Opinion About the Bulletin," 1952/02/25, 1952/05/17, 1952/07/11, 1952/07/29, 1952/09/28, 1953/01/19, 1953/03/24, 1953/05/28, and 1953/06/15 (F11, B6, DHB Papers, SSC).

207. Ahluwalia, *Reproductive Restraints*, 95.

208. Klausen, *Race, Maternity, and the Politics of Birth Control in South Africa*, 152.

209. McKinnon, "Pathfinding for the Pathfinder Fund in the Field of Family Planning from the Year 1960–1966," 1971 (F76, ERM Papers, SL), tape 3, 12–13.

210. Extract from report, "Written 1961 for YWCA Magazine—Not Published" (F2907, B184, CG Papers, FACLM).

211. See, for example, Jean Allman, "Making Mothers: Missionaries, Medical Officers and Women's Work in Colonial Asante, 1924–1945," *History Workshop* 38 (1994): 23–47; Anna Davin, "Imperialism and Motherhood," *History Workshop* 5 (Spring 1998): 9–65; Anne-Emmanuelle Birn, "Skirting the Issue: Women and International Health in Historical Perspective," *American Journal of Public Health* 89, no. 3 (March 1999): 399–407; Susan Pedersen, "The Maternalist Moment in British Colonial Policy: The Controversy over 'Child Slavery' in Hong Kong 1917–1941," *Past & Present* 171, no. 1 (2001): 161–202; Lara Putnam, "Global Child-Saving, Transatlantic Maternalism, and the Pathologization of Caribbean Childhood, 1930s–1940s," *Atlantic Studies* 11, no. 4 (October 2014): 491–514.

212. Dorothy Brush, "Keynote," *ATW* 6, 1952/06 (B6, DHB Papers, SSC), 1.

213. "Report of the Hon. Adviser for Field Work Services," c. 1958 (F18, B7, DHB Papers, SSC), 2.

214. Dorothy H. Brush to Professor St. Clair Drake, "Letter," 1959/05/23 (F1, B8, DHB Papers, SSC), 1.

215. Dorothy Brush to Edris, "Letter," 1959/07/29 (F18, B2, MS 23, DHB Papers, SSC).

216. "Highlights of the Middle East Tour," 1956/05/11 (F2894, B184, CG Papers, FACLM).

217. Edith to Clarence, Letter, 1957/10/14 (F2902, B184, CG Papers, FACLM), 1.

218. E. R. McKinnon, "Jordan Report No. I," 1966/01/02–14 (F101, ERM Papers, SL), 1.

219. McKinnon, "Jordan Report No. I," 1.

220. "Pathfinding in Family Planning for Pathfinder Fund" (F559, SMBG Papers, SL), 5.

221. "Haiti," *ATW* 8, 1952/10 (B6, DHB Papers, SSC), 3; "African Journey," *ATW* 26, 1954/06 (B6, DHB Papers, SSC), 2; "Islands," *ATW* 38, 1955/10 (B6, DHB Papers, SSC), 3.

222. Mrs. K. K. Goh to Dorothy, "Letter," c. 1950s/07/23 (F16, B8, DHB Papers, SSC), 1.

223. Pip (C. P. B.) to Dorothy, "Letter," 1960/03/20 (F12, B1, DHB Papers, SSC), 2.

224. Dorothy Brush to Rufus [Day], "Letter," 1962/01/18 (F17, B1, DHB Papers, SSC), 1.

225. Brush to Gamble, "Letter," 1958/06/24 (F23, B1, DHB Papers, SSC), 2.

226. Edris to Mrs. Dorothy Brush, "Letter," 1959/07/11 (F13, B8, DHB Papers, SSC), 1.

227. Edris to Brush, "Letter," 1.

228. Rice-Wray to Brush, "Letter," 1962/08/20 (F18, B2, DHB Papers, SSC), 2.

229. Rice-Wray to Brush, "Letter," 2.

230. Espinosa Tavares, "'They Are Coming in So Fast That if We Had Publicity about the Clinic We Would Be Swamped,'" 82.

231. Brush to Edris, "Letter," 1959/07/29 (F18, B2, DHB Papers, SSC), 1.

232. Dorothy Brush to Tze-kuan Shu Kan, "Letter," 1959/11/07 (F6, B2, DHB Papers, SSC), 1.

233. Family Planning Association of China to Mrs. Charles F. Brush, "Letter," 1959/11/22 (F4, B8, DHB Papers, SSC), 1–2.

234. On their continued engagement later, see Dorothy Brush to Sai Poh (Mrs. Goh Kok Kee), "Letter," 1960/11/21 (F26, B1, MS 23, DHB Papers, SSC), 1.

235. McKinnon, "Pathfinding for the Pathfinder Fund in the Field of Family Planning from the Year 1960–1966," 1971 (F76, ERM Papers, SL), tape 1, 11.

236. Edna to Bernadine and Charles, "Letter," 1965/12/29 (F104, ERM Papers, SL).

237. Hanna Rizk to Mrs. Dorothy Brush, "Letter," 1955/011/10 (F19, B2, DHB Papers, SSC).

238. Clarence to Edith, Letter, 1955/12/02 (F2895, B184, CG papers, FACLM).

239. Clarence to Edith, Letter.

NOTES TO PAGES 59–61 › 207

240. Edna R. McKinnon, "The Inter Report No. II of Second Trip to Indonesia," 01–17/06/1962 (F97, ERM Papers, SL), 4.

241. Margaret to Helen, Letter, 1956/02/27 (F2862, B182, CG Papers, FACLM).

242. Margaret to "Folks," Letter, 1956/11 (F2862, B182, CG Papers, FACLM), 1.

243. Margaret to "Folks," Letter, 1.

244. Margaret to "Folks," Letter, 2.

245. Roots, "Summary of What It Takes to Get 3 Reels Film Released from Customs in Dacca," 1959 (F20, B7, DHB Papers, SSC).

246. "Margaret Roots," n.d. (F559, SMBG Papers, SL), 2–3.

247. Extract from report, "Written 1961 for YWCA Magazine—Not Published" (F2907, B184, CG Papers, FACLM), 3.

248. Dorothy Brush to John, "Letter," 1969/07/06 (F4, B2, DHB Papers, SSC), 2.

249. McKinnon, "Pathfinding for the Pathfinder Fund in the Field of Family Planning from the Year 1960–1966," 1971 (F76, ERM Papers, SL), tape 3, 8–9.

250. McKinnon, "Pathfinding for the Pathfinder Fund," tape 3, 8–9.

251. McKinnon, "Pathfinding for the Pathfinder Fund," tape 3, 8–9.

252. Edna R. McKinnon, "Report No II on Saudi Arabia," 1966/01/28–02/17 (F101, ERM Papers, SL), 1.

253. Edith M. Gates, "An Exploratory Tour into South America," c. 1959 (F19, B7, DHB Papers, SSC), 2.

254. Margaret F. Roots, "Report to Pathfinder Fund: Burma," 1959/11 (F20, B7, DHB Papers, SSC), 2.

255. Margaret to Clarence, Letter, 1957/03/01 (F2863, B182, CG Papers, FACLM).

256. Schoen, *Choice and Coercion*, 220.

257. Edith M. Gates, "Progress Report, Lagos, Nigeria," 1959/04, 2; Edith M. Gates, "Ibadan, Nigeria—Visit," 1959/04/20–27 (F19, B7, DHB Papers, SSC), 1.

258. Edna R. McKinnon, "Report of Visit to Liberia No. I," 1964/03/05–24 (F102, ERM Papers, SL), 1.

259. Edna McKinnon, "Report to F.E.A.R.," 1960/10/23–27 (F96, ERM Papers, SL); Edna R. McKinnon, "Report of Second Trip to Ethiopia," 1965/04/01–06/02 (F106, ERM Papers, SL).

260. "Amy Bailey Great Family Planning Pioneer," *JFPA News* 1, December 1970 (J2235, Rare Books and Pamphlets, NLJ), 6.

261. Fred T. Sai, interview by Deborah McFarlane, "Transcript of audio recording, March 11, 2004" (PRHOHP, SSC), 34.

262. See, for example, Amy Kaler, "A Threat to the Nation and a Threat to the Men: The Banning of Depo-Provera in Zimbabwe, 1981," *Journal of Southern African Studies* 24, no. 2 (June 1998): 347–76; Laura Briggs, "Discourses of 'Forced Sterilization' in Puerto Rico."

208 ‹ NOTES TO PAGES 63–71

CHAPTER TWO

1. I have used a pseudonym for the patient to protect privacy. 1/4/108/645, MFC, NAJ.

2. Bourbonnais, *Birth Control in the Decolonizing Caribbean*, chap. 3.

3. Farquharson to How-Martyn, "Letter," 1939/12/29 (4/108/1315, MFC, NAJ).

4. May Farquharson to Mrs. Kennedy, "Letter," 1940/05/03 (4/108/945, MFC, NAJ).

5. Farquharson to Mrs. How-Martyn, "Letter," 1939/01/04, 1940/06/17 (4/108/1315, MFC, NAJ); these disparaging opinions also come out in other letters in this file.

6. See Bourbonnais, *Birth Control in the Decolonizing Caribbean*, chap. 1.

7. Bourbonnais, *Birth Control in the Decolonizing Caribbean*, 30–75.

8. Sonja A. Sinclair and Barbara Boland, "Characteristics of the Population," in *Recent Population Movements in Jamaica* (Kingston, Jamaica: Cicred Series, 1974), 17.

9. Henrice Altink, *Destined for a Live of Service: Defining African-Jamaican Womanhood, 1865–1938* (Manchester and New York: Manchester University Press, 2011).

10. Cohen, "Private Lives in Public Spaces," 10.

11. "Poland," *ATW* 74, 1959/04 (B7, DHB Papers, SSC), 7.

12. "Great Britain," *ATW* 3, 1952/03 (F12, B6, DHB Papers, SSC), 3.

13. "U.S.A.," *ATW* 34, 1955/04 (F12, B6, DHB Papers, SSC), 3.

14. See, for example, Letter, May Farquharson to British Drug Houses, 24 October 1953 (4/108/1095, MFC, NAJ), 1; Nurse Campbell, "Report on my Visit and Work at Spaldings from June 4th to the 13th 1945" (4/108/832, MFC, NAJ).

15. "Singapore," *ATW*; International Planned Parenthood Federation, 44, 1956/04 (F12, B6, DHB Papers, SSC), 2. See also "Hong Kong," *ATW* 66, 1958/06 (B7, DHB Papers, SSC), 6; Familia, "Annual Report," 1960/02/29 (F13, B8, DHB Papers, SSC), 1; Huston, *Motherhood by Choice*, 101; Klausen, *Race, Maternity, and the Politics of Birth Control in South Africa*, 102.

16. "Fertility Control in Africa," *ATW* 61, 1958/01 (B7, DHB Papers, SSC), 3; "Kenya," Morain, "Field Report for Mrs Brush by Mrs Morain, Africa," 1959/01–02 (F1, B8, DHB Papers, SSC), 1; Fred T. Sai, interview by Deborah McFarlane, "Transcript of audio recording, March 11, 2004" (PRHOHP, SSC), 32–33.

17. Gordon, *The Moral Property of Women*, 18. See also McLaren and McLaren, *The Bedroom and the State*, 18.

18. Gordon, *The Moral Property of Women*, 21.

19. "Madras," *ATW* 13, 1953/03 (F12, B6, DHB Papers, SSC), 3; Grace Ebun Delano, interview by Rebecca Sharpless, "Transcript of audio recording, October 7–8, 2003" (PRHOHP, SSC), 34–36; "I.P.P.F. Contacts and Some Selected Names from Miss Gates's Reports," 1957/07/11 (F9, B1, MS 23, DHB Papers, SSC), 4.

20. Jamaica Family Planning League, "Marital Status of Patients," 1942, 10 (4/108/2107, MFC, NAJ).

21. Gordon, *The Moral Property of Women*, 223.

NOTES TO PAGES 71–74 › 209

22. Necochea López, *A History of Family Planning in Twentieth-Century Peru*, 83.

23. Roots, "Report to Pathfinder Fund: Burma," 1959/11 (F20, B7, DHB Papers, SSC), 2.

24. Edris Rice-Wray, "Report on Trip to El Salvador, Honduras, Costa Rica and Guatemala in the Interest of Planned Parenthood," 1960/04 (F21, B7, DHB Papers, SSC), 1.

25. Dorothy Brush, "The Masses Are People," *ATW* 2, 1952/02 (F12, B6, DHB Papers, SSC), 1.

26. May Farquharson to M. Houghton, "Letter," 1952/05/27 (4/107/2102-3, MFC, NAJ).

27. "France," *ATW* 5, 1952/05 (F12, B6, DHB Papers, SSC), 3.

28. "Research," *ATW* 30, 1954/12 (F12, B6, DHB Papers, SSC), 1.

29. Bourbonnais, *Birth Control in the Decolonizing Caribbean*, 141.

30. Klausen, *Abortion under Apartheid*, 39.

31. Gordon, *The Moral Property of Women*, 16–17.

32. Gordon, *The Moral Property of Women*, 26; McLaren and McLaren, *The Bedroom and the State*, 32–37; Necochea López, *A History of Family Planning in Twentieth-Century Peru*, 67.

33. "Borneo," *ATW* 37, 1955/09 (F12, B6, DHB Papers, SSC), 3.

34. Necochea López, *A History of Family Planning in Twentieth-Century Peru*, 83.

35. "Borneo," *ATW* 37, 1955/09 (F12, B6, DHB Papers, SSC), 3.

36. Klausen, *Abortion under Apartheid*, 50.

37. Brush, "The Masses Are People," 1.

38. Ahluwalia, *Reproductive Restraints*, 61.

39. Linder, *Crusader for Sex Education*, 186.

40. Dorothy Brush, Letter to "My Dear Elliot," 1960/09/02 (F18, B8, DHB Papers, SSC). On other concerns over Emko, see Löwy, "Defusing the Population Bomb in the 1950s," 589.

41. Brush to Day, "Letter," 1962/01/18 (F17, B1, DHB Papers, SSC), 1.

42. Margaret F. Roots, "Report to Pathfinder Fund," 1959/06 (F9, B8, DHB Papers, SSC), 1; Roots, "Report to Pathfinder Fund: Burma," 1959/11 (F20, B7, DHB Papers, SSC), 1.

43. Necochea López, "Gambling on the Protestants," 356–57.

44. "National Organization," 5–6 ("IPPF General, 1952–58" Folder, B40, MS Papers, SSC).

45. E. R. McKinnon, "Interim Report for the Pathfinder Fund," 14/07/1961 (F97, ERM Papers, SL), 1.

46. Edna R. McKinnon, "Report of a Trip to Indonesia," 26/06–22/08, 1961 (F97, ERM Papers, SL), 1.

47. Necochea López, "Gambling on the Protestants," 360–61.

48. Edith How-Martyn to May, Letter, 1939/05/14 (4/108/1315, MFC, NAJ), 1.

49. Edith How-Martyn to May, Letter, 1939/04/23 (4/108/1315, MFC, NAJ), 2.

210 ‹ NOTES TO PAGES 75–79

50. J. L. Varma to Sir Arthur Farquharson, 1938/07/24 (4/108/1447, MFC, NAJ).

51. Farquharson to Society of Cultural Relations with Soviet Russia, "Letter" 1938/07/01 (4/108/1339, MFC, NAJ).

52. See "Makers of Contraceptives (File)," 4/108/912-974; Director, The British Drug Houses Ltd., to Miss May Farquharson, "Letter," 1953, 01.28 (4/108/1174, MFC, NAJ).

53. Clinic balance sheets (4/108/2002, MFC, NAJ). See also "Posted to Mrs. Allwood, Vermont, Chapelton," 1941/11/29 (4/108/614, MFC, NAJ).

54. "Confidential: Advice to Mothers on Birth Control" (4/108/1187, MFC, NAJ), 1.

55. "Confidential: Advice to Mothers on Birth Control" (4/108/1187, MFC, NAJ), 1–7. See also "Contraceptive Sponges," n.d. (4/108/1076, MFC, NAJ); "An Improvised Method of Using Volpar Paste," n.d. (4/108/1079, MFC, NAJ); and "Hygienic Methods of Family Limitation," n.d. (4/108/1179, MFC, NAJ).

56. Klausen, *Race, Maternity, and the Politics of Birth Control in South Africa*, 111.

57. "Clinics," *ATW* 4, 1952/04 (F12, B6, DHB Papers, SSC), 3.

58. Farquharson to ANC Lieut. Colonel B. L. Raina, "Letter," 1952/08/23 (4/108/1067, MFC, NAJ).

59. Farquharson to Messrs. Holland-Rantos Company Mrs. Kennedy, Inc., "Letter," 1939/06/03 (4/108/950, MFC, NAJ).

60. "Malaya," *ATW* 2, 1952/02 (F12, B6, DHB Papers, SSC), 2.

61. Edna McKinnon, "Report to F.E.A.R.," 23–27/10/1960 (F96, MC325, ERM Papers, SL).

62. Robinson, "The Evolution of Population Policies and Programs in the Arab Republic of Egypt," 21.

63. "Towards Personal Merdeka," *ATW* 55, 1957/05 (B7, DHB Papers, SSC), 2.

64. "Big News from Hong Kong," *ATW* 51, 1957/01 (B7, DHB Papers, SSC), 4.

65. Family Planning Association of Hong Kong, "Quarterly Bulletin," 1960/06 (F8, B8, DHB Papers, SSC), 5.

66. Espinosa Tavares, "'They Are Coming in So Fast That if We Had Publicity about the Clinic We Would Be Swamped,'" 85.

67. Cohen, "Private Lives in Public Spaces," 98–99.

68. Takeuchi-Demirci, *Contraceptive Diplomacy*, 46.

69. "Report on the First Indian Ocean Regional Conference of the International Planned Parenthood Federation," Lahore, Pakistan, 1962 (F10, B6, DHB Papers, SSC), 98.

70. Asociacion Mexicana Pro-Bienestar de la Familia, "Bulletin No. 1," 1960/01 (F13, B8, DHB Papers, SSC), 1.

71. Familia, "Annual Report," 1960/02/29 (F13, B8, DHB Papers, SSC), 5.

72. Family Planning Association of China, "Monthly Activity Report," 1963/09 (F4, B8, DHB Papers, SSC), 2.

73. Adaline Pendleton Satterthwaite, "Diary 1966 (Thailand and Taipei)," 3/10/66 (B14, APS Papers, SSC).

74. Sarah Lewis to Dr. Gamble, "Letter," 1960/12/31 (F21, B7, DHB Papers, SSC), 1.

NOTES TO PAGES 79–83 › 211

75. Nefissa Hussein Eissa, "Family Planning in Egypt," *Journal of Family Welfare* 3 (1957/03): 2.

76. Family Planning Association of Ceylon, "Thirteenth Annual Report," 1965–66 (F3, B8, DHB Papers, SSC), 9.

77. "Finland," *ATW* 73, 1959/03 (B7, DHB Papers, SSC), 2.

78. "Indonesia," *ATW* 72, 1959/02 (B7, DHB Papers, SSC), 3.

79. Baron, "The Origins of Family Planning," 39.

80. "Family Planning Association of China," 1965/06 ("China" File 4/4, B57, MS Papers, SSC), 1–4.

81. Family Planning Association of Singapore, "Ninth Annual Report," 1958/01/01–1958/12/31 ("FPA Singapore Annual Reports" File, B58, MS Papers, SSC), 32.

82. "Switzerland," *ATW* 3, 1952/03 (F12, B6, DHB Papers, SSC), 4.

83. "Northern Rhodesia," *ATW* 70, 1958/12 (B7, DHB Papers, SSC), 5.

84. Ceylon, "Eleventh Annual Report 1963–1964," 1964 (F3, B8, DHB Papers, SSC), 6.

85. Familia, "Bulletin No. II," 1960/07/01 (F13, B8, DHB Papers, SSC), 4.

86. Barbara Cadbury, "Report from the Canadian Federation of Societies for Population Planning," 1964 ("Canada" file, B57, MS Papers, SSC), 1.

87. "New Zealand," *ATW* 21, 1954/01 (F12, B6, DHB Papers, SSC), 4.

88. Manon Parry, *Broadcasting Birth Control*, 85–86.

89. Bourbonnais, *Birth Control in the Decolonizing Caribbean*, 153–71.

90. IPPF, "Fifth Report: 1st June, 1959–31st December, 1961," 1961, 12.31 (4/108/564, MFC, NAJ), 11.

91. IPPF, "Fourth Report," London, England, 1957/01/01–1959/05/31 (F10, B6, DHB Papers, SSC), 79.

92. Hari Sen to Mrs. G. J. Watumull, "Letter," 1959/11/26 (F9, B8, DHB Papers, SSC), 1.

93. "Hong Kong," *ATW* 95, 1961/05 (B7, DHB Papers, SSC), 3.

94. Violet Allwood, "Letter to the Editor: The Population Problem," *Daily Gleaner*, October 30, 1940, 8.

95. "Egypt," *ATW* 41, 1956/01 (F12, B6, DHB Papers, SSC), 2. See also "Denmark," *ATW* 14, 1953/04 (F12, B6, DHB Papers, SSC), 3; "Burma: Mrs. Cadbury Reports," *ATW* 94, 1961/04 (B7, DHB Papers, SSC), 2; Roots, "Report to Pathfinder Fund: Burma," 1959/11 (F20, B7, DHB Papers, SSC), 1.

96. George W. and Barbara Cadbury, "Report on Visit to Burma," 1951/02 (File "Burma," B57, MS Papers, SSC).

97. FPATT, "25 Years of Family Planning in Trinidad and Tobago," *FPA Bulletin*, September 1981 (WI Serial HQ766.5 T8 A1 F796 B9/C, AJL, UWI), 1.

98. "Italy," *ATW* 64, 1958/04 (B7, DHB Papers, SSC), 3.

99. "African Journey," *ATW* 26, 1954/06 (F12, B6, DHB Papers, SSC), 2.

100. Edith M. Gates, "An Exploratory Tour into South America," 1959 [c.] (F19, B7, DHB Papers, SSC), 4.

101. "Need," *ATW* 4, 1952/04 (B6, DHB Papers, SSC), 3.

102. "Italy," *ATW* 49, 1956/11 (F12, B6, DHB Papers, SSC), 3.

103. "Need," *ATW* 4, 1952/04 (B6, DHB Papers, SSC), 3.

104. Letter to Dr. Mendoza, 1932/10/31 (in file "Mexico," B58, MS Papers, SSC).

105. "Ceylon," *ATW* 24, 1954/04 (F12, B6, DHB Papers, SSC), 3.

106. "The Family Planning Association of Winnipeg," 1960/04/01–31/03/1961 ("Canada" file, B57, MS Papers, SSC), 2.

107. Singapore Family Planning Association, "10th Annual Report," 1960 (F671, MC229, MME Papers, SL), 26.

108. "Union of South Africa," *ATW* 30, 1954/12 (F12, B6, DHB Papers, SSC), 4.

109. "Union of South Africa," 4.

110. "Birth of International Planned Parenthood Federation," *ATW* 11, 1953/01 (F12, B6, DHB Papers, SSC), 1.

111. "Birth of International Planned Parenthood Federation," 1.

112. Sarah to Dorothy, "Letter," 1960/02/11 (F13, B8, DHB Papers, SSC), 1.

113. George and Barbara Cadbury, "Report on Visit to Indonesia," 12/1960 (F97, ERM Papers, SL), 18.

114. "The Old Man," *ATW* 32, 1955/02 (F12, B6, DHB Papers, SSC), 1.

115. China, "Monthly Activity Report," 1963/09 (F4, B8, DHB Papers, SSC), 1.

116. Bourbonnais, *Birth Control in the Decolonizing Caribbean*, 132–46.

117. McLaren and McLaren, *The Bedroom and the State*, 24–27.

118. Jadwiga E. Pieper Mooney, *The Politics of Motherhood: Maternity and Women's Rights in Twentieth-Century Chile* (Pittsburgh: University of Pittsburgh Press, 2009), 54–55.

119. MacNamara, *Birth Control and American Modernity*, 94.

120. S. E. Duff, "'Dear Mrs Brown': Social Purity, Sex Education and the Women's Christian Temperance Union in Early Twentieth Century South Africa," *Social History* 45, no. 4 (2020): 476–79.

121. Cohen, "Private Lives in Public Spaces," 111.

122. Jamaica Family Life Project, "Which One?," Kingston, JA: The Gleaner Co., Ltd., 1956 (4/108/1898, MFC, NAJ).

123. Lewis Walsley, "China," *ATW* 59, 1957/11 (B7, DHB Papers, SSC), 2.

124. Ashford, *Development and Women's Reproductive Health in Ghana*, 175.

125. "Let Others Take Note," *ATW* 87, 1960/09 (B7, DHB Papers, SSC), 4.

126. Sreenivas, *Reproductive Politics and the Making of Modern India*, 194.

127. "Jamaica," *ATW* 23, 1954/03 (F12, B6, DHB Papers, SSC), 4.

128. "Puerto Rico," *ATW* 31, 1955/01 (F12, B6, DHB Papers, SSC), 4.

129. "Propaganda Over the Air," *ATW* 55, 1957/05 (B7, DHB Papers, SSC), 3.

130. Family Planning Association of China, "Monthly Activity Report," 1963/01 (F4, B8, DHB Papers, SSC), 5.

131. "Family Planning Songs," n.d. (4/108/1300, MFC, NAJ).

NOTES TO PAGES 88–91 › 213

132. "Operation Calypso," *ATW* 66, 1958/06 (B7, DHB Papers, SSC), 3.

133. "Films," *ATW* 70, 1958/12 (B7, DHB Papers, SSC), 8.

134. "Leaflets," *ATW* 25, 1954/05 (F12, B6, DHB Papers, SSC), 4.

135. "Leaflets," 4. See also "Ceylon," *ATW* 29, 1954/11 (F12, B6, DHB Papers, SSC), 2; Edith M. Gates, "Progress Report on Zanzibar," 1959/06/11–15 (F19, B7, DHB Papers, SSC), 2.

136. Gates, "Progress Report on Zanzibar," 1959/06/11–15 (F19, B7, DHB Papers, SSC), 2.

137. "Filed Activity Report: Family Planning Association of China," 1962/06 (F4, B8, DHB Papers, SSC), 4–5.

138. "Booklets," *ATW* 67, 1958/09 (B7, DHB Papers, SSC), 4.

139. Ceylon, "Eleventh Annual Report 1963–1964," 1964 (F3, B8, DHB Papers, SSC), 9.

140. "Family Planning Films," *ATW* 3, 1952/03 (F12, B6, DHB Papers, SSC), 4.

141. Edna R. McKinnon, "The Inter Report No. II of Second Trip to Indonesia," 01–17/06/1962 (F97, ERM Papers, SL), 4.

142. Ministry of Health Singapore, "Family Planning Handbook for Speakers and Lay Workers," c. 1960 (F671, MME Papers, SL), 1.

143. Ministry of Health Singapore, "Family Planning Handbook," 2.

144. Ministry of Health Singapore, "Family Planning Handbook," 7.

145. Ministry of Health Singapore, "Family Planning Handbook," 6, 13.

146. Ministry of Health Singapore, "Family Planning Handbook," 7.

147. Zimmerman, *Too Hot to Handle*, 108.

148. Sylvie Burgnard, "The Family Planning Service and the Pill in Geneva (1965–1980): A Step Towards Women's Emancipation?," *The History of the Family* 20, no. 1 (2014): 26.

149. Sharpless, "Population Science, Private Foundations, and Development Aid: The Transformation of Demographic Knowledge in the United States, 1945–1965," 187–88. See also Whitworth, *Feminism and International Relations*, 80, 83; Sreenivas, *Reproductive Politics and the Making of Modern India*, 166–67.

150. Planned Parenthood Movement in the Philippines, "Let Us Plan for Healthy Happy Children," cover page (F260, EHM Papers, SL).

151. Planned Parenthood Movement in the Philippines, "Let Us Plan for Healthy Happy Children," 2.

152. Whitworth, *Feminism and International Relations*, 94.

153. See, for example, Gordon, *The Moral Property of Women*, 242–43.

154. Rusterholz, *Women's Medicine*, 127.

155. Eunjoo Cho, "Making the 'Modern' Family: The Discourse of Sexuality in the Family Planning Program in South Korea," *Sexualities* 19, no. 7 (2016): 802–18.

156. Parry, *Broadcasting Birth Control*, 3.

157. Sreenivas, *Reproductive Politics and the Making of Modern India*, 171.

214 ‹ NOTES TO PAGES 91–93

158. Ginsburg and Rapp, "Introduction," 6.

159. MacNamara, *Birth Control and American Modernity*, 28–29.

160. Connelly, *Fatal Misconception*, 257; see also Sreenivas, *Reproductive Politics and the Making of Modern India*, 185.

161. Leslie K. Dwyer, "Spectacular Sexuality: Nationalism, Development and the Politics of Family Planning in Indonesia," in *Gender Ironies of Nationalism: Sexing the Nation*, ed. Tamar Mayer (London and New York: Routledge, 2000), 43–44.

162. "Report on the First Indian Ocean Regional Conference of the International Planned Parenthood Federation," Lahore, Pakistan, 1962 (F10, B6, DHB Papers, SSC), 88.

163. Bourbonnais, *Birth Control in the Decolonizing Caribbean*, 156.

164. Bourbonnais, *Birth Control in the Decolonizing Caribbean*, 155.

165. Fan, "Hong Kong: Evolution of the Family Planning Program," 197.

166. Singapore Family Planning Association, "10th Annual Report," 1960 (F671, MME Papers, SL), 37.

167. "Family Planning Scheme on Tebrau Estate," n.d. (F98, ERM Papers, SL), 1.

168. Takeuchi-Demirci, *Contraceptive Diplomacy*, 173.

169. "More News from Africa," *ATW* 79, 1959/11 (B7, DHB Papers, SSC), 1.

170. Maria Luisa de Marchi to Mr. Clarence J. Gamble, "Letter," 1959/08/12 (F20, B7, DHB Papers, SSC), 1.

171. C. V. Lawrence, "Report on My Visit to the Creche" (4/108/1297, MFC, NAJ).

172. Federation, "Fifth Report: 1st June, 1959–31st December, 1961," 1961/12/31 (4/108/564, MFC, NAJ), 11.

173. Farquharson to Executive Secretary Mrs. Gasperro, I.P.P.F., "Letter," 1961/10/24 (4/108/2017, MFC, NAJ).

174. "Barbados," *ATW* 105, 1962/05 (B7, DHB Papers, SSC), 2.

175. Federation, "Fifth Report: 1st June, 1959–31st December, 1961," 1961/12/31 (4/108/564, MFC, NAJ), 11.

176. "A Three Month Report of the Pathfinder Fund Project in Johore," 02–04/1961 (F98, ERM Papers, SL), 2.

177. Singapore Family Planning Association, "10th Annual Report," 1960 (F671, MME Papers, SL), 36.

178. "Results of an experimental service programme in family planning conducted by the Johore Family Planning Association in the District of Johore, Bahru," 01/02/1061–01/02/1962 (F97, MC325, ERM Papers, SL), 2.

179. Barbara Cadbury, "Warsaw," *ATW* 107, 1962/09 (B7, DHB Papers, SSC), 4.

180. Adaline Pendleton Satterthwaite, "Diaries, 1972 (Peru and Venezuela)," 6/23/72 (B14, APS Papers, SSC).

181. Simon Frazer to Vera [Houghton], "Letter," 1959/02/08 (F2, B2, MS 23, DHB Papers, SSC), 1.

NOTES TO PAGES 93–95 › 215

182. Jamaica Family Planning League, "Perseverance in Attendance at Clinic, Kingston, May 5, 1939 to May 9, 1955," 1955/05/09 (4/108/2106, MFC, NAJ).

183. Ceylon, "Thirteenth Annual Report," 1965–66 (F3, B8, DHB Papers, SSC), 22; Klausen, *Race, Maternity, and the Politics of Birth Control in South Africa*, 93; MacNamara, *Birth Control and American Modernity*, 111; Edna R. McKinnon, "Report to F.E.A.R," 23–27/10/1960 (F96, ERM Papers, SL).

184. Edith Gates, "Progress Report on Zanzibar," 1959/06/11–15 (F19, B7, DHB Papers, SSC), 1.

185. Quoted in Bourbonnais, *Birth Control in the Decolonizing Caribbean*, 147.

186. "Report on the First Indian Ocean Regional Conference of the International Planned Parenthood Federation," Lahore, Pakistan, 1962 (F10, B6, DHB Papers, SSC), 53.

187. "The Return Visit," *ATW* 52, 1957/02 (B7, DHB Papers, SSC), 4.

188. Klausen, *Race, Maternity, and the Politics of Birth Control in South Africa*, 125.

189. "Hong Kong," *ATW* 45, 1956/05 (F12, B6, DHB Papers, SSC), 3.

190. Ceylon, "Eleventh Annual Report 1963–1964," 1964 (F3, B8, DHB Papers, SSC), 32.

191. Philip Stoughton to Miss May Farquharson, Letter, 1940/02/09 (4/108/970, MFC, NAJ), 1.

192. May Farquharson to Mrs. Campbell, "Letter," 1955/02/09 (4/108/1177, MFC, NAJ).

193. Farquharson to Mr. Cowell Lloyd, "Letter," 1944/01/15 (4/108/1007, MFC, NAJ).

194. "Berlin Express," *ATW* 60, 1957/12 (B7, DHB Papers, SSC), 1.

195. Edith M. Gates, "An Exploratory Tour into South America," 1959 [c.] (F19, B7, DHB Papers, SSC), 1; "Puerto Rico Conference," *ATW* 36, 1955/06 (F12, B6, DHB Papers, SSC), 3.

196. Ministry of Health Singapore, "Family Planning Handbook for Speakers and Lay Workers," c. 1960 (F671, MC229, MME Papers, SL), 24–25.

197. MacNamara, *Birth Control and American Modernity*, 12–13.

198. Patricia Mohammed, "A History of the Family Planning Association of Trinidad and Tobago," 1986 ("Family Planning" File, CGD, UWI), 12. See also Maria Cancro, "Report on Domestic Propaganda and Distribution of Leaflets," 1957/07/23 ("IPPF Minutes, 1953–1964" Folder, B40, MS Papers, SSC), 3.

199. Ashford, *Development and Women's Reproductive Health in Ghana*, 173.

200. "Report on the First Indian Ocean Regional Conference of the International Planned Parenthood Federation," Lahore, Pakistan, 1962 (F10, B6, DHB Papers, SSC), 127; Ceylon, "Eleventh Annual Report 1963–1964," 1964 (F3, B8, DHB Papers, SSC), 9.

201. "India," *ATW* 38, 1955/10 (F12, B6, DHB Papers, SSC), 3; "Women and Family Growth," *ATW* 59, 1957/11 (B7, DHB Papers, SSC), 1; "Japan," *ATW* 17, 1953/09 (F12, B6, DHB Papers, SSC), 3; Bourbonnais, *Birth Control in the Decolonizing Caribbean*, 154.

202. "Results of an experimental service programme in family planning conducted by the Johore Family Planning Association in the District of Johore, Bahru," 01/02/1061–01/02/1962 (F97, MC325, ERM Papers, SL), appendix—"Personal Comments by Mrs. Edna R. McKinnon."

203. Huston, *Motherhood by Choice*, 155–56.

204. "Puerto Rico Conference," *ATW* 36, 1955/06 (F12, B6, DHB Papers, SSC), 3.

205. Dorothy H. Brush to Dr. Adenyi-Jones, "Letter," 1959 [c] (F1, B8, DHB Papers, SSC), 1–2.

206. "Japan," *ATW* 17, 1953/09 (F12, B6, DHB Papers, SSC), 3; "U.S.A.," *ATW* 30, 1954/12 (F12, B6, DHB Papers, SSC), 2; "Brakes," *ATW* 71, 1959/01 (B7, DHB Papers, SSC), 3; Federation, "Fourth Report," London, England, 1957/01/01–1959/05/31 (F10, B6, DHB Papers, SSC), 92.

207. IPPF, "Asian tour 1960/61, Reports from Mr. and Mrs. G. W. Cadbury," 16 (IPPF: Reports: General, 1959–61 Folder, B40, MS Papers, SSC).

208. "African Journey," *ATW* 26, 1954/06 (F12, B6, DHB Papers, SSC), 3.

209. "The Family Planning Association of Winnipeg," 1960/04/01–31/03/1961 ("Canada" file, B57, MS Papers, SSC), 3.

210. "Family Planning Scheme on Tebrau Estate," n.d. (F98, ERM Papers, SL), 1.

211. Edna R. McKinnon, "Report No II on Saudi Arabia," 1966/01/28–02/17 (F101, ERM Papers, SL), 2.

212. "Annual Reports," *ATW* 58, 1957/10 (B7, DHB Papers, SSC), 2. See also "African Journey," *ATW* 26, 1954/06 (F12, B6, DHB Papers, SSC), 2.

213. Federation, "Fourth Report," London, England, 1957/01/01–1959/05/31 (F10, B6, DHB Papers, SSC), 92.

214. Ministry of Health Singapore, "Family Planning Handbook for Speakers and Lay Workers," c. 1960 (F671, MME Papers, SL), 2.

215. "Report on the First Indian Ocean Regional Conference of the International Planned Parenthood Federation," Lahore, Pakistan, 1962 (F10, B6, DHB Papers, SSC), 84.

216. "Report on the First Indian Ocean Regional Conference of the International Planned Parenthood Federation," 88.

217. "Report on the First Indian Ocean Regional Conference of the International Planned Parenthood Federation," 89.

218. Ceylon, "Eleventh Annual Report 1963–1964," 1964 (F3, B8, DHB Papers, SSC), 46.

219. Family Planning Association, "Sixth Annual Report," 1959/09 ("Ceylon" file, B57, MS Papers, SSC), 12.

220. Dorothy Brush, to "Nassau/Bermuda," 1958? (F18, B7, DHB Papers, SSC), 2.

221. "Madras," *ATW* 13, 1953/03 (F12, B6, DHB Papers, SSC). See also Bourbonnais, *Birth Control in the Decolonizing Caribbean*, 150; Klausen, *Race, Maternity, and the Politics of Birth Control in South Africa*, 97–99.

NOTES TO PAGES 97–99 › 217

222. Huston, *Motherhood by Choice*, 47. See also Cohen, "Private Lives in Public Spaces," 110.

223. Huston, *Motherhood by Choice*, 47.

224. Cohen, "Private Lives in Public Spaces," 105.

225. Vera Houghton to Dorothy, "Letter," 1958/05/06 (F2, B2, MS 23, DHB Papers, SSC), 1.

226. Nafis Sadik, interviewed by Rebecca Sharpless, "Transcript of the Audio Recording, July 24, 2003" (PRHOHP, SSC), 11.

227. Farquharson, May, to Dr. Lightbourne, "Letter," 1954/04/05 (4/108/1092, MFC, NAJ).

228. "Report on the First Indian Ocean Regional Conference of the International Planned Parenthood Federation," 72; Sect. Jamaica Family Planning League to Messrs Gilmont Products Ltd., "Letter," 1958/06/18 (4/108/1712, MFC, NAJ), 1.

229. J. D. Cobban, Export Marketing Manager, The British Drug Houses Ltd to Miss Mae [*sic*] Farquharson, "Letter," 1950/07/24 (4/108/1175, MFC, NAJ), 1.

230. Mallikak (Ghosh) to Mrs. Watumull, "Letter," 1968/11/06 (F9, B8, DHB Papers, SSC), 2–3.

231. Frazer to [Houghton], "Letter," 1959/02/08 (F2, B2, MS 23, DHB Papers, SSC), 1.

232. Löwy, "Defusing the Population Bomb in the 1950s," 587.

233. "Results of an experimental service programme in family planning conducted by the Johore Family Planning Association in the District of Johore, Bahru," 01/02/1061–01/02/1962 (F97, ERM Papers, SL), 5.

234. Johore Family Planning Association to Dr. C. J. Gamble, Letter, 1961/10/01 (F98, ERM Papers, SL), 1.

235. "Scientists Meet in Exeter," *ATW* 57, 1957/09 (B7, DHB Papers, SSC), 3.

236. "Oliver Bird Lecture," *ATW* 97, 1961/09 (B7, DHB Papers, SSC), 2.

237. Fort George, Stony Hill to ANC Lieut. Colonel B. L. Raina, Simla, India, "Letter," 1952/08/26 (4/108/1067, MFC, NAJ), 1.

238. May Farquharson to Gen. Secretary Family Planning Association Miss Irene James, "Letter," 1952/04/28 (4/108/232, MFC, NAJ), 1.

239. Vera Houghton to Miss May Farquharson, "Letter," 1952/05/05 (4/108/530, MFC, NAJ), 1.

240. "Research Projects," *ATW* 56, 1957/06 (B7, DHB Papers, SSC), 1; "Research," *ATW* 30, 1954/12 (F12, B6, DHB Papers, SSC), 1.

241. The "Pill," *ATW* 40, 1955/12 (F12, B6, DHB Papers, SSC), 2.

242. Singapore Family Planning Association, "Seventh Annual Report," 1956/01/01–1956/12/31 ("Singapore" file, B59, MS Papers, SSC), 15.

243. "Hong Kong," *ATW* 45, 1956/05 (F12, B6, DHB Papers, SSC), 3.

244. "Two Aspects of Sterilization," *ATW* 104, 1962/04 (B7, DHB Papers, SSC), 2.

245. "Kuala Lumpur," *ATW* 79, 1959/11 (B7, DHB Papers, SSC), 4.

218 ‹ NOTES TO PAGES 100–107

246. López, *A History of Family Planning in Twentieth-Century Peru*, 90.

247. Bourbonnais, *Birth Control in the Decolonizing Caribbean*, 70.

248. Letter to Miss May Farquharson, "Letter," 1944/02/09 (4/108/1188, MFC, NAJ), 4. (Name removed for confidentiality.)

249. Letter to Miss May Farquharson, "Letter," 3.

250. May Farquharson to Dr. Peat, "Letter," 1955/07/27 (4/108, MFC, NAJ), 1.

251. May Farquharson to Barbara, "Letter," 1955/08/10 (4/108/1278, MFC, NAJ), 1.

252. May Farquharson to Barbara, "Letter," 1956/06/14 (4/108/1278, MFC, NAJ), 1.

253. See, for example, "Blanket" to Violettina, "Letter," 1956/03/05 (4/108/1936, MFC, NAJ).

254. May Farquharson, "Plea from a Pioneer," *ATW* 45, 1956/05 (F12, B6, DHB Papers, SSC), 1.

255. "Agenda: Annual General Meeting to Be Held October 18th 1956," 1956/10/18 (4/108/802, MFC, NAJ), 1.

256. Ahluwalia, *Reproductive Restraints*, 17.

257. IPPF, "IPPF Sixth Report," London, England, 1963 (F10, B6, DHB Papers, SSC), 36.

258. IPPF, "IPPF Sixth Report," 36.

CHAPTER THREE

1. Adaline Pendleton Satterthwaite, "Diary 1966 (Thailand and Taipei)," 3/12/66 (APS Papers, SSC).

2. Adaline Pendleton Satterthwaite, "Diary 1966 (Thailand and Taipei)," 3/14/66 (APS Papers, SSC).

3. Adaline Pendleton Satterthwaite, "Diary 1966 (Thailand and Taipei)," 3/31/66 (APS Papers, SSC).

4. Adaline Pendleton Satterthwaite, "Diary 1966 (Thailand and Taipei)," 10/12/66 (APS Papers, SSC).

5. Adaline Pendleton Satterthwaite, "Diary 1968 (Pakistan)," 5/30/68 (B14, APS Papers, SSC).

6. Adaline Pendleton Satterthwaite, "Diary 1968 (Pakistan)," 7/31/68 (B14, APS Papers, SSC).

7. Adaline Pendleton Satterthwaite, "Diaries, Jun–Dec 1971 (Pakistan)," 10/1/71 (B14, APS Papers, SSC).

8. Warren C. Robinson and John A Ross, "Family Planning: The Quiet Revolution," in Robinson and Ross, *The Global Family Planning Revolution*, 421–22.

9. Connelly, *Fatal Misconception*; Hartmann, *Reproductive Rights and Wrongs*; Solinger and Nakachi, *Reproductive States*.

10. Connelly, *Fatal Misconception*, 185.

11. Connelly, *Fatal Misconception*, 206. For more on Ford's support of population programs, see Kathleen McCarthy, "From Government to Grass-Roots Reform:

The Ford Foundation's Population Programmes in South Asia, 1959–1981," *Voluntas: International Journal of Voluntary and Nonprofit Organizations* 6, no. 3 (1993): 292–316.

12. Connelly, *Fatal Misconception*, 159.

13. Connelly, *Fatal Misconception*, 186.

14. Connelly, *Fatal Misconception*, 231.

15. Cueto, Brown, and Fee, *The World Health Organization: A History*, 156.

16. Connelly, *Fatal Misconception*, 232.

17. Parry, *Broadcasting Birth Control*, 1, 89. For a full discussion of the film, see Patrick Ellis and Jesse Olszynko-Gryn, "Communicating Overpopulation to a Global Audience: Disney's *Family Planning* (1968)," *Journal of Global History* (2024): 1–24.

18. Takeshita, *The Global Biopolitics of the IUD*.

19. Connelly, *Fatal Misconception*.

20. Whitworth, *Feminism and International Relations*, 97.

21. Margaret Sanger, "Special Poll of Opinions," 1958/08/28 ("IPPF General, 1952–58" Folder, B40, MS Papers, SSC), 1.

22. Dorothy Brush, "Report of the Hon. Adviser for Field Work Services," c. 1958 (F18, B7, DHB Papers, SSC), 2.

23. Sreenivas, *Reproductive Politics and the Making of Modern India*, 26, 91–123.

24. Bourbonnais, *Birth Control in the Decolonizing Caribbean*, 195, 199.

25. "Straws in the Wind," *ATW* 80, 1959/12 (B7, DHB Papers, SSC), 2.

26. Baron, "The Origins of Family Planning," 38.

27. Baron, "The Origins of Family Planning," 48.

28. Huston, *Motherhood by Choice*, 64.

29. Adaline Pendleton Satterthwaite, interviewed by James Reed, "Transcript," 1974 (SROHP, SL), 1–8.

30. Satterthwaite, interviewed by James Reed, "Transcript," 10.

31. Satterthwaite, interviewed by James Reed, "Transcript," 9–10.

32. Adaline Pendleton Satterthwaite, "Contraceptive Clinical Trials in Puerto Rico," n.d. (B21, APS Papers, SSC), 4.

33. A. P. Satterthwaite, "Clinical Experience with New Contraceptive Technology," *Fourth National Congress of Iranian Gynecologists and Obstetricians*, Shiraz, Iran, 1966/04/18 (B20, APS Papers, SSC), 1.

34. Satterthwaite, "Clinical Experience with New Contraceptive Technology," 15.

35. Satterthwaite, "Clinical Experience with New Contraceptive Technology," 12.

36. Satterthwaite, "Clinical Experience with New Contraceptive Technology," 15.

37. Kathryn Lankford, "More Than a Way Station: Ground-Level Experiences in the Field Trials of Oral Contraceptives and IUDs in Puerto Rico, 1956–1966" (PhD diss., Department of History, Michigan State University, 2021), 106–18.

38. Satterthwaite, interviewed by James Reed, "Transcript," 17–18.

39. Satterthwaite, interviewed by James Reed, "Transcript," 20. See Lankford, "More Than a Way Station," 11–12, on the structure of the trials.

40. Gordon, *The Moral Property of Women*, 288; Corrêa, *Population and Reproductive Rights*, 458.

41. Briggs, *Reproducing Empire*.

42. Lankford, "More Than a Way Station," 88.

43. Lankford, "More Than a Way Station," 187.

44. Lankford, "More Than a Way Station," 216–24.

45. Schoen, *Choice and Coercion*, 30.

46. Satterthwaite, interview by James Reed, "Transcript" (SROHP, SL), 21.

47. Lankford, "More Than a Way Station," 206.

48. Lankford, "More Than a Way Station," 11.

49. Lankford, "More Than a Way Station," 29, 219–21.

50. Lankford, "More Than a Way Station," 226, see also 227–28.

51. Lankford, "More Than a Way Station," 222.

52. Lankford, "More Than a Way Station," 26–28, 45–46, 73–77.

53. Lankford, "More Than a Way Station," 275.

54. Quoted in Lankford, "More Than a Way Station," 266.

55. Lankford, "More Than a Way Station," 212. On early pill doses, see Wendy Kline, "Bodies of Evidence: Activists, Patients, and the FDA Regulation of Depo-Provera," *Journal of Women's History* 22, no. 3 (Fall 2010): 72.

56. Lankford, "More Than a Way Station," 212–13.

57. Lankford, "More Than a Way Station," 230.

58. Lankford, "More Than a Way Station," 271.

59. Lankford, "More Than a Way Station," 277.

60. Lankford, "More Than a Way Station," 271.

61. Barbara Cadbury, "Warsaw," *ATW* 107, 1962/09 (B7, DHB Papers, SSC), 4.

62. Gordon, *The Moral Property of Women*, 322–23.

63. Gordon, *The Moral Property of Women*, 322–23.

64. Takeshita, *The Global Biopolitics of the IUD*, 43.

65. Takeshita, *The Global Biopolitics of the IUD*, 43.

66. Lankford, "More Than a Way Station," 239.

67. Takeshita, *The Global Biopolitics of the IUD*, 31. See also Sanjam Ahluwalia and Daksha Pamar, "From Gandhi to Gandhi: Contraceptive Technologies and Sexual Politics in Postcolonial India, 1947–1977," in Solinger and Nakachi, *Reproductive States*, 135.

68. A. P. Satterthwaite, "Progress Report on Intrauterine Contraception," 1963/04, Ryder Memorial Hospital, Humacao, Puerto Rico (Ryder: oral contraceptives reports, B21, APS Papers, SSC), 4.

69. Lankford, "More Than a Way Station," 176.

NOTES TO PAGES 115–118 › 221

70. Lankford, "More Than a Way Station," 180.

71. Lankford, "More Than a Way Station," 182.

72. Richmond K. Anderson to Dr. Lucien A. Gregg, 1965/05/04 ("Puerto Rico: Population Council Field Staff," F1493, B157, PC Papers, RAC).

73. Satterthwaite, interviewed by James Reed, "Transcript" (SROHP, SL), 37.

74. Adaline Pendleton Satterthwaite, Letter to Sharon, 1975/09/20 ("Unfpa: Dacca: Corr, 1974–81," B22, APS Papers, SSC).

75. Adaline Pendleton Satterthwaite, "Diary, 1966 (Thailand–Taipei)," 5/26/66 (B14, APS Papers, SSC). See also Allan G. Rosenfield and Caroline J. Min, "The Emergence of Thailand's National Family Planning Program," in Robinson and Ross, *The Global Family Planning Revolution*, 221–25.

76. Satterthwaite, "Diary, 1966 (Thailand–Taipei)," 7/26/66.

77. Huston, *Motherhood by Choice*, 91.

78. Adaline P. Satterthwaite, "Family Health Research in Thailand—a Report to the Ministry of Health, March 15 to June 15, 1967," 1967/06/15 ("Thailand Reports 1966–67," B20, APS Papers, SSC), 6.

79. Satterthwaite, "Diary, 1966 (Thailand–Taipei)," 4/2/66.

80. Satterthwaite, "Diary, 1966 (Thailand–Taipei)," 9/8/66, 6/7/66, 12/27/66.

81. Satterthwaite, "Diary, 1966 (Thailand–Taipei)," 4/2/66, 6/28/66, and 11/1/66.

82. Family Planning Association of China, "Monthly Activity Report," 1964/05 (F4, B8, DHB Papers, SSC), 3.

83. Baron, "The Origins of Family Planning," 36.

84. Huston, *Motherhood by Choice*, 48. See also Darshi Thoradeniya, "Birth Control Pill Trials in Sri Lanka: The History and Politics of Women's Reproductive Health (1950–1980)," *Social History of Medicine* 33, no. 1 (2020): 267–87.

85. Necochea López, "Gambling on the Protestants," 363.

86. Espinosa Tavares, "'They Are Coming in So Fast That if We Had Publicity about the Clinic We Would Be Swamped,'" 77, 88.

87. Rice-Wray to Brush, "Letter," 1962/08/20 (F18, B2, MS 23, DHB Papers, SSC), 2. Espinosa Tavares, "'They Are Coming in So Fast That if We Had Publicity about the Clinic We Would Be Swamped,'" 81–83.

88. Rice-Wray to Brush, "Letter," 1962/08/20 (F18, B2, MS 23, DHB Papers, SSC), 2.

89. Satterthwaite, "Diary 1966 (Thailand and Taipei)," 4/11/66, 6/17/66, and 10/17/66 (B14, APS Papers, SSC).

90. Richard Moore, "Family Planning in Iran, 1960–79," in Robinson and Ross, *The Global Family Planning Revolution*, 40.

91. Satterthwaite, "Diary 1966 (Thailand and Taipei)," 10/17/66.

92. Connelly, *Fatal Misconception*, 205.

93. Adaline P. Satterthwaite to Dr. Arturo Zelaya, "Letter," 1966/01/17 ("Puerto Rico: Population Council Field Staff," F1492, B157, PC Papers, RAC), 3.

94. Satterthwaite, "Diary, 1966 (Thailand–Taipei)," 5/19/66.

95. Satterthwaite, "Diary, 1966 (Thailand–Taipei)," 10/10/66.

96. Ahluwalia and Pamar, "From Gandhi to Gandhi," 136.

97. Baron, "The Origins of Family Planning," 39.

98. China, "Monthly Activity Report," 1963/01 (F4, B8, DHB Papers, SSC), 2.

99. Sai Poh to Dorothy, "Letter," 1960/07/18 (F26, B1, DHB Papers, SSC).

100. Satterthwaite, "Diary 1966 (Thailand–Taipei)," 4/14/66.

101. Satterthwaite, "Diary 1966 (Thailand–Taipei)," 4/20/66.

102. Satterthwaite, "Diary 1966 (Thailand–Taipei)," 12/27/66.

103. Adaline Pendleton Satterthwaite, "Diary, 1969 (New York–Pakistan)," 11/18/69 (B14, APS Papers, SSC).

104. James T. Fawcett, Aree Somboonsuk, and Sumol Khaisang, "Diffusion of Family Planning Information by Word of Mouth Communication," November 1966 ("Thailand Reports 1966–67," B20, APS Papers, SSC), 2.

105. Fawcett, Somboonsuk, and Khaisang, "Diffusion of Family Planning Information," 2, 13.

106. Fawcett, Somboonsuk, and Khaisang, "Diffusion of Family Planning Information," 10.

107. Adaline Pendleton Satterthwaite, "Diary, 1967 (Thailand and Pakistan)," 2/17/67, and "Diaries, 1970 (Pakistan)," 7/30/70 (B14, APS Papers, SSC).

108. Fawcett, Somboonsuk, and Khaisang, "Diffusion of Family Planning Information," 4.

109. Huston, *Motherhood by Choice*, 88.

110. Huston, *Motherhood by Choice*, 88.

111. Rosenfield, "The Emergence of Thailand's National Family Planning Program," 224.

112. Fawcett, Somboonsuk, and Khaisang, "Diffusion of Family Planning Information," 6.

113. Adaline P. Satterthwaite, "Family Health Research in Thailand—a Report to the Ministry of Health, March 15 to June 15, 1967," 1967/06/15 ("Thailand Reports 1966–67," B20, APS Papers, SSC), 9.

114. See, for example, figures at Adaline Pendleton Satterthwaite, "Diary, 1966 (Thailand–Taipei)," 3/8/66, "Diary 1968 (Pakistan)," 3/30/68, "Diary, 1969 (New York–Pakistan)," 11/10/69, "Diaries, 1970 (Pakistan)," 1/5/70 (B14, APS Papers, SSC); Satterthwaite, "Family Health Research in Thailand," 9. See also George F Brown, "Morocco: First Steps in Family Planning," in Robinson and Ross, *The Global Family Planning Revolution*, 78; Ashford, *Development and Women's Reproductive Health in Ghana*, 170–71.

115. Takeshita, *The Global Biopolitics of the IUD*, 66.

116. Ahluwalia and Pamar, "From Gandhi to Gandhi," 137.

117. Satterthwaite, "Diary, 1967 (Thailand and Pakistan)," 5/18/67.

118. Satterthwaite, "Diary, 1966 (Thailand–Taipei)," 6/17/66.

119. Satterthwaite, "Diary, 1966 (Thailand–Taipei)," 10/11/66.

120. Satterthwaite, "Diary, 1966 (Thailand–Taipei)," 10/6/66. See also Ahluwalia and Pamar, "From Gandhi to Gandhi," 137.

121. Adaline Pendleton Satterthwaite, "Clinical Experience with New Contraceptive Technology," *Fourth National Congress of Iranian Gynecologists and Obstetricians*, Shiraz, Iran, 1966/04/18 ("Thailand: Trip to Iran, 1966," B20, APS Papers, SSC).

122. Silvia de Zordo, "Programming the Body, Planning Reproduction, Governing Life: The '(Ir-) Rationality' of Family Planning and the Embodiment of Social Inequalities in Salvador De Bahia (Brazil)," *Anthropology & Medicine* 19 (2012): 214.

123. Satterthwaite, "Diary 1967 (Thailand and Pakistan)," 7/22/67.

124. Satterthwaite, "Diary 1966 (Thailand and Taipei)," 3/9/66.

125. Dario Merchán López and A. P. Satterthwaite, "Comparative Study of Copper T and Lippes Loops at the Maternidad Concepcion Palacios," 1972 ("Venezuela: corr. & rpts, 1972–73," B20, APS Papers, SSC), 2, 9.

126. Takeshita, *The Global Biopolitics of the IUD*, 53–54.

127. Satterthwaite, "Diary, 1966 (Thailand–Taipei)," 6/15/66, 7/11/66.

128. Satterthwaite, "Diary, 1967 (Thailand and Pakistan)," 9/14/67, 10/30/67.

129. Satterthwaite, "Diary, 1967 (Thailand and Pakistan)," 2/28/67, 3/1/67, 3/2/67.

130. Satterthwaite, "Diary, 1967 (Thailand and Pakistan)," 7/11/67.

131. Matthew R. Dudgeon and Marcia C. Inhorn, "Gender, Masculinity and Reproduction: Anthropological Perspectives," in Dudgeon and Inhorn, eds., *Reconceiving the Second Sex: Men, Masculinity, and Reproduction* (New York: Berghahn Books, 2009), 75–78. See also Ginsburg and Rapp, "Introduction," 7.

132. Takeshita, *The Global Biopolitics of the IUD*, 66.

133. "Intrauterine Devices," *ATW* 106, 1962/06 (B7, DHB Papers, SSC), 1–2.

134. Lu Chieh, "A Follow-Up Survey of a Cohort of Loop Acceptors," Taipei, Taiwan: Family Planning Association of China, 1968/04 (F4, B8, DHB Papers, SSC), 1.

135. Chieh, "A Follow-Up Survey of a Cohort of Loop Acceptors," 3.

136. Bourbonnais, *Birth Control in the Decolonizing Caribbean*, 212.

137. Satterthwaite, "Diary, 1966 (Thailand–Taipei)," 6/17/66, see also 4/5/66.

138. Satterthwaite, "Diary, 1966 (Thailand–Taipei)," 4/2/66.

139. Satterthwaite, "Diary 1967 (Thailand and Pakistan)," 6/1/67.

140. Satterthwaite, "Diary 1967 (Thailand and Pakistan)," 6/1/67.

141. Takeshita, *The Global Biopolitics of the IUD*, 4, 47–48.

142. Takeshita, *The Global Biopolitics of the IUD*, 43.

143. Kline, "Bodies of Evidence," 71.

144. Takeshita, *The Global Biopolitics of the IUD*, 59.

145. Adaline Pendleton Satterthwaite, "Diary, 1966 (Thailand–Taipei)," 6/22/66.

146. Ashford, *Development and Women's Reproductive Health in Ghana*, 169.

147. Satterthwaite, "Diary 1967 (Thailand and Pakistan)," 2/22/67.

224 ‹ NOTES TO PAGES 124–127

148. Satterthwaite, "Diary, 1967 (Thailand and Pakistan)," 2/24/67.

149. Satterthwaite, "Diary, 1967 (Thailand and Pakistan)," 3/6/67. On subsequent controversies over Depo-Provera trials, see Kline, "Bodies of Evidence."

150. See "Monthly Report—March, 1967," 1967/03 ("Thailand: Monthly Reports," F1932, B201, PC Papers, RAC), and newspaper clippings: "Birth Curb Not Feasible Says Prapas," *Bangkok Post*,1967/04/06 and "Birth Control Recommended—Food Production Cannot Keep Up," *Prachathipatai* 1967/04/06 ("Thailand Reports 1966–67," B20, Adaline P. Satterthwaite Papers, SSC).

151. Newspaper clipping: "Doctor Expresses Views—Birth Control Should Be Free of Controls,"1967/04/24 ("Thailand Reports 1966–67," B20, APS Papers, SSC), 2.

152. Adaline P. Satterthwaite to Dr. N. R. E. Fendall, "Letter," 1967/05/26 ("Thailand: Ministry of Public Health: Satterthwaite, Adaline P.," F1653, B171, PC Papers, RAC), 1.

153. Richmond K. Anderson to General Netr, "Letter," 1967/05/04 ("Thailand: National Research Council," F1654, B172, PC Papers, RAC), 1.

154. Warren C. Robinson, "Family Planning Programs and Policies in Bangladesh and Pakistan," in Robinson and Ross, *The Global Family Planning Revolution*.

155. Adaline Pendleton Satterthwaite, "Diary, 1967 (Thailand and Pakistan)," 9/19/47 (B14, APS Papers, SSC).

156. Adaline Pendleton Satterthwaite, "Diary, 1967 (Thailand and Pakistan)," 8/4/67 (B14, APS Papers, SSC).

157. Ahluwalia and Pamar, "From Gandhi to Gandhi," 136.

158. Ahluwalia and Pamar, "From Gandhi to Gandhi," 140–41.

159. Connelly, *Fatal Misconception*, 224–30.

160. Dwyer, "Spectacular Sexuality," 40. See also Takeshita, *The Global Biopolitics of the IUD*, 127; and Terence H. Hull, "Formative Years of Family Planning in Indonesia," in Robinson and Ross, *The Global Family Planning Revolution*, 235–56.

161. Baron, "The Origins of Family Planning," 50.

162. Yap Mui Teng, "Singapore: Population Policies and Programs," in Robinson and Ross, *The Global Family Planning Revolution*, 206–7.

163. Thoradeniya, "Altruism, Welfare, or Development Aid?," 438–41.

164. Bourbonnais, *Birth Control in the Decolonizing Caribbean*, 208.

165. Nafis Sadik, interviewed by Rebecca Sharpless, "Transcript of the Audio Recording, July 24, 2003" (PRHOHP, SSC), 8.

166. Sadik, interviewed by Sharpless, "Transcript," 10.

167. Sadik, interviewed by Sharpless, "Transcript," 13–14.

168. Sadik, interviewed by Sharpless, "Transcript," 22.

169. Satterthwaite, "Diary 1967 (Thailand and Pakistan)," 5/5/67.

170. See Sreenivas, *Reproductive Politics and the Making of Modern India*, 130–31.

171. Satterthwaite, "Diary 1968 (Pakistan)," 1/10/68.

172. Satterthwaite, "Diary, 1966 (Thailand–Taipei)," 4/1/66.

173. Robinson, "Family Planning Programs and Policies in Bangladesh and Pakistan," 329.

174. Satterthwaite, "Diary, 1967 (Thailand and Pakistan)," 7/29/67.

175. Satterthwaite, "Diary 1969 (Pakistan)," 8/22/69; Satterthwaite, "Diary 1968 (Pakistan)," 1/8/68, 1/17/68, 1/20/68.

176. Satterthwaite, "Diary, 1969 (New York–Pakistan)," 3/3/69.

177. Satterthwaite, "Diary, 1967 (Thailand and Pakistan)," 6/27/67.

178. Satterthwaite, "Diary, 1969 (New York–Pakistan)," 10/2/69.

179. Satterthwaite, "Diary 1968 (Pakistan)," 5/30/68 and 12/7/68.

180. Satterthwaite, "Diary, 1967 (Thailand and Pakistan)," 12/15/67.

181. Enver Adil to Mr. Q. G. Ahad, "Letter," 1967/02/21 ("Pakistan: Monthly Reports," F1915, B199, PC Papers, RAC).

182. Satterthwaite, "Diary 1967 (Thailand and Pakistan)," 9/29/67.

183. Satterthwaite, "Diary 1967 (Thailand and Pakistan)," 9/4/67.

184. Satterthwaite, "Diary 1967 (Thailand and Pakistan)," 10/05/67.

185. Satterthwaite, "Diary, 1969 (New York–Pakistan)," 3/3/69; "Diary, 1967 (Thailand and Pakistan)," 10/6/67; "Diary 1968 (Pakistan)," 1/3/68.

186. Satterthwaite, "Diary 1968 (Pakistan)," 7/30/68.

187. Satterthwaite, "Diary 1968 (Pakistan)," 12/20/68.

188. Satterthwaite, "Diary, 1967 (Thailand and Pakistan)," 7/4/67. See also Satterthwaite, "Diary, 1969 (New York–Pakistan)," 8/16/69, 8/18/69, and 9/30/69.

189. Adaline Pendleton Satterthwaite, "Medical Aspects of the Pakistan Family Planning Program" ("Pakistan: reports, 1984, n.d.," B20, APS Papers, SSC), 7. See also Satterthwaite, "Diary, 1966 (Thailand–Taipei)," 5/6/66; and Satterthwaite, "Diary 1968 (Pakistan)," 5/30/68.

190. Satterthwaite, "Diary 1968 (Pakistan)," 1/13/68.

191. Satterthwaite, "Diary 1967 (Thailand and Pakistan)," 8/5/67, 9/4/67, 12/11/67, and 12/14/67.

192. Satterthwaite, "Diary, 1969 (New York–Pakistan)," 8/22/69.

193. Satterthwaite, "Diary, 1969 (New York–Pakistan)," 4/2/69.

194. Satterthwaite, "Diaries, 1970 (Pakistan)," 2/11/70.

195. Satterthwaite, "Diary, 1969 (New York–Pakistan)," 9/29/69. See also Adaline P. Satterthwaite to Dr. Richmond K. Anderson, "Letter," 1969/10/17 (F1303, B137, PC Papers, RAC).

196. Adaline Satterthwaite, "Discussion Paper: III. Program Organization and Administration: Delivery of Services," 1968/02/20 ("Catalogued Reports," B400, FF Papers, RAC), 2.

197. Satterthwaite, "Diary 1968 (Pakistan)," 3/9/68 and 12/7/68.

198. Satterthwaite, "Diary, 1967 (Thailand and Pakistan)," 6/20/67, 6/27/67, and 7/15/67.

199. Adaline Pendleton Satterthwaite to Sharon, "Letter," 04/13/1975 ("UNFPA: Dacca: Corr, 1974–81," B22, APS Papers, SSC), 1.

200. Satterthwaite, "Diaries, 1970 (Pakistan)," 2/26/70.

201. Satterthwaite, "Diary 1968 (Pakistan)," 7/19/68.

202. Satterthwaite, "Diary 1968 (Pakistan)," 12/7/68.

203. Satterthwaite, "Diary, 1969 (New York–Pakistan)," 2/1/69.

204. Satterthwaite, "Diary 1968 (Pakistan)," 5/29/68, 7/7/68, 7/19/68, 8/2/68, and 9/13/68.

205. Satterthwaite, "Diary 1968 (Pakistan)," 2/29/68 and 3/5/68.

206. Satterthwaite, "Diary 1968 (Pakistan)," 7/24/68.

207. Satterthwaite, "Diary 1968 (Pakistan)," 5/29/68.

208. Satterthwaite, "Diary 1968 (Pakistan)," 8/1/68, 8/7/68, and 11/26/68.

209. Satterthwaite, "Diary, 1969 (New York–Pakistan)," 2/25/69.

210. Satterthwaite, "Diary, 1969 (New York–Pakistan)," 5/14/69.

211. Satterthwaite, "Diary, 1969 (New York–Pakistan)," 7/4/69 and 7/28/69.

212. Satterthwaite, "Diary, 1969 (New York–Pakistan)," 10/4/69 and 9/22/69.

213. Satterthwaite, "Diaries, 1970 (Pakistan)," 2/6/70.

214. Satterthwaite, "Diaries, 1970 (Pakistan)," 10/7/70.

215. Satterthwaite, "Diary 1970 (Pakistan)," 4/29/70 and 6/23/70.

216. "Pakistan: Annual Report for 1969–70," 1970 ("Pakistan: reports, 1984, n.d.," B20, APS Papers, SSC), 1.

217. Adaline Pendleton Satterthwaite, "Diaries, Jun–Dec 1971 (Pakistan)," 7/23/71 (B14, APS Papers, SSC).

218. Adaline Pendleton Satterthwaite, "Diary 1971—Jan–May (Pakistan)," 7/12/71 (B14, APS Papers, SSC).

219. Satterthwaite, "Diary 1971—Jan–May (Pakistan)," 4/19/71.

220. Satterthwaite, "Diary 1971—Jan–May (Pakistan)," 5/11/71. See also Nafis Sadik, interviewed by Rebecca Sharpless, "Transcript of the Audio Recording, July 24, 2003" (PRHOHP, SSC), 36–37.

221. Sanhueza, "Family Planning in Chile," 105.

222. Soledad Zárate Campos, "Planificación Familiar En La Guerra Fría Chilena," 215.

223. Pieper Mooney, "Re-Visiting Histories of Modernization, Progress, and (Unequal) Citizenship Rights," *History Compass* 8 (2010): 1041.

224. Soledad Zárate Campos, "Planificación Familiar En La Guerra Fría Chilena," 215.

225. Roberto and Jane T. Bertrand Santiso-Gálvez, "Guatemala: The Pioneering Days of the Family Planning Movement," in Robinson and Ross, *The Global Family Planning Revolution.*

226. Necochea López, *A History of Family Planning in Twentieth-Century Peru*, 100.

227. Necochea López, *A History of Family Planning in Twentieth-Century Peru*, 126, 367.

228. Sanhueza, "Family Planning in Chile," 107–9.

229. Carranza, "In the Name of Forests," 133–35.

230. Anthony R. and Guillermo Lopez-Escobar Measham, "Against the Odds: Colombia's Role in the Family Planning Revolution," in Robinson and Ross, *The Global Family Planning Revolution*, 123.

231. Anthony R. and Guillermo Lopez-Escobar Measham, "Against the Odds: Colombia's Role in the Family Planning Revolution," 126.

232. Satterthwaite, "Diary 1971—Jun–Dec (Pakistan)," 10/23/71. See also Sanhueza, "Family Planning in Chile," 107; Carranza, "In the Name of Forests," 133–35.

233. Satterthwaite, "Diaries, 1972 (Peru and Venezuela)," 6/28/72, 10/7/72; Satterthwaite, "Diary, Jan–Oct 1974 (Dom. Rep.–Mexico)," 8/30/74 (B15, APS Papers, SSC).

234. Transcript of debate, "Television Canal 8, Caracas, Venezuela, Programa 'Buenos Dias!,' 11 de Octubre de 1972" (F1836, B193, PC Papers, RAC).

235. Satterthwaite, "Diaries, 1972 (Peru and Venezuela)," 6/26/72.

236. Satterthwaite, "Diary 1971—Jun–Dec (Pakistan)," 10/19/71.

237. Satterthwaite, "Diaries, 1972 (Peru and Venezuela)," 1/28/72.

238. Satterthwaite, "Diaries, 1972 (Peru and Venezuela)," 3/17/72.

239. Satterthwaite, "Diary 1971—Jan–May (Pakistan)," 5/25/71.

240. Satterthwaite, "Diaries, 1972 (Peru and Venezuela)," 6/28/72.

241. Satterthwaite, "Diaries, Jun–Dec 1971 (Pakistan)," 10/1/71.

242. Satterthwaite, "Diaries, 1972 (Peru and Venezuela)," 9/22/72.

243. Satterthwaite, "Diary 1971—Jan–May (Pakistan)," 6/9/71.

244. Satterthwaite, "Diaries, 1972 (Peru and Venezuela)," 2/22/72.

245. Adaline Pendleton Satterthwaite, "Diaries, 1973 (Venezuela–Bangladesh)," 07/9–12/73 (B15, APS Papers, SSC).

246. Satterthwaite, "Diaries, 1973 (Venezuela–Bangladesh)," 09/3–7/73.

247. Satterthwaite, "Diaries, 1972 (Peru and Venezuela)," 11/3/72.

248. Satterthwaite, "Diary notes, 1973 (Venezuela–Bangladesh)," 05/21–25/73 (B15, APS Papers, SSC).

249. Satterthwaite, "Diaries, 1972 (Peru and Venezuela)," 9/28/72, 10/1/72, 10/19/72, 11/3/72, and 11/6/72.

250. Adaline Pendleton Satterthwaite, interviewed by James Reed, "Transcript," 1974 (SROHP, SL), 51.

251. Satterthwaite, "Diaries, 1972 (Peru and Venezuela)," 10/2/72.

252. Satterthwaite, "Diaries, Jun–Dec 1971 (Pakistan)," 9/11/71.

253. Satterthwaite, "Diaries, 1972 (Peru and Venezuela)," 10/17/72.

254. Satterthwaite, "Diaries, 1972 (Peru and Venezuela)," 6/23/72. See also Satterthwaite, "Diaries, Jun–Dec 1971 (Pakistan)," 9/11/71.

255. Satterthwaite, "Diary 1971—Jan–May (Pakistan)," 5/24/71.

256. Satterthwaite, "Diary, Jan–Oct 1974 (Dom. Rep.–Mexico)," 2/1/74.

257. Satterthwaite, "Diary 1968 (Pakistan)," 12/16/68. Satterthwaite, interviewed by Reed, "Transcript," 47.

258. Satterthwaite, "Diaries, 1972 (Peru and Venezuela)," 1/13/72.

259. Satterthwaite, "Diaries, Jan–May 1971 (Pakistan)," 5/24/71. See also Satterthwaite, "Diaries, 1972 (Peru and Venezuela)," 2/21/72.

260. Adaline Pendleton Satterthwaite to Sharon, "Letter," 04/13/1975 ("UNFPA: Dacca: Corr, 1974–81," B22, APS Papers, SSC), 1.

261. Satterthwaite, "Diary 1968 (Pakistan)," 1/21/69.

262. Satterthwaite, "Diaries, 1972 (Peru and Venezuela)," 1/13/72.

263. Satterthwaite, "Diary 1973 (Venezuela–Bangladesh)," 11/14/73, 11/15/73, and 11/24–27/73 (B15, APS Papers, SSC); Satterthwaite, "Diary, Jan–Oct 1974 (Dom. Re.–Mexico)."

264. Satterthwaite, "Diary, Jan–Oct 1974 (Dom. Re.–Mexico)," 3/29/74.

265. Satterthwaite, interviewed by James Reed, "Transcript," 37.

266. A. P. Satterthwaite, "Clinical Experience with New Contraceptive Technology," *Fourth National Congress of Iranian Gynecologists and Obstetricians*, Shiraz, Iran, 1966/04/18 ("Thailand: Trip to Iran, 1966," B20, APS Papers, SSC), 8.

267. Satterthwaite, interviewed by Reed, "Transcript," 38.

268. Satterthwaite, interviewed by Reed, "Transcript," 47.

269. Satterthwaite, interviewed by Reed, "Transcript," 50.

270. Satterthwaite, interviewed by Reed, "Transcript," 51.

271. Joan Dunlop, interview by Rebecca Sharpless, "Transcript of audio recording, April 14–15, 2004" (PRHOHP, SSC), 4–5.

272. Dunlop, interview by Sharpless, "Transcript of audio recording," 6.

273. Dunlop, interview by Sharpless, "Transcript of audio recording," 7.

274. Joan M. Dunlop to Mr. John D. Rockefeller III, "Memorandum," 1974/02/19 ("Rockefeller—Correspondence," B1, JD Papers, SSC), 1.

275. Dunlop to Rockefeller, "Memorandum," 2.

276. Dunlop to Rockefeller, "Memorandum," 2.

277. Connelly, *Fatal Misconception*, 314; Dobos, "Global Challenges, Local Knowledges," 219–21; Maud Anne Bracke, "Women's Rights, Family Planning, and Population Control: The Emergence of Reproductive Rights in the United Nations (1960s–70s)," *International History Review* 44, no. 4 (2021): 12.

278. Connelly, *Fatal Misconception*, 310–16.

279. Saul Halfon, *The Cairo Consensus: Demographic Surveys, Women's Empowerment, and Regime Change in Population Policy* (Lanham, MD: Lexington Books, 2007), 66; Jutta M Joachim, *Agenda Setting, the UN, and NGOs: Gender Violence and Reproductive Rights* (Washington, DC: Georgetown University Press, 2007), 146.

280. Ahluwalia and Pamar, "From Gandhi to Gandhi," 129–30, 143–48.

281. Connelly, *Fatal Misconception*, 329, 332; Mathieu Caulier, "The Population Revolution: From Population Policies to Reproductive Health and Women's Rights Politics," *International Review of Sociology* 20, no. 2 (July 2010): 357–58.

282. McCarthy, "From Government to Grass-Roots Reform," 306–8.

283. Whitworth, *Feminism and International Relations*, 101–2.

284. Dunlop, interview by Sharpless, "Transcript of audio recording."

285. Satterthwaite, "Diaries, 1973 (Venezuela–Bangladesh)," 9/29/73.

286. Adaline Pendleton Satterthwaite to K. C. [Bai Kopal], "Letter," 1981/10/15 ("General Correspondence, 1979–82," B12, APS Papers, SSC), 1.

287. Satterthwaite, interviewed by Reed, 53.

288. Joan B. Dunlop to "Colleague," "Letter," 03/31/1993 ("General Correspondence, 1993–94," B12, APS Papers, SSC).

289. "Women's Voices '94: Women's Declaration on Population Policies," 1993/03/04 (F12, WRR Papers, AA), 21.

290. Sreenivas, *Reproductive Politics and the Making of Modern India*, 113.

291. Lisa Ann Richey, "Global Knowledge/Local Bodies: Family Planning Service Providers' Interpretations of Contraceptive Knowledge(s)," *Demographic Research* 18, no. 17 (2008): 486.

292. Indeed, a review of programs published in 1993 found that fourteen government programs were "strong," twenty-nine "moderate," thirty-eight "weak," and seventeen "very weak" or non-existent. Corrêa, *Population and Reproductive Rights*, 15.

293. Connelly, *Fatal Misconception*, 361.

294. Connelly, *Fatal Misconception*, 362.

CHAPTER FOUR

1. T. K. Sundari Ravindran, interview by Nicole Bourbonnais, "Transcript, July 13, 14, and 15, 2021" (RROHP, GGI), 27.

2. Corrêa, *Population and Reproductive Rights*, 457.

3. Selected transcripts for these projects are available online, others by request to the archive, while others are private. For PRHOHP, SSC, see: https://findingaids.smith.edu/repositories/2/resources/802; For the OHP, WLP: https://learningpartnership.org/learning-center/learning-center-overview/about-oral-history-project. For the RROHP, GGI: https://www.graduateinstitute.ch/academic-departments/international-history-and-politics/oral-history-archive.

4. Connelly, *Fatal Misconception*, xii.

5. Mindy Jane and Laura Reichenbach Roseman, "Global Reproductive Health and Rights: Reflecting on ICPD," in Laura Reichenbach and Mindy Jane Roseman, eds., *Reproductive Health and Human Rights: The Way Forward* (Philadelphia: University of Pennsylvania Press, 2009), 3–4.

6. Connelly, *Fatal Misconception*, 353–55; Maud Anne Bracke, "Contesting 'Global Sisterhood,'" 822.

7. Bashford, *Global Population*, 346.

8. Bracke, "Contesting 'Global Sisterhood,'" 818.

9. Adrienne Germain to Distribution, "Inter-Office Memorandum," 1985/08/21 ("Ford Foundation" file, B1, JD Papers, SSC), 5.

10. Germain to Distribution, "Inter-Office Memorandum," 5–6.

11. Bracke, "Women's Rights, Family Planning, and Population Control."

12. Petchesky, *Global Prescriptions*, 34.

13. Petchesky, *Global Prescriptions*, 4; Bice Maiguashca, "Theorizing Knowledge from Women's Political Practices: The Case of the Women's Reproductive Rights Movement," *International Feminist Journal of Politics* 7, no. 2 (2005): 212–13; Bracke, "Contesting 'Global Sisterhood.'"

14. Gita Sen and Caren Grown, *Development, Crisis and Alternative Visions: Third World Women's Perspectives* (New York: Routledge, 1987).

15. "Women's Voices '94—A Declaration on Population Policies," *Population and Development Review* 19, no. 3 (1993): 637–40. See also Joachim, *Agenda Setting, the UN, and NGOs*, 149.

16. CEPIA and IWHC, "Reproductive Health and Justice."

17. Gita Sen et al., eds., *Population Policies Reconsidered: Health, Empowerment, and Rights* (Boston: Harvard School of Public Health, 1994); Corrêa, *Population and Reproductive Rights*.

18. For compelling accounts of the role of these three women in particular, see Connelly, *Fatal Misconception*, 360–69; Caulier, "The Population Revolution"; and Michelle Goldberg, *The Means of Reproduction: Sex, Power, and the Future of the World* (London: Penguin Books, 2010).

19. See Amy J. Higler, "International Women's Activism and the 1994 Cairo Population Conference," in Mary K. Meyler and Elisabeth Prügl, eds., *Gender Politics in Global Governance* (Lanham, MD: Rowman & Littlefield Publishers, 1998), 125–26.

20. Bracke, "Women's Rights, Family Planning, and Population Control," 2. See also Petchesky, *Global Prescriptions*, 3–4.

21. Adetoun Ilumoka, interview by Nicole Bourbonnais, "Transcript, July 9 and 10, October 10, 2021" (RROHP, GGI), 3–4.

22. See "Report to the Pathfinder Fund of Mrs. Edna McKinnon, Field Representative: Nigeria," 1964/11/28–1965/02/05; and "Lagos, Nigeria Report No. I," 1964/07/04–30 (F105, ERM Papers, SL).

23. Peggy Antrobus, interview by Nicole Bourbonnais, "Transcript, November 29 and 30, December 7, 2021" (RROHP, GGI), 5.

24. See Sharpless, "Population Science, Private Foundations, and Development Aid"; Merchant, *Building the Population Bomb*.

25. Caulier, "The Population Revolution," 356–57.

26. Claudia García-Moreno, interview by Nicole Bourbonnais, "Transcript, July 21 and 26, 2021" (RROHP, GGI).

27. T. K. Sundari Ravindran, interview by Nicole Bourbonnais, "Transcript, July 13, 14, and 15, 2021" (RROHP, GGI).

28. Amparo Claro, interview by Nicole Bourbonnais, "Transcript, January 31 and March 7, 2022" (RROHP, GGI).

NOTES TO PAGES 153–155 › 231

29. Asia Samachar, "An Extraordinary Woman," 2018/02/20, https://www.wings.sg/wp-content/uploads/2019/10/sc-asiasamachar-20180220.pdf.

30. Ravindran, interview by Bourbonnais, 4.

31. García-Moreno, interview by Bourbonnais, 4.

32. Rosalind Petchesky, interview by Nicole Bourbonnais, "Transcript, October 18 and October 25, 2021" (RROHP, GGI), 4.

33. Frances Kissling, interview by Rebecca Sharpless, "Transcript of audio recording, 13–14 September, 2002" (PRHOHP, SSC) 2; Noeleen Heyzer interview, "Audio Recording," 2016 (OHP, WLP), track 1.

34. Noeleen Heyzer interview, audio recording, 2016 (OHP, WLP), track 1.

35. Marieme Helie Lucas interview, audio recording, 2015 (OHP, WLP), track 1.

36. García-Moreno, interview by Bourbonnais, 3.

37. Jacqueline Pitanguy interview, audio recording, 2015 (OHP, WLP), track 1. See also García-Moreno, interview by Bourbonnais, 4; and Gita Sen, interview by Nicole Bourbonnais, "Transcript, September 12, 19 and 28, 2022" (RROHP, GGI), 4.

38. Ravindran, interview by Bourbonnais, 3.

39. Ravindran, interview by Bourbonnais, 7. See also Amparo Claro, interview by Nicole Bourbonnais, "Transcript, January 31 and March 7, 2022" (RROHP, GGI), 3.

40. Noeleen Heyzer interview, "Audio Recording," 2016 (OHP, WLP), 7:35.

41. Adrienne Germain, interview by Rebecca Sharpless, "Transcript of audio recording, 19–20 June, 25 September 2003" (PRHOHP, SSC), 10; Peggy Antrobus, interview by Nicole Bourbonnais, "Transcript, November 29 and 30, December 7, 2021" (RROHP, GGI), 5, 8, 41; on the latter, see Rosalind Petchesky, interview by Nicole Bourbonnais, "Transcript, October 18 and October 25, 2021" (RROHP, GGI); Amparo Claro, interview by Nicole Bourbonnais, "Transcript, January 31 and March 7, 2022" (RROHP, GGI), 4–5.

42. Sandra Kabir, interview by Deborah McFarlane, "Transcript of audio recording, 13–14 March, 2004" (PRHOHP, SSC).

43. Frances Kissling, interview by Rebecca Sharpless, "Transcript of audio recording, 13–14 September, 2002" (PRHOHP, SSC), 8.

44. Marge Berer, interview by Nicole Bourbonnais, "Transcript, November 1 and 3, 2021" (RROHP, GGI), 6. See also Joan Dunlop, interview by Rebecca Sharpless, "Transcript of audio recording, April 14–15, 2004" (PRHOHP, SSC).

45. Jacqueline Pitanguy interview, audio recording, 2015 (OHP, WLP), 1:02:13.

46. Heyzer eventually did give birth, although in a complicated pregnancy (Noeleen Heyzer interview, "Audio Recording," 2016 [OHP, WLP], track 1); Antrobus adopted her children (Peggy Antrobus, interview by Nicole Bourbonnais, "Transcript, November 29 and 30, December 7, 2021" (RROHP, GGI), 5).

47. Claudia García-Moreno, interview by Nicole Bourbonnais, "Transcript, July 21 and 26, 2021" (RROHP, GGI), 7–8.

48. Florence Manguyu, interview by Nicole Bourbonnais, "Transcript, April 26, May 3 and May 12, 2023" (RROHP, GGI), 21.

49. Claudia García-Moreno, interview by Nicole Bourbonnais, "Transcript, July 21 and 26, 2021" (RROHP, GGI), 8.

50. Noeleen Heyzer interview, "Audio Recording," 2016 (OHP, WLP), track 1.

51. Adetoun Ilumoka, interview by Nicole Bourbonnais, "Transcript, July 9 and 10, October 10, 2021" (RROHP, GGI), 13, 15–17.

52. Ravindran, interview by Nicole Bourbonnais (RROHP, GGI), 5.

53. Frances Kissling, interview by Rebecca Sharpless, "Transcript of audio recording, 13–14 September, 2002" (PRHOHP, SSC); Adrienne Germain, interview by Rebecca Sharpless, "Transcript of audio recording, 19–20 June, 25 September 2003" (PRHOHP, SSC); Joan Dunlop, interview by Rebecca Sharpless, "Transcript of audio recording, April 14–15, 2004" (PRHOHP, SSC); Jacqueline Pitanguy interview, audio recording, 2015 (OHP, WLP); Marge Berer, interview by Nicole Bourbonnais, "Transcript, November 1 and 3, 2021" (RROHP, GGI).

54. See, for example, Peggy Antrobus, interview by Nicole Bourbonnais, "Transcript, November 29 and 30, December 7, 2021" (RROHP, GGI), 4–7; Adetoun Ilumoka, interview by Nicole Bourbonnais, "Transcript, September 7, October 7 and October 10, 2021" (RROHP, GGI), 17–18; Gita Sen, interview by Nicole Bourbonnais, "Transcript, September 12, 19 and 28, 2022" (RROHP, GGI), 8–9.

55. Gita Sen, interview by Nicole Bourbonnais, "Transcript, September 12, 19 and 28, 2022" (RROHP, GGI), 5–7, 12.

56. Rosalind Petchesky, interview by Nicole Bourbonnais, "Transcript, October 18 and October 25, 2021" (RROHP, GGI), 6.

57. Petchesky, interview by Bourbonnais, 20.

58. Petchesky, interview by Bourbonnais, 14.

59. Amparo Claro, interview by Nicole Bourbonnais, "Transcript, January 31 and March 7, 2022" (RROHP, GGI), 6, 16.

60. Claro, interview by Bourbonnais, 7.

61. Joan Dunlop, interview by Rebecca Sharpless, "Transcript of audio recording, April 14–15, 2004" (PRHOHP, SSC), 6.

62. Adrienne Germain, interview by Rebecca Sharpless, "Transcript of audio recording, 19–20 June, 25 September 2003" (PRHOHP, SSC), 21.

63. Germain, interview by Rebecca Sharpless, 58, 76.

64. García-Moreno, interview by Bourbonnais, 14–15.

65. García-Moreno, interview by Bourbonnais, 16.

66. García-Moreno, interview by Bourbonnais, 16, 19.

67. Sandra Kabir, interview by Deborah McFarlane, "Transcript of audio recording, 13–14 March, 2004" (PRHOHP, SSC), 91.

68. Kabir, interview by McFarlane, 19.

69. Kabir, interview by McFarlane, 20–21.

70. Kabir, interview by McFarlane, 24.

71. Kabir, interview by McFarlane, 86.

72. Adrienne Germain, interview by Rebecca Sharpless, "Transcript of audio recording, 19–20 June, 25 September 2003" (PRHOHP, SSC), 128.

NOTES TO PAGES 158–161 › 233

73. Joan B. Dunlop, "Bangladesh Site Visit Report," 1984/12/30–1985/01/08 ("IWHC—General," B1, Joan B. Dunlop Papers, SSC-MS-00707, SSC), 2.

74. Ravindran, interview by Bourbonnais, "Transcript, July 13, 14, and 15, 2021" (RROHP, GGI), 8.

75. Ravindran, interview by Bourbonnais, 9.

76. Ravindran, interview by Bourbonnais, 8.

77. Ravindran, interview by Bourbonnais, 12.

78. Maggie Bangser, "Trip Report: March 9–22, 1988, Institute for Social Studies and Action," 1988/05 ("IWHC—General," B1, JD Papers, SSC), 26.

79. Dunlop, "Colombia Trip Notes," 1985/12 ("IWHC—General," B1, JD papers, SSC), pt. 2, 7.

80. Dunlop, "Colombia Trip Notes," pt. 1, 1, pt. 2, 2.

81. "Draft: A Time to Celebrate, a Time to Act: The International Women's Health Coalition, 1984–1995," 1995 ("History/Evaluations by Dixon-Mueller, '86 and '96," B1, AG Papers, SSC), 7.

82. Nelson, *More Than Medicine*; Nelson, *Women of Color and the Reproductive Rights Movement*; Silliman et. al, *Undivided Rights*; Luna, *Reproductive Rights as Human Rights*; Price, "What Is Reproductive Justice?"

83. Silliman, *Undivided Rights*, 69–92.

84. See, for example, Peggy Antrobus, interview by Nicole Bourbonnais, "Transcript, November 29 and 30, December 7, 2021" (RROHP, GGI), 10, 16; Ravindran, interview by Bourbonnais, 11, 20; Adetoun Ilumoka, interview by Nicole Bourbonnais, "Transcript, July 9 and 10, October 10, 2021" (RROHP, GGI), 41; García-Moreno, interview by Bourbonnais, "Transcript, July 21 and 26, 2021" (RROHP, GGI), 8; Gita Sen, interview by Nicole Bourbonnais, "Transcript, September 12, 19 and 28, 2022" (RROHP, GGI), 3–4.

85. Ravindran, interview by Bourbonnais, 11, Jacqueline Pitanguy interview, audio recording, 2015 (OHP, WLP), track 1.

86. Sen, interview by Bourbonnais, 13; see also 10.

87. Antrobus, interview by Bourbonnais, 16.

88. Antrobus, interview by Bourbonnais, 51.

89. Ravindran, interview by Bourbonnais, 9.

90. Sen, interview by Bourbonnais, 6–7.

91. Rosalind Petchesky, interview by Nicole Bourbonnais, "Transcript, October 18 and October 25, 2021" (RROHP, GGI), 14.

92. Petchesky, interview by Bourbonnais, 21–22.

93. Ravindran, interview by Bourbonnais, 21–22.

94. For the use of similar techniques in the women's health movement in the United States, see Kline, "Bodies of Evidence."

95. Adrienne Germain, interview by Rebecca Sharpless, "Transcript of audio recording, 19–20 June, 25 September 2003" (PRHOHP, SSC), 62.

96. Antrobus, interview by Nicole Bourbonnais, 18–19, 22; Noeleen Heyzer interview, "Audio Recording," 2016 (OHP, WLP); Joan Dunlop, interview by Rebecca Sharpless, "Transcript of audio recording, April 14–15, 2004" (PRHOHP, SSC), 78–79; Ravindran, interview by Bourbonnais, 15; Sen, interview by Bourbonnais, 15.

97. Price, "What Is Reproductive Justice?"; Luna, *Reproductive Rights as Human Rights.*

98. Bracke, "Contesting 'Global Sisterhood,'" 817, 820–21.

99. Rosalind P. Petchesky and Jennifer A. Weiner, "Global Feminist Perspectives on Reproductive Rights and Reproductive Health: A Report on the Special Sessions Held at the Fourth International Interdisciplinary Congress on Women," Hunter College, New York City, 1990/06/03–07 (F31, WRR Papers, AA), 6.

100. Ravindran, interview by Bourbonnais, 21.

101. Petchesky and Weiner, "Global Feminist Perspectives on Reproductive Rights and Reproductive Health," 12.

102. Petchesky and Weiner, "Global Feminist Perspectives on Reproductive Rights and Reproductive Health," 14.

103. Petchesky and Weiner, "Global Feminist Perspectives on Reproductive Rights and Reproductive Health," 6.

104. Joan Dunlop and Adrienne Germain to London Group, "International Women's Health Coalition Memorandum," 1992/11/30 (F17, WRR Papers, AA), "Appendix VI, List of Participants, London Meeting."

105. Adrienne Germain, interview by Rebecca Sharpless, "Transcript of audio recording, 19–20 June, 25 September 2003" (PRHOHP, SSC), 151.

106. Joan Dunlop, interview by Rebecca Sharpless, "Transcript of audio recording, April 14–15, 2004" (PRHOHP, SSC), 95–97.

107. García-Moreno, interview by Bourbonnais, 19, 21.

108. Dunlop, interview by Sharpless, 97.

109. See, for example, the changes suggested by WGNRR and Loes Keysers: "Draft 3: Women's Declaration on World Population Policies: Comments," 1993/01/08 (F33, WRR Papers, AA), 2.

110. For the original publication, see "Women's Voices '94—A Declaration on Population Policies," *Population and Development Review* 19, no. 3 (1993): 637–40.

111. "Women's Voices '94," 637–40. See also Joachim, *Agenda Setting, the UN and NGOs,* 149.

112. Higler, "International Women's Activism and the 1994 Cairo Population Conference," 133–34; Joachim, *Agenda Setting, the UN, and NGOs,* 150–51.

113. Joachim, *Agenda Setting, the UN and NGOs,* 151.

114. Maiguashca, "Theorizing Knowledge from Women's Political Practices," 215.

115. Joachim, *Agenda Setting, the UN, and NGOs,* 214–15. See also ANTIGENA, "A Criticism of 'Women's Declaration of Population Policies,'" 1993 (F14, WRR Papers, AA).

116. "Declaration of People's Perspectives on 'Population' Symposium," Comilla, Bangladesh, 1993/12/12–15 (F14, WRR Papers, AA), 1.

117. "Meetings Scheduled for 1992, 1993 and 1994," 1992 (F33, WRR Papers, AA), 1–3.

118. Antrobus, interview by Bourbonnais, 25; Corrêa, *Population and Reproductive Rights: Feminist Perspectives from the South*, viii–ix.

119. Antrobus, interview by Bourbonnais, 16.

120. Antrobus, interview by Bourbonnais, 25.

121. Corrêa, *Population and Reproductive Rights*, 8.

122. Corrêa, *Population and Reproductive Rights*, 47.

123. CEPIA and IWHC, "Women's Voices '94: A Proposal for an International Conference," 1993/04 ("IWHC—General, 1994–1998," B2, JD Papers, SSC); CEPIA and IWHC, "Reproductive Health and Justice," 1. For a more detailed discussion of the evolving goals and nature of the conference, see Nicole C. Bourbonnais, forthcoming, "Rio '94: International Visions of Reproductive Rights and Justice on the Eve of Cairo," in Maud Bracke et al. eds., *From Rights to Justice: Global Reproductive Politics since 1945* (Berkeley: University of California Press).

124. CEPIA and IWHC, "Reproductive Health and Justice," 2.

125. "List of Conference Participants," in CEPIA and IWHC, "Reproductive Health and Justice," 10–22.

126. Ravindran, interview by Bourbonnais, 24.

127. García-Moreno, interview by Bourbonnais, 17.

128. CEPIA and IWHC, "Reproductive Health and Justice," 1.

129. Sen, interview by Bourbonnais, 19.

130. Sen, interview by Bourbonnais, 20; García-Moreno, interview by Bourbonnais, 17.

131. Adrienne Germain, interview by Rebecca Sharpless, "Transcript of audio recording, 19–20 June, 25 September 2003" (PRHOHP, SSC), 154.

132. Sen, interview by Bourbonnais, 33.

133. CEPIA and IWHC, "Reproductive Health and Justice," 4.

134. CEPIA and IWHC, "Reproductive Health and Justice," 4.

135. CEPIA and IWHC, "Reproductive Health and Justice," 5.

136. CEPIA and IWHC, "Reproductive Health and Justice," 5.

137. CEPIA and IWHC, "Reproductive Health and Justice," 6.

138. CEPIA and IWHC, "Reproductive Health and Justice," 7.

139. CEPIA and IWHC, "Reproductive Health and Justice," 5.

140. Published as "Reproductive Rights/Human Rights," *Women's Global Network for Reproductive Rights* 44, 1993/07/09 (F16, WRR Papers, AA), 4.

141. Luna, *Reproductive Rights as Human Rights*, 67.

142. Solinger, *Reproductive Justice: An Introduction*, 9.

143. Quoted in Luna, *Reproductive Rights as Human Rights*, 150.

144. Luna and Luker, "Reproductive Justice."

145. Germain, interview by Sharpless, 156. See also Halfon, *The Cairo Consensus*, 69.

146. Petchesky, *Global Prescriptions*, 35.

147. Higler, "International Women's Activism and the 1994 Cairo Population Conference," 135–36.

148. García-Moreno, interview by Bourbonnais, 23.

149. Antrobus, interview by Bourbonnais, 26–27.

150. Halfon, *The Cairo Consensus*, 64.

151. Germain, interview by Sharpless, 161.

152. Halfon, *The Cairo Consensus*, 64.

153. García-Moreno, interview by Bourbonnais, 21.

154. Jacqueline Pitanguy interview, audio recording, 2015 (OHP, WLP), 1:02:25.

155. García-Moreno, interview by Bourbonnais, 26.

156. Dunlop, interview by Sharpless, 123, Germain, interview by Sharpless, 157–59, 168–69.

157. Sandra Kabir, interview by Deborah McFarlane, "Transcript of audio recording, 13–14 March, 2004" (PRHOHP, SSC), 52. See also Rosalind Petchesky, interview by Nicole Bourbonnais, "Transcript, October 18 and October 25, 2021" (RROHP, GGI), 24.

158. Dunlop, interview by Sharpless, 109.

159. T. Ravindran, interview by Bourbonnais, 27.

160. Joachim, *Agenda Setting, the UN and NGOs*, 365–66.

161. See Halfon, *The Cairo Consensus*; Maiguashca, "Theorizing Knowledge from Women's Political Practices."

162. García-Moreno, interview by Bourbonnais, 22.

163. Joachim, *Agenda Setting, the UN and NGOs*, 156.

164. United Nations, "Population and Development: Programme of Action Adopted at the International Conference on Population and Development" (Cairo, 5–13 September); see also Halfon, *The Cairo Consensus*, 65–82.

165. Luna, *Reproductive Rights as Human Rights*, 69.

166. Germain, interview by Sharpless, 169–70.

167. Dunlop, interview by Sharpless, 128.

168. Jacqueline Pitanguy interview, audio recording, 2015 (OHP, WLP), track 3, 57:00–1:02:25.

169. Amparo Claro, interview by Nicole Bourbonnais, "Transcript, January 31 and March 7, 2022" (RROHP, GGI), 23.

170. Adetoun Ilumoka, interview by Nicole Bourbonnais, "Transcript, July 9–10, October 10, 2021" (RROHP, GGI), 43–44.

171. Marge Berer, interview by Nicole Bourbonnais, "Transcript, November 1 and 3, 2021" (RROHP, GGI), 19–22, 27.

172. Peggy Antrobus, interview by Nicole Bourbonnais, "Transcript, November 29 and 30, December 7, 2021" (RROHP, GGI), 30.

173. Chandra Talpade Mohanty, "Under Western Eyes: Feminist Scholarship and Colonial Discourses," *boundary 2* 12, no. 3 (1984): 334, 352.

174. Bracke, "Women's Rights, Family Planning, and Population Control," 15; Joachim, *Agenda Setting, the UN and NGOs*, 81–82.

175. Ravindran, interview by Bourbonnais, 13. See also Bracke, "Women's Rights, Family Planning, and Population Control," 16.

176. Sen, interview by Bourbonnais, 19, 29.

177. Ilumoka, interview by Bourbonnais, "Transcript, July 9–10, October 10, 2021" (RROHP, GGI), 40–43.

178. On this debate, see, for example, Morgan, "Reproductive Rights or Reproductive Justice?"; Bracke, "Contesting 'Global Sisterhood,'" 823.

179. Morgan, "Reproductive Rights or Reproductive Justice?"; Luker, "Reproductive Justice"; Price, "What Is Reproductive Justice?"

180. Morgan, "Reproductive Rights or Reproductive Justice?," 144.

181. Higler, "International Women's Activism and the 1994 Cairo Population Conference," 124.

182. Germain, interview by Sharpless, 151.

183. Noeleen Heyzer interview, "Audio Recording," 2016 (OHP, WLP), track 1, 44:56.

184. Antrobus, interview by Bourbonnais, 24; Petchesky, interview by Bourbonnais, 22–24; Frances Kissling, interview by Rebecca Sharpless, "Transcript of audio recording, 13–14 September, 2002" (PRHOHP, SSC), 59–60, 79.

185. Kissling, interview by Sharpless, 76.

186. Corrêa, *Population and Reproductive Rights*, 103.

187. Antrobus, interview by Bourbonnais, 47.

188. Ravindran, interview by Bourbonnais, 24. For a similar position, see Petchesky, interview by Bourbonnais, 29; Antrobus, interview by Bourbonnais, 12.

189. Jacqueline Pitanguy interview, audio recording, 2015 (OHP, WLP), track 3.

190. Germain, interview by Sharpless, 166.

191. Berer, interview by Bourbonnais, 19, 27.

192. Solinger and Nakachi, "Reproductive States," 15, 22.

193. Ravindran, interview by Bourbonnais, 27; Higler, "International Women's Activism and the 1994 Cairo Population Conference," 138; Petchesky, *Global Prescriptions*, 42–54.

194. Petchesky, *Global Prescriptions*, 42–54.

195. Petchesky, *Global Prescriptions*, 42–54. See also Cueto, *The World Health Organization: A History*, 167–68.

196. Petchesky, interview by Bourbonnais, 24.

197. Pitanguy interview, Track 3, 1:04:50; Dunlop, interview by Sharpless, 131; Ravindran, interview by Bourbonnais, 30.

198. Pieper Mooney, "Re-Visiting Histories of Modernization, Progress, and (Unequal) Citizenship Rights."

199. Solinger, "Reproductive States," 25–26.

200. Betsy Hartmann, "10 Reasons Why Population Control Is Not the Solution to Global Warming," *Different Takes* 57 (Winter 2009): 1–4.

201. Jade S. Sasser, "Sexual Stewardship: Environment, Development, and the Gendered Politics of Population," in *Routledge Handbook of Gender and Environment*, ed. Sherilyn MacGregor (New York: Routledge, 2017), 354. See also Jade S. Sasser, *On Infertile Ground: Population Control and Women's Rights in the Era of Climate Change* (New York: NYU Press, 2018).

202. Luna, *Reproductive Rights as Human Rights*, 126.

203. Kabir, interview by McFarlane, 98–99.

204. Petchesky, interview by Bourbonnais, 23.

205. Richey, "Global Knowledge/Local Bodies"; de Zordo, "Programming the Body, Planning Reproduction, Governing Life."

206. Richey, "Global Knowledge/Local Bodies."

207. McCarthy, "From Government to Grass-Roots Reform." See also Kissling, interview by Sharpless, 145; Petchesky, interview by Bourbonnais, 23; Sen, interview by Bourbonnais, 30; Claro, interview by Bourbonnais, 7–9.

208. Sen, interview by Bourbonnais, 31.

209. Marieme Helie Lucas interview, audio recording, 2015 (OHP, WLP), track 2, 25:30; Germain, interview by Sharpless, 80, 103, 124, 164; Ravindran, interview by Bourbonnais, 12.

210. Claro, interview by Bourbonnais, 18.

211. Antrobus, interview by Bourbonnais, 14.

212. Ravindran, interview by Bourbonnais, 10.

213. Ravindran, interview by Bourbonnais, 28.

214. Ravindran, interview by Bourbonnais, 22.

215. Ravindran, interview by Bourbonnais, 28.

216. Loes Keysers, "The Costs of the Women and Health Gains at the UN Conferences: New Challenges for the Women's Health Movement," in *8th International Women and Health Meeting*. Rio de Janeiro, Brazil: 1997/03/17 (F33, WRR, AA), 8.

217. Lopez, *Matters of Choice*, 121.

218. Lopez, *Matters of Choice*, 121.

219. Connelly, *Fatal Misconception*, 364.

220. Antrobus, interview by Bourbonnais, 41.

221. Corrêa, *Population and Reproductive Rights*, 87.

222. Antrobus, interview by Bourbonnais, 29–30.

EPILOGUE

1. Cynthia Enloe, *Bananas, Beaches and Bases: Making Feminist Sense of International Politics*, 2nd ed. (Berkeley: University of California Press, 2014).

2. Sreenivas, *Reproduction and the Making of Modern India*, 89. One could think, for example, of the birth control advocacy of Subhas Chandra Bose and B. R. Ambedkar in India (Ahluwalia, *Reproductive Restraints*, 62–63), or the proletarian movement in Japan (Takeuchi-Demirci, *Contraceptive Diplomacy*, 44).

Bibliography

ARCHIVAL COLLECTIONS

Atria Archives, Amsterdam, the Netherlands (AA)
Women's Reproductive Rights Papers (WRR Papers)
Francis A. Countway Library of Medicine, Boston, United States (FACLM)
Clarence Gamble Papers (CG Papers)
Geneva Graduate Institute Archives, Geneva, Switzerland (GGI)
Reproductive Rights Oral History Project (RROHP)
National Archives of Jamaica, Spanishtown, Jamaica (NAJ)
May Farquharson Collection (MFC)
National Library of Jamaica, Kingston, Jamaica (NLJ)
Rare Books and Pamphlets
Rockefeller Archive Centre, Sleepy Hollow, United States (RAC)
Ford Foundation Papers (FF Papers)
Population Council Papers, Accession 2 (PC Papers)
Schlesinger Library, Cambridge, MA, United States (SL)
Edna Rankin McKinnon Papers (ERM Papers)
Emily Hartshorne Mudd Papers (EHM Papers)
Martha May Eliot Papers (MME Papers)
Sarah Merry Bradley Gamble Papers (SMBG Papers)
Schlesinger-Rockefeller Oral History Project (SROHP)
Sophia Smith Collection, Northampton, MA, United States (SSC)
Adaline Pendleton Satterthwaite Papers (APS Papers)
Adrienne Germain Papers (AG Papers)
Dorothy Hamilton Brush Papers (DHB Papers)
Joan Dunlop Papers (JD Papers)
Margaret Sanger Papers (MS Papers)
Population and Reproductive Health Oral History Project (PRHOHP)
University of the West Indies, St. Augustine, Trinidad (UWI)
Center for Gender and Development (CGD)
Alma Jordan Library (AJL)
Wellcome Library, London, United Kingdom (WL)
Family Planning Association Papers (FPA Papers)
Women's Learning Partnership, Online Archive (WLP)
Oral History Project (OHP)

BOOKS, ARTICLES, AND CHAPTERS

Ahluwalia, Sanjam. *Reproductive Restraints: Birth Control in India, 1877–1947*. Urbana and Chicago: University of Illinois Press, 2008.

Ahluwalia, Sanjam, and Daksha Pamar. "From Gandhi to Gandhi: Contraceptive Technologies and Sexual Politics in Postcolonial India, 1947–1977." In *Reproductive States: Global Perspectives on the Invention and Implementation of Population Policy*, edited by Rickie Solinger and Mie Nakachi, 124–55. Oxford: Oxford University Press, 2016.

Akin, Ayse. "Emergence of the Family Planning Program in Turkey." In *The Global Family Planning Revolution: Three Decades of Population Policies and Programs*, edited by Warren C. Robinson and John A. Ross, 85–102. New York: World Bank, 2007.

Allman, Jean. "Making Mothers: Missionaries, Medical Officers and Women's Work in Colonial Asante, 1924–1945." *History Workshop* 38 (1994): 23–47.

Altink, Henrice. *Destined for a Live of Service: Defining African-Jamaican Womanhood, 1865–1938*. Manchester and New York: Manchester University Press, 2011.

Anderson, Benedict. *Imagined Communities: Reflections on the Origin and Spread of Nationalism*. New York: Verso, 1983.

Antrobus, Peggy. *The Global Women's Movement: Origins, Issues and Strategies*. Global Issues. London: Zed Books, 2004.

Ashford, Holly. *Development and Women's Reproductive Health in Ghana, 1920–1982*. New York: Routledge, 2022.

Barnett, Michael. *Empire of Humanity: A History of Humanitarianism*. Ithaca, NY, and London: Cornell University Press, 2011.

Baron, Beth. "The Origins of Family Planning: Aziza Hussein, American Experts, and the Egyptian State." *Journal of Middle East Women's Studies* 4, no. 3 (Fall 2008): 31–57.

Bashford, Alison. *Global Population: History, Geopolitics and Life on Earth*. New York: Colombia University Press, 2014.

———. "Nation, Empire, Globe: The Spaces of Population Debate in the Interwar Years." *Comparative Studies in Society and History* 49, no. 1 (2007): 170–201.

———. "Population, Geopolitics, and International Organizations in the Mid Twentieth Century." *Journal of World History* 19, no. 3 (Sept 2008): 327–47.

Bashford, Alison, and Phillipa Levine, eds. *The Oxford Handbook of the History of Eugenics*. Oxford: Oxford University Press, 2010.

Berg, Annika. "A Suitable Country: The Relationship between Sweden's Interwar Population Policy and Family Planning in Postindependence India." *Berichte zur Wissenschaftsgeschichte* 33, no. 3 (2010): 297–320.

Birn, Anne-Emanuelle. "Skirting the Issue: Women and International Health in Historical Perspective." *American Journal of Public Health* 89, no. 3 (March 1999): 399–407.

Bourbonnais, Nicole C. *Birth Control in the Decolonizing Caribbean: Reproductive Politics and Practices on Four Islands, 1930–1970*. New York: Cambridge University Press, 2016.

———. "'A Grande Causa': Missionários do Planeamento Familiar no Fim do Império [The "Great Cause": Family Planning Missionaries at the End of Empire]." *Ler História* 85 (2024).

———. "The Intimate Labor of Internationalism: Maternalist Humanitarians and the Mid-20th Century Family Planning Movement." *Journal of Global History* 17, no. 3 (November 2022): 515–38.

———. "Population Control, Family Planning, and Maternal Health Networks in the 1960s/70s: Diary of an International Consultant." *Bulletin of the History of Medicine* 93, no. 3 (2019): 335–64.

———. "Rio '94: International Visions of Reproductive Rights and Justice on the Eve of Cairo." In *From Rights to Justice: Global Reproductive Politics since 1945*, edited by Maud Bracke, Catherine Burns, Jesse Olszynko-Gryn, and Raul Necochea Lopez. Berkeley: University of California Press, forthcoming.

Bracke, Maud Anne. "Contesting 'Global Sisterhood': The Global Women's Health Movement, the United Nations and the Different Meanings of Reproductive Rights (1970s–80s)." *Gender & History* 35 (2023): 811–29.

———. "Women's Rights, Family Planning, and Population Control: The Emergence of Reproductive Rights in the United Nations (1960s–70s)." *International History Review* 44, no. 4 (2021): 751–71.

Bradley, Marc Philip. "Decolonization, the Global South, and the Cold War, 1919–1962." In *The Cambridge History of the Cold War Volume 1, Origins, 1945–1962*, edited by Melvyn P. Leffler and Odd Arne Westad, 464–85. Cambridge: Cambridge University Press, 2012.

Briggs, Laura. "Discourses of 'Forced Sterilization' in Puerto Rico: The Problem with the Speaking Subaltern." *differences: A Journal of Feminist Cultural Studies* 10, no. 2 (1998): 30–66.

———. *Reproducing Empire: Race, Sex, Science, and U.S. Imperialism in Puerto Rico.* Berkeley: University of California Press, 2002.

Briggs, Laura, Faye Ginsburg, Elena R. Gutiérrez, Rosalind Petchesky, Rayna Rapp, Andrea Smith, and Chikako Takeshita. "Roundtable: Reproductive Technologies and Reproductive Justice." *Frontiers: A Journal of Women Studies* 34, no. 3 (2013): 102–25.

Brown, B. B. "Facing the 'Black Peril': The Politics of Population Control in South Africa." *Journal of Southern African Studies* 13, no. 2 (1987): 256–73.

Brown, George F. "Morocco: First Steps in Family Planning." In *The Global Family Planning Revolution: Three Decades of Population Policies and Programs*, edited by Warren C. Robinson and John A. Ross, 71–82. New York: World Bank, 2007.

———. "Tunisia: The Debut of Family Planning." In *The Global Family Planning Revolution: Three Decades of Population Policies and Programs*, edited by Warren C. Robinson and John A. Ross, 59–69. New York: World Bank, 2007.

Browner, Carole H., and Carolyn F. Sargent, eds. *Reproduction, Globalization, and the State: New Theoretical and Ethnographic Perspectives.* Durham, NC: Duke University Press, 2011.

———. "Towards Global Anthropological Studies of Reproduction: Concepts, Methods, Theoretical Approaches." In *Reproduction, Globalization, and the State: New Theoretical and Ethnographic Perspectives*, edited by Carole H. Browner and Carolyn F. Sargent. Durham, NC: Duke University Press, 2011.

Burgnard, Sylvie. "The Family Planning Service and the Pill in Geneva (1965–1980): A Step Towards Women's Emancipation?" *The History of the Family* 20, no. 1 (2014): 24–40.

Campbell, Chloe. *Race and Empire: Eugenics in Colonial Kenya.* Manchester and New York: Manchester University Press, 2007.

Carranza, María. "'In the Name of Forests': Highlights of the History of Family Planning in Costa Rica." *Canadian Journal of Latin American and Caribbean Studies: Special Issue: Landscapes of Latin American Health* 35, no. 69 (January 2010): 119–54.

Carter, Eric D. "Population Control, Public Health, and Development in Mid Twentieth Century Latin America." *Journal of Historical Geography* 62 (October 2018): 96–105.

Caulier, Mathieu. "The Population Revolution: From Population Policies to Reproductive Health and Women's Rights Politics." *International Review of Sociology* 20, no. 2 (July 2010): 357–58.

CEPIA and IWHC. "Reproductive Health and Justice: International Women's Health Conference for Cairo '94." Conference Report. Rio de Janiero, Brazil: CEPIA and IWHC, 1994.

Chávez, Ana María Medina. "The Social Context of the Birth Control Debate in Colombia in the 1960s and 1970s: Politics, Medicine and Society." *Historia, ciencias, saude—Manguinhos* 21, no. 4 (2014): 1467–73.

Cho, Eunjoo. "Making the 'Modern' Family: The Discourse of Sexuality in the Family Planning Program in South Korea." *Sexualities* 19, no. 7 (2016): 802–18.

Claeys, Vicky. "Brave and Angry: The Creation and Development of the International Planned Parenthood Federation (IPPF)." *The European Journal of Contraception & Reproductive Health Care : The Official Journal of the European Society of Contraception* 15 (December 2010): S67–76.

Cohen, Deborah A. "Private Lives in Public Spaces: Marie Stopes, the Mothers' Clinics and the Practice of Contraception." *History Workshop* 35 (Spring 1993): 95–116.

Connelly, Matthew. *Fatal Misconception: The Struggle to Control World Population.* Cambridge, MA: The Belknap Press of Harvard University Press, 2008.

———. "Population Control Is History: New Perspectives on the International Campaign to Limit Population Growth." *Comparative Studies in Society and History* 45, no. 1 (January 2003): 122–47.

Cooper, Frederick, and Randall Packard. "Introduction." In *International Development and the Social Sciences*, edited by Frederick Cooper and Randall Packard, 1–41. Berkeley: University of California Press, 1997.

———, eds. *International Development and the Social Sciences.* Berkeley: University of California Press, 1997.

Cornwall, Andrea, Sonia Corrêa, and Susie Jolly. *Development with a Body: Making the Connections between Sexuality, Human Rights and Development.* London: Zed Books, 2008.

Corrêa, Sonia, and Rebecca Reichmann. *Population and Reproductive Rights: Feminist Perspectives from the South.* London: Zed Books, 1994.

Critchlow, D T. "Birth Control, Population Control, and Family Planning: An Overview." *Journal of Policy History: JPH* 7, no. 1 (1995): 1–21.

Cueto, Marcos, Theodore M. Brown, and Elizabeth Fee. *The World Health Organization: A History.* Cambridge: Cambridge University Press, 2019.

Dalsgaard, Anne Line. *Matters of Life and Longing: Female Sterilisation in Northeast Brazil.* Denmark: Museum Tusculanum Press, 2004.

Davin, Anna. "Imperialism and Motherhood." *History Workshop* 5 (Spring 1998) 9–85.

Deverell, Colville. "The International Planned Parenthood Federation—Its Role in Developing Countries." *Demography* 5, no. 2 (1 January 1968): 574–77.

de Zordo, Silvia. "Programming the Body, Planning Reproduction, Governing Life: The '(Ir-) Rationality' of Family Planning and the Embodiment of Social Inequalities in Salvador De Bahia (Brazil)." *Anthropology & Medicine* 19, no. 2 (2012): 207–23.

Dobos, Corina. "Global Challenges, Local Knowledges: Politics and Expertise at the World Population Conference in Bucharest, 1974." *East Central Europe* 45 (2018): 215–44.

BIBLIOGRAPHY › 245

Dudgeon, Matthew R., and Marcia C. Inhorn. "Gender, Masculinity and Reproduction: Anthropological Perspectives." In *Reconceiving the Second Sex: Men, Masculinity, and Reproduction*, edited by Matthew R. Dudgeon and Marcia C. Inhorn, 72–102. New York: Berghahn Books, 2009.

Duff, S. E. "'Dear Mrs Brown': Social Purity, Sex Education and the Women's Christian Temperance Union in Early Twentieth-Century South Africa." *Social History (London)* 45, no. 4 (October 2020): 476–99.

Dwyer, Leslie K. "Spectacular Sexuality: Nationalism, Development and the Politics of Family Planning in Indonesia." In *Gender Ironies of Nationalism: Sexing the Nation*, edited by Tamar Mayer, 25–64. London and New York: Routledge, 2000.

Dykeman, Wilma. *Too Many People, Too Little Love: Edna Rankin McKinnon, Pioneer for Birth Control*. Austin, TX: Holt, Rinehart and Winston, 1974.

Ellis, Patrick, and Jesse Olszynko-Gryn. "Communicating Overpopulation to a Global Audience: Disney's *Family Planning* (1968)." *Journal of Global History* (2024): 1–24.

El Shakry, Omnia. "Reproducing the Family: Biopolitics in Twentieth-Century Egypt." In *Reproductive States: Global Perspectives on the Invention and Implementation of Population Policy*, edited by Rickie Solinger and Mie Nakachi. Oxford: Oxford University Press, 2016.

Enloe, Cynthia. *Bananas, Beaches and Bases: Making Feminist Sense of International Politics*, 2nd ed. Berkeley: University of California Press, 2014.

Espinosa Tavares, Martha Liliana. "'They Are Coming in So Fast That if We Had Publicity about the Clinic We Would Be Swamped': Edris Rice-Wray, the First Family Planning Clinic in Mexico (1959), and the Intervention of US-Based Private Foundations." *Journal of Women's History* 34 (2022): 76–96.

Fan, Susan. "Hong Kong: Evolution of the Family Planning Program." In *The Global Family Planning Revolution: Three Decades of Population Policies and Programs*, edited by Warren C. Robinson and John A. Ross, 193–200. New York: World Bank, 2007.

Fisher, Kate. "'She Was Quite Satisfied with the Arrangements I Made': Gender and Birth Control in Britain 1920–1950." *Past & Present* 169 (2000): 161–93.

Gawin, Magdalena. "The Sex Reform Movement and Eugenics in Interwar Poland." *Studies in History and Philosophy of Biological and Biomedical Sciences* 39, no. 2 (June 2008): 181–86.

Ginsburg, Faye D., and Rayna Rapp. "Introduction: Conceiving the New World Order." In *Conceiving the New World Order: The Global Politics of Reproduction*, 1–18. Berkeley: University of California Press, 1995.

Goldberg, Michelle. *The Means of Reproduction: Sex, Power, and the Future of the World*. London: Penguin Books, 2010.

Gordon, Linda. *The Moral Property of Women: A History of Birth Control Politics in America*. Chicago: University of Illinois Press, 2002.

Greenhalgh, Susan. *Just One Child: Science and Policy in Deng's China*. Berkeley: University of California Press, 2008.

Gunn, Simon, and Lucy Faire. *Research Methods for History*. Edinburgh: Edinburgh University Press, 2012.

Halfon, Saul. *The Cairo Consensus: Demographic Surveys, Women's Empowerment, and Regime Change in Population Policy*. Lanham, MD: Lexington Books, 2007.

Hartman, Saidiya, *Wayward Lives, Beautiful Experiments: Intimate Histories of Social Upheaval*. New York: W. W. Norton and Company, 2019.

Hartmann, Betsy. "Liberal Ends, Illiberal Means: National Security, 'Environmental Conflict' and the Making of the Cairo Consensus." *Indian Journal of Gender Studies* 13, no. 2 (2006): 195–227.

———. *Reproductive Rights and Wrongs: The Global Politics of Population Control.* Boston: South End Press, 1995 [1987].

———. "10 Reasons Why Population Control Is Not the Solution to Global Warming." *Different Takes* 57 (Winter 2009): 1–4.

Heisel, Donald F. "Family Planning in Kenya in the 1960s and 1970s." In *The Global Family Planning Revolution: Three Decades of Population Policies and Programs,* edited by Warren C. Robinson and John A. Ross, 393–417. New York: World Bank, 2007.

Herrin, Alejandro N. "Development of the Philippines' Family Planning Program: The Early Years, 1967–80." In *The Global Family Planning Revolution: Three Decades of Population Policies and Programs,* edited by Warren C. Robinson and John A. Ross, 277–97. New York: World Bank, 2007.

Higler, Amy J. "International Women's Activism and the 1994 Cairo Population Conference." In *Gender Politics in Global Governance,* edited by Mary K. Meyler and Elisabeth Prügl, 122–41. Lanham, MD: Rowman & Littlefield, 1998.

Hilton, Mathew, et al. "History and Humanitarianism: A Conversation." *Past and Present* 241 (November 2018): e1–e38.

Hirsch, Jennifer. "Catholics Using Contraceptives: Religion, Family Planning, and Interpretive Agency in Rural Mexico." *Studies in Family Planning* 39, no. 2 (June 2008): 93–104.

Hodges, Sarah. *Contraception, Colonialism and Commerce: Birth Control in South India, 1920–1940.* Burlington, Ashgate Publishing Ltd., 2008.

Hull, Terence H. "Formative Years of Family Planning in Indonesia." In *The Global Family Planning Revolution: Three Decades of Population Policies and Programs,* edited by Warren C. Robinson and John A. Ross, 235–56. New York: World Bank, 2007.

Huston, Perdita. *Motherhood by Choice: Pioneers in Women's Health and Family Planning.* New York: The Feminist Press at the City University of New York, 1992.

Ittmann, Karl. *A Problem of Great Importance: Population, Race and Power in the British Empire, 1918–1973.* Berkeley: University of California Press, 2013.

Janssens, Angélique. "'Were Women Present at the Demographic Transition?': A Question Revisited." *History of the Family* 12 (2007): 43–49.

Joachim, Jutta. *Agenda Setting, the UN, and NGOs: Gender Violence and Reproductive Rights.* Washington, DC: Georgetown University Press, 2007.

———. "Framing Issues and Seizing Opportunities: The UN, NGOs, and Women's Rights." *International Studies Quarterly* 47, no. 2 (2003): 247–74.

Joffe, Carole. *The Regulation of Sexuality: Experiences of Family Planning Workers.* Philadelphia: Temple University Press, 1986.

Johnson, Jennifer. "The Origins of Family Planning in Tunisia: Reform, Public Health, and International Aid." *Bulletin of the History of Medicine* 92, no. 4 (2018): 664–93.

Jones, Margaret. "Infant and Maternal Health Services in Ceylon, 1900–1948: Imperialism or Welfare?" *Social History of Medicine: The Journal of the Society for the Social History of Medicine* 15, no. 2 (August 2002): 263–89.

Kaler, Amy. *Running after Pills: Politics, Gender, and Contraception in Colonial Zimbabwe.* Portsmouth: Heinemann, 2003.

BIBLIOGRAPHY › 247

———. "A Threat to the Nation and a Threat to the Men: The Banning of Depo-Provera in Zimbabwe, 1981." *Journal of Southern African Studies* 24, no. 2 (June 1998): 347–76.

Kashani-Sabet, Firoozeh. *Conceiving Citizens: Women and the Politics of Motherhood in Iran*. Oxford and New York: Oxford University Press, 2011.

———. "Iran's Population Policies: A Historical Debate." In *Reproductive States: Global Perspectives on the Invention and Implementation of Population Policy*, edited by Rickie Solinger and Mie Nakachi, 196–217. Oxford: Oxford University Press, 2016.

Kim, Taek Il, and John A. Ross. "The Korean Breakthrough." In *The Global Family Planning Revolution: Three Decades of Population Policies and Programs*, edited by Warren C. Robinson and John A. Ross, 177–92. New York: World Bank, 2007.

Klancher Merchant, Emily. *Building the Population Bomb*. Oxford: Oxford University Press, 2021.

Klausen, Susanne. *Abortion under Apartheid: Nationalism, Sexuality, and Women's Reproductive Rights in South Africa*. Oxford: Oxford University Press, 2015.

———. *Race, Maternity, and the Politics of Birth Control in South Africa, 1910–39*. Basingstoke, Hampshire, and New York: Palgrave Macmillan, 2004.

Klein, Marian van der, Rebecca Jo Plant, Nichole Sanders, and Lori R. Weintrop. *Maternalism Reconsidered: Motherhood, Welfare and Social Policy in the Twentieth Century*. New York: Berghahn Books, 2012.

Kline, Wendy. "Bodies of Evidence: Activists, Patients, and the FDA Regulation of Depo-Provera." *Journal of Women's History* 22, no. 3 (Fall 2010): 64–87.

Knudsen, Lara M., and Betsy Hartmann. *Reproductive Rights in a Global Context: South Africa, Uganda, Peru, Denmark, the United States, Vietnam, Jordan*. Nashville: Vanderbilt University Press, 2006.

Ladd-Taylor, Molly. "Toward Defining Maternalism in U.S. History." *Journal of Women's History* 5, no. 2 (1993): 110–13.

Laite, Julia. "Traffickers and Pimps in the Era of White Slavery." *Past & Present* 237, no. 1 (November 2017): 237–69.

Lankford, Kathryn. "More Than a Way Station: Ground-Level Experiences in the Field Trials of Oral Contraceptives and IUDs in Puerto Rico, 1956–1966." PhD diss., Department of History, Michigan State University, 2021.

Linder, Doris H. *Crusader for Sex Education: Elise Ottesen-Jensen (1886–1973) in Scandinavia and on the International Scene*. Lanham, MD: University Press of America, 1996.

Lopera López, Juan Alejandro. "Paternidad O Procreación Responsable: Iglesia Católica, Acción Cultural Popular Y Control De La Natalidad En Colombia (1964– 1978)." *Historia y Sociedad* 31 (July–December 2016): 235–67.

Lopez, Iris. *Matters of Choice: Puerto Rican Women's Struggle for Reproductive Freedom*. New Brunswick, NJ: Rutgers University Press, 2008.

Lopreite, Debora. "Travelling Ideas and Domestic Policy Change: The Transnational Politics of Reproductive Rights/Health in Argentina." *Global Social Policy* 12, no. 2 (August 2012): 109–28.

Löwy, Ilana. "Defusing the Population Bomb in the 1950s: Foam Tablets in India." *Studies in History and Philosophy of Biological and Biomedical Sciences* 43 (2012): 583–93.

Luna, Zakiya. *Reproductive Rights as Human Rights: Women of Color and the Fight for Reproductive Justice*. New York: New York University Press, 2020.

Luna, Zakiya, and Kristin Luker. "Reproductive Justice." *Annual Review of Law and Social Science* 9 (2013): 327–52.

MacNamara, Trent. *Birth Control and American Modernity: A History of Popular Ideas*. Cambridge: Cambridge University Press, 2018.

Magnússon, Sigurõur Gylfi, and István M. Szijártó. *What Is Microhistory? Theory and Practice*. Oxon: Routledge Press, 2013.

Maiguashca, Bice. "Theorizing Knowledge from Women's Political Practices: The Case of the Women's Reproductive Rights Movement." *International Feminist Journal of Politics* 7, no. 2 (2005): 207–32.

Margulies, L. "History of Intrauterine Devices." *Bulletin of the New York Academy of Medicine* 51, no. 5 (May 1975): 662–67.

McCarthy, Kathleen. "From Government to Grass-Roots Reform: The Ford Foundation's Population Programmes in South Asia, 1959–1981." *Voluntas: International Journal of Voluntary and Nonprofit Organizations* 6, no. 3 (1995): 292–316.

McLaren, Angus, and Arlene T. McLaren. *The Bedroom and the State: The Changing Practices and Politics of Contraception and Abortion in Canada, 1880–1997*. Toronto: McClelland & Stewart, 1986.

Measham, Anthony R., and Guillermo Lopez-Escobar. "Against the Odds: Colombia's Role in the Family Planning Revolution." In *The Global Family Planning Revolution: Three Decades of Population Policies and Programs*, edited by Warren C. Robinson and John A. Ross, 121–35. New York: World Bank, 2007.

Moore, Richard. "Family Planning in Iran, 1960–79." In *The Global Family Planning Revolution: Three Decades of Population Policies and Programs*, edited by Warren C. Robinson and John A. Ross, 32–57. New York: World Bank, 2007.

Morgan, John. "Anglicanism, Family Planning and Contraception: The Development of a Moral Teaching and Its Ecumenical Implications." *Journal of Anglican Studies* 16, no. 2 (2018): 147–69.

Morgan, Lynn M. "Reproductive Rights or Reproductive Justice? Lessons from Argentina." *Health and Human Rights Journal* 17, no. 1 (2015): 136–47.

Murphy, Michelle. "Technology, Governmentality, and Population Control." *History and Technology* 26, no. 1 (March 2010): 69–76.

Nakachi, Mie. "Liberation without Contraception? The Rise of the Abortion Empire and Pronatalism in Socialist and Postsocialist Russia." In *Reproductive States: Global Perspectives on the Invention and Implementation of Population Policy*, edited by Rickie Solinger and Mie Nakachi, 290–328. Oxford: Oxford University Press, 2016.

Nandagiri, Rishita. "What's So Troubling About 'Voluntary' Family Planning Anyway? A Feminist Perspective." *Population Studies* 75, no. S1 (2021): 221–34.

Narayan, Uma. *Dislocating Cultures: Identities, Traditions and Third World Feminisms*. London: Taylor and Francis, 1997.

Necochea López, Raúl. "Gambling on the Protestants: The Pathfinder Fund and Birth Control in Peru, 1958–1965." *Bulletin of the History of Medicine* 88, no. 2 (2014): 344–71.

———. *A History of Family Planning in Twentieth-Century Peru*. Chapel Hill: University of North Carolina Press, 2014.

BIBLIOGRAPHY › 249

Nelson, Jennifer. *More Than Medicine: A History of the Feminist Women's Health Movement*. New York and London: New York University Press, 2015.

———. *Women of Color and the Reproductive Rights Movement*. New York and London: New York University Press, 2003.

Nguyen, Thuy Linh. "Overpopulation, Racial Degeneracy and Birth Control in French Colonial Vietnam." *Journal of Colonialism & Colonial History* 19, no. 3 (2018).

Oudshoorn, Nelly. *The Male Pill: A Biography of a Technology in the Making*. Durham, NC, and London: Duke University Press, 2003.

Packard, Randall M. *A History of Global Health: Interventions into the Lives of Other Peoples*. Baltimore: Johns Hopkins University Press, 2016.

Parry, Manon. *Broadcasting Birth Control: Mass Media and Family Planning*. New Brunswick, NJ: Rutgers University Press, 2013.

Pearce, Tola Olu. "Population Policies and the 'Creation' of Africa." *Africa Development* 19, no. 3 (1994): 61–76.

Pedersen, Susan. "The Maternalist Moment in British Colonial Policy: The Controversy over 'Child Slavery' in Hong Kong 1917–1941." *Past & Present* 171, no. 1 (2001): 161–202.

Petchesky, Rosalind P. *Global Prescriptions: Gendering Health and Human Rights*. London: Zed Books, 2003.

Pieper Mooney, Jadwiga E. *The Politics of Motherhood: Maternity and Women's Rights in Twentieth-Century Chile*. Pittsburgh: University of Pittsburgh Press, 2009.

———. "Re-Visiting Histories of Modernization, Progress, and (Unequal) Citizenship Rights: Coerced Sterilization in Peru and in the United States." *History Compass* 8, no. 9 (2010): 1026–54.

Pigg, Stacey Leigh. "'Found in Most Traditional Societies': Traditional Medical Practitioners between Culture and Development." In *International Development and the Social Sciences*, edited by Frederick Cooper and Randall Packard, 259–90. Berkeley: University of California Press, 1997.

Price, Kimala. "What Is Reproductive Justice? How Women of Color Activists Are Redefining the Pro-Choice Paradigm." *Meridians: feminism, race, transnationalism* 10, no. 2 (2010): 42–65.

Putnam, Lara. "Global Child-Saving, Transatlantic Maternalism, and the Pathologization of Caribbean Childhood, 1930s–1940s." *Atlantic Studies* 11, no. 4 (October 2014): 491–514.

Reichenbach, Laura, and Mindy Jane Roseman. *Reproductive Health and Human Rights: The Way Forward*. Philadelphia: University of Pennsylvania Press, 2009.

Reverby, Susan M. "Ethical Failures and History Lessons: The U.S. Public Health Service Research Studies in Tuskegee and Guatemala." *Public Health Review* 34, no. 1 (2012): 1–18.

Richey, Lisa. "Family Planning and the Politics of Population in Tanzania: International to Local Discourse." *Journal of Modern African Studies* 37, no. 3 (1999): 457–87.

———. "Global Knowledge/Local Bodies: Family Planning Service Providers' Interpretations of Contraceptive Knowledge(s)." *Demographic Research* 18, no. 17 (2009): 469–98.

Roberts, Dorothy. *Killing the Black Body: Race, Reproduction, and the Meaning of Liberty*. New York: Pantheon Books, 1997.

Robinson, Warren C. "Family Planning Programs and Policies in Bangladesh and Pakistan." In *The Global Family Planning Revolution: Three Decades of Population*

Policies and Programs, edited by Warren C. Robinson and John A. Ross, 325–39. New York: World Bank, 2007.

Robinson, Warren C., and Fatma H. El-Zanaty. "The Evolution of Population Policies and Programs in the Arab Republic of Egypt." In *The Global Family Planning Revolution: Three Decades of Population Policies and Programs*, edited by Warren C. Robinson and John A. Ross, 1–31. New York: World Bank, 2007.

Robinson, Warren C., and John A. Ross, eds. "Family Planning: The Quiet Revolution." In *The Global Family Planning Revolution: Three Decades of Population Policies and Programs*, edited by Warren C. Robinson and John A. Ross, 421–49. New York: World Bank, 2007.

———. *The Global Family Planning Revolution: Three Decades of Population Policies and Programs*. New York: World Bank, 2007.

Roseman, Mindy Jane, and Laura Reichenbach. "Global Reproductive Health and Rights: Reflecting on ICPD." In *Reproductive Health and Human Rights: The Way Forward*, edited by Laura Reichenbach and Mindy Jane Roseman, 3–20. Philadelphia: University of Pennsylvania Press, 2009.

Rosenfield, Allan G., and Caroline J. Min. "The Emergence of Thailand's National Family Planning Program." In *The Global Family Planning Revolution: Three Decades of Population Policies and Programs*, edited by Warren C. Robinson and John A. Ross, 221–33. New York: World Bank, 2007.

Ross, Loretta, and Rickie Solinger. *Reproductive Justice: An Introduction*. Berkeley: University of California Press, 2017.

Rusterholz, Caroline. "English Women Doctors, Contraception and Family Planning in Transnational Perspective (1930s–70s)." *Medical History* 63, no. 2 (April 2019): 153–72.

———. *Women's Medicine: Sex, Family Planning and British Female Doctors in Transnational Perspective, 1920–70*. Manchester: Manchester University Press, 2020.

Sanhueza, Hernán. "Family Planning in Chile: A Tale of the Unexpected." In *The Global Family Planning Revolution: Three Decades of Population Policies and Programs*, edited by Warren C. Robinson and John A. Ross, 105–20. New York: World Bank, 2007.

Santiso-Gálvez, Roberto, and Jane T. Bertrand. "Guatemala: The Pioneering Days of the Family Planning Movement." In *The Global Family Planning Revolution: Three Decades of Population Policies and Programs*, edited by Warren C. Robinson and John A. Ross, 137–54. New York: World Bank, 2007.

Sasser, Jade S. *On Infertile Ground: Population Control and Women's Rights in the Era of Climate Change*. New York: NYU Press, 2018.

———. "Sexual Stewardship: Environment, Development, and the Gendered Politics of Population." In *Routledge Handbook of Gender and Environment*, edited by Sherilyn MacGregor, 345–56. New York: Routledge, 2017.

Scaglia, Ilaria. *The Emotions of Internationalism: Feeling International Cooperation in the Alps in the Interwar Period*. Oxford: Oxford University Press, 2019.

Schoen, Johanna. *Choice and Coercion: Birth Control, Sterilization, and Abortion in Public Health and Welfare*. Chapel Hill and London: University of North Carolina Press, 2005.

Sen, Gita, Adrienne Germain, and Lincoln C. Chen, eds. *Population Policies Reconsidered: Health, Empowerment, and Rights*. Boston: Harvard School of Public Health, 1994.

Sen, Gita, and Caren Grown. *Development, Crisis, and Alternative Visions: Third World Women's Perspectives*. New York: Routledge, 1987.

Sethna, Christabelle. "The Evolution of the Birth Control Handbook: From Student Peer-Education Manual to Feminist Self-Empowerment Text, 1968–1975." *Canadian Bulletin of Medical History* 23, no. 1 (2006): 89–117.

Sharpless, John. "Population Science, Private Foundations, and Development Aid: The Transformation of Demographic Knowledge in the United States, 1945–1965." In *International Development and the Social Sciences,* edited by Frederick Cooper and Randall Packard, 176–200. Berkeley: University of California Press, 1997.

Silliman, Jael, Marlene Gerber Fried, Loretta Ross, and Elena Gutiérrez. *Undivided Rights: Women of Color Organizing for Reproductive Justice.* Boston: South End Press, 2004.

Silvia, Adam M. "Modern Mothers for Third World Nations: Population Control, Western Medical Imperialism, and Cold War Politics in Haiti." *Social History of Medicine* 27, no. 2 (2014): 260–80.

Sinclair, Sonja A., and Barbara Boland, "Characteristics of the Population." In *Recent Population Movements in Jamaica,* 11–23. Kingston, Jamaica: Cicred Series, 1974.

Singh, Jyoti Shankar. *Creating a New Consensus on Population: The Politics of Reproductive Health, Reproductive Rights and Women's Empowerment,* 2nd ed. Abingdon, Oxon: Earthscan from Routledge, 2009.

Soledad Zárate Campos, María, and Maricela González Moya. "Planificación Familiar En La Guerra Fría Chilena: Política Sanitaria Y Cooperación Internacional, 1960–1973." *Historia Crítica* 55 (January–March 2015): 207–30.

Solinger, Rickie, and Mie Nakachi. "Reproductive States: Global Perspectives on the Invention and Implementation of Population Policy." In *Reproductive States: Global Perspectives on the Invention and Implementation of Population Policy,* edited by Rickie Solinger and Mie Nakachi, 1–32. Oxford: Oxford University Press, 2016.

———, eds. *Reproductive States: Global Perspectives on the Invention and Implementation of Population Policy.* Oxford: Oxford University Press, 2016.

Sreenivas, Mytheli. *Reproductive Politics and the Making of Modern India.* Seattle: University of Washington Press, 2021.

Stearns, Peter. "Social History Present and Future." *Journal of Social History* 37, no. 1 (2003): 9–19.

Takeshita, Chikako. *The Global Biopolitics of the IUD—How Science Constructs Contraceptive Users and Women's Bodies.* Cambridge, MA, and London: MIT Press, 2011.

Takeuchi-Demirci, Aiko. "Birth Control and Socialism: The Frustration of Margaret Sanger and Ishimoto Shizue's Mission." *Journal of American–East Asia Relations* 17, no. 3 (2010): 257–80.

———. *Contraceptive Diplomacy: Reproductive Politics and Imperial Ambitions in the United States and Japan.* Stanford, CA : Stanford University Press, 2018.

Talpade Mohanty, Chandra. "Under Western Eyes: Feminist Scholarship and Colonial Discourses." *boundary 2* 12, no. 3 (1984): 333–58.

Teng, Yap Mui. "Singapore: Population Policies and Programs." In *The Global Family Planning Revolution: Three Decades of Population Policies and Programs,* edited by Warren C. Robinson and John A. Ross, 201–19. New York: World Bank, 2007.

Tey, Nai Peng. "The Family Planning Program in Peninsular Malaysia." In *The Global Family Planning Revolution: Three Decades of Population Policies and Programs,* edited by Warren C. Robinson and John A. Ross, 257–76. New York: World Bank, 2007.

Thiery, M. "Pioneers of the Intrauterine Device." *The European Journal of Contraception & Reproductive Health Care: The Official Journal of the European Society of Contraception* 2, no. 1 (March 1997): 15–23.

Thomas, Lynn M. *Politics of the Womb: Women, Reproduction and the State in Kenya.* Berkeley: University of California Press, 2003.

Thoradeniya, Darshi. "Altruism, Welfare, or Development Aid? Swedish Aid for Family Planning in Ceylon, 1958 to 1983." *East Asian Science, Technology and Society* 10 (2016): 423–44.

———. "Birth Control Pill Trials in Sri Lanka: The History and Politics of Women's Reproductive Health (1950–1980)." *Social History of Medicine* 33, no. 1 (2020): 267–87.

Timm, Annette F. *The Politics of Fertility in Twentieth-Century Berlin.* New York: Cambridge University Press, 2010.

Tuladhar, Jayanti M. "Emergence and Development of Nepal's Family Planning Program." In *The Global Family Planning Revolution: Three Decades of Population Policies and Programs*, edited by Warren C. Robinson and John A. Ross, 363–76. New York: World Bank, 2007.

United Nations. "Population and Development: Programme of Action Adopted at the International Conference on Population and Development." Cairo, 5–13 September 1994.

Watkins, Elizabeth Siegel. *On the Pill: A Social History of Oral Contraceptives, 1950–1970*, reprint ed. Baltimore: Johns Hopkins University Press, 2001.

Wells-Wilbon, Rhonda. "Family Planning for Low-Income African American Families: Contributions of Social Work Pioneer Ophelia Settle Egypt." *Social Work* 60, no. 4 (October 2015): 335–42.

White, Tyrene. "China's Population Policy in Historical Context." In *Reproductive States: Global Perspectives on the Invention and Implementation of Population Policy*, edited by Rickie Solinger and Mie Nakachi, 329–68. Oxford: Oxford University Press, 2016.

Whitworth, Sandra. *Feminism and International Relations: Towards a Political Economy of Gender in Interstate and Non-Governmental Institutions.* New York: St. Martin's Press, 1994.

"Women's Voices '94—A Declaration on Population Policies." *Population and Development Review* 19, no. 3 (1993): 637–40.

Zimmerman, Jonathan. *Too Hot to Handle: A Global History of Sex Education.* Princeton, NJ, and Oxford: Princeton University Press, 2015.

Index

Page numbers in italics refer to figures and tables.

abortion: activists, 47–48, 156, 202n141; compromises made on rights for, 174–75; early methods of, 4–5, 72. *See also* contraceptive methods

Abzug, Bella, 168

activism (family planning): birth control, 28–30, 69, 86; conversion of men to cause and, 95–96; early family planning and, 5–6, 34–35, 46; against government programs, 20; history of international aid and, 5–6; leadership at Women's Declaration/ Rio Conference and, 147, *148–50*, 151, 156, *166*; links between state and non-state, 109; reproductive rights of 1970s through 1990s and, 142–43, 159; university experience from 1960s through 1970s and, 155–56; women-centered approach in, 158–59; for women of color, 159–61, 164–66. *See also* advocates (family planning); International Planned Parenthood Federation (IPPF); Pathfinder Fund; reproductive rights; women (within family planning movement)

Adil, Enver, 128

advocates (family planning): characteristics of, 27–28, 33; friction between, 56–61; history of local, 29; humanitarianism and, 17–18, 46–56, 60–61; kinship among, 54; motivations of, 45–49; personal experiences and, 48–50; religion and,

35–36, 50–51; women as, 25–26, 41–43, 52–54, 70–71. *See also* activism (family planning)

Ahluwalia, Sanjam, 9

Ahsan, Ali K., 130

AIDS crisis, 157

Aiken, Maymie (Madame de Mena), 69

Allen, Lillie, 159

Allwood, Violet, 82

Anderson, Kristen, 177

Antrobus, Kenneth, 151, 155

Antrobus, Peggy, *148*, 151–52, 160, 163–65, 168, 171, 174, 177–81

Armar, Augustus A., 48

Around the World. See under International Planned Parenthood Federation (IPPF)

Asavasena, Winich, 116, 118

Avery, Byllye, 159

Bacalao, Ela, 132–33

Bailey, Amy, 29, 48, 69

Bangladesh Women's Health Coalition (BWHC), 157–58

Barroso, Carmen, 177

Belgium Society for Sexual Advice, 35

Ben Sheikh, Tewhida, 43, 47

Berer, Marge, *150*, 152–53, 155–56, 159, 161–62, 171, 175

Besant, Annie, 28

Birth Control International Information Centre (BCIIC), 29

INDEX

birth control leagues and associations, 28–30, 69–70. *See also* clinics (family planning); family planning; population control
Blacker, C. P., 46, 57–58
Bracke, Maud, 146
Bradlaugh, Charles, 28
Brando, Marlon, 124
Briggs, Laura, 111
British Malthusian League, 28
Brush, Dorothy: on advocacy, 97; concerns of about expanding IPPF, 109; contraception methods and, 73; duality and, 27; Fernando and, 26; international work and, 32–33; kinship among other advocates, 54; politics and, 56
Brush Foundation. *See* Brush, Dorothy

Cadbury, Barbara, 35, 100
Cairo. *See* United Nations International Conference on Population and Development (ICPD): Cairo
Chan, Violet, 53
chemical methods of contraception, 4, 71, 74, 98. *See also* contraceptive methods
Chinnatamby, Siva, 47–48, 53, 97
Cho, Eunjoo, 90
Claro, Amparo, *148*, 153, 156, 171, 177
climate change and environmentalism, 8–10, 12, 45–46, 145, 167, 176
clinics (family planning): early models of, 76–77; intimate atmosphere of, 77–78; letters asking for advice sent to, 70; need for, 82–84; obstacles to access to, 96–97; services provided by early, 79–80. *See also* family planning
Cohen, Deborah A., 77, 86
colonialism: birth control pill trials in Puerto Rico and, 111–13; history of family planning and, 10; humanitarian movements vs., 56, 59–61; population control and, 137
Committee for Abortion Rights and Against Sterilization Abuse (CARASA), 156
Concepcion, Mercedes, 35

condoms, 4–5, 71. *See also* contraceptive methods
"Confidential Advice for Mothers, The," 75
Connelly, Matthew, 9, 107–8
contraceptive methods: birth control pill, 99, 111–14, 124; donors to and research on, from 1960 to 1970, 108; early birth control advocates and, 5; early twentieth century and, 71–74; history of, 4–6, *4*, *6*; importance of different types of, 19; men's role in, 94–95; obstacles of, 97–101; pamphlets about, 75–76, 86, 89–90; passed from generations of women, 71–72; religious and cultural norms and, 5, 50–51; research trials on, 117–18, 124; universal appeal of, 84–86. *See also* chemical methods of contraception; clinics (family planning); condoms; diaphragms and cervical caps; IUDs (intra-uterine devices)
Corrêa, Sonia, *148*, 164–65, 174, 180
Coulibaly, Sidi, 48

Daily Gleaner, 63, 70, 82
"Declaration of People's Perspective on Population," 164
Delano, Grace Ebun, 49
Development, Crises, and Alternative Perspectives (DAWN), 146
Development Alternatives with Women for a New Era (DAWN): history of, 146; *Population and Reproductive Rights*, 146; race and gender and, 160; "Rio Statement on Reproductive Health and Justice," 146; "Women's Declaration on Population Policies," 146. *See also* women (within family planning movement)
Diallo, Dázon Dixon, 162
diaphragms and cervical caps, 4, 19, 73–74, 97. *See also* contraceptive methods
Diaz Lovera, Armando, 134
Donetz, Sonia, 53
Dunlop, Joan, 136–38, *150*, 152, 155, 157–58, 162–63, 171

Dusitin, Nikorn, 119–20
Dwyer, Leslie, 91

Ecce Homo (Nietzsche), 50
Emergency Period (India), 9, 137
Erb Na Bangxang, 124
Essay on the Principle of Population, An (Malthus), 8
ethics of trials, 112–13
eugenics movement: history of, 7–9; human rights violations and, 9–10; neo-Malthusian and, 8; sterilization laws and, 8–9

family planning: appeals to progressive thinking, 91; colonialism and imperialism and, 10, 56, 59–61, 111–13, 137; early activists of, 5–6, 34–35; early associations of, 36–37; factors that influence, 3–4; global studies about, 13–17; international aid and, 6–7, 107–9; link to reproductive rights activism, 151–53; media use and, *87*, 88–91; missionary relationships with communities, 91–101; from 1940s through 1960s, 80–82, *82*; from 1960s through 1970s, 107–8; obstacles of, 96–101; "planned parenthood" and, 30; politics and, 11; population control and, 7; religion and, 11, 35–36, 44–45; reproductive rights and, 12; resistance to, 93; social ostracism and, 45; as tool of social advance, 86–91, *87*. *See also* clinics (family planning); government plans for family planning
Family Planning (Disney), 107, *108*
Family Planning Association (FPA): of Ceylon, 25–26, 36, 44, 79, 94, 97; of China, *40, 41*; of Hong Kong, *78*, 99; of Singapore, 89, 93, 99; of Thailand, *81*
"Family Planning Handbook for Speakers and Lay Workers," 89
Family Planning International Assistance (FPIA), 157
Farquharson, May: contraception and, 74–75, 86, 94, 97–98; frustrations within movement, 94–95; history of,

68–69; letters between Mrs. Allen and, 63–66, 100; resignation of, 99–100; views on family planning, 69
Fazelbhoy, Zarina, 46
feminism: DAWN and, 146; funding for feminist organizations, 177–78; government policies of population control and, 137; history of family planning programs and, 11–12; imperialism and, 172–73; leaders at action/policy research centers, 152, 154; leadership at Women's Declaration/Rio Conference, 147, *148–50*, 151; within population organizations in 1970s, 138; race and, 160, 172–73; reproductive rights approach and, 12, *156*, 161–65, 174–75; Sanger and, 7; support of family planning after WWII, 46. *See also* women (within family planning movement)
Fernando, E. L., 97
Fernando, Sylvia, 25, 45, 93
Foo, Rosalind, 53
Ford Foundation, 107, 136, 138, 157
Frazer, Simon, 93
Fung Hsien-mei, 85

Gamble, Clarence, 31, 46, 59, 111
Gamble, Sarah, 51, 79
García-Moreno, Claudia, 152–55, 157, 163, 166, 169–70, 174
Gates, Edith, 32, 34, 55, 57, 59–61
gender roles (within family planning movement): contraception and, 95–96; division of labor and, 17; experiences with pregnancy and childbirth and, 155; feminism and, 160; sexism and, 157
Germain, Adrienne, 136–38, *150*, 152, 157–58, 161–62, 166, 168–69, 171, 173–75
Global South. *See* Development Alternatives with Women for a New Era (DAWN); women (within family planning movement)
Goh Kok Kee, Constance, 33, 40, 45, 50, 53, 57, 109

Gordon, Linda, 71
government plans for family planning:
in Egypt, 126; in India, 125, *126*; in
Indonesia, 126; lack of support for,
133–34; in Pakistan, 124–25, 127–29;
in Singapore, 126; in Sri Lanka, 126;
target numbers for treatment within,
128–31

Hartmann, Betsy, 9, 176
Helie Lucas, Marieme, *148*, 154
Heyzer, Noeleen, *149*, 154–55, 173,
231n46
Higler, Amy, 173
Houghton, Vera, 98–99
How-Martyn, Edith, 29, 69
"How to Establish a Birth Control Clinic"
(Stone), 76
Humanae Vitae, 50–51, 132
Human Betterment League of North
Carolina, 31
humanitarians. *See* advocates (family
planning)
Hussein, Aziza, 33, 109, 117
Hyde Amendment, 156

Ilumoka, Adetoun, *149*, 151, 155, 171–72
International Planned Parenthood
Federation (IPPF): *Around the World*
newsletter of, 27, 32–33, 36, 44, 52–
55, 83–84, 87–88, 93; contraception
methods and, 73–74, 95–96, 98–99;
creation of, 6, 30; early fieldwork
program of, 31–34; family planning
associations and, 36–37; funding by,
61; goals of, 30; Mexico City Policy
and, 144; name tensions within, 37,
58, 199n79; organization members
(1926–1959) of, 36–37, *38–39*;
"Planned Parenthood and Women's
Development" program, 138; political
tensions and, 56–58; role of men in,
108. *See also* Pathfinder Fund
International Reproductive Rights
Research and Action Group
(IRRRAG), 161
International Women's Health Coalition
(IWHC), 145, 158–59

IUDs (intra-uterine devices):
complications of, 120–24, 133;
early experimentation of, 114–15;
history of, 5; promotion of, 108,
118–20; resistance to use of, 129;
Satterthwaite work diary about, 103–
4; target numbers for, 128–29. *See
also* contraceptive methods

Jackson, Margaret, 114
Jacobs, Aletta, 28
Jacobs, Beth, 33
Jamaica Family Planning League (JFPL),
69, 81, 88. *See also* Farquharson, May
Jaramillo, Mario, 47
Joffe, Carole, 13
Jolly, Elizabeth M., *53*

Kabir, Sandra, *148*, 154, 157, 169, 176
Kato, Shidzue, *53*
Keysers, Loes, 162, 164, 178
Kissling, Frances, *150*, 154–56, 174
Klausen, Susanne, 55

LaBadie, Alma, 69
Laite, Julia, 16
Lankford, Kathryn, 111, 113
Latin America: demand for family
planning in, 133; local family planning
clinics in during 1960s, 132–33;
resistance to population control
in, 131
Liaquat Ali Khan, Ra'ana, 128
Lightbourne, Hyacinth, 76
Lin Yutang, 46
Lippes, Jack, 117, 122
Lopez, Iris, 14, 179

MacNamara, Trent, 17, 85, 91
Malik, Hameda, 53
Malthus, Thomas, 8
Manguyu, Florence, *149*, 155
Manley, Michael, 160
Margalit, Avishai, 18
Marriage Hygiene, 29
Mashima, Chimo, 52
McCormick, Katharine, 99
McDaniel, Edwin B., 124

INDEX › 257

McKinnon, Edna Rankin, 32, *42*, 51, 54–55, 57, 59–61, 93, 95
Mendoza, Ofelia, 33
Mexico City Policy, 144, 157, 170
Mohanty, Chandra Talpade, 172
Moizuddin, Mohammad, 96–97
Moore, Hugh, 8
Morgan, Lynn, 173

National Archives of Jamaica, 68
National Black Women's Health Project (NBWHP), 159
Necochea López, Raúl, 14, 31, 132
neo-Malthusian, history of, 8
New Culture Movement (China), 29
Nigerian Women's Union, 46

One Child Policy (China), 9, 137
Osborn, Fairfield, 8
Ottesen-Jensen, Elise, 30, 48, 51–52, *53*
Our Bodies, Ourselves (Boston Women's Health Collective), 158

Pakistan, 125–31
Parry, Manon, 80, 90–91
Pathfinder Fund: contraception and, 74; creation of, 6; early fieldwork program of, 31–34; family planning associations and, 36–37; funding and, 61; leadership and, 57; religion and, 50; resistance to, 93; tensions within, 59–62; trial of Enovid contraceptive pill, 111. *See also* International Planned Parenthood Federation (IPPF)
Petchesky, Rosalind, *150*, 154, 156, 161–62, 167–68, 175–77
Pill, The (documentary), 112–13
Pillay, A. P., 29
Pincus, Gregory, 99
Pitanguy, Jacqueline, *148*, 154–55, 169, 171, 174
Poh, Sai, 119
Population and Reproductive Rights (Corrêa and Reichmann), 165, 174–75, 180
population control: colonialism and, 10, 137; decolonization

and, 8; environmentalism and, 8; family planning and, 7; history of government programs for, 6–9; human rights violations and, 9; movement from 1960s through 1970s, 107–8; Pakistan's government policy for, 125–31; problems in international policies of, 136–39; reproductive rights and, 12. *See also* eugenics movement; family planning; government plans for family planning
Population Council: changes within, 138; creation of, 6; critiques of, 134–36; IUD project and, 119–20; from 1960s through 1970s, 107–8; professionalization and role of men in 1960s, 108; promotion of contraceptive methods and, 118–19; Satterthwaite and, 115, *116*, 124
Population Policies Reconsidered (Sen et al.), 146
Preparatory Committees (PrepComs), 168–71. *See also* United Nations International Conference on Population and Development (ICPD): Cairo
pro-natalist politics, 144

Quamina, Elizabeth, 47

racism: by early fieldworkers, 59–61; experienced by women activists, 156; within philanthropic organizations and programs, 157; within reproductive rights movement, 172–73
Radhakrishnan, Sarvepalli, 56
Ramali, A., 36
Rama Rau, Dhanvanthi, 26, 33, 52, *53*
Ransome-Kuti, Funmilayo, 46
Ravindran, T. K. Sundari, 141, 148, 152–54, 156, 158–59, 161–62, 165, 170, 174, 178
Reagan, Ronald, 144
Reed, James, 135
Regulations on Health According to Islamic Law (Ramali), 36
Reichmann, Rebecca, 174

religion: conflicts with family planning work and, 44–45; contraception and, 5; critiques of population programs by, 11; humanitarianism and, 50–51; support of family planning and, 35–36; against women's movement, 170

"Reproductive Health and Justice" (Rio de Janeiro): conference organizers, *147*, *148–50*; conference participants, 166; "Rio Statement on Reproductive Health and Justice," 146, 167–68

Reproductive Health Matters, 161

reproductive justice: politics and, 172–73, 176; "Rio Statement," 167–68; as transnational reproductive rights movement, 143; women of color and, 12, 168. *See also* reproductive rights; "Rio Statement on Reproductive Health and Justice"; United Nations International Conference on Population and Development (ICPD): Cairo

reproductive rights: agenda at International Conference on Population and Development (Cairo), 142–43; broad, holistic approach to, 159–60; building framework for, 161–63; diversity and, 165–66; feminism and, 12, 156, 161–65; funding and, 177–78; implementation issues, 176–77; racism and imperialism within movement of, 172–73; reproductive freedom vs., 179; tension within movement of, 174–76; use of term, 144–45; vision for, 180–81. *See also* activism (family planning); International Conference on Population and Development (ICPD): Cairo; reproductive justice

Rice-Wray, Edris, 44, 58, 95–96, 111, 118

Richey, Lisa, 177

"Rio Statement on Reproductive Health and Justice," 146, *166*, 167–68. *See also* reproductive justice; Women's Declaration

Rockefeller, John D., III, 136

Rockefeller Foundation, 107

Roland, Edna, 162

Roots, Margaret, 32, 50–51, 57, 59–60

Ross, Loretta, 168

Rusterholz, Caroline, 43, 90

Sadik, Nafis, 127, 131, 140, 142

Sanger, Margaret: *Around the World* newsletter and, 33, 52, *53*; birth control clinics and, 29–30; contraception and, 73; ideology of, 7; International Planned Parenthood Federation (IPPF) and, 30; on role of men in movement, 108–9

Sasser, Jade, 176

Sasson, Tehila, 15

Satterthwaite, Adaline Pendleton (Penny): background, 109–11, *110*; birth control pill and, 111–14, *112*; on contraception options, 118; feminism and, 138–39; IUDs and, 114–15, 119–24, 133; Population Council and, 115, *116*, 124, 130–31; on Puerto Ricans and contraception, 111; work diary excerpts of, 103–4; work history of, 105–6; work in Latin America, 131–36; work in Pakistan, 125–31; work in Thailand, 116–24

Schoen, Johanna, 14, 112

Scott, Julia, 159

Sen, Gita, *148*, 152, 156, 160–61, 166–67, 177

sex reform advocates, 46

sexuality, 156

Snidvongs, M. L. Kashetra, 116

Soin, Kanwaljit, *149*, 153

Sreenivas, Mytheli, 52, 109, 185

Stearns, Peter, 15

sterilization: activism, 156; compulsory eugenic sterilization laws and policies, 8–9, 99–100; Family Planning Associations and, 99; mass, 9

Stone, Abraham, 76

Stopes, Marie: birth control clinics and, 29–30; contraception and, 73; ideology of, 7

Swedish National League for Sex Education (RFSU), 30

Takeshita, Chikako, 115, 123
Takeuchi-Demirci, Aiko, 17
Thailand: early family planning activism in, 51, 53–54, *81*; 1960s contraceptive research and programs, 103, 116–24, *116*. See also Satterthwaite, Adaline Pendleton (Penny)
Thomas, Franklin A., 138
Tze-kuan Shu Kan, 37, 54, 58

"Under Western Eyes" (Mohanty), 172
United Nations Family Planning Association (UNFPA), 6, 107, 140, 142
United Nations International Conference on Population and Development (ICPD): Bucharest, 10, 137–38; Cairo, 11–12, 141–43, 161–71, *166*, 168–71; Mexico City, 144; Rome, 25; timeline of, 144; women's roles in, 161–71. See also Preparatory Committees (PrepComs)

vasectomy campaigns, 128
Vejjabul, Hoon Pierra, 53
Venezuela, 131–36

Wadia, Avabai, 33, 109
Walt Disney Company, 107–8
"Which One?" (Jamaica Family Life Project), 86
Whitworth, Sandra, 90
Wirth, Tim, 169
women (within family planning movement): activism and, 20–21, 109, 161–62; as advocates, 25–26, 70–71; depicted within *Around the World* newsletter, 52–54; early fieldworkers of, 30–34; early local

actors of, 34, 39–45; of Global South, 146; leaders at action/policy research centers, 152; leadership at Women's Declaration/Rio Conference, 147, *148–50*, 151, *166*, 168–71; leaders of core organizations of population control, 152; letters illustrating interactions between FPA and, 63–66; passing of traditional contraception methods, 71–72; resistance to family planning, 93–94; roles in early years, 18; roles within International Conference on Population and Development (Cairo), 141–42; timeline of influential committees and conferences from 1970s through 1990s, 144–45; women-centered approach for, 158–61; "World Plan of Action," 144. See also Development Alternatives with Women for a New Era (DAWN); feminism; United Nations International Conference on Population and Development (ICPD): Cairo
Women's Declaration: core foundations of, 163; criticism of, 163–64; initiators of, 162–63. See also "Rio Statement on Reproductive Health and Justice"
Women's Environment and Development Organization (WEDO), 168
Women's Political Union, 36
World Health Organization (WHO), 11
"World Plan of Action," 144
World Population Plan of Action, 137
World War II, 30

Zalduondo, Celestina, 53, 84
Zeidenstein, George, 138